ANASTAS MIKOYAN

ANASTAS MIKOYAN

AN ARMENIAN REFORMER IN KHRUSHCHEV'S KREMLIN

PIETRO A. SHAKARIAN

INDIANA UNIVERSITY PRESS

This book is a publication of

Indiana University Press
Office of Scholarly Publishing
Herman B Wells Library 350
1320 East 10th Street
Bloomington, Indiana 47405 USA

iupress.org

First Printing 2025

Cataloging information is available from the Library of Congress.

ISBN 978-0-253-07354-9 (hdbk.)
ISBN 978-0-253-07355-6 (pbk.)
ISBN 978-0-253-07357-0 (ebook)
ISBN 978-0-253-07356-3 (web PDF)

IN MEMORY OF

Stephen F. Cohen (1938–2020),
scholar, mentor, friend

CONTENTS

ACKNOWLEDGMENTS

In Russia, it is customary to say that everyone has their own fate (*sud'ba*). My fate, which would lead me to Russia, Armenia, and eventually the authorship of this book, has its roots in my family history. Over one hundred years ago, in 1915, my Armenian grandfather embarked on a voyage, leaving behind an empire where Armenians were the official enemies of the state and the unofficial victims of one of the first genocides of the new century. Then only a teenager, he departed from his beloved Constantinople and set sail for Constanta, Romania. My siblings and I were repeatedly told the story of how our grandparents met, married in Bucharest, and in 1945 bore our father, just as Romania became a "People's Republic" under Stalin's influence. The Romanian authorities eventually permitted the family to leave the country in 1960, given their status as Nansen passport holders. They spent one year in Beirut, Lebanon, living in the Bourj Hammoud neighborhood, before emigrating to America, first to Queens, New York, and then to Cleveland, Ohio. In the old country, countless friends and acquaintances fed my family numerous stories about an America cast as a veritable "miracle land" of "milk and honey" where the streets were "paved with gold." However, in New York and Cleveland, they came face-to-face with the gritty reality of America's fast-paced, hard-nosed northern metropolises. Upon arrival in the New World, my grandfather asked, incredulously, "This is America?"

Nevertheless, it was that same America that enabled my father to become a successful architect and to meet my mother—the daughter of an immigrant working-class Hungarian father and a second-generation Slovak mother—while commuting to college in Cleveland. For me, growing up in a "European household," political jokes and anecdotes were common. However, it was ultimately the dynamic history of the Russian Revolution, fueled by accounts like those of Jack Reed, that ignited a fire within me, making me a veritable fixture in the

Cleveland Public Library for the next several years. As a teenager, I was especially interested in Armenia's Soviet past, including the role of Anastas Mikoyan in de-Stalinization. My interest was only fueled by accounts of Mikoyan's travels to America, including the account of his 1959 visit to Cleveland penned by George E. Condon, the *Plain Dealer*'s legendary quick-witted Irish American columnist. According to Condon, Mikoyan's "mustache twitched" and his eyes became "misty" at the sight of Cleveland's Terminal Tower, which called to mind the tower at Lomonosov Moscow State University. "Now you're talking! This is my kind of town!" the statesman reportedly declared.

It would be difficult to imagine this work without several individuals and institutions that provided me indispensable assistance along the way. Particular gratitude goes first and foremost to Indiana University Press and to Bethany Mowry, Sophia Hebert, Carol McGillivray, Dave Miller, and Samantha Heffner for seeing the potential in this study and bringing it to publication. The Centre for Historical Research at the National Research University–Higher School of Economics (HSE) in St. Petersburg, Russia, provided crucial support for my endeavor to expand my former dissertation into a full-fledged book within the framework of the university's Basic Research Program. Not unlike the former Hermitage director Boris Piotrovskii and his book on Urartu, I managed to complete this work amid a period of intense global upheaval. Along the way, I was extremely fortunate to have the encouragement, input, and fellowship of my wonderful and creative colleagues at HSE, especially Aleksandr Reznik, Ekaterina Kalemeneva, and Adrian Selin, but also Tatiana Borisova, Kirill Chunikhin, Evgenii Egorov, Igor Kuziner, Marina Loskutova, Daria Moskvina, Aleksandra Nedopekina, Evgeniia Platonova, Nikolai Ssorin-Chaikov, Maria Starun, and Ekaterina Vasilik, among many others. Stefan Gužvica was especially helpful in elucidating questions on Yugoslav federalism relevant to this study. I also owe much gratitude to Aleksandr Semyonov for his input and guidance during his tenure as the director of the Centre for Historical Research. Additionally, I am deeply grateful to Tatiana Kolesnikova, Marina Kozhemiakina, Anastasia Kotiashkina, Maria Pechnikova, Svetlana Liubavina, and Samira Akhmedova for their support and assistance. Further gratitude goes to Elena Kosareva, Tamara Vladimirova, and others at the HSE St. Petersburg Library for acquiring much-needed resources for this work. Special recognition is due to my students at HSE for their intellectual curiosity, critical engagement, and in-class insights.

Outside the university, I am particularly indebted to the staffs of the various archives in Russia where I conducted research. In Moscow, these included the Russian State Archive (GARF), the Russian State Archive of Socio-Political History (RGASPI), the Russian State Archive of Contemporary History (RGANI), and the Russian State Archive of Literature and Art (RGALI). In particular, the indefatigable Aleksei Trefakhin of GARF expertly handled all my requests alongside those of others. I am also thankful to Liudmila Kosheleva, Marina Astakhova, and Natalia Kirillova of RGASPI for their support and assistance. Additional gratitude goes to Sergei Filippov of Memorial in Moscow, who provided me with copies of rare documents from the Russian Presidential Archive (APRF) and the Central Archive of the FSB (TsA FSB RF). The latter were xeroxed by scholars at Memorial in 1992 during a period of unprecedented archival access in Russia. I am likewise thankful to the staffs of the libraries wherein I spent many long hours conducting research, including the National Library of Russia in St. Petersburg and the Russian State Library and the State Public Historical Library of Russia in Moscow.

Prior to my fellowship in Petersburg, I had the great fortune of spending a year as an adjunct professor of history at the American University of Armenia (AUA) in Yerevan. In addition to teaching, my time at AUA gave me the opportunity to greatly expand my work. The institution itself was ideally situated within walking distance of the Armenian Archives and Yerevan's Fundamental Scientific Library. Before my time at AUA, I spent much time in Armenia, which I visit regularly. Overall, I am deeply appreciative of the many academics who guided me through my research in the Armenian Republic, before, during, and after my time at AUA. These scholars include my colleagues at the university, in particular Anna Aleksanyan, Siranush Dvoyan, Suren Aghasi Manukyan, Harout Marashlian, Tigran Matosyan, Naira Sahakyan, and Ashot Voskanyan, among many others. Additional gratitude goes to Sharistan Melkonian and Vahram Ter-Matevosyan for their support of my work, as well as to Bella Avagyan at the AUA Armenian General Benevolent Union (AGBU) Papazian Library. As with HSE, special recognition goes to my students at AUA. Their in-class intellectual engagement and curiosity played no small role in shaping this monograph.

Outside of AUA, I am deeply appreciative of the staff of the National Archives of Armenia (HAA) in Yerevan, in particular former director Amatuni Virabyan, Kino-Foto-Fono Branch director Avag Harutyunyan, and research archivist Varditer Grigoryan, among many others. Special gratitude is due to Tatev Vardanian of the Armenian National Library for her indispensable assistance to this project. Additional thanks are due to the various individuals at the Fundamental Scientific Library, the History Museum of Armenia, the Charents Museum of Literature and Arts, the Yeghishe Charents House-Museum, the Aram Khachaturian Museum, the Yervand Kochar Museum, the Avetik Isahakyan House-Museum, and outside Yerevan, the Mikoyan Brothers Museum in Alaverdi. I also owe great thanks to several other individuals in Armenia, including Hrant Akopian, Rouben Galichian, Mark Grigorian, Ashkhen Hakobyan, Syuzanna Khojamiryan, Nelly Manucharyan, Davit Matevossian, Sergey Minasyan, Sona

Mnatsakanyan, Mariam Saghatelyan, and Gayane Shagoyan, among many others. I am immensely grateful to the Calouste Gulbenkian Foundation in Lisbon and the AGBU in New York for providing generous financial assistance for my research in Armenia.

This book was also the result of several years of prior study at various universities in the United States. In the PhD program in history at the Ohio State University (OSU), I was extremely fortunate to have the guidance and encouragement of my advisor and good friend David Hoffmann, who has continued to provide me invaluable assistance in my ongoing endeavors. Additional acknowledgment goes to my coadvisor Nick Breyfogle, my dissertation committee members Scott Levi and Claudia Buchmann, and many other individuals at OSU, including Greg Anderson, Ashley Bowerman, and Eileen Kunkler. This book would have also been impossible without the generous assistance of an American Councils Title VIII Research Scholar grant, which allowed me to conduct research in Yerevan and Moscow during the 2019–20 academic year at OSU. As an MA student at the University of Michigan in Ann Arbor, I was fortunate to work under the tutelage of Ronald Grigor Suny, as well as Olga Maiorova, Alaina Lemon, and many others whose insights helped lay the groundwork for this current study. At John Carroll University in Cleveland, I must thank my first professor in Russian history, Jim Krukones, as well as Maria Marsilli, Matt Berg, Michael Eng, and several others. Further appreciation goes to all those who assisted me in the acquisition of much-needed materials at the Harlan Hatcher Graduate Library at the University of Michigan, the Cleveland Public Library, the New York Public Library, and the Thompson Memorial Library at the Ohio State University.

However, the one person to whom I owe particular gratitude is the late historian Stephen F. Cohen of New York University and Princeton University, a close friend and mentor. His biography of Nikolai Bukharin sparked my interest in the genre of political biography, and his book *The Victims Return* fueled my interest in Mikoyan's role in de-Stalinization and alternative paths in Soviet history. In fact, in May 2014, during my time as a graduate student at the University of Michigan, it was Dr. Cohen who suggested to me the idea of writing my dissertation on Mikoyan. Both he and his wife, Katrina vanden Heuvel, offered invaluable input and assistance throughout the development of this monograph. At their Manhattan apartment, amid Chinese takeout and deep conversations on all things Russian, Dr. Cohen even dubbed me the newest member of the "Tucker-Cohen school," referring to his own mentor, Robert C. Tucker. Tragically, Dr. Cohen passed away on September 18, 2020, after a five-month battle with cancer. In one of our final communications, just weeks before his passing, I shared with him a transcript from GARF of Mikoyan's 1964 meeting with rehabilitated Old Bolsheviks in Baku. He was a scholar's scholar to the very end. Although he was never able to see this book reach publication, I am certain that he would be very proud of me. It is to his memory that I have dedicated this work.

Further gratitude is due to several individuals for their support and assistance, including George Bournoutian, Tatyana Bystrova-McIntyre, Samuel Casper, Riccardo Cucciolla, Asya Darbinyan, Edward and Françoise Djerejian, Etienne Forestier-Peyrat, Aleksandr Gevorkyan, Lilit Grigoryan, Hripsime Haroutunian, Nataliya Kibita, Denis Kozlov, Maike Lehmann, Michael Loader, Alex Marshall, Zhores Medvedev, Andreas Oberender, Serguei Oushakine, Zaroui Pogossian, William Risch, Paul Robinson, Arsène Saparov, Ara Sarafian, William Taubman, Alexander Titov, and Artyom Tonoyan, among countless others. Particular acknowledgment goes to the participants of the June 2022 Conference of Political Historians of the Post-War Soviet Union, where I presented my work. The latter was held at the University of Glasgow and was organized by Michael Loader with support from David Smith, the university's Alec Nove Chair in Russian and East European Studies. Additionally, certain portions of this monograph, particularly from chapter 6, were previously published in the article "Towards a More Perfect Union?" for the journal *Europe-Asia Studies*, based at the University of Glasgow. I thank the editors of that journal for granting me permission to reprint the material from my earlier article. Additional thanks are due to Ara Sanjian and Gerald Ottenbreit Jr. at the Armenian Research Center at the University of Michigan–Dearborn, and to Marc Mamigonian and Ani Babaian at the National Association for Armenian Studies and Research (NAASR) in Belmont, Massachusetts. Gratitude is likewise due to Vahe Apelian for granting permission to use his translations of Antranig Dzarugian's *Hin yerazner, nor chambaner.* I am further thankful to those who consented to be interviewed for this work, specifically Vladimir Mikoyan and Tatiana Shahumyan in Moscow and the late Sergei Khrushchev in Cranston, Rhode Island. Here I must especially recognize Vladimir Mikoyan, grandson of Anastas and son of Sergo, for his astute knowledge, assistance, patience, warmth, and friendship. Gratitude is likewise due to Ashkhen Mikoyan, daughter of Stepan, for her assistance on this research.

Finally, I owe an enormous debt of gratitude to my family, and in particular, my parents, Berj and Carol Shakarian. Both are my pillars who have been there for me in every respect. They were the ones who created the spark in me that grew into my passion for the history of Russia, Armenia, and Eurasia. Upon noticing my strong curiosity for this part of the world as a plucky West Side Cleveland kid, they fueled my interest with books, invaluable intellectual exchanges, and loving patience and generosity. They are truly the tops, and, if there is one thing of which I am certain, it is that I could never top them. I will forever value their love, encouragement, and contributions to my growth as a young man, at the start of a career as a historian of Russia and the former Soviet Union.

NOTE ON TRANSLATION AND TRANSLITERATION

This book draws extensively on source material in the Russian and Armenian languages. All English translations herein are my own, unless noted otherwise. For transliteration, this study follows the Library of Congress (LoC) standards for both Russian and Armenian, without diacritical marks. For Russian, the soft sign "ь" is transliterated with an apostrophe, following the LoC system. Exceptions are made only for the names of prominent political groups (e.g., "Bolshevik" instead of "Bol'shevik") and individuals (e.g., "Olga Shatunovskaia" instead of "Ol'ga Shatunovskaia"). For clarity of pronunciation, the Russian letter "ё" is rendered as "io," except in prominent names, such as Khrushchev, Gorbachev, and Ponomarev. Following the LoC guidelines for Armenian, all Armenian surnames terminate with the suffix "-yan" rather than "-ian" (e.g., "Mikoyan," as opposed to "Mikoian"). Exceptions are made for certain Western Armenian individuals, such as Antranig Dzarugian, as well as Armenian surnames that appear in the transliterated titles of Russian works. Additional exceptions are made for two prominent Eastern Armenian figures—the composer Aram Khachaturian and the writer Hrant Matevossian. The former is the most common romanization of Khachaturian's surname, while the latter is the form of Matevossian's surname preferred by the Matevossian family. Diverging from the LoC system, I opted to transliterate the vowel letter "ե" as "ye" rather than "e" in those cases when it appears in the initial position (e.g., "Yerevan" instead of "Erevan," "Yeghegnadzor" instead of "Eghegnadzor," "Yeghishe" instead of "Eghishe," etc.). Similarly, the vowel letter "ո" when placed in the initial position is transliterated as "vo" (as in "voch'") rather than "o" (e.g., "Voghji" instead of "Oghji").

For ease of reading, the names of prominent Armenian figures follow their most common transliterated form, without apostrophes (e.g., "Charents" instead of "Ch'arents'," "Tumanyan" instead of "T'umanyan," "Kochinyan" instead of "K'ochinyan," etc.). The same approach applies to Armenian place names (e.g., "Vayots Dzor" instead of "Vayots' Dzor," "Talin" instead of "T'alin," "Artik" instead of "Art'ik," etc.) and names of prominent political parties (e.g., "Dashnaktsutyun" instead of "Dashnakts'ut'yun"). Exceptions are made only for transliterated titles of Armenian books and articles. For residents of settlements and regions in Armenia, the demonyms used in the text follow the Armenian form, terminating with the suffix "-ts'i" but without the apostrophe (e.g., Yerevantsi, Alaverdtsi, Ghapantsi, Loretsi, Gorisetsi, etc.). For the sake of precision, I opted to transliterate rather than translate the Russian names of Soviet administrative units (e.g., *oblast', krai, okrug, raion*, etc.), as these terms carried specific meanings within the Soviet administrative hierarchy, just as they do within the administrative hierarchy of today's Russian Federation. These terms are all rendered in lowercase when referring to specific entities (e.g., "Groznyi oblast'," "Altai krai," "Prigorodnyi raion," etc.). Exceptions are made only for autonomous regions (e.g., "Nagorno-Karabakh Autonomous Oblast'") and military districts (e.g., "Transcaucasian Military Okrug").

For the larger territory of historical Armenia, the geographic term *haykakan lernashkharh* is rendered as "Armenian Plateau" rather than "Armenian Highland" or "Armenian Upland." Depending on the context, Nagorno-Karabakh is rendered as either "Mountainous Karabakh" or "Nagorno-Karabakh," following the LoC Russian transliteration of "Karabakh" rather than Armenian or Azerbaijani variants. Similarly, the transliteration of the name "Nakhichevan'" follows the LoC Russian system. Finally, in acknowledgment of the long-standing connections between the North and South Caucasus, I decided to use the general terms "Caucasia" or "the Caucasus" as much as possible. Where distinction is necessary, the term "North Caucasus" is used to denote the area north of the Greater Caucasus range, while the "South Caucasus" is referred to as "Transcaucasia" (*zakavkaz'e*), given the specific Soviet and pre-Soviet historical contexts.

TERMS AND ABBREVIATIONS

agitprop	agitation and propaganda
AO	autonomous oblast'
ARF / ARF-D / Dashnaktsutyun / Dashnaks	Armenian Revolutionary Federation
Armenkom	Armenian Committee of the Bolshevik Party
ASSR	Autonomous Soviet Socialist Republic
CPSU (Russian: KPSS)	Communist Party of the Soviet Union
druzhba narodov	friendship of peoples
gorkom	city committee
Gosekonomsovet	State Scientific-Economic Council
Gosplan	State Planning Committee
Gossnab	State Supply Committee
Gosstroi	State Construction Committee
guberniia	governorate (alternatively, province)
Gulag	labor camp administration system
Hunchaks	Social Democrat Hunchakian Party
Kavburo	Caucasus Bureau of the Communist Party
kolkhoz	collective farm
kolkhoznik	member of a collective farm
Komsomol	Communist Youth League

krai	territory
kraikom	territorial (alternatively, regional) committee
marz	province [Armenian]
NEP	New Economic Policy
NKAO	Nagorno-Karabakh Autonomous Oblast'
NPNSC (Russian: NPNGS)	Nationality Policy and National-State Construction
obkom	provincial committee
oblast'	province [Russian]
OGPU / NKVD / KGB	Joint State Political Directorate / People's Commissariat for Internal Affairs / Committee for State Security
okrug	region (alternatively, district)
Orgburo	Organizational Bureau of the Central Committee
orgkom	organizing committee
ORPO	Department of Leading Party Organs
Politburo	Political Bureau of the Central Committee
raikom	district committee
raion	district [Russian]
revkom	Revolutionary Committee
RSDRP(b)	Russian Social Democratic Workers' Party (Bolsheviks)
samizdat	self-publishing
SFSR	Soviet Federative Socialist Republic
shrjan	district [Armenian]
sovkhoz	state farm
sovnarkhoz	People's Economic Council [Russian]
Sovnarkom	Council of People's Commissars
SSR	Soviet Socialist Republic
uezd	county (alternatively, district)
vozhd'	leader
zhoghtntkhorh	People's Economic Council [Armenian]

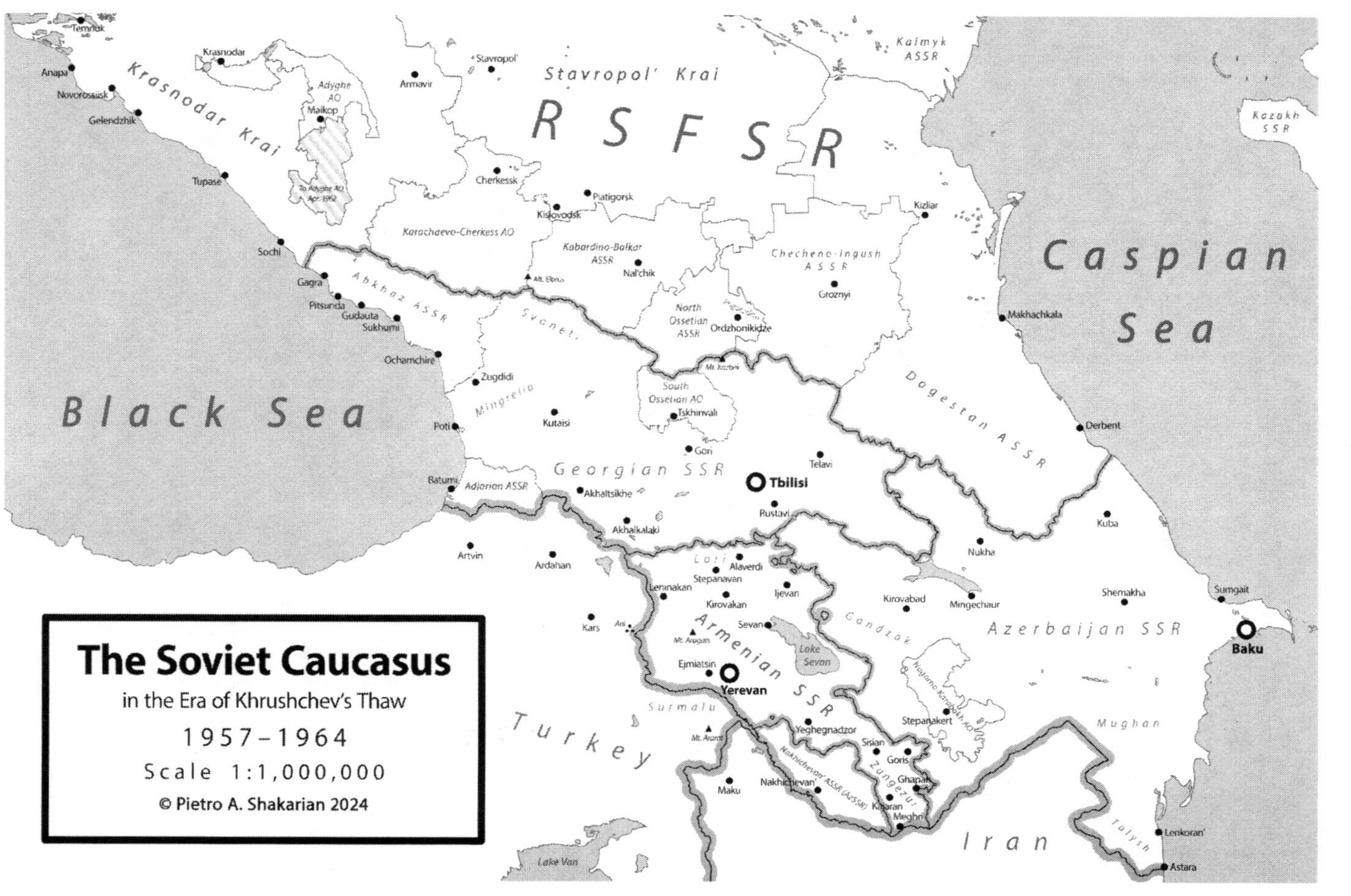
The Soviet Caucasus
in the Era of Khrushchev's Thaw
1957–1964
Scale 1:1,000,000
© Pietro A. Shakarian 2024
Black Sea
Caspian Sea
RSFSR
Stavropol' Krai
Krasnodar Krai
Kalmyk ASSR
Kazakh SSR
Adyghe AO
To Adyghe AO Apr. 1962
Karachaevo-Cherkess AO
Kabardino-Balkar ASSR
Checheno-Ingush ASSR
North Ossetian ASSR
South Ossetian AO
Dagestan ASSR
Abkhaz ASSR
Adjarian ASSR
Georgian SSR
Armenian SSR
Azerbaijan SSR
Nagorno-Karabakh AO
Nakhichevan' ASSR (AzSSR)
Svaneti
Mingrelia
Lori
Gandzak
Zangezur
Surmalu
Mughan
Talysh
Turkey
Iran
Lake Sevan
Lake Van
Mt. Elbrus
Mt. Kazbek
Mt. Aragats
Mt. Ararat
Temriuk
Anapa
Novorossiisk
Gelendzhik
Krasnodar
Maikop
Tupase
Sochi
Gagra
Pitsunda
Gudauta
Sukhumi
Ochamchire
Zugdidi
Poti
Batumi
Armavir
Stavropol'
Cherkessk
Kislovodsk
Piatigorsk
Nal'chik
Ordzhonikidze
Groznyi
Kizliar
Makhachkala
Derbent
Kuba
Nukha
Shemakha
Sumgait
Baku
Lenkoran'
Astara
Kutaisi
Tskhinvali
Gori
Telavi
Tbilisi
Rustavi
Akhaltsikhe
Akhalkalaki
Artvin
Ardahan
Kars
Ani
Leninakan
Stepanavan
Alaverdi
Kirovakan
Ijevan
Sevan
Ejmiatsin
Yerevan
Kirovabad
Mingechaur
Stepanakert
Yeghegnadzor
Sisian
Goris
Ghapan
Kajaran
Meghri
Nakhichevan'
Maku

ANASTAS MIKOYAN

Introduction

Soviet Armenian statesman and longtime Politburo member Anastas Ivanovich Mikoyan (1895–1978) is perhaps best known in both the West and the post-Soviet space as a political survivor, weathering every Soviet leader "from Il'ich to Il'ich, without heart attack and paralysis."[1] His reputation in this regard was undoubtedly augmented by the larger theme of survival in the history of his native republic, Armenia. It was Mikoyan who famously served as Stalin's foreign trade commissar, a position that granted him the exceptional privilege to travel to the United States in the 1930s and to bring back to the Soviet Union the culinary innovations that he witnessed.[2] It was also Mikoyan who became well known as a master of international diplomacy, forging Soviet diplomatic ties with revolutionary Cuba and then playing a key role in defusing the Cuban Missile Crisis.[3] Less well known is the pivotal role that Mikoyan—once a loyal Stalinist—played in dismantling and rejecting the repressive Stalinist legacy after the death of Iosif Stalin in 1953. In addition to his more general role in de-Stalinization, the statesman served as the Kremlin's leading reformer on nationality matters under the leadership of Nikita Khrushchev (1894–1971) during the era of the Thaw (1953–64). A son of Sanahin, Armenia, Mikoyan believed that the ethnic diversity of the USSR was a strength that should be embraced, not a danger that needed to be suppressed.

The Khrushchev-era nationality policy, as guided by Mikoyan, represented a significant departure from the state violence and centralization characteristic of Stalin's approach to nationalities during the height of his power. One might call this departure a form of de-Stalinization in the nationality sphere, if one defines de-Stalinization as the rejection of the policies and methods that characterized the rule of Stalin as the leader of the USSR from 1928 to 1953.[4] This de-Stalinization was reflected in Mikoyan's work on the nationality issue in several areas. These included (1) the rehabilitation of repressed national cultural figures; (2) the effort to combat national nihilism, in addition to national chauvinism; (3) the patronage of national republics like Armenia; (4) the use of historical narratives to promote peaceful relations among national groups; (5) the return and rehabilitation of deported nationalities; (6) the development of a new nationality platform for the CPSU's 1961 Party Program; and (7) the drafting of a new constitution envisioning a greater devolution of powers to national republics and autonomies, emphasizing their rights vis-à-vis Moscow.

Mikoyan's ideas in the realm of nationality policy were a crucial part of Khrushchev's reforms, which represented a selective but wide-ranging (and politically risky) attempt to reject Stalinist methods and policies. They also reflected the larger zeitgeist of the Thaw (*ottepel'*), with its renewed emphasis on Soviet society and the Soviet people, as best represented by the greater focus on domestic economic investment and the political aspiration to increase the role of the citizen in the governing process. As a historical period, the Thaw famously derived its name from Il'ia Ehrenburg's eponymous 1954 novella. More generally, one may define this era as the watershed moment in Soviet history following Stalin's death in 1953, characterized by a "new pluralism" of opinions and media as well as an "intense exchange of ideas, greater personal security, and higher living standards," in the words of Denis Kozlov and Eleonory Gilburd.[5] Mikoyan's rejection of Stalinist centralization and state violence was emblematic of this historical shift, and he firmly believed that the best possible future for the development of the USSR's various national groups was within a reformed and democratized Soviet socialist framework. In fact, from his perspective as an Armenian and as a non-Russian, multiethnicity and Soviet socialism were inextricably intertwined.

The spirit of Mikoyan's approach toward the nationality issue was perhaps best articulated in the speech that he delivered in the Armenian capital Yerevan on March 11, 1954. In it, he effectively foreshadowed the countrywide process of de-Stalinization and underscored the necessity of a flexible line toward Soviet nationalities—two policies that preoccupied him for the remainder of his life and career. In that address, the statesman argued for a form of managed national expression, condemning both national nihilism (i.e., indifference to the concerns of Soviet nationalities) and national chauvinism (i.e., an aggressive sense of pride and superiority of one national group over another).[6] The idea was not new in the context of the larger history of the Soviet nationality policy. Nevertheless, Mikoyan gave it new life during the Thaw, and after laying out his vision in Yerevan, moved to implement it as Khrushchev's point man on nationality matters. In this regard, Mikoyan built on the political and personal trust that he had earned with Khrushchev, especially after his pivotal support for the Soviet premier in defeating the attempted power seizure by the "Anti-Party Group" of

Malenkov, Molotov, and Kaganovich in June 1957. Mikoyan's staunch support for Khrushchev in the latter instance was motivated to a significant degree by his anti-Stalinist and pro-reformist policies.[7]

Mikoyan sought to extend the reformist agenda to the nationality question. His approach, which harkened back to earlier variations of the Soviet nationality policy, was based on two principles—state unity and a respect for ethnic and cultural diversity. The state would discard policies advocating for assimilation and centralization in favor of those advocating for greater political and economic devolution and cultural expression among non-Russian nationalities. For example, at Mikoyan's insistence, the concept of the merger (*sliianie*), or assimilation, of smaller nations into larger ones was officially abandoned by the Party. This concept was based on the Marxist dialectical idea that national differences would cease to have any relevance with the realization of communism and that the Soviet nationality policy was a step toward the inevitable process of a merger.[8] This idea was substituted by Mikoyan with that of the rapprochement (*sblizhenie*) of nations. Instead of assimilation, *sblizhenie* advocated coexistence among the peoples of the USSR and respect for local cultures within the framework of a united Soviet state. Another feature of the Thaw-era nationality policy was the tendency toward greater decentralization from Moscow to the republics, including greater political and economic devolution.[9] In the view of Mikoyan and other reformers in the Soviet leadership, decentralization not only formed a key component of the rejection of the Stalinist legacy but also held the promise for a more democratic and representative brand of Soviet socialism. Stalinist state violence and mass repression were likewise rejected in favor of the return of deported nationalities like the Chechens and the Ingush and the rehabilitation of national cultural figures like Yeghishe Charents and Aksel Bakunts.

However, while stressing decentralization and a greater space for national expression, the Khrushchev government also emphasized the importance of the unity of the state. Consequently, it worked to check those national or cultural expressions it deemed "anti-Soviet" or threatening to state unity, echoing Mikoyan's 1954 articulation of the dual struggle against national nihilism and national chauvinism. This approach formed the foundation for the "tug of war" that developed between Moscow and the republics during the Thaw, with both sides struggling to agree on which forms of national expression were acceptable and which were not.[10] Additionally, Moscow's nationality policy had its limitations, and Mikoyan's lofty visions often clashed with more complicated political realities. The state's inability to address the long-standing grievances of the Armenians of Nagorno-Karabakh (Artsakh) represented one such case. Another was the government's decision to allow for the return of certain deported nationalities (e.g., the Ingush and Balkars) but not others (e.g., the Crimean Tatars and

Volga Germans). Sometimes the Stalinist legacy complicated the state's aims at redressing past wrongs, as the Ingush-Ossetian territorial dispute over the Prigorodnyi raion demonstrated. Most significantly, the approach toward nationality policy favored by Mikoyan was contested, and it did not find universal approval among Kremlin elites. Mikoyan's struggle to secure the removal of the *sliianie* concept from the CPSU's 1961 Party Program reminds us of this reality, as does the struggle of the Chechens and Ingush to return to their native lands.

The study of Mikoyan's contributions to Thaw-era nationality policy reform is also a study of the politics of difference. As historians Jane Burbank and Frederick Cooper have written, this notion of a "politics of difference" could be interpreted differently by different empires and multiethnic states. "In some empires," they wrote, "[it] could mean recognizing the multiplicity of peoples and their varied customs as an ordinary fact of life; in others it meant drawing a strict boundary between undifferentiated insiders and 'barbarian' outsiders." Of these two models of managing difference, the former might be described as "inclusive" and the latter as "exclusive." The "inclusive" model generally fit the Russian state throughout most of its history, but particularly in the years of the Thaw-era USSR. For Mikoyan, difference was "a fact and an opportunity, not an obsession."[11] As this study illustrates, Mikoyan's ethnic background, and his origins from one of the most ethnically and confessionally diverse regions of the Russian Empire, profoundly affected his outlook toward the governance of multicultural societies.

National distinctiveness defined Mikoyan's experience as an Armenian. It was the historic kingdom of Armenia that became the first state in the world to accept the Christian faith, an event traditionally dated by Armenians to the year AD 301.[12] Armenian identity was further distinguished by the invention of the unique Armenian alphabet by Mesrop Mashtots in AD 406.[13] Mikoyan was deeply familiar with this history from the time of his boyhood in the village of Sanahin, nestled in the mountainous Armenian region of Lori on the southern periphery of the Russian Empire. From an early age, he was immersed in an Armenian environment, growing up in a large and loving, but poor, Armenian family. By his own account, Mikoyan first learned to read and write Armenian from a monk at the local tenth-century Sanahin monastery.[14] The Armenian experience was further enhanced by Mikoyan's education at the Nersisyan School in Tiflis and the Gevorgyan Seminary at Ejmiatsin, the center of the Armenian Apostolic Church. His intimate understanding of the Armenian and Caucasian worlds, as well as his later practical experience managing difference in the North Caucasus, proved to be assets for Khrushchev in the nationality sphere.

In fact, as sociologist Liliana Riga highlighted, Mikoyan's personal biography serves as a prime example of the reality that "Bolshevism's Russian-inflected class universalism was especially appealing in those social locations across the Russian

Empire most affected by socioethnic or imperial exclusions." The statesman's Caucasian context profoundly impacted his decision to join the Bolsheviks in his youth, underscoring the fact that "ethnic dynamics within the socialist class-revolutionary movement" were "constitutively built into [its] core . . . through the identities and experiences of its social carriers."[15] Indeed, in addition to his avowed belief in revolutionary Marxism, Mikoyan's commitment to the reconstitution of the multiethnic Russian state was driven by the promise of geopolitical security for his native Armenia as well as the prospect of peaceful relations among the different ethnic groups of the Caucasus.[16] The context was the violent breakdown of tsarist authority in Caucasia in 1918–20 and the catastrophic 1915 Armenian Genocide, a calamity that preoccupied Mikoyan in his writings decades later.

Mikoyan's favored approach to managing difference in the multiethnic Soviet Union falls into the category that political scientists have dubbed "territorial pluralism"—that is, a style of governance "aimed specifically at the accommodation of distinct ethnic, linguistic, religious, cultural, and national communities."[17] However, due to the Communist Party's monopoly on political power in the USSR, some Western scholars of territorial pluralism have dismissed the Soviet federal model as a form of "sham federalism"—that is, representative on paper but not in practice.[18] In fact, as chapter 6 documents, the work of the constitutional subcommittee on Nationality Policy and National-State Construction (NPNSC) reveals that Soviet federalism and Soviet politics were much more dynamic than these scholars had assumed. The subcommittee, which was chaired by Mikoyan and included the first secretaries of four union republics, took into consideration not only questions about the self-governance of nationalities but also questions about the fundamental nature of the Soviet state structure. Ultimately, the members of the subcommittee, led by Mikoyan, were grappling with centuries-old questions regarding the ways in which Russia as a multiethnic state should be governed. Should the state be centralized? If not, how much power should be delegated to the union republics? What kind of state is the Soviet Union—a federation, a confederation, or a union state? Why are the differences among these forms of state so significant? Should the republics be permitted to secede? Should certain autonomous republics, like Tataria or Iakutia, be elevated to the status of union republics, like Ukraine or Armenia? If so, what should be the criteria? What benefits and obligations should the state provide to each type of national community within the country?

Mikoyan's efforts to answer these questions and others are reflected in each chapter of this study. Chapter 1 provides a backdrop for Mikoyan's nationality reform efforts by exploring the 1937 Yerevan intervention and Mikoyan's role in the Stalinist repressions in Armenia. Supervised personally by Stalin, the

1937 Yerevan episode constituted a major central intervention by Moscow into the affairs of a union republic and exemplified Stalin's disregard for local self-governance, something that Mikoyan would challenge in his later reform efforts. Perhaps even more significantly, Mikoyan's lingering guilt from his role as a participant in Stalinist state violence would guide his later de-Stalinization initiatives, beginning with his March 1954 speech in Yerevan. Chapter 2 highlights Mikoyan's Yerevan address as a policy speech that provided the framework for the Thaw-era Soviet nationality policy. In that address, the statesman also called for the rehabilitation of the futurist Armenian poet Yeghishe Charents, a victim of Stalin's Great Purge.[19] By invoking the name of Charents, Mikoyan enabled the process of the post-Stalin rehabilitation of former "*vragi naroda*" ("enemies of the people"), including national cultural figures. In this respect, the speech helped set the stage for Nikita Khrushchev's broader reassessment of Stalin and his cult of personality two years later, at the Twentieth Party Congress. Moreover, it became symbolic as a starting point for the Thaw in Soviet Armenia. Subsequent chapters demonstrate the ways in which Mikoyan worked to develop his 1954 nationality policy framework during the Thaw.

Chapter 3 examines Mikoyan's efforts to highlight his native republic, Armenia, as a model of Soviet success in the nationality sphere and the ways in which those efforts cultivated his Armenian patronage network. It further highlights the limitations of Mikoyan and his Armenian network in relation to the issue of Nagorno-Karabakh, revealing fundamental contradictions within the Soviet state structure and underscoring the necessity for reform. Chapter 4 follows Mikoyan's efforts to invoke historical narratives to promote the much-vaunted Soviet concept of *druzhba narodov* ("friendship of peoples") in the context of the Caucasus. These narratives not only reflected his long-standing commitment to the geopolitical unity of the multiethnic Russian state but also constituted one of many possible responses from Moscow to the rising demands for greater national expression during the Thaw. Chapter 5 examines Mikoyan's role in the rehabilitation and return of nationalities deported by Stalin to Central Asia during World War II, in particular the Chechens and the Ingush. It highlights that the return of these peoples to their native lands and the restoration of their autonomous republics became a highly contested issue within the Soviet leadership. While reform-minded officials like Mikoyan favored the return of these peoples, security officials such as KGB chief Ivan Serov opposed such initiatives. Chapter 6 deals with Mikoyan's contributions to the nationality platform of the CPSU's Third Party Program and his chairmanship of the NPNSC Subcommittee of Khrushchev's Constitutional Commission of the 1960s. It argues that Mikoyan's work on these initiatives indicated a general trend toward greater decentralization and, ultimately, democratization of the Soviet state and system under Khrushchev.

This monograph contributes to the study of Russia as a multiethnic, multiconfessional space, a topic of analysis that has flowered since 1991, with the advent of the "archival revolution" and the rise of what scholars have dubbed the "imperial turn" in Russian/Soviet studies. Since that time, critical exploration of Soviet nationality policy has focused primarily on the earlier decades of Soviet history, from Lenin's New Economic Policy (NEP) to the death of Stalin.[20] Only recently have scholars proceeded to move beyond these periods, facing a new question—how did Soviet nationality policy evolve in the decades following Stalinism? This question is a challenging one for scholars to address, largely due to the institutional centralization and reorganization of the Soviet state that occurred with the adoption of the Stalin constitution of 1936.[21] In other words, the loss of specific nationality policy institutions in this process made it more difficult, although not impossible, for scholars to identify a centrally coordinated policy toward nationality issues in subsequent years through archival sources.

Consequently, historians have sought to investigate Soviet nationality policy in the post-Stalin years from the perspective of national autonomies, such as Buriatia, or union republics, such as Ukraine, Latvia, Georgia, or Azerbaijan.[22] As one might expect, these very specific examinations found that the evolution of national identity in the postwar USSR was primarily driven by local factors, although the influence of the center undoubtedly left its mark. Nevertheless, some scholars have sought to move beyond these confines in the effort to identify a central approach toward nationality in the post-Stalin years. For example, Michael Loader convincingly argued for the significance of Lavrentii Beria's "new course" on nationality policy in the post-Stalin power struggle between Beria and Khrushchev.[23] In the contexts of Ukraine and Belorussia, other historians have similarly identified the significance of Beria's attempts to use the nationality policy to advance his position in the post-Stalin power struggle.[24] At the same time, it is clear from the writings of these scholars that although Beria, in tandem with Khrushchev, implemented a series of nationality reforms, these actions alone did not constitute a coherent policy and in fact were intended to achieve short-term political aims. In contrast to Mikoyan in 1954, Beria did not articulate a guiding philosophy or framework toward the nationality issue. For example, it is unclear what position (if any) Beria held in relation to the *sliianie* concept.

As noted earlier, this study argues that the overall trend from Moscow was toward more, not less, decentralization. This argument speaks to earlier Western interpretations of the Thaw-era nationality policy. In seeking to identify Moscow's approach toward nationalities in the wake of Khrushchev's 1958 educational reform and the defeat of Latvia's "national communists," several Western scholars concluded that the Kremlin became less tolerant of political decentralization by the early 1960s.[25] This argument was first advanced by Robert Conquest, who contended that the 1961 Party Program constituted a "wide-ranging rebuff" against local aspirations and even a "provocation" toward them by indirectly expressing Moscow's supposed intention to "gradually dissolve the separate republics."[26] Many other Western scholars have subsequently echoed these interpretations, perceiving Khrushchev's policies of the late 1950s and early 1960s as aiming toward the "eventual assimilation [of national groups] into one larger community" and therefore legitimizing "the Russification of non-Russian nationalities."[27] However, the evidence of Mikoyan's work on the Third Party Program and the NPNSC Subcommittee indicates that, far from being a rejection of local aspirations, these reform efforts represented an official rejection of "Russification" by the CPSU. Indeed, a better explanation for the rollback against nationally minded leaderships in republics like Latvia is that it constituted part of the larger "tug of war" between Moscow and local republican elites who "began to test the limits of what [the center] would tolerate."[28]

The personality of Mikoyan stands at the center of this study. Through the genre of political biography, it seeks to examine Mikoyan's personal role in post-Stalin nationality reform as a means of delving into much broader questions, not only about Soviet nationality policy but also about the possibilities of political reform in the Soviet Union and the management of diversity in multiethnic societies generally. In this respect, the work is not dissimilar to Stephen F. Cohen's classic biography on Nikolai Bukharin. Moreover, it follows a general renewed interest in the genre of political biography in the field of Russian and Soviet studies internationally. This trend is perhaps best illustrated not only by the recent biographies of Gorbachev by William Taubman, Brezhnev by Susanne Schattenberg, and the young Stalin by Ronald Grigor Suny but also by the forthcoming biographies of Lev Trotskii by Aleksandr Reznik and Mikhail Suslov by Alex Marshall. A key study that influenced this work as a political biography has been *The Bolsheviks and the Russian Empire*, by Liliana Riga. As noted earlier, Riga persuasively makes the case that ethnic experiences and dynamics were key in influencing the thought and radicalization of early Bolshevik leaders, including Mikoyan. Building on Riga's work, this study further contends that ethnicity not only influenced Mikoyan's attraction toward revolutionary politics but also profoundly influenced his thinking on nationality policy, especially in the post-Stalin years.

Similarly, in her research on post-Stalin Soviet Armenia, historian Maike Lehmann contends that the Soviet experience led to the emergence of a hybrid identity in the national republics, fusing together an all-union Soviet (i.e., state and socialist) identity with a national identity (i.e., a sense of belonging to a specific ethnic, national, cultural, or ethnoreligious community). She calls this phenomenon "Apricot socialism," referring to "yet another variation of the revolutionary red in the Soviet everyday." Specifically, she noted that "the apricot, being the Armenian national fruit, whose skin often samples the whole color spectrum between crimson red and light orange, serves me as a metaphor for how people in Soviet Armenia imagined the rules and goals of the Soviet community." To be sure, such identities were constructs or "imagined communities," in the words of Benedict Anderson. However, although "imagined," they nevertheless came into existence as tangible forms of self-identification, whether they represented subjective senses of belonging to "national communities" (e.g., Armenians) or "state and socialist communities" (e.g., Soviets). In Lehmann's argument, these identities blended in the Soviet era to form a "very Soviet hybrid of national and socialist elements."[29] My research concurs with her findings, maintaining that Soviet and national identities not only constituted a hybrid Soviet-national identity but also actively influenced the course of Soviet politics, as the case of Mikoyan illustrates.

Some scholars have been tempted to view the Soviet Union's efforts to manage difference in the framework of a "colonial empire." This view has gained traction in Western scholarship in recent years, with increased calls to "decolonize" Russian and Soviet studies in the Western world. However, as Adeeb Khalid persuasively argued, the application of the colonial framework to the Soviet case simply "does not work." "The Soviet Union's cultural agenda—mass education in indigenous languages, fighting illiteracy, public health, political mobilization—had more in common with those of the mobilizational states of the interwar era," Khalid stressed. Furthermore, he noted that Soviet attempts to "engineer society—land reform, organization of marginal groups in society, reshaping the body social—have no parallels in the colonial empires of the era."[30] Although the colonial model cannot be applied to the USSR, this study demonstrates that we can learn much about the dynamic and multifaceted history of the Soviet state by examining it from the perspective of individuals from national republics like Armenia. Mikoyan's contributions to Thaw-era nationality reform and de-Stalinization further underscore the fact that such individuals actively influenced larger all-union political processes.

This study is built on information from a variety of sources—archival materials from Russian and Armenian archives, memoirs, personal interviews, and newspaper articles. From Russia, this study is indebted to the major Russian federal archives in Moscow—the Russian State Archive of Socio-Political History (RGASPI), the Russian State Archive (GARF), the Russian State Archive of Contemporary History (RGANI), and the Russian State Archive of Literature and Art (RGALI). Additionally, this work draws on copies of documents from the Russian Presidential Archive (APRF) and the Central Archive of the FSB (TsA FSB RF) acquired through the international society Memorial in Moscow. From

Armenia, this study draws on materials from the Central, Social-Political, and Kino-Foto-Fono branches of the Armenian National Archives (HAA) in Yerevan. Several libraries were instrumental in the development of this monograph. In the former Soviet Union, these included the National Library of Russia in St. Petersburg, the Russian State Library and the State Public Historical Library of Russia in Moscow, and the National Library of Armenia and the Fundamental Scientific Library of the Armenian National Academy of Sciences in Yerevan. Important resources were also secured through the HSE St. Petersburg Library and the AUA AGBU Papazian Library. The National Library of Armenia was especially helpful in providing access to Soviet Armenian newspapers *Khorhrdayin Hayastan* (later *Sovetakan Hayastan*) and *Kommunist*, as well as local Party papers, like the Meghri-based *Koltntesayin Gyugh*, which are inaccessible in the West. In the United States, this project would be incomplete without the superb collections of the Harlan Hatcher Library at the University of Michigan, the Cleveland Public Library, the New York Public Library, and the Thompson Memorial Library at the Ohio State University.

Memoirs have proved to be crucial in piecing together the historical puzzle of Mikoyan. These include Mikoyan's own memoirs, which have proved to be fairly reliable and which largely correspond with the documentary materials held at the Russian and Armenian archives, as well as the accounts of other memoirs. Nevertheless, as Mikoyan himself confessed, "any memoirs are inevitably of a subjective character."[31] Indeed, while much of what Mikoyan wrote can be corroborated in the archives, he also omitted several important episodes from his life, many of which are covered in this book. Mikoyan began publishing his memoirs in the mid-1960s in the Soviet magazine *Iunost'*, followed by two volumes published by Politizdat in the 1970s.[32] Due to censorship, the two Politizdat volumes leave out significant information, especially the second volume.[33] According to Sergo Mikoyan, a third volume of his father's memoirs was supposed to be published but was canceled after his death in 1978, reportedly due to the influence of Suslov.[34] The publications of the two Russian volumes were soon followed by Armenian translations.[35] It is quite significant that the memoirs were translated into Armenian and not into any other Soviet language. The aim was to elucidate historical questions for Armenian-speaking audiences, both in the USSR and in the Armenian diaspora, especially as they related to the Baku Commune and the civil war in Transcaucasia. When the translations were published, they were very well received by Armenian audiences abroad.[36] One Armenian diasporan from Paris even requested the publication of Mikoyan's memoirs in Classical Armenian orthography, although such an idea was never realized.[37] Additionally, in 1988, an English translation of the first volume was published in the United

States, with a foreword by W. Averell Harriman and a preface and annotations by Harrison E. Salisbury.[38] This study draws on the most recent edition of Mikoyan's memoirs published after the Soviet dissolution.

Mikoyan had five sons with his wife, Ashkhen—Stepan, Vladimir, Aleksei, Vano, and Sergo. Two of these sons—Stepan and Sergo—have left us with memoirs. Stepan's memoirs were published both in Russian and in an English translation by his daughter Ashkhen.[39] Sergo's memoirs are less accessible; only an earlier, incomplete draft was published in Yerevan in 2007, in an Armenian translation by Eduard and Svetlana Avagyan under the title *Hayrs Anastas Mikoyane* (*My Father Anastas Mikoyan*). Fortunately, Vladimir Mikoyan, the son of Sergo and his first wife, Alla Kuznetsova, has generously provided me with a complete copy of his father's original Russian manuscript, entitled "Anastas Mikoian: Zhizn', otdannaia narodu" ("Anastas Mikoyan: A Life Devoted to the People"). Sergo completed these memoirs in the autumn of 2009, just months before he died of leukemia in March 2010. Both the Armenian translation and the Russian manuscript are cited throughout this work, as the Armenian version includes details that are not included in the Russian text, and vice versa. In addition, this study draws on in-person interviews with Vladimir Mikoyan, Sergei Khrushchev, and Tatiana Shahumyan, as well as several published memoirs, including those of Vahram Alazan, Yeghishe Astsatryan, Elena Bonner, Izabella Charents, Iunus Desheriev, Antranig Dzarugian, Regina Ghazaryan, Nikita Khrushchev, Anton Kochinyan, Dinmukhamed Kunaev, Nami Mikoyan (Geurkova), Aleksandr Mil'chakov, Aram Piruzyan, Olga Shatunovskaia, and Nikita Zarobyan, among many others. Of these, the memoirs of the Armenian officials Kochinyan and Astsatryan merit special attention as they devote entire chapters to Mikoyan's role as a patron for Armenia, providing fascinating insights into the world of informal Soviet politics.

The subject of this book is extremely timely and relevant to ongoing developments in the former Soviet Union. The history of the Soviet ethno-federal state and the management of multiethnicity have received renewed interest across the post-Soviet world in the wake of the war in Ukraine, ongoing conflicts in the Caucasus, the centenary of the formation of the USSR, and the passing of Mikhail Gorbachev. In Russia in particular, these events have sparked much discussion and introspection about potential alternative paths in Soviet history and whether the union of republics could have been preserved, or whether the Soviet nationality policy had been a "failure" or a "success."[40] The history of Mikoyan's role in the development of post-Stalin nationality reform can serve as an important addition to such discussions, as well as those regarding the management of diversity within contemporary post-Soviet Russia. Indeed, as this study highlights, Mikoyan's contributions to political reform in the Soviet Union were genuinely extraordinary, which makes it all the more tempting to overstate them. Every biographer is at least somewhat guilty of this sin, including, possibly, this author. Nevertheless, if this book at least succeeds in illuminating an important yet little-known aspect of the Khrushchev Thaw to both Soviet and world history, it will have more than done its job.

1 | Prelude

Yerevan 1937

One cannot fully comprehend the significance of Mikoyan's efforts to de-Stalinize Soviet nationality policy without first examining his role in the Great Purge in Armenia in September 1937, on the orders of Stalin.[1] Mikoyan's participation comprised part of the 1937 Yerevan intervention, also known as the "Armenian Affair," arguably one of the most significant political events in the Soviet Caucasus of the 1930s.[2] A major intervention by the Soviet central government into the affairs of a union republic, it was supervised personally by Stalin and served as a vivid illustration of the center's disregard for local self-governance in this period. Moreover, and perhaps even more significantly, Mikoyan's role as a participant in Stalinist state violence would go on to haunt him and this sense of guilt informed his later de-Stalinization efforts, including his calls to rehabilitate national cultural figures such as the poet Yeghishe Charents. Consequently, the Yerevan intervention would have a lasting impact on Mikoyan and his later actions regarding nationality policy reform during the Thaw. Indeed, it was in the immediate aftermath of this episode that he assumed the post of a Supreme Soviet deputy for nationalities representing Yerevan, a position from which he would later deliver his March 1954 speech, laying the groundwork for his reforms in the nationality sphere.

THE GREAT PURGE IN ARMENIA

At the time of the 1937 intervention, Mikoyan was the people's commissar of food production and deputy chairman of the Council of Ministers. He had little direct involvement in the affairs of Soviet Armenia, which had been under the jurisdiction of the Transcaucasian SFSR from the founding of the USSR in 1922 to the Stalin constitution of 1936.[3] Contrary to those historians who assert that

Mikoyan and Georgii Malenkov unleashed the Great Purge in Armenia, the Purge was in fact already in its active phase when Stalin dispatched Malenkov and later Mikoyan to Yerevan.[4] The history dates back to 1936, with the conflict between popular Soviet Armenian leader Aghasi Khanjyan and Georgian First Secretary Lavrentii Beria. Khanjyan's local support base in Armenia presented a serious threat to Beria's pretensions to regional leadership.[5]

No member of Khanjyan's network was more fiercely opposed to Beria than Armenian Party leader Nerses "Nersik" Stepanyan, "a man of penetrating mind, iron logic and high principles" who "never hid in the shadows, even during a period when thousands of honest people faced repression." Stepanyan openly criticized Beria's pretentious "little book" on the history of the Bolsheviks in Transcaucasia, considering it to be a "dangerous work that falsified the history of the Party." On one occasion, he even likened Beria personally to Ottoman sultan Abdul Hamid II.[6] Stepanyan was also known for his sensitivity toward national cultures and for his support of Armenian writers, such as Yeghishe Charents and Aksel Bakunts.[7] Beria managed to silence him through Armenia's Second Secretary Amatuni Amatuni (Vardapetyan) and the head of the Armenian NKVD Khachik Mughdusi. By May 21, 1936, these cronies managed to secure Stepanyan's arrest on behalf of Beria.[8] However, Stepanyan remained firm on his convictions even after his arrest, stating, "I accuse . . . I exposed and will expose . . . I will not retreat from the positions of Lenin!"[9] He would eventually be executed by the Armenian NKVD on July 8, 1937, alongside Bakunts and Drastamat Ter-Simonyan.[10] At the very moment that he was shot, Stepanyan reportedly shouted, "To hell with Stalin!" ("*Korch'i Staline*"), while Bakunts and Ter-Simonyan defiantly sang "The Internationale" immediately before their execution.[11]

Stepanyan's arrest was soon followed by the death of Khanjyan on July 9, 1936. Although it was officially reported as a "suicide" at the time, an official Soviet investigation in January 1956 concluded that Khanjyan did not commit suicide and that Beria personally shot him in his office in Tbilisi.[12] The poet Charents, a close friend of Khanjyan, saw the assassination at the hands of Beria as an ominous sign of the violence to come.[13] Indeed, Beria soon denounced Khanjyan posthumously in a lengthy editorial entitled "Scatter the Enemies of Socialism to Dust." The op-ed was published on the second page of *Pravda* on August 19, the day when the first Moscow trial against the "Trotskiite-Zinovievite terrorist center" commenced.[14] In his text, Beria called for greater "vigilance" against "Trotskiites and Zinovievites" and highlighted Khanjyan as an example of those who lacked such "vigilance." He accused the former Armenian first secretary of protecting Stepanyan and his "counter-revolutionary terrorist group" while also providing support to "rabid nationalist elements among the Armenian intelligentsia." He further "revealed" Khanjyan's correspondence with the "bourgeois" Armenian diasporan writer Arshag Chobanian, who advocated incorporating Akhalkalaki (Javakhk/Javakheti), Nagorno-Karabakh, and Nakhichevan' into Soviet Armenia.[15]

With Khanjyan posthumously disgraced, Beria moved to liquidate his network entirely, a formula that he would later repeat with brutal efficiency in Abkhazia with Nestor Lakoba and his network.[16] Toward that end, Beria promoted Amatuni to the office of Armenian first secretary and Mughdusi to the post of minister of internal affairs. These local loyalists proceeded to unleash a vicious campaign of state violence in Armenia, with the aim of eliminating Khanjyan's support base.[17] Some of Armenia's most prominent cultural figures were swallowed up in the ensuing repressions, including Charents, Bakunts, Vahram Alazan, Gurgen Mahari, Vahan Totovents, and Vagharshak Norents, all of whom were loyal to the Soviet system and to the ideals of the Bolshevik Revolution. An atmosphere of pervasive fear gripped the republic as the local NKVD worked to "unmask" and destroy real or imagined "enemies" of Beria and Stalin. Mughdusi became especially infamous among Armenians for his penchant for cruelty and sadism.[18]

On the all-union level, the notorious Central Committee plenum of February–March 1937 in Moscow officialized Stalin's campaign of mass repression and painted a portrait of a country saturated with spies and saboteurs, even at the highest levels of the Party and the state.[19] The subsequent all-union plenum of June 1937 built on this theme, with the feared NKVD chief Nikolai Ezhov revealing his "unmasking" of "enemies" in various state and Party organs and ominously setting the stage for an even greater, more intensive purge throughout the country.[20] The Armenian Party leadership dutifully demonstrated that Yerevan was in full accordance with these all-union trends and eagerly tied them to the ongoing campaign to liquidate Khanjyan's network. In a letter to Stalin from June 1937, Amatuni boasted that in the ten months since the "exposure" of Khanjyan, 1,365 people had been arrested under his leadership, including 900 "Dashnak-Trotskiites." However, he stressed that continued "enemy attacks" throughout the republic "left no doubt that there were still enemy nests in Armenia that should be uprooted."[21]

Amatuni framed the repressions as part of the ideological struggle against the Specifists, a group of Armenian Marxists with prerevolutionary origins who advocated tailoring Marxism to Armenian national conditions.[22] In the draft of his letter to Stalin, he even went so far as to claim that it was "unlikely that the enemy had harmed any other part of the Soviet Union as much as Armenia" due to the purported influence of the Specifists.[23] Amatuni further alleged that "for almost all the years of Soviet power," Armenia's Communist Party had been led by men who supported the Specifists, including prominent Old Bolshevik Sahak Ter-Gabrielyan.[24] However, the decision of Amatuni and Mughdusi to target Ter-Gabrielyan would prove to be a fatal miscalculation.[25] Ter-Gabrielyan was known to be critical of Beria and reportedly viewed him as "an upstart, an adventurer, a forceful brute," and "a dangerous bastard" (*opasnyi merzavets*). For his part, Beria "did not like and did not trust" Ter-Gabrielyan.[26] Ter-Gabrielyan had been under suspicion by the Armenian NKVD as early as August 1936, one month after the murder of Khanjyan.[27] He was arrested by the NKVD in Moscow on June 25, 1937, and held at Butyrka prison before being transferred to Armenia on July 3.[28] At the Armenian NKVD headquarters in Yerevan, Ter-Gabrielyan was harshly interrogated by Mughdusi's men Ivan Gevorkov and Yeghbayr Nikoghosyan, at Mughdusi's direction. Ter-Gabrielyan then either jumped or was pushed from the third-floor window of the building, falling to his death approximately ten meters (thirty-three feet) to the ground on August 21, 1937.[29]

The death of Ter-Gabrielyan and the circumstances surrounding it soon caught the attention of Stalin. Angered by the death and by the decision of the local leadership not to inform him about it, Stalin dictated a letter to Malenkov, addressed to the Armenian Central Committee, dated September 8.[30] "The Government of the USSR and the Central Committee of the CPSU believe that the situation in Armenia, on an economic and Party and cultural level, is proceeding extremely badly [*iz rukh von plokho*]," he began. Stalin went on to detail that agriculture had "collapsed" and that "industrial enterprises under construction are in stagnation." He strongly insinuated that the Armenian Central Committee was misusing or stealing centrally distributed funds. "It is difficult to say where the money goes," Stalin wrote. He condemned cultural construction as "lackluster" and stated that Party work "had again deviated from the Party line." He maintained that "the Trotskiites and other anti-Party elements are not adequately rebuffed by the Party leadership of Armenia."[31]

On Ter-Gabrielyan's death, Stalin was not timid at all in suspecting foul play and placed direct blame on the authorities in Yerevan:

> The most recent events, in connection with Ter-Gabrielyan's "suicide," put into clear focus all the maximum rot and decay that sums up the state of the Party and Soviet organizations in Armenia. It is hard to imagine that Ter-Gabrielyan jumped out of the window. It is completely inconsistent with his timid and prudent nature. It is much more likely that he was thrown out of the window to shut him up so that he could not expose the enemies of Soviet power. It is rather bizarre that the leadership of Armenia did not consider it necessary to inform the Council of People's Commissars or the Central Committee about this [incident]. They apparently wanted to conceal this flagrant fact and naïvely assumed that they could get away with it.[32]

Announcing that the Central Committee and the Council of People's Commissars "cannot allow the enemies of the Armenian people to walk freely in Armenia,"

Stalin ordered the immediate arrest of Mughdusi and Chairman of the Council of People's Commissars Abraham Guloyan. Both men, Stalin asserted, "cannot but bear direct responsibility for all the outrages that have been revealed." To make the full force of the Soviet state felt on the Armenian Communist Party, he concluded that Malenkov would be sent to Yerevan to conduct an on-site investigation.[33]

THE ARRIVAL OF MALENKOV AND THE NKVD BRIGADE

Malenkov left Moscow for Yerevan by train on September 9, with a mandate from the all-union Central Committee. He was accompanied by his personal assistant Dmitrii Sukhanov and an NKVD brigade led by Mikhail Litvin and including interrogators Piotr Fedotov, Lazar' Al'tman, Kirill Geiman, Grigorii Arsenovich, and Mikhail Iakhontov.[34] Stalin's personal decision to include Litvin, an obedient deputy of Ezhov, was a natural choice.[35] The visiting group also included Malenkov's close associates Vladimir Donskoi and editor of the magazine *Partstroitel'stvo*, Dmitrii Smirnov.[36] On such assignments, Malenkov was known to always bring along Donskoi, whom Sukhanov later described as a "drunkard," a "morphine addict," a "loafer," and, most importantly, a "specialist" in fabricating materials against regional Party leaders.[37] As Khrushchev famously recalled, Malenkov was accustomed to "running errands" such as these for Stalin and others.[38] During this period, Stalin had dispatched him to oversee the brutal purge of local Party leaderships throughout the USSR, including in Soviet Belorussia and various parts of the Russian SFSR, such as the Tatar ASSR.[39]

On the way to Armenia, the entourage first stopped for half a day in Tbilisi. In the Georgian capital, Malenkov, accompanied by Donskoi, met with Beria to discuss "the procedure for 'investigation' and repression" against the Armenian leadership.[40] Beria's concern in Armenia was tied to the fate of his protégés, Amatuni and Mughdusi. As Georgia's first secretary, he had possessed near-total power in his native republic, where he ruthlessly terrorized his own people.[41] In Yerevan and Baku, he exercised informal power through his clients, but now with the fatal miscalculations of Amatuni and Mughdusi, he was losing control in Yerevan. Indeed, in his decision to purge Beria's cronies, Stalin undoubtedly aimed to test the loyalty of his increasingly prominent Mingrelian hangman. Would Beria support his Armenian deputies or Stalin? In the end, Beria reaffirmed his loyalty to Stalin and took the loss of his deputies in stride, paving the way for his promotion to the leadership of the all-union NKVD. Moreover, in his consultations with Malenkov, Beria agreed to participate in developments in Yerevan to ensure that his cronies would be followed by politically palatable successors. Sukhanov later testified that it was during the Yerevan intervention that Beria and Malenkov developed a close friendship, which formed the basis for their later political alliance.[42]

For his part, Malenkov, who had just successfully brutalized the Tatar leadership in Kazan', wasted no time in doing what he did best.[43] In the morning hours of September 14, he and his retinue descended on Yerevan, arriving "incognito," in the words of Liparit Barseghyan, unbeknownst to the Armenian Central Committee or the Armenian Sovnarkom.[44] Beria, who arrived separately by car, was already there waiting for them.[45] His close ally, the brutal Azerbaijani First Secretary Mir Jafar Bagirov, was also present.[46] Colonel (later General) G. A. Petrov, head of the Armenian section of the Soviet border guards, was summoned to a meeting in Malenkov's railroad car with strict orders not to inform his superior, Mughdusi. When he arrived at the car, Petrov was escorted by an NKVD officer to a private room. There he met with members of the NKVD brigade, who asked him a series of questions to which he "could not give immediate answers." Malenkov then emerged from the adjoining compartment. "Don't be shy, Comrade Petrov," he said, before presenting the colonel with a copy of Stalin's September 8 letter.[47] He then instructed Petrov to arrest Mughdusi, Guloyan, Gevorkov, Nikoghosyan, Vahram Chituni, and others, and to "urgently take measures to close the state border."[48] Malenkov and Litvin likewise decided to order the arrest of Armenia's chief of police, Aleksandr Dulgarov, as well as the police officer who happened to be on duty at the NKVD building at the time of Ter-Gabrielyan's fall.[49]

At the Armenian NKVD headquarters in Yerevan, Petrov personally arrested Mughdusi, who, bewildered, asked his former subordinate, "What's wrong?"[50] Under arrest, Mughdusi—the once-feared Armenian NKVD chief—was now at the mercy of Malenkov and Litvin. According to Petrov, both Litvin and Malenkov personally participated in the interrogation of Mughdusi. Together with their NKVD men, they beat him violently and continuously until he began to "confess" to his manifold crimes.[51] When Mughdusi initially refused to confess to throwing Ter-Gabrielyan out of the window, Litvin reportedly showed him a copy of Stalin's letter and told him, "You fool! Don't you understand that since the letter says that you threw him out, I can't very well go back [to Moscow] and say [to Stalin] that 'you were wrong, Mughdusi didn't do such a thing.' If I did that, then they would shoot me too."[52]

Beatings were also employed in the interrogation of Guloyan, to extract the necessary "confessions" of "counter-revolutionary" conspiracy.[53] The same fate awaited Gevorkov, who was in Leninakan and needed to be brought to Yerevan. When Malenkov learned of his whereabouts, he reportedly told Petrov, "If he escapes to Turkey, then your head is off."[54] In addition to Malenkov and Litvin, Beria personally attended Gevorkov's interrogation, which took place in Gevorkov's office at the Armenian NKVD building, in the same room where Ter-Gabrielyan had been interrogated on the fateful night of his death. Petrov later recounted that when he arrived in the office, Beria, Malenkov, and Litvin were already there examining the scene, especially the window from which Ter-Gabrielyan fell. The border guards escorted Gevorkov into the room. Once Gevorkov saw who was present, he fell to his knees and began weeping. He begged for forgiveness and insisted that Ter-Gabrielyan had thrown himself out. Beria, Malenkov, and Litvin were less than sympathetic. "What are you drooling about?" they snarled. "Tell us how you threw Ter-Gabrielyan out the window." However, Gevorkov reportedly insisted on his version of events throughout the interrogation.[55]

Others arrested in Armenia during this time likewise recounted being violently beaten and tortured by Malenkov, Litvin, and their NKVD men.[56] Donskoi reportedly participated in these interrogations as well.[57] The former head of Armenia's cotton trust, Arshak Hovhannisyan, testified that after one interrogation, Malenkov theatrically declared that "the greatest humanist Maksim Gor'kii once said: 'if the enemy does not surrender, destroy him.'"[58] In the case that the arrestees refused to "confess" even after torture, the NKVD men Al'tman and Gaiman would "correct" the interrogation protocols to ensure that they did.[59] Together with the NKVD brigade, Malenkov preferred to conduct his work from the NKVD headquarters in Yerevan rather than the republic's Central Committee building. "All [government] organs in the capital were paralyzed," recalled Armen Ananyan, former chairman of Armenia's Central Executive Committee and an "accidental" survivor of the interrogations. "Malenkov was the boss, with his brigade. Every night, batches of responsible workers were arrested, without the involvement of the prosecutor or the Central Committee of the Party. They filled the cellars of the Armenian Ministry of Internal Affairs."[60]

On the following day, September 15, the Armenian Party plenum commenced at 6:00 p.m. in the meeting hall of the Armenian Central Committee building.[61] According to Petrov, the atmosphere at the plenum was "very active and stormy."[62] The Armenian Central Committee members were surrounded by escorts of armed border guards.[63] The proceedings were opened by Amatuni, who gave the floor to Malenkov, the official plenary chairman. Malenkov briefly discussed the Ter-Gabrielyan case and then read aloud Stalin's letter to the attendees. Once he finished, he loudly concluded, "Signed Stalin," and held up the letter with Stalin's signature for all to see.[64] Then, accusing the entire Armenian Party organization of "political blindness," Malenkov declared that he and Beria had "managed to uncover a whole counter-revolutionary conspiracy within just a few hours of their stay in Yerevan."[65] He further boasted of arresting Guloyan and extracting a quick confession from him after one hour, which he then read aloud to those present, reportedly alongside the confession of Mughdusi.[66] "Such inveterate counter-revolutionaries as Guloyan and Mughdusi sat right under your nose and engaged in counter-revolution," Malenkov told the attendees. "You didn't expose them, and we needed to come from Moscow, arrest them, and, one hour after arrest, extract a confession like the one that I just read to you. And how many hundreds of enemies like Guloyan remain in the ranks of the Armenian Communist Party? Enemies who you still have not unmasked?"[67]

On the same day, Malenkov and Litvin telegraphed Stalin and updated him about the arrests of Mughdusi, Guloyan, and the others.[68] Stalin was personally supervising all developments closely from Moscow. Although Amatuni spoke at the proceedings and was not yet officially in disgrace, he would not remain in office for long. Stalin tasked the visiting group, and primarily Malenkov, to investigate Amatuni. However, the "investigation" was far from impartial, for Stalin had already made up his mind that Amatuni was "guilty," and now he wanted his surrogates to produce proof of his "treason." At 8:30 p.m. (20:30), Stalin and Viacheslav Molotov sent a message to Litvin and Malenkov. "We do not trust Amatuni, and we consider him to be a Trotskiite," they wrote. "However, there is no need to arrest him just yet. We need to collect materials on him first." In the meantime, Stalin and Molotov instructed Malenkov and Litvin on how to conduct the plenum. They further ordered Malenkov to arrest Abkhaz Party leader Aleksei Agrba and Azerbaijan's second secretary Atanes Akopov, who was of Armenian origin.[69] On September 18, Malenkov dutifully informed Stalin and Ezhov that he had arrested both Agrba and Akopov after "light" and "short" interrogations.[70]

Until Stalin's men "found" the desired evidence against Amatuni, the plenum focused on the "guilt" of several lower Armenian officials instead, specifically Amatuni's deputy, Stepan Akopov (no relation to Atanes), beginning on September 16.[71] Sukhanov later claimed that Malenkov and Donskoi even encouraged some Armenian officials to attack each other in their plenary speeches, to underscore the "dysfunction and squabbling that allegedly existed within the Party organization of Armenia."[72] Behind the scenes, Malenkov reported to Stalin on the progress of the plenum and detailed the "confession" of Guloyan as well as the arrests of several other Armenian officials.[73] However, as the plenum proceeded, it initially appeared as if Amatuni might escape the fate of his henchmen. During the plenum's evening session on September 17, Malenkov even motioned to establish a commission on its outcome, including himself, Litvin, Amatuni, and several lower Armenian officials.[74] In reality, Stalin remained adamant on Amatuni's removal, characterizing the change in Armenia's leadership as "necessary" in his letter to Malenkov and Litvin on the same day.[75] Unsurprisingly, during the plenum's morning session on September 18, its work was abruptly interrupted at the motion of Malenkov for a three-day recess "to study a number of special issues."[76] Malenkov clearly needed more time to secure the evidence that Stalin demanded to ensure Amatuni's ouster.

The necessary evidence soon emerged from the scholar Ashot Hovhannisyan, who previously served as Armenia's first secretary for much of the NEP period. Hovhannisyan was dismissed by the Soviet government from his post in 1927 for his alleged sympathies to the Specifist movement. He was arrested by the NKVD in Moscow on July 8, 1937, and then transferred to Yerevan.[77] On September 19, Hovhannisyan penned a lengthy letter to Ezhov, denying the charges of "counter-revolutionary right-wing nationalism." He also denounced several prominent Armenian politicians, intellectuals, and cultural figures for holding such views, including Myasnikyan, Lukashin, Charents, and many others.[78] Amid these extensive denunciations, Hovhannisyan revealed incriminating material about Amatuni's alleged ideological transgressions. Specifically, he alluded to a letter that he claimed was written by Amatuni from July 1927 in which he confessed his disagreement on the Party's approach to Specifism.[79] The letter reflected poorly on Amatuni and appeared especially ironic given his own zealous efforts to "root out" Specifism in Armenia. It was just the evidence that Malenkov needed to secure the removal of the Armenian leader.

Hovhannisyan first reported the letter to Nikolai Kudriavtsev, the deputy head of the ORPO of the CPSU Central Committee, on March 3, 1937, as part of a general testimony about Amatuni's alleged history of ideological deviations.[80] According to Hovhannisyan, that history dated back to his record of dissent on Party positions at the Institute of Red Professors in Moscow in the 1920s. Especially damning were Hovhannisyan's revelations of Amatuni's alleged "ideological vacillations of the Trotskiite order." He noted that Amatuni "declared to me frankly (apparently out of respect for me as an elder comrade) that he had many doubts about the correctness of the Party line with respect to Trotskii. The conversation was brief and to the point. I resolutely declared to him that his doubts were groundless, that Trotskii disagreed with the Party on the principal, fundamental questions of Leninism and that the severity of the struggle against him was necessary." Hovhannisyan further noted that "there were rumors" that Amatuni left his earlier post in Yerevan in 1930 due to "some kind of incorrect Party line" and that his name was associated with disgraced Georgian Bolshevik Vissarion "Beso" Lominadze.[81]

However, it was Amatuni's July 1927 letter to Hovhannisyan that proved to be the most explosive and damning piece of evidence that Hovhannisyan had against him. In it, Amatuni wished Hovhannisyan well after his forced departure from Armenia's first secretaryship. However, and even more critically, Amatuni—the same man who ruthlessly devastated his own people for even the slightest disagreement with the Party line—openly admitted his doubts about the Party's approach toward Specifism. "I recall the debate about the so-called 'Specifism' even during the life of Comrade [Aleksandr] Myasnikov," he wrote. "It appeared in articles by [Aramayis] Yerzikyan and you, the latter of which I had only heard about but did not get the chance to read. I think that there is a basis for serious disagreement. There are facts that speak against the Central Committee." Amatuni recommended that Hovhannisyan contact Khanjyan, Avis Nurijanyan, and "others" with the aim of having them "rally around" Hovhannisyan, presumably for him to stage a political comeback as Armenia's first secretary.[82] Hovhannisyan thought this idea to be "strange."[83]

Amatuni wrote his letter with not only "deep respect" but also the utmost discretion. Although "unsure" if he would receive an answer from Hovhannisyan, Amatuni wrote, "I still beg of you, as much as it is possible, to write to me. . . . If necessary, I promise not to disclose your thoughts. In general, I am ready to accept any condition, just to hear your true word about what is happening."[84] For his part, Hovhannisyan testified that he found this "conspiratorial" tone also to be "strange." His perception was heightened by the fact that it was personally delivered to him by Armenian Party leader Gurgen Gumedin and not through the mail.[85] Although Amatuni "sought to receive an answer to the letter," Hovhannisyan "left it unanswered," and, shortly after receiving it, "left Armenia altogether and forgot about Amatuni and his message entirely." Hovhannisyan maintained that he was prompted to review his personal archive and reassess the letter due to the Moscow trials of 1936–37 and a speech that Amatuni delivered before the Yerevan Party *aktiv* on October 2, 1936, in which he accused Hovhannisyan of "national-deviationism" and "Specifism." Although he "hesitated for a long time" about how to deal with it, Hovhannisyan ultimately decided that he "did not have the right to keep this letter" and that it was "necessary" to bring it to the attention of the authorities. In fact, he felt the matter to be so serious that he urged the all-union Central Committee, rather than the Central Committee of Armenia, to give the message a "proper assessment" and to "draw conclusions from it and from all that can be ascertained about Amatuni and his Party characteristics."[86]

Meanwhile, with the sword of Damocles over his head, Amatuni desperately attempted to prove his fidelity and devotion to Stalin. On September 19, he chaired a regular session of the Armenian Politburo, during which he dismissed three members of Armenia's Central Committee for "political reasons" and expelled the head of the Armenian Party Archives from the Party. He also formally appointed Petrov as the interim head of the Armenian NKVD, even though de facto authority over the republic's internal affairs was still exercised by the all-union NKVD brigade.[87] The meeting further highlighted incidents of supposed "sabotage" across the republic in connection with economic failures in the agricultural and industrial spheres in the context of the second Five-Year Plan. Amatuni specifically sought to investigate alleged acts of sabotage in nine

Armenian raions—Ijevan, Dilijan, Shamshadin, Stepanavan, Alaverdi, Nor Bayazet, Aparan, Sevan, and Meghri (on the Iranian border).[88]

The allegations of sabotage quickly caught the attention of Malenkov, who chaired a meeting on that same day (September 19) to discuss the matter with members of the Armenian Party Central Committee Apparat, the Yerevan Party Gorkom, and other Armenian Party officials. The discussion focused on developments across six raions in northern Armenia—Alaverdi, Stepanavan, Amasia (on the Turkish border), Shamshadin, Ijevan, and Dilijan.[89] The officials gave Malenkov the information that he expected and wanted to hear, informing him about acts of sabotage and "wrecking" by hidden "Dashnak" and "Trotskiite" networks in most of these raions and calling for tough action to be taken. Some attributed these acts to "poor Party work," while others, understanding the evolving direction of events, attributed them to the negligence of the Armenian Party leadership or the local NKVD. "We must examine why the NKVD refused to arrest 16 Dashnaks [in Ijevan] and why these Dashnaks are still free," one official told Malenkov.[90] Several officials identified local Party leaders and their families by name as "known Dashnaks" or "Trotskiites" who "needed to be exposed." Others named individuals with "family ties" to persons arrested as alleged "Dashnaks" and "Trotskiites."[91] Still others informed on local leaders and their families who expressed sympathetic views of Armenia's former first secretary Aghasi Khanjyan.[92] In response, Malenkov encouraged local investigations into these allegations.[93] He also notified Stalin about them.[94] In the end, instead of helping Amatuni, these reports only added to the case against him as a politically unreliable leader. Moreover, and more ominously, they built a case for more mass repressions in Armenia.

THE ROLE OF MIKOYAN

On the following day, Mikoyan arrived in Yerevan to join Malenkov and Litvin.[95] The inclusion of Mikoyan was a last-minute addition by Stalin. On September 15, Stalin personally received Mikoyan at around 7:00 p.m. (19:00) and spoke with him for two hours in the presence of Ezhov and Molotov.[96] Two days later, on September 17, he notified Malenkov and Litvin that Mikoyan would be joining them in Yerevan on September 20, the anniversary of the execution of the twenty-six Baku commissars, whose fate Mikoyan had narrowly escaped by chance.[97] Stalin's selection of this date was significant, serving as a not-so-subtle hint to Mikoyan to "behave accordingly" and to exclude any deviation from the prepared scenario. Anticipating Amatuni's downfall even before the Hovhannisyan revelations became known, Stalin instructed Malenkov to chat with Mikoyan about the "necessary changes in the composition of the Armenian leadership and new candidates."[98] On the day of Mikoyan's arrival, Stalin further told Malenkov to update Mikoyan about incidents of "wrecking" in the republic and ordered him to return to Moscow on the day of Mikoyan's speech on September 22, not September 25 or 26 as he originally planned.[99] Ultimately, however, Stalin apparently decided to keep Malenkov in Yerevan to keep an eye on Mikoyan until the end of the plenum on September 23.[100] Mikoyan did not take part in the investigative aspect of the intervention.[101] As will be seen, the scope of his mission included condemning Amatuni in a speech before the plenum, determining the post-Amatuni Armenian leadership, and consenting to whatever repressive measures Malenkov and Litvin demanded in response to the "sabotage" allegations. He would also sign off on a stricter regime for the Armenian-Turkish border.

As the Soviet press noted later that year, Mikoyan was sent to Armenia personally "on the instructions of Great Stalin."[102] Stalin's decision to involve Mikoyan was guided by his specific considerations for both the Soviet Armenian statesman and the Armenian Party leadership. By including the most prominent Armenian political figure in the USSR, Stalin aimed to send a strong signal to the Armenian leadership from Moscow in response to Ter-Gabrielyan's death. Indeed, as Mikoyan wryly recalled, his presence "would make the importance of the Central Committee's pest control efforts more convincing for the Armenian Communists."[103] However, Stalin primarily wanted to test the loyalty of Mikoyan, who in fact had a history of being directly involved in saving, or attempting to save, many people from the repressions.[104] The Great Purge weighed heavily on the Armenian statesman. At home, Mikoyan's son Stepan witnessed several somber conversations between his father and his mother in Armenian regarding the arrests and repressions. "Such conversations," he recounted, "were always conducted in a serious, anxious, and, on my mother's part, often mournful tone, which drew my attention even more. I do not remember a single case in which celebration, gloating, or satisfaction sounded in someone's words."[105] The fact that Stalin sent Mikoyan to Armenia as a late addition to the visiting group, and not alone, indicates that the *vozhd'* did not trust him to execute such a mission without the "support" of others.[106] "These very circumstances," noted Mikoyan's son Sergo, "suggest that Stalin did not consider [my father] an ardent supporter of repressions." Obedience to Stalin, he wrote, was "absolutely obligatory" for his father's personal and political survival.[107]

"Already after the suicide of Sergo [Ordzhonikidze], Stalin decided to taint me with participation in the repressions," recalled Mikoyan years later. "He was very annoyed by my negative attitude toward them, which I did not hide. I stood up for many of those arrested."[108] Of Ter-Gabrielyan's fall, Mikoyan recounted that Stalin had deduced that Mughdusi's men had "probably thrown [him] out because he knew too much." "And so," Mikoyan wrote, "Stalin gave me an order, backed up by the decision of the Politburo, to go with his letter to Armenia, where 'the pests and Trotskiites had dug in.' . . . I could not refuse the assignment of the Politburo."[109] Sergo Mikoyan years later wrote that "unfortunately, my own father, Anastas Mikoyan, despite having plenty of common sense, inner honesty and decency, was fanatical enough to subdue these inborn qualities to the goals of *the Party*."[110] As historian Sheila Fitzpatrick notes, the 1937 Armenian episode was the only known instance of Mikoyan being sent out to do Stalin's bidding in the republics, and he "did a poor job, from Stalin's point of view."[111]

"In Yerevan, everything went according to Stalin's scenario," recalled Mikoyan.[112] The plenum reconvened on the evening of September 22, with its focus no longer only Akopov but also Amatuni.[113] Now an "enemy of the people," the Armenian first secretary would be swallowed up by the very violence that he had unleashed. The first speaker that evening was Amasia Raikom Secretary Hmayak Galustyan, a rising star in the Party.[114] On behalf of the visiting group from Moscow, Galustyan read aloud the letter that Amatuni had addressed to the "nationalist enemy of the people" Hovhannisyan, as well as Hovhannisyan's testimony to Kudriavtsev about Amatuni's ideological vacillations. After Galustyan, several others came to the podium to launch blistering denunciations of Amatuni and "his treason, double-dealing, Trotskiism, and Lominadzeism," as well as "his role in the counter-revolutionary organization of Mughdusi and others."[115] One of the speakers—Armenian Central Committee agitprop chief Gino Shaghgamyan—had attended the meeting with Malenkov on September 19.[116]

Finally, at the end of the evening, Mikoyan came to the podium to speak. The drama in the hall was amplified by the arrival of Beria. Unnerved by Beria's sudden theatrical entry, Mikoyan feared that he had come to arrest him if he did not do Stalin's bidding. However, he managed to maintain his composure. "Beria's appearance in the hall was a surprise to me," Mikoyan recalled. "He came in when I spoke from the rostrum. I do not rule out that the expression on my face changed at that moment. I quickly arrived at the conclusion that Stalin ordered him to come to arrest me right there at the plenum. However, I hope that I managed to hide my alarm and that he did not notice. Later, I realized that this was also part of the scenario: fearing my unpredictability, they wanted to drive me into a corner and show me that I have no choice but to submit completely."[117] Mikoyan was not alone in his unease. As another Armenian attendee later testified, "the presence of Beria at the plenum had a dispiriting effect on almost everyone."[118]

Casting aside his unease with Beria, Mikoyan delivered an extempore speech from the rostrum based on a series of hastily composed handwritten notes.[119] In his address, he raised the issue of Amatuni's ideological dalliances with Specifism, citing the July 1927 letter to Hovhannisyan.[120] The speech was met with "thunderous applause" and an "ovation" from the audience.[121] According to an account of the proceedings from an anti-Stalinist Armenian émigré, Amatuni, who was present, rejected all charges. "You lie," he reportedly told Mikoyan.[122] In response, Mikoyan pulled the incriminating 1927 letter from his pocket. The beleaguered Amatuni then reached into his own pocket. Guards immediately surrounded him, and Mikoyan told him to "hand it over." Amatuni produced a revolver and gave it to the guards. The chamber erupted in chaos. Amatuni's brother, Vardges Vardapetyan, reportedly "hurled a few upbraiding words at Mikoyan."[123]

Mikoyan fulfilled Stalin's task—he successfully assured the final downfall of Amatuni. At the same time, he did not accomplish this act without his own share of involvement in the Purges in Armenia, however unwilling he may have been to participate. Always disinclined toward violent solutions to problems, Mikoyan evidently never forgave himself for his role in these repressions, becoming the one member of Stalin's circle "most distraught by his conscience."[124] Indeed, as Mikoyan himself confessed many years later in private company, "we were all bastards then."[125] This burden of guilt was heightened by the fact that his native Armenia was involved, just over twenty years after the Armenian Genocide of 1915.[126] In his official October 1937 report on Armenia, Litvin noted that the visiting NKVD brigade had arrested 1,183 people during the intervention period, including 100 Armenian officials and 936 "Dashnaks."[127] Those arrested were broadly divided into two categories by the NKVD, in accordance with Ezhov's infamous Order 00447. Category 1 consisted of the "most active" group of "anti-Soviet elements," subject to "immediate arrest and, after consideration of their case by the [NKVD] troikas, to be shot." Category 2 consisted of "all the remaining less active but nonetheless hostile elements." These were to be arrested and confined in concentration camps for a term of eight to ten years, "while the most vicious and socially dangerous among them" were "subject to confinement for similar terms in prisons as determined by the troikas."[128]

Order 00447 had set Armenia's quota (*limit*) for executions of Category 1 "anti-Soviet elements" at five hundred, based on the plan proposed by Amatuni in his message to Stalin and Ezhov from July 9.[129] After the arrival of Malenkov and his retinue in Yerevan, the number of individuals convicted in this category quickly surpassed Amatuni's original quota. According to Litvin, the total number of Category 1 repressions during the Yerevan intervention alone was five hundred.[130] These repressions were fueled by the local Armenian demands to combat "sabotage," in an era when regional officials sought to demonstrate their "vigilance" and loyalty to Moscow by exceeding quotas for "smashing enemies." Therefore, for Malenkov, Litvin, and the NKVD brigade, Amatuni's original quota was much too low, and they evidently demanded increasing it by an additional seven hundred names. It was left to Mikoyan, then the most senior Party leader in Yerevan, to communicate this monstrous demand to Moscow.[131] However, he was apparently uncomfortable with conveying such a request to the Kremlin alone and insisted that it be sent as a collective request on behalf of him, Malenkov, and Litvin. Consequently, in a message sent to Stalin and Ezhov on September 22, Mikoyan, Malenkov, and Litvin requested an additional seven hundred Category 1 repressions for a "real purge of Armenia" amid "the revelation of a growing body of evidence regarding the free revelry of Dashnaks and other anti-Soviet elements." The original quota of five hundred, the authors noted, was "already exhausted."[132] Ezhov was more than happy to oblige and even topped the original request. "I propose shooting an additional 1,500 people," he callously wrote to Stalin, who approved the increase with a characteristic "*za*" ("for"). In his proposal to Stalin, Ezhov likewise ignored the collective character of the request, mentioning only Mikoyan and not Malenkov or Litvin, given Mikoyan's senior rank.[133] Nevertheless, Stalin was also aware of the original, collective message, which he also signed "*za*."[134]

In addition, Mikoyan recounted receiving a list "prepared by the NKVD of the republic, in agreement with Moscow," with the names of three hundred individuals, which he was then forced to sign.[135] Rather than the local Armenian NKVD, it is much more likely that such a list would have been prepared by the visiting all-union NKVD brigade, which had effectively run the republic's internal affairs commissariat since the arrival of Malenkov and his entourage on September 14. Moreover, although Mikoyan recalled that the list was for persons "subject to arrest," the circumstances suggest that it would have been for Category 2 "anti-Soviet elements," subject to imprisonment in accordance with Order 00447. According to Mikoyan, Malenkov was the first to see this document. Looking through the list, Mikoyan noticed the name of an old friend, Danush Shahverdyan. "He was my senior comrade and my mentor for Party work during the years of my youth," he later recalled.[136] Indeed, it was Shahverdyan who had first introduced the young Mikoyan to the writings of Lenin.[137] Mughdusi's Armenian NKVD had arrested him on February 23, 1937, and his wife, Elizaveta, on March 26.[138] They accused Shahverdyan of "Trotskiite-nationalist" espionage and made similar charges against Elizaveta, based on the couple's earlier outreach to the Armenian diaspora.[139] However, in a letter to Mikoyan from August 3, 1954, Armenian Party veteran Ado Adoyan recounted that the real reason for the case against Shahverdyan was his refusal to endorse Beria's falsifications on the history of the Bolsheviks in Transcaucasia.[140]

At the time of the September 1937 intervention, Shahverdyan was still in detention and remained under active investigation.[141] The visiting NKVD brigade tied his case to those of other arrested officials in an elaborate conspiracy to "separate Armenia from the USSR," claiming that he was a spy who was laying the groundwork for this plot via his diaspora connections. Toward that end, they claimed that he was responsible for allowing a "large number of spies and saboteurs to penetrate into the Soviet Union."[142] The Soviet press further tied the Shahverdyan case to that of Stepan Akopov, claiming that Akopov was a "Dashnak agent" who had received "generous gifts from abroad" that allegedly came via the "famous spy-Dashnak" Shahverdyan.[143] Although Mikoyan wrote that he immediately struck Shahverdyan's surname ("*familiia*") off the NKVD list, it was to no avail.[144] On May 27, 1939, Shahverdyan appeared in front of a military tribunal of the Transcaucasian Military Okrug and was sentenced to ten years' imprisonment, with loss of rights for five years and confiscation of half of his personal property.[145] "Obviously," Mikoyan later recalled, "Beria informed the local NKVD that my signature was needed as a mere formality, and that my considerations could be dismissed, even though I was a member of the Politburo and I arrived there with a letter from Stalin."[146] Unaware of the ill-fated move to save him, Shahverdyan attempted to appeal to Mikoyan twice, but again to no avail.[147] He apparently died in prison on October 24, 1941.[148]

CONCLUSION OF THE PLENUM

In the morning session of the plenum on September 23, the attendees adopted a letter to Stalin "to the cries of 'ura' and stormy applause."[149] The letter slavishly praised "the brilliant leader of nations" and "the father and liberator of the Armenian people" for his "historical letter on the situation in Armenia" and for "unmasking" the "entire knot of the rot in the leadership of the Armenian Central Committee and the Soviet Armenian government with ingenious insight."[150] The Armenian Party also owned up to its lack of vigilance. "The Bolsheviks of Armenia," the letter stated, "were unable to discern in time how the enemies of the people sitting in our state and Party leadership—Amatuni, Guloyan, Akopov, Mughdusi, and [Gevorg] Hanesoghlyan and others, cloaked themselves with speeches about fidelity to the Party and the fight against enemies." It asserted that "in reality, they carried out heinous acts of wrecking and allowed the enemies of the people—Dashnaks, Trotskiites, and a whole spy-wrecking cabal—to walk freely throughout Armenia." Following Malenkov's talking points, the Armenian Party then blamed itself for its "criminal lack of concern" toward the threat of "Khanjyanism" in the aftermath of Khanjyan's "provocative suicide." They cited their own inability to "root out" this "threat" as resulting in "vile work" perpetuated by "enemies" using "heinous fascist methods to cover up their odious counter-revolutionary deeds."[151]

The letter pointed to the alleged instances of "wrecking" and "sabotage" throughout the republic that local leaders raised in their September 19 meeting with Malenkov. It blamed the "wreckers" for Armenia's poor agricultural performance and stagnant industrial development. The plenary letter asserted that, although the Armenian Party had "opened the main hornet's nest and smashed it" through the guidance of Stalin's "greatest insights" and "finest leadership instincts," enemies nevertheless "still existed." Ominously, the letter declared that every "enemy" down "to the last scoundrel" would be "erased from the land of the Armenian SSR." The authors vowed to "destroy and clean spy-wrecking Dashnak-Trotskiite rubbish from our beautiful land" and to "decisively take up the liquidation of the consequences of sabotage and subversive work" against the Armenian Party by "rotten and deceitful people," who would be "quickly removed from the path forward."[152] The Armenian Party leaders promised "to learn all the lessons" from the episode and "to cultivate in every Bolshevik, worker, and kolkhoznik" a sense of "revolutionary offensive vigilance" against "enemies of the people." Young cadres in the Party would be promoted to "give all their energy to the cause of socialism, to deploy genuine Bolshevik work, and to elevate the Armenian SSR to the ranks of the advanced republics of the great Soviet Union in the nearest future." The letter concluded with the customary praise of "our native [*rodnoi*] father, the great leader [*vozhd'*] of nations, Comrade Stalin."[153]

In the evening, in the final, closed session of the Armenian Party plenum, the attendees formally removed the "exposed counter-revolutionary enemies of the people" Amatuni and Akopov from their posts and from the Armenian Central Committee. Dismissed from the membership of the Party, their cases were to be referred to the NKVD. Still other prominent names—Mughdusi, Guloyan, Gevorkov, and Kostikyan—were expelled from the Central Committee.[154] Malenkov personally arrested Amatuni at the plenum.[155] The NKVD charged the former Armenian first secretary with being a "leading member of an anti-Soviet, nationalist, right-Trotskiite organization in Armenia," which "set as its goal the separation of the Armenian SSR from the USSR" and the "creation of an 'independent' bourgeois Armenian state."[156] Under arrest, Amatuni, the man who once terrorized Armenia, was now subjected to violent and grueling NKVD interrogation, personally supervised by Beria and Litvin. Years later, one of their NKVD men, Arsenovich, whom Beria once ordered to beat a man "half to death," recounted hearing the "screams and groans" of Amatuni and the other arrestees as they were tortured.[157] The choice methods of Beria and Litvin soon yielded the desired results. Amatuni "confessed" to his "role" in the "vast counter-revolutionary nationalist right-Trotskiite conspiracy," naming the names of his various "accomplices."[158] He and the other arrestees would all appear on Stalin's execution lists and be shot in 1938.[159]

With Amatuni ousted, Stalin tasked the visiting Moscow group with selecting a new Armenian first secretary. Mikoyan and Malenkov sought to bring in an Armenian leader from outside the republic. Their choice was Grigorii Arutinov, who would serve as the republic's Party boss for over a decade. An Armenian from

Georgia who spoke only Russian and had to learn Armenian, Arutinov was serving as the second secretary of the Tbilisi Gorkom at the time. He was proposed by Beria, who sought to retain his influence in Armenia. Others have speculated that his expectations for the new Armenian leader were laced with wicked cynicism, motivated by a desire to rid Georgia of a potential political rival. "Let the Armenians eat him alive," Beria purportedly remarked.[160] Moreover, Arutinov's relations with Beria would later become complicated by the latter's role in the deaths of his brother, Sergo, and brother-in-law, Artiom Geurkov. Geurkov, who served as first secretary of the Adjarian ASSR on the Georgian Black Sea coast, committed suicide under the threat of NKVD arrest in October 1937.[161] His young daughter, Nami, came to live with Arutinov and his family in Yerevan in 1939.[162]

With a new first secretary selected, Mikoyan telephoned Stalin from Yerevan. "The plenum of the Central Committee expelled Amatuni and Akopov from the Party and transferred their cases to the NKVD," Mikoyan said. "Malenkov, Beria, and I are proposing Grigorii Arutinov, the second secretary of the Tbilisi Gorkom as the first secretary. For the second secretary of the Central Committee, we propose [Ashot] Margaryan, a member of the Central Committee of Georgia and the editor of an Armenian newspaper, who previously worked in Armenia. For the third secretary, we propose Comrade [Hmayak] Galustyan, who was earlier intended to be nominated as second secretary. Inform us of your opinion."[163] Stalin immediately issued a joint response with Molotov, stating that the Central Committee "did not object" to the proposed appointments. "If the plenum should have any doubts," they added, "then it should be given the opportunity to discuss the issue in detail and resolve it independently."[164] At the plenum, Mikoyan moved to have the new leadership choices approved by the attendees and proactively promoted Mushegh Danelyan to head the Armenian Sovnarkom and Matsak Papyan to head the Central Executive Committee. Danelyan assumed the chairmanship of the plenum. Additionally, both Mikoyan and Malenkov advanced several candidates for the Armenian Politburo.[165]

After the plenum, Malenkov returned to Moscow and met with Stalin on the evening of September 26. Mikoyan was received by Stalin later, on the evening of October 3, in a meeting that was also attended by Malenkov.[166] For his part, Arutinov, having arrived in Yerevan from Tbilisi, chaired his first Armenian Politburo session on September 29.[167] In December, Mikoyan would assume the post of a Supreme Soviet deputy for nationalities representing Yerevan, allowing him to retain a supervisory role in Armenia to assist Arutinov in his relations with Moscow.[168] This partnership would be solidified by the marriage of Nami Geurkova to Mikoyan's son Aleksei in 1950.[169] Although these developments appeared to signal the beginning of a political "stabilization" in the Armenian Republic, repressions continued into late 1937 and 1938. These were overseen first by the all-union

NKVD brigade, which had been running Armenia's internal affairs commissariat directly since September 14, and then under Armenia's new internal affairs chief, Viktor Khvorostian, who assumed office on October 20.[170] On September 25, Litvin reported to Ezhov that "a significant number of active Dashnak emigrants, who had been at large, were revealed. We continue to carry out arrests."[171] Despite their recent appointments by Mikoyan at the September plenum, Danelyan, Galustyan, and Margaryan were all arrested by mid-November, with Danelyan arrested by the NKVD brigade in Yerevan and Galustyan and Margaryan arrested by Beria's NKVD men in Georgia.[172]

Armenian philosopher Artavazd Minasyan recounted years later that, after Yerevan, Mikoyan arrived in the Nakhichevan' ASSR and briefly visited the town of Ordubad, near the border with Iran.[173] This trip was likely connected with measures to strengthen the USSR's southwestern borders in the aftermath of the September plenum in Armenia. The fears over the vulnerability of the Armenian frontier were earlier raised by Amatuni in a letter to Stalin on July 5. In his letter, Amatuni underscored that Armenia's borders with Iran and Turkey were especially porous and susceptible to infiltration and that the previous Armenian authorities had taken the "wrong attitude" toward the matter. "The present situation on the borders of Armenia," he wrote, "is such that it is not difficult for any saboteur or spy to slip through to our side, or vice versa, for the enemy [from within] to slip beyond the cordon." In a section of the letter underlined by Stalin, Amatuni further noted that there were "close to 40 villages at the border itself, as well as many villages in the vicinity of the border." He likewise emphasized the existence of cross-border familial ties and the fact that a "large number" of border residents had previously been exiled or imprisoned. Consequently, on behalf of the Armenian Central Committee, Amatuni sought permission to evict "five hundred households" from the border area to "remote lands" in the "next three to five months." The request was personally signed by Stalin and approved by other members of the Politburo, including Mikoyan, who had little choice in the matter.[174] The internal deportees were to be exiled to Kazakhstan, and, in another letter to Stalin, Amatuni noted that those to be deported would include previously convicted "smugglers, participants in anti-Soviet speeches, and members of their families."[175]

From Stalin's perspective, the recent events in Armenia underscored that these earlier measures were demonstrably inadequate. His perception was undoubtedly reinforced by the greater context of the rise of Adolf Hitler and the increased likelihood of a German attack on the Soviet Union. The fact that neighboring Turkey maintained warm relations with Berlin at the time only added to the apparent need to bolster border security.[176] Therefore, on September 27, the all-union Central Committee in conjunction with the Council of People's Commissars advanced and approved an eleven-point resolution, "On the Protection of the Borders of the Armenian SSR and the Nakhichevan' ASSR." The resolution called for the establishment of a restricted border zone that would include all eight Armenian raions bordering Turkey—Amasia, Leninakan, Artik, Talin, Sardarabad, Vagharshapat (Ejmiatsin), Ghamarlu, and Vedi.[177] As the name implied, it would also encompass the exclave of Nakhichevan'. Sandwiched between Iran and Soviet Armenia, Nakhichevan' was a historically Armenian territory that became an ASSR of Soviet Azerbaijan in 1921, in accordance with the treaties of Moscow and Kars between Kemalist Turkey and the Russian SFSR.[178] Significantly, as a result of these same 1921 treaties, Turkey acquired the Surmalu uezd with Mount Ararat and a strip of land between the Araks and Kara-su rivers, allowing it to share a small but strategic border with the Nakhichevan' ASSR and, by extension, Soviet Azerbaijan.[179]

Although the advancement of the September 27 Armenia-Nakhichevan' resolution came amid the immediate context of the 1937 Yerevan intervention, it nevertheless formed part of a broader pattern of "securitization" of the USSR's external borders on the eve of the Second World War.[180] The resolution obligated residents of the border zone to provide identification photographs on their passports, while those living particularly close to the Turkish border would be obligated to have special stamps on their passports from Soviet border guards. The zone was to be included within the scope of the earlier July 1935 resolution of the Central Executive Committee and the Council of People's Commissars "On Entry and Residence in Border Strips." That resolution required residents of other parts of the USSR to obtain special permission from the NKVD to visit the restricted border area. The September 27 resolution further called for the NKVD to evict from the zone "all unreliable elements and all Kurdish households." Residing along both sides of the USSR's borders with Turkey and Iran, the Kurds were added later to the text.[181] Although their culture thrived in NEP-era Armenia, they had already come under the scrutiny of Soviet authorities at the onset of Stalin's rule.[182] In addition to these measures, the September 27 resolution called for the deployment of another 1,700 Soviet border guards to the restricted zone, as well as specifically ethnic Russian military units, based in Yerevan and Nakhichevan'. The decision was signed by Stalin, Mikoyan, Kliment Voroshilov, and Lazar' Kaganovich and approved by Vlas Chubar' and Mikhail Kalinin.[183]

Despite its political significance, the Yerevan intervention received only limited publicity in the Soviet press, although local reporting at the time reflected the general course of events.[184] Stalin personally dispatched *Pravda* journalist Mikhail Kotliarov to Yerevan to cover the story.[185] The choice of reporter was obvious to Stalin, as he knew that Amatuni strongly disliked Kotliarov's coverage of Armenian affairs.[186] When the reporter arrived in Yerevan, he was informed by Mikoyan that the press was not permitted to cover the plenum until its aftermath.[187] It was only on September 26 that *Khorhrdayin Hayastan* and the Russian-language *Kommunist* officially reported on the "unmasking" of Amatuni, Akopov, and others at the plenum, as well as the appointments of Arutinov, Margaryan, and Galustyan.[188] The press revealed more specific details on September 28, in an article by Kotliarov printed on the second page of *Pravda* entitled "The Affairs of the Enemies of the Armenian People." Written for *Pravda*'s all-union audience, the article described Hovhannisyan's evidence against Amatuni, the allegations of mass sabotage, Shahverdyan's alleged "spy" activities, the dismissal of Amatuni and his associates, and the plenum's adoption of a letter to Stalin.[189] The following day, *Khorhrdayin Hayastan* printed the article in Armenian translation on its front page, while *Kommunist* reprinted the Russian original on its second page.[190] Mikoyan's role in the intervention was not publicly acknowledged by the Soviet press until the end of the year when he participated in the Supreme Soviet elections.[191]

Overall, the 1937 Yerevan intervention represented one of the most significant events in the politics of the Soviet Caucasus of the 1930s. The intervention allowed Stalin to test Mikoyan's loyalty as well as Beria's. It signaled the beginning of the Beria-Malenkov political alliance and resulted in strengthening security along the Soviet-Turkish frontier as part of the larger securitization of Soviet external borders in advance of World War II. Most significantly of all, the Yerevan intervention would have a lingering impact on political developments beyond the Stalin era itself. During the Thaw, Malenkov's role came under scrutiny as part of the "Anti-Party Group" proceedings.[192] Meanwhile, Mikoyan's sense of personal guilt informed his proactive position on de-Stalinization. In fact, he perceived this episode not only as a source of guilt but also as a clear reflection of Stalinist centralization and disregard for the autonomy of national republics.[193] His sensitivity to the centralization issue would later have a direct impact on his nationality policy reform efforts during the Thaw. Significantly, it was from Mikoyan's post as a Supreme Soviet deputy for Armenia that he would deliver his March 1954 speech in Yerevan, in which he articulated the framework of the post-Stalin nationality policy.

2 | Yerevan 1954

On March 10, 1954, Mikoyan traveled to the Armenian capital, Yerevan, to meet with his voters for the Supreme Soviet elections of that year. He commenced his electoral trip with a visit to Sergei Merkurov's monument to Iosif Stalin in the city's Victory Park.[1] Although many in Yerevan would not yet realize it, the speech that Mikoyan was to deliver the next day, on March 11, would contribute to the process that would eventually result in the removal of that very Stalin statue. In the speech, he articulated the essence of the Soviet nationality policy during the Thaw and helped enable the process of the post-Stalin rehabilitation of former "enemies of the people." The address was to set the stage for Khrushchev's broader reassessment of Stalin at the Twentieth Party Congress in February 1956. As such, it held significance not only for Soviet Armenia but also for the Soviet Union at large, enjoying widespread publication across the country, with a booklet print run of one hundred thousand copies.[2]

Mikoyan argued for a policy of managed national expression, with controls to ensure that expressions of national sentiment did not veer into manifestations that were chauvinistic (i.e., advocating an aggressive sense of pride and superiority of one national group over another) or opposed to official Soviet ideology. "Bourgeois nationalism" was to be condemned, but the state needed to avoid what Mikoyan called "national nihilism"—that is, an indifference to national cultures and sensitivities. Although the idea itself was not new and harkened back to earlier variations of the Soviet nationality policy, the Yerevan address infused it with new meaning. Underscoring the dangers of "national nihilism," Mikoyan called for a "Thaw" in national cultural expression, highlighting the need to republish the works of the Armenian national authors Rafael Patkanyan and Raffi and to revive the memory of NEP-era Soviet Armenian leader Aleksandr Myasnikyan.

Nevertheless, although Mikoyan stressed the need to combat "national nihilism" and "bourgeois nationalism," he did not offer specific details about these ideas. Moscow and the union republics struggled to define these concepts throughout the 1950s and 1960s, seeking to identify the parameters between those forms of national expression that were acceptable and those that were not in what some scholars have called a "tug of war."[3]

The framework for approaching multiethnicity that Mikoyan articulated in Yerevan proved lasting and consequential. Through Mikoyan's influence, it came to form the basis for subsequent nationality policy reform efforts by the Khrushchev government. It is no coincidence that the nationality platform of the CPSU's Third Party Program is so strikingly evocative of the content of Mikoyan's Yerevan speech. Moreover, the program's platform on nationality was then used as the basis for Mikoyan's work as the chairman of the Subcommittee on Nationality Policy and National-State Construction (NPNSC), part of Khrushchev's constitutional reform commission of the 1960s. The two basic principles that guided Mikoyan's speech—state unity and a respect for ethnic and cultural diversity—also guided these later reform efforts, which represented a rejection of assimilationist tendencies within the CPSU. In taking this approach, Mikoyan was informed by his background as a non-Russian within the Soviet leadership and by his identity as someone who was at once both Soviet *and* Armenian, reflecting the phenomenon that Maike Lehmann called "Apricot socialism."[4]

Additionally, Mikoyan's speech was significant for its role in the process of enabling de-Stalinization and the rehabilitation of political prisoners through his call to rehabilitate the poet Yeghishe Charents, a victim of Stalin's Purges. After the arrest of Lavrentii Beria, Mikoyan began receiving several letters from those requesting the rehabilitation of loved ones—many of whom had connections to Mikoyan's revolutionary Bakuvian/Caucasian network. Mikoyan's speech was intended as a signal indicating that the cases of the repressed would be reviewed and that it was possible for former "enemies" to have their names cleared of any wrongdoing. Despite this political significance, the address has rarely been placed in the larger context of Soviet history. Many historians of Russia and the Soviet Union have written about Mikoyan's role in de-Stalinization at the all-union level.[5] Likewise, several historians of Armenia, beginning with Mary Kilbourne Matossian, have identified the significance of Mikoyan's Yerevan address as a key starting point for the Thaw in the Armenian Republic.[6] However, it is necessary to examine both sides of the story together. In placing developments in Armenia in dialogue with broader Soviet history, this chapter highlights the full significance of the speech and the ways in which it impacted the broader process of de-Stalinization and Mikoyan's role in it. Moreover, it traces the lasting impact of the speech on the development of the Thaw and de-Stalinization in Armenia. The subsequent flowering of Armenian national expression culminated in the 1965 Yerevan demonstrations, demanding recognition of the 1915 Genocide, and in the 1988 Karabakh (Artsakh) movement, advocating unification between Soviet Armenia and Nagorno-Karabakh.[7] As historian Razmik Panossian noted, "the Yerevan protests [of 1965] did not occur in a vacuum" and "were a product of the post-Stalin thaw and the slow emergence of national issues in the late 1950s and early 1960s."[8] Truly, the impact of Mikoyan's 1954 speech on modern Armenian history cannot be underestimated.

This chapter commences by exploring the immediate context of the Soviet Union after Stalin's death, specifically as it related to changing interpretations of the Soviet nationality policy, political shifts within Soviet Armenia, and Mikoyan's motivations for delivering his Yerevan address. Mikoyan's speech is critically explored, alongside his draft material and notes, specifically the final portion, entitled "Toward an All-Encompassing Strengthening of the Friendship of Peoples," dealing with the nationality issue. Finally, it examines the immediate impact of the speech on de-Stalinization and political developments in Armenia, specifically arguing that the speech both set the stage for Khrushchev's address at the Twentieth Party Congress and signaled the start of the Thaw in the Armenian context.

SETTING THE STAGE AFTER STALIN

In his 1954 speech, Mikoyan articulated the essence of a post-Stalin Soviet nationality policy that balanced an expanded space for national expression with controls to prevent manifestations of national chauvinism. In this sense, it would be a return to earlier variations of the Soviet nationality policy, with Mikoyan moving the needle back from Stalinist repression. However, the speech did not represent the first effort to revamp the Soviet nationality policy in the early months following Stalin's death. Beria attempted to use the nationality issue to bolster his position amid the ensuing power struggle within the Soviet leadership. Dmitrii Shepilov later recounted that it was "painfully transparent" that Beria's approach toward the nationality question "was not intended in any way to promote any valid political goals, such as correcting what was wrong and distorted in the relationship between Moscow and the republics" or "fortifying and expanding further the sovereignty of allied [i.e., union] and autonomous republics and the bonds of friendship among the different nationalities." "No," Shepilov concluded, "Beria was angling for support among the people of the national republics and within their leading strata."[9] Beria had begun to cast himself as the champion for nationalities as early as the Nineteenth Party Congress in October 1952. Behind the scenes, beginning in April 1953, both he and Khrushchev experimented with a more flexible nationality policy in what became informally known as "Beria's New Course."[10] This series of reform policies had an immediate impact on Beria's power base in Georgia but primarily affected the western parts of the Soviet Union, specifically the Baltics, Belorussia, and Western Ukraine.[11] Together, Beria and Khrushchev sought to use the New Course policies to secure the support of the union republics and non-Russian nationalities in the post-Stalin power struggle.[12] However, neither of them sought to publicly articulate or define a new overarching framework or philosophy toward the nationality question, as Mikoyan would in his Yerevan speech of March 1954.

The downfall of Beria in 1953 created new political realities in Soviet Armenia in advance of Mikoyan's speech. The ascendant Khrushchev sought a clean sweep of the leaderships in all three of the Caucasus republics to rout out any lingering influence of Beria.[13] This sweep included not only staunch Beria loyalists Bagirov and Mirtskhulava but also Arutinov. The latter had a more ambiguous and at times antagonistic relationship with Beria, despite the fact that it was Beria who proposed his appointment to Armenia's highest office in 1937. Nevertheless, any affiliation with Beria was a decisive factor for Khrushchev, who preferred to err on the side of caution while dismantling the support base of his Georgian rival. According to Mikoyan's son Sergo, his father initially opposed Arutinov's removal but eventually came to accept it, given that he was in the minority politically.[14] Meanwhile, Arutinov's political opponents within Armenia, most prominently Shmavon Arushanyan, saw Beria's downfall as an opportune time to remove the Armenian first secretary from his post.[15] At the November 1953 plenum of the Armenian Central Committee in Yerevan, Arutinov faced numerous denunciations from local Party members.[16] As Yeghishe Astsatryan noted, only a few prominent voices dared to defend the embattled leader.[17] Although Arutinov was dismissed from office by the plenum, he avoided the violent fates of Beria and Bagirov and instead became the director of a sovkhoz near Ejmiatsin.[18] In his place, the plenum unanimously elected Suren Tovmasyan as the republic's new first secretary on November 30, at the motion of all-union Central Committee Secretary Piotr Pospelov.[19] Arutinov later passed away in Tbilisi on November 9, 1957.[20] Mikoyan sent a letter expressing "deep condolences" to his widow, Nina, the following day.[21] He would later defend Arutinov's legacy at a meeting with Soviet Armenian historians in Yerevan in March 1962.[22]

Beria's downfall encouraged victims of Stalinism to be more proactive about their cases, as evidenced by the large volume of direct appeals that Mikoyan received shortly after Beria's arrest, both from victims of repression and from family members of repressed persons. Most of these requests came from individuals of various ethnic backgrounds (Armenian, Russian, Georgian, Jewish) who maintained ties with Mikoyan dating back to his revolutionary years in the Caucasus.[23] "After Stalin's death," Mikoyan recalled, "requests began to come to me from family members of repressed persons, requesting review of their cases.

Many appealed to me through Lev Stepanovich Shahumyan."[24] The sheer volume of letters had a profound impact on Mikoyan and prompted him to act. Scholar Samuel Casper has argued that the statesman was influenced in this regard by a sense of obligation to his Caucasian (specifically Bakuvian) patronage network.[25] However, the influence of Mikoyan's Armenian background was arguably just as significant. For instance, the poet Yeghishe Charents, who became the symbol of Mikoyan's de-Stalinization efforts and the Thaw in Armenia, had no personal connection with Mikoyan aside from his Armenian background. Similarly, Mikoyan's decision to invoke the names of the Armenian national figures Raffi and Patkanyan reflected his personal love for the works of these writers.[26] Finally, in addition to his Bakuvian patronage network, Mikoyan had a separate Armenian network that included some of the republic's highest officials. These two networks often overlapped with one another as factors influencing his work on de-Stalinization. Therefore, Mikoyan's decision to invoke Charents in his speech was intended to send a message both to a specifically Armenian audience and to those in his Bakuvian network who would have been familiar with Charents in the Soviet cultural context. The ideological factor was no less important. As Mikoyan himself said throughout his life, he, very much like Khrushchev and the first wave of Bolshevik revolutionaries, strongly believed in the original promise of the revolution. He therefore viewed Stalin's dictatorship as a deviation from "Lenin's true path."[27]

Additionally, Mikoyan's personal burden of guilt from his own participation in Stalinist state violence has been cited by historians and memoirists as a motivation for his proactive stance on de-Stalinization.[28] Many of Mikoyan's closest friends had been victims of the Purges, including several of his Nersisyan School classmates.[29] Gulag survivor Olga Shatunovskaia, the daughter of Bakuvian Jewish parents, had earlier worked alongside Mikoyan in the Baku revolutionary movement, serving as the secretary of Stepan Shahumyan. She later played a major role in de-Stalinization at the personal encouragement of Mikoyan.[30] The repressions also directly impacted the Mikoyan family. Alla Kuznetsova, the young wife of Mikoyan's son, Sergo, was the daughter of Central Committee Party Secretary Aleksei Kuznetsov, who, together with several other prominent Party figures, was killed by Stalin in the notorious Leningrad Affair of 1949–50.[31] Mikoyan knew and respected Kuznetsov as a "charming, gregarious, and sincere man," while he and his wife, Ashkhen, considered Alla to be the daughter that they never had. "The girl was charming, beautiful, and cheerful," Mikoyan recounted. "She had an everlasting smile and was always joking around, which Ashkhen and I really liked."[32] The Leningrad ordeal devastated the family, and, as Mikoyan later recounted, it personally caused him "great anxiety that a time similar to 1936–38 might return again, but only in a somewhat newer setting, and perhaps with some newer methods."[33] Mikoyan's sense of personal anxiety was undoubtedly heightened by Stalin's very public attacks against him at the Central Committee plenum following the Nineteenth Party Congress. Indeed, the statesman himself most certainly would have fallen victim to a new wave of repressions had Stalin lived longer.[34] Shortly after Stalin's death in 1953, Mikoyan invited Kuznetsov's children to his dacha, where he told them in no uncertain terms, "Your father was not an enemy of the people. This you should know!"[35] He subsequently became personally involved in securing the release of Kuznetsov's widow, Zinaida Dmitrievna, from imprisonment in the city of Vladimir in February 1954.[36] Kuznetsov himself was officially rehabilitated posthumously only a few months later, on April 30, 1954, by the decision of the Military Collegium of the Soviet Supreme Court.[37]

In this context, Mikoyan decided that he could no longer wait. He had to make a public gesture to signify that a new period of change had arrived and to communicate to others that he would be willing to act on their behalf to redress the crimes of Stalinism. A natural place for Mikoyan to begin was the rehabilitation of the fiery poet Yeghishe Charents. Charents was the embodiment of the revolutionary zeitgeist that characterized the era of Lenin's New Economic Policy (NEP) in the Armenian context. A bohemian and a committed communist, he fervently believed in the promise of the Bolshevik Revolution and tied it to the fate of the Armenian people in his writings and verse.[38] A friend of Khanjyan and Nersik Stepanyan, Charents was targeted by Mughdusi's NKVD men as early as November 1936, when they opened a criminal case against him and restricted him from leaving Yerevan. On November 16, they charged the poet with being one of the leaders of a "Trotskiite-nationalist terrorist organization" and subjected him to interrogation. On November 29, Charents faced a second charge of an alleged "provocation toward the incitement of ethnic hatred."[39] He was formally arrested by the Armenian NKVD on the personal orders of Mughdusi on July 27, 1937, and died on November 27 in NKVD custody under unclear circumstances.[40]

Discussions of Charents's rehabilitation preceded Mikoyan's speech. The history dates back to the Yerevan intervention of 1937. Although the Soviet press did not publicize the intervention, many in Armenia were aware of it and sent hundreds of appeals to Malenkov and Mikoyan to investigate and redress the abuses of Amatuni's administration. According to Dmitrii Sukhanov, this development was encouraged by Malenkov, who, upon his arrival in Yerevan, ordered Vladimir Donskoi to collect statements expressing dissatisfaction with the Armenian leadership. Malenkov sought to use these statements in his plenary speeches as "proof" of the dysfunction within the local Party organization. This task was apparently not difficult, and Donskoi managed to complete it "very quickly."[41] Appeals were not limited to complaints against Party leaders or calls to reconsider cases against Party members; they also included statements informing on alleged "Dashnaks" and other "enemies." Colonel G. A. Petrov of the Soviet border guards, who acted as the local people's commissar, recalled that he was "informed daily about bundles of letters" and that "literally heaps of slanderous statements against Party members and non-Party persons poured in."[42] Word that the Moscow group was receiving appeals apparently reached the Nakhichevan' ASSR as well. Artavazd Minasyan recounted that, during a subsequent visit by Mikoyan to the town of Nakhichevan', "an incredible crowd of people" threw "hundreds of letters from both sides [of the central street] right into Mikoyan's path." "Bagirov said to me: 'Give an order to collect all these letters!'" Minasyan recalled. "Immediately, huge sacks were found and were filled up with the letters in minutes."[43]

Back in Yerevan, the number of complaints received by the visiting Moscow group became so great that the post-Amatuni Armenian government had to establish an investigative commission for appeals directed to Malenkov and Mikoyan.[44] From September 26 to October 1, it heard and resolved 306 individual cases.[45] Beginning on September 28, its work began to focus exclusively on appeals addressed only to Mikoyan.[46] In many ways, the 1937 commission served as a crude predecessor to the much more thorough review commission that Mikoyan would oversee with the Soviet Armenian leadership after the deaths of Stalin and Beria. However, unlike the 1954 review commission, in which Mikoyan worked closely with Yerevan, neither Mikoyan nor Malenkov took a direct role in the work of the 1937 commission. The existing source materials do not indicate which Armenian officials served on the commission, although Second Secretary Ashot Margaryan was involved with its work.[47]

Additionally, the era and its circumstances limited the scope of the commission, and the most egregious cases from the Amatuni-Mughdusi period would remain uninvestigated until the Thaw, dashing the hopes of many. Armenian philosopher Henri Gabrielyan recounted that initially, many in the republic "thought that the representative of the Central Committee [Malenkov] had arrived with a mandate to sort out the situation objectively," especially regarding the death of Khanjyan. However, he noted that not only did Malenkov "not understand the matter" but he "continued the work that Amatuni had begun at the command of Beria, i.e. the extermination of Party *aktiv*."[48] Similarly, another eyewitness recounted that when the "Malenkov commission" appeared in Armenia, "we decided that Moscow had learned about the horrors in Yerevan and that the commission would sort it out and that truth would triumph." However, he recounted, "instead of the expected victory of truth and justice, the arrival of the Malenkov commission was characterized by an intensification of repressions in prison and a pogrom against the remaining Old Bolsheviks who were still at large."[49] One of the most prominent unresolved cases was that of Charents. On

September 25, his wife, Izabella, in a beautifully handwritten letter, appealed personally to Mikoyan to intervene to save her husband, underscoring his innocence, illness, and morphine addiction.[50] However, her letter never reached Mikoyan. Khvorostian's Armenian NKVD arrested Izabella on November 23 and subsequently exiled her to Kazakhstan for a period of five years, as the spouse of an "enemy of the people."[51]

The death of Stalin in 1953 created new conditions for the full reinvestigation and eventual rehabilitation of Charents as well as redress for the wrongful exile of his wife. The official process of rehabilitating the poet commenced on December 10, 1953, after the arrest of Beria and about two weeks before his execution on December 23.[52] The waters would be tested by the Armenian writer Hrachya Kochar, likely with backstage encouragement from Mikoyan. Earlier, Kochar infamously denounced Charents and his works to the Armenian Writers' Union in April 1937. "Charents is a stone that has fallen on the path of Armenian poetry," he declared. "That stone must be removed as soon as possible."[53] Seven months later, on November 27, 1937, the poet died in an NKVD jail cell.[54] Remarkably, seventeen years later, the same Kochar chaired the rehabilitation commission tasked with reviewing the case of Charents.[55] Moreover, the writer publicly walked back his earlier charges and called for the exoneration of the poet at the Seventeenth Congress of the Armenian Communist Party in February 1954.

The Seventeenth Armenian Party Congress commenced with a speech on February 14 by First Secretary Tovmasyan. In his address, Tovmasyan called for waging a struggle against the "harmful ideological theory of the cult of personality [*kul't lichnosti*]" in propaganda work and stressed the "leading, guiding, and transformative role of the Party," the "decisive role of the popular masses in history," and the "role of the Soviet state as the main instrument in the construction of communism."[56] Tovmasyan's invocation of the "cult of personality" was by no means the earliest use of this concept by a Soviet official after the death of Stalin. Malenkov was the first known individual to employ the phrase in relation to Stalin at a meeting of the Presidium of the CPSU Central Committee on March 10, 1953.[57] Nevertheless, the Armenian first secretary's words set the stage for Kochar's speech on the third day of the Armenian Party Congress on February 16, 1954. In his address, Kochar condemned manifestations of "national nihilism" among the former Soviet Armenian authorities.[58] He further invoked the most recent use of the phrase by Pospelov at the November 1953 plenum in Yerevan.[59] Kochar called for a broader reassessment of the Armenian revolutionary movement and greater sensitivity toward Armenian national culture. At one point, he even referenced Mikoyan's recommendation to the author Derenik Demirchyan to write a novel on the inventor of the Armenian alphabet, Mesrop Mashtots, despite Mashtots's association with the Armenian Church.[60]

It was in that context that Kochar called for the republication of the works of the writer Raffi.[61] Born near Salmast in northwestern Iran as Hakob Melik Hakobyan, Raffi was among the foremost figures in nineteenth-century Russian Armenian national literature, alongside Khachatur Abovyan.[62] His popular novels, such as *Khent'e* (*The Fool*), spoke to the revolutionary nationalist and socialist zeitgeist among Armenians in the late nineteenth century.[63] However, during the Stalin era, Soviet Armenian authorities denounced Raffi for his "bourgeois nationalism" and for allegedly downplaying the role of the Russian people in helping the Armenian national movement.[64] "The question of Raffi is not a question of a single writer," Kochar stated. "It is a question of the assessment of the history of our people, the assessment of the values created by our people. Raffi expressed the national liberation aspirations of our people. His struggle was directed against the Sultan's regime, against the most severe regime of that time." After praising Raffi as a "brilliant master of the artistic word" who fought for the Armenian people "with the pen of a great writer," he noted that "in an effort to denigrate Raffi, people hid the influence of Russian literature on Raffi, the influence of Chernyshevskii on him. Raffi was a man of Russian orientation and an ardent defender of this orientation."[65]

Nevertheless, Kochar was not unequivocal in his praise of Raffi and tempered his acclamation with criticism. "Raffi has reactionary elements in his work," he noted. "His hatred in some places turns into aggressive nationalism." However, he stressed that these "nationalist elements did not constitute the whole creative spirit of Raffi" and that "the spirit of his creativity is the aspiration for liberation, the hope of our people." He concluded that it would be "wrong to deny Raffi, just as it is wrong to unquestioningly accept him completely." He reminded his audience that Stepan Shahumyan, the famous Armenian Bolshevik and revolutionary mentor of Mikoyan, counted Raffi and the playwright Aleksandr Shirvanzade among his favorite Armenian authors. Furthermore, he warned that, if rejected, such "valuable cultural achievements" as Raffi's novels would be claimed by the archenemies of Soviet Armenia—the Dashnaks. "Nothing should be left to the Dashnaks, the heirs of the Armenian bourgeoisie," Kochar stated. "What the nihilists discard is seized by the enemy and declared his own."[66]

Kochar's discussion on Raffi served as an opening for raising the much more serious case of Charents. The exoneration of such a prominent former "enemy of the people" was not a light matter, and the fact that the subject was broached by one of his original denouncers made it even more significant. By highlighting the shortcomings of Raffi and subsequently other Armenian national figures, such as Gabriel Aivazovskii and Levon Shant, Kochar made it easier to walk back his own denunciations of Charents and to open a discussion on his legacy. Such a discussion was particularly significant in the post-Stalin context as Charents's case was not only a cultural question but also a fundamentally political one. As Kochar told the delegates,

> We note the historical limitations of these writers and criticize the flaws in their work, but we will not abandon their heritage. There have been similarly contradictory writers in our time, and one such writer was Yeghishe Charents. However, our people are not indifferent to Charents's literary heritage, no matter how locked-up it is. This heritage, of course, has its bright and dark sides. It is impossible to erase from Soviet literature Charents's poems about Lenin, his talented lyrical works exposing the Dashnaks, his fiery verses, his realistic poem "Commander Shavarsh." At the same time, vicious works with unacceptable content, such as "Along the Crossroads of History," should not be included in the literature. Politically immature works by Charents are also weak in an artistic sense and are not accepted by the people. But the people remember and love the best works of Charents. His oscillations were an expression of Beria's anti-Leninist policy in Transcaucasia. Certainly, Charents's ideological errors cannot be justified, but it is necessary to clarify them. His fully sound works cannot remain locked up. They belong to the main canon of our Soviet culture.[67]

Significantly, Kochar's last line was greeted by thunderous applause from the delegates, implying widespread sympathy among them for Charents.[68]

In addition to Raffi and Charents, Kochar addressed the fate of those Armenians who had been exiled to the Altai krai in 1949.[69] His statements on this matter were wrapped in strong condemnations of Arutinov, in keeping with the general criticisms of Armenia's former first secretary at the time. Condemning Arutinov as an "agent of Beria," Kochar sharply criticized the Altai deportations, noting that "thousands of innocent people" had been exiled, including "even communists with their children, pioneers, and Komsomol members." For this "base deed," he held both Beria and Arutinov responsible, regardless of Arutinov's actual position on the issue. "With this," he told his audience, "Beria and Arutinov politically discredited and dismembered our people." Kochar called on the Armenian government to redress the issue of the Altai exiles immediately. He noted that "it was time for the Armenian Council of Ministers and the Central Committee to review this question, because if this issue is just left for review by some [lower] commissions, it will drag on for years."[70] Overall, Kochar's statements on the Altai deportations and Armenian national writers successfully tested the waters for what was possible and set the stage for what was to transpire in Yerevan on March 11.

MIKOYAN'S YEREVAN SPEECH, MARCH 1954

On the evening of March 11, during his Supreme Soviet electoral visit to Armenia, Mikoyan delivered his address at Yerevan's Spendiarov Opera Theatre, under large portraits of Stalin and Lenin.[71] In contrast to the convivial countenance seen in his subsequent visits to the Armenian Republic, Mikoyan appeared pensive and anxious, uncertain about the potential reaction from his Armenian audience. Donning his reading glasses, he delivered his address, primarily in Russian and partially in Armenian.[72] Beginning in February 1954, Mikoyan composed at least three complete drafts of his speech before delivering the final version in Yerevan.[73] The draft material is significant as it highlights the evolution of Mikoyan's thought and provides a raw, unfiltered, and more direct version of the views that he publicly expressed. During the drafting process, Mikoyan prepared his discussion on Armenian national issues separately, with the intention of eventually including all or part of it in the final address. In this separate overview, he discussed not only major Armenian cultural figures but also Russian-Armenian relations, the Armenian Genocide, and the Armenian national revolutionary movement. His passages on Raffi and Patkanyan originated from this text, and he first introduced them in the second draft of the speech.[74] Meanwhile, Mikoyan saved his thoughts on the other national issues, such as the Genocide, for his memoirs written decades later.[75]

The most pivotal part of Mikoyan's address was the final portion, entitled "Toward an All-Encompassing Strengthening of the Friendship of Peoples" ("*Vsemerno ukrepliat' druzhbu narodov*"), which he originally called "Friendship of Peoples: Questions of Armenia" ("*Druzhba narodov: Voprosy Armenii*").[76] In this concluding portion, lasting approximately fifteen minutes, Mikoyan commenced by praising the successes of the Soviet nationality policy, emphasizing the central role of Lenin in its formation. By contrast, he gave Stalin only passing mention, despite the influential role of the *vozhd'* in the early development of the nationality policy. Mikoyan then proceeded to laud the Communist Party and the Russian proletariat for assisting the peoples of the Caucasus in their revolutionary struggle against the tsarist "prison house of nations" as well as the "Musavatist-Dashnak-Menshevik counter-revolutionaries" and "Anglo-Turkish and all other interventionists." Invoking the 1918 Baku Commune, Mikoyan emphasized the "feat of the courageous twenty-six Baku commissars" who "heroically died by the interventionists' bullets." He further quoted Lori-born Armenian writer Hovhannes Tumanyan, "a champion of the *druzhba narodov*" and a "devotee of internationalism" who invoked the great Armenian troubadour Sayat-Nova. "It is not by chance that the great *ashugh* [bard] Sayat-Nova wrote his songs in Armenian, in Georgian, and in Azerbaijani," Mikoyan told his audience.[77]

After again condemning Armenian Dashnaks, Azeri Musavatists, Georgian Mensheviks, and even Ukrainian nationalists, Mikoyan then singled out the most "despicable agent of international imperialism" of them all—Beria. Beria, he maintained, "worked, with dirty tricks, to tarnish the sacred feeling of the *druzhba narodov* of the USSR, to undermine the alliance among peoples, and above all with the Russian people, to activate bourgeois nationalist elements in the union republics, and in particular in Transcaucasia."[78] Such words must have had strong resonance among Mikoyan's Armenian audience, especially given Beria's role in decimating Armenia's leading Party cadres and cultural figures during the Stalinist repressions. "In the company of international spies can be found, as on Noah's Ark, 'two of every creature,'" Mikoyan continued, referencing the Genesis flood narrative. He then related this Noah's Ark reference to Mount Ararat, the spiritual and cultural symbol of the Armenian people, visible from Yerevan but located across the border in NATO member Turkey.[79] In a nod to contemporary Cold War geopolitics, Mikoyan reminded his Yerevantsi audience of this reality:

> By the way, Noah's Ark also comes to mind because, as the newspapers have continuously reported, American "scientific expeditions" are underway to systematically search for the ark near the border with Armenia, in full view of you, from Yerevan. Such "expeditions" claim to be based on the Biblical reference to Mount Ararat and that it was there that forefather Noah supposedly anchored his ship. Well, how can you not remember the words of that remarkable friend of the Armenians, the great Russian writer [Aleksandr] Griboedov, who put into the mouth of one of his heroes the most fitting words for just such an occasion: "could you not find a better place to walk?"[80]

The last line, quoted from the character of Pavel Famusov in Griboedov's *Woe from Wit*, reflected Mikoyan's long-standing anxiety over the proximity of Yerevan to the Turkish border.[81]

Then came the essence of the statesman's speech, in which he articulated the framework for what would eventually become the guiding philosophy of the Soviet nationality policy under Khrushchev. Although the Soviet government would continue the fight against "bourgeois nationalism," Mikoyan stressed that it had to wage an equally fierce struggle against what he called "national nihilism"—an indifference toward or even denial of national cultures and traditions. The phrase was not new. It was earlier employed by Pospelov and Kochar in the Armenian context, while its earliest known use was by Stalin himself in his closing address before the Constituent Congress of the Tatar-Bashkir Soviet Republic in Moscow on May 16, 1918. In that speech, Stalin stressed, "To neglect the national question, to ignore and deny it, as some of our comrades do, does not yet mean the defeat of nationalism. Far from it! National nihilism only harms the cause of socialism, playing into the hands of bourgeois nationalists."[82] Ironically, Mikoyan would now use this same phrase to signify the beginning of a de-Stalinization in the nationality sphere, rejecting the centralization and repression characteristic of the Stalinist approach toward nationalities and national republics. In the earliest draft of his speech, the phrase that Mikoyan employed was "great power and local chauvinism."[83] However, this expression apparently did not encompass everything that he sought to address—specifically, the problem of not only chauvinistic nationalism but also indifference to and disregard of national cultures more generally. "The Communist Party," he told his audience, "had always fought against both bourgeois nationalism and national nihilism and nihilistic attitudes toward cultural heritage." Later in the speech, he added, "Everyone knows that our Party, recognizing the importance of everything progressive, carefully preserves the cultural heritage of the people. We are critically mastering this heritage and using it for the development of socialist culture."[84]

Mikoyan then turned to the "nihilistic" suppression of national cultures during the Stalin era, highlighting Armenia as an example. "The harmfulness of nihilism," he stressed, "is evidenced by such facts from local Armenian life as the attitude toward the representatives of Armenian literature Rafael Patkanyan and Raffi."[85] He maintained that "the matter reached such a point that a monument to Patkanyan in Ejmiatsin was removed, and what is more, by people who call themselves 'communists'!"[86] He further noted that these same individuals "ceased publication of works of classical Armenian literature by Raffi." Echoing Kochar's earlier appeals at the Seventeenth Armenian Party Congress, Mikoyan stated, "Of course, there are nationalistic shades in some works of Patkanyan and Raffi. But, on this basis, is it really possible to abandon a cultural heritage that reflected a number of pages of the heroic struggle of the Armenian people against the Persian and Turkish enslavers? Is it possible to abandon a cultural heritage that celebrated the life and labor of the people with love and sublime sensibility?" The statesman proceeded to underscore Raffi's revolutionary credentials. "It is not by chance," he said, "that Raffi devoted his first work with admiration to Mikael Nalbandyan, an associate of Chernyshevskii."[87] The earliest draft of Mikoyan's speech, dating back to February 1954, makes no mention of Raffi or Patkanyan at all.[88] Mikoyan would introduce these figures, as well as Aleksandr Myasnikyan, beginning in the second draft of the speech, from March 5.[89] He would not add Charents until the third draft of the speech on March 11, the same day that he was to deliver it in Yerevan.[90] For Mikoyan, the memory of Raffi and Patkanyan was a personal matter. His love for Raffi dated back to his Nersisyan School days in Tiflis. "I read everything that came into my hands," he later recalled. "During the first years at the seminary I read only Armenian books, because I did not yet know Russian. With great interest I read the historical novels of the Armenian writer Raffi—*Davit Bek, Samvel,* and others. I was fascinated by the romantic struggle of the Armenian people against foreign oppressors, and Raffi's novels left an indelible impression on my mind."[91]

Therefore, when Mikoyan first added the two writers to the second draft of his speech, the wording was much stronger and more passionate than in the final version that he delivered in Yerevan. In it, he skewered the former Soviet Armenian authorities for their "nihilistic" attitudes toward Raffi and Patkanyan:

> It would be wrong to consign a number of leading representatives of the Armenian people to the reactionary camp on the basis that they did not reach revolutionary democratic conclusions. One cannot deny the democratic progressive ideas in their creative output. This is occurring because some dogmatists and ignoramuses have isolated the analysis of the worldviews and creative works of these leading figures from the historical contexts in which they acted. They then proceeded to stick various labels on them. However, it is impossible to mix the era of Patkanyan and Raffi with the later imperialist era when the Armenian counter-revolutionary bourgeoisie created its own traitorous Dashnak Party. It was precisely this confusion of different eras that led to this nihilistic denial of the progressive roles of Patkanyan and Raffi.[92]

Before this passage appeared in the second draft of the speech, Mikoyan first developed it in the separate overview that he wrote on Armenian history and culture in preparation for his address.[93] The content on Raffi and Patkanyan from that overview would be added to the speech in the second draft. The only major difference was that, in the overview, Mikoyan also mentioned Armenian writer Stepanos Nazaryan alongside Patkanyan and Raffi. When Mikoyan added the text to the second draft, he removed Nazaryan from the passage and made a few minor changes to the subsequent paragraph on Raffi, marking them in blue pencil on the overview.[94] Evidently, Mikoyan decided that the time was not quite right to reference Nazaryan, another Armenian writer maligned by official Stalinist dogma. However, Nazaryan too would eventually be exonerated, after his daughter Elizaveta appealed directly to Mikoyan in a letter addressed to him on May 14, 1954, two months after he delivered his Yerevan address.[95]

While developing the second draft of the speech, Mikoyan sought the counsel of Armenian historian and Party official Aramayis Mnatsakanyan. Thus, on March 5, at the request of Mikoyan's assistant Dmitrii Koroliov, Mnatsakanyan prepared a "Note on Cultural Heritage" ("*Spravka o kul'turnom nasledii*"). The note provided Mikoyan with a "brief summary on the attitude toward the heritage of the writers Raffi and Patkanyan, on the destruction of the mockup of the *History of Armenia*, and on A. F. Myasnikyan." By the "destruction of the mockup of the *History of Armenia*," Mnatsakanyan was referring to the decision by the previous Soviet Armenian authorities to "*burn up* the mockup of the second volume" of the official school textbook on Armenian history. The reason was that "warm words were said about some Armenian literary, political, and military figures of the pre-Soviet era and today." Mnatsakanyan noted that the book's authors were "accused of making nationalistic mistakes" and added that because of this "national-nihilistic approach" and "incorrect attitude," Armenian schools still had "not yet received a textbook on the history of their own people." The historian further emphasized the "clearly wrong attitude" of the former leadership of Armenia toward Raffi and Patkanyan, and he underscored that "selected misinterpretations" of Patkanyan based on his condemnations of Ottoman oppression "should not serve as a basis for declaring such a great master of artistic words a nationalist." It was Mnatsakanyan who brought Mikoyan's attention to the removal of the Patkanyan monument at Ejmiatsin, noting that only after a "public outcry" was the monument was "restored in another location."[96]

Following his discussion of Raffi and Patkanyan, after a three-second pause, Mikoyan dropped a bombshell. He exonerated the purged poet Charents. "The former leadership of the republic of Armenia also incorrectly treated the legacy of the talented Armenian poet of the Soviet era, Yeghishe Charents," Mikoyan told his audience. The hall immediately erupted in thunderous applause, lasting approximately thirty seconds.[97] The intensity of the applause was such that one could hear in it not only a consensus among Mikoyan's audience that the cases against Charents and others had been unjust but also that a new political reality was on the horizon. "Charents devoted his work to celebrating the revolutionary activities of the masses and the founder of our Party and the Soviet state, the great Lenin," Mikoyan continued. "Charents's works are distinguished for their high skill, imbued with revolutionary pathos and Soviet patriotism. They must become the property of the Soviet reader." This line was received with a second, albeit shorter, round of thunderous applause from Mikoyan's audience.[98]

Mikoyan's references to Charents were entirely absent in the first and second drafts of his address.[99] Mnatsakanyan likewise did not mention the poet at all in his "Note on Cultural Heritage."[100] Apparently, Mikoyan deliberately decided to wait until the very last moment to add Charents to the speech. When he finally did so in the third draft, his language on the poet's fate was stronger and much more direct than in the version he delivered in Yerevan. In the original, Mikoyan slammed the actions of the former Soviet Armenian authorities toward Charents as "inadmissible" (*nedopustimyi*). By contrast, in the final version delivered in Yerevan, he softened his wording considerably, to state that the former Soviet Armenian government had been merely "incorrect" (*nepravil'nyi*) about Charents. Additionally, Mikoyan originally praised Charents for his "*genuinely* revolutionary pathos" in the third draft of the speech. The more dramatic-sounding "genuinely" (*podlinnyi*) was removed by Mikoyan in the final version. Similarly, Mikoyan toned down "the *most* (*naibolee*) talented Armenian poet" in the third draft to simply "the talented Armenian poet" in the final address.[101] It is significant that, unlike Kochar at the Seventeenth Armenian Party Congress, Mikoyan's assessments of Charents and his work were entirely positive and not tempered by any negative criticisms, indicating that Mikoyan did not agree with the notion that Charents had been guilty of any "ideological errors."

In addition to Charents, Mikoyan bemoaned the fact that the Armenian Old Bolshevik Aleksandr Myasnikyan had all but vanished from the pages of Soviet Armenian history. "It seems strange," he remarked, "that the memory of one of our most prominent Party figures has been forgotten here—Myasnikyan-Myasnikov, Aleksandr Fiodorovich." Like Charents, the name Myasnikyan was greeted with loud and enthusiastic applause from the audience.[102] The revolutionary statesman had been appointed by Lenin to lead Armenia amid the 1921 anti-Bolshevik uprising in Zangezur led by Garegin Nzhdeh and the Dashnaks. As in Georgia, Lenin favored a moderate policy in Armenia and Myasnikyan came to embody this approach, playing an instrumental role in the stabilization and rebuilding of the Armenian Republic during the NEP years.[103] It was with good reason that Norwegian humanitarian Fridtjof Nansen praised Myasnikyan for his "wise moderation" in governance.[104] Charents once described the appearance of the Armenian revolutionary as "forceful and striking." "Of all the descriptions that have occurred to me," the poet wrote, "the one that seems to fit him best is, 'cast in bronze,' which I have applied to him in my poems. Not his imposing face alone, but his entire being seemed to be made of bronze, projecting an image of complete self-sufficiency and self-control." Charents further reflected on Myasnikyan's commanding presence. "The eyes were dominant, a deep hazel, the whites with a greyish shade, his glance exerting an almost physical impact," he recounted. "Few could withstand the power of that glance, and refrain from lowering their eyes under its hypnotic pressure."[105] Tragically, Myasnikyan died in a plane crash in 1925—an "accident" that, some allege, was the work of Beria.[106]

"The working people of Armenia in particular should keep the bright memory of Aleksandr Myasnikyan sacred in their hearts," Mikoyan told his Yerevantsi audience.[107] Indeed, to this day, Myasnikyan is fondly remembered in Armenia as a wise and pragmatic statesman who got the republic back on its feet under NEP.[108] If Charents symbolized the cultural wing of Mikoyan's call for a "re-Leninization" in the nationality sphere, then Myasnikyan symbolized its political wing. Again, like Raffi and Patkanyan, Myasnikyan was not added by Mikoyan until the second draft of his speech.[109] In his "Note on Cultural Heritage" to Mikoyan, the scholar Mnatsakanyan expressed similar sentiments on Myasnikyan, bemoaning the fact that "such a bright face was consigned to oblivion" and that "no works were published on his activities." In fact, he noted, "only one article was published in *Izvestiia* by the Armenian Academy of Sciences in 1947 on the military activities of Myasnikyan in 1917–21." Mnatsakanyan attributed this omission to the "negative consequences" of national nihilistic approaches toward Armenian history. Instead, he concluded that Myasnikyan's work as a Party and state figure and his "tireless efforts to strengthen friendship among the peoples of Transcaucasia" should "serve as an example of Party loyalty and the strengthening of international ties among our peoples."[110] Mnatsakanyan himself would later help fill the gap by authoring his own biography of Myasnikyan and citing Mikoyan's Yerevan speech in the preface of his work.[111]

Following his praise of Myasnikyan, Mikoyan advised his audience to "preserve and fully develop" the "wonderful traditions of internationalism that were laid down in the Caucasus before the October Revolution" by Caucasian Bolsheviks of various national backgrounds, including Shahumyan, Ordzhonikidze, Spandaryan, Kirov, Azizbekov, Japaridze, and Fioletov. As a precautionary measure, he also mentioned Stalin first among these names in one of only four references to the recently deceased *vozhd'* in the entire speech.[112] Building on this "internationalist" call, Mikoyan raised the issue of language, a potentially sensitive topic that would later become a major issue for the nationality question during Khrushchev's reform of the educational system in 1958.[113] Instruction in the union republics had been in the native languages since the revolution, and knowledge of Russian as a second language became compulsory beginning in 1938.[114] Although strongly defending the position of the native republican languages in his speech and emphasizing voluntary Russian-language instruction, Mikoyan placed special emphasis on the need for improving the quality of Russian education. His position was later echoed in the nationality section of the 1961 Soviet Party Program. "The Russian language is now becoming the property of every Soviet citizen, along with his native language," he said. "It is a powerful means for cultural growth. We just need to improve the quality of the teaching of the Russian language. We need to ensure that everyone who has graduated from a secondary institution—the Armenian, the Georgian, the Azerbaijani, the Ukrainian—has a good command of Russian."[115]

To underscore the importance of Russian, Mikoyan even quoted the 1927 poem "To Our Youth" by the futurist poet Vladimir Maiakovskii.[116] In the first and second drafts of his speech, he also invoked his old revolutionary comrade Shahumyan to highlight the important role of Russian in breaking down barriers among the many national groups of the USSR. "In his letters to Lenin," Mikoyan originally wrote, "Stepan Shahumyan, one of the foremost authorities on the nationality question in our Party, emphasized the enormous importance of the Russian language. Lenin responded with an exhaustive answer about the role of Russian in maintaining and developing communication among the working people of the various nationalities inhabiting Russia. Lenin and the Bolsheviks have always spoken out against any form of coercion toward non-Russian peoples."[117] This function of learning the language was especially relevant given Mikoyan's experience witnessing nationalist violence in the Caucasus with the collapse of the tsarist state in 1918–20. In the final version of his speech, Mikoyan told his audience, "There was once a time, now left forever behind us, when the peoples of Transcaucasia shared blood and tears. The blood shed by our peoples was not in vain. It cemented the friendship of the socialist nations of Transcaucasia and the friendship among all the peoples of our Motherland. Now the time has come when it is possible to share the joy and happiness of great creative labor, the creative joy of overcoming difficulties on the path of building communism."[118] Mikoyan concluded his speech in Armenian, with customary praise for the Eastern Bloc, the Soviet socialist homeland, "the indestructible friendship of peoples" (*zhoghovurdneri ankhortakeli barekamut'yune*), and the Communist Party.[119] The statesman decided to conclude the address in Armenian at the last moment, on the day that he was to speak in Yerevan.[120]

Mikoyan's Yerevan speech provided the framework for what would become the essence of Moscow's approach toward nationality policy during the Thaw: a return to greater national expression and a greater respect for national differences within the structure of a united multiethnic state. "National chauvinism" in the vein of the Dashnak or Musavatist "counter-revolutionaries" or damaging policies by figures such as Beria would be swiftly condemned. At the same time, national writers, like Raffi and Patkanyan, would be celebrated, and expressions of "national nihilism" would not be tolerated. The ideological context of Mikoyan's articulated policy approach was the notion of the "return to Leninism," and who better to represent this return than the poet Charents and the statesman Myasnikyan? That both figures were major symbols of the NEP era in Armenia and representatives of "Leninist ideals" only underscored this point. The fact that Charents was a prominent victim of Stalin's repressions made the ideological message doubly significant. It was a signal not only that the country was "returning to Leninism" but also that Stalin was an aberration from Lenin's "true vision" of the revolution and that it was now possible for former "enemies" to become "heroes" again. Thus, the speech also helped create the conditions for Khrushchev's broader reassessment of Stalin at the Twentieth Party Congress. The significance was sharpened by the irony that Mikoyan delivered the address for the voters of Yerevan's Stalin electoral okrug, which was later renamed the Lenin electoral okrug by the time of his 1962 visit. "My father was the first to bring to his homeland Armenia a feeling of liberation from the 'Great Terror', from the fear of doing something wrong," recalled Sergo Mikoyan. "It was he who [in 1954] reprimanded the ideologists who had not yet been released from their inertia."[121]

COMING IN FROM THE COLD

The significance of the speech was not lost on those who heard it. To family members of the victims of Stalin's repressions, the speech, and specifically the reference to the poet Charents, served as a cue that the government (and Mikoyan specifically) would be willing to reinvestigate the cases of their loved ones. Mikoyan had already received numerous rehabilitation requests from those in his Caucasian Old Bolshevik circle, many of whom were of Armenian background. However, immediately after his March 1954 speech in Yerevan, he received a "rash of letters from the relatives of Caucasian Old Bolsheviks" at his door.[122] Charents's close friend, artist Regina Ghazaryan, recalled that "it was Mikoyan who, for the first time after many years of silence, uttered the name CHARENTS in his speech before the auditorium of the [Yerevan] Opera Theatre. Accompanied by the heartfelt joy and enthusiastic applause of the people, it was he who noted the importance of Charents's legacy and who called for his works to be republished." Ghazaryan was personally entrusted by Charents to hide his unpublished manuscripts after his arrest. She buried them, but Mikoyan's speech inspired her to run out that very night "in a half delirious state" to exhume them from their place of hiding.[123] In the words of scholar Vartan Matiossian, "[after] sixteen years of silence, Mikoyan's reference [to Charents] was an explicit signal to bring the poet back to life."[124] Of the speech, the Armenian diasporan writer Antranig Dzarugian similarly wrote, "the name and the literary works of Charents had remained under lock. Suddenly they burst free. Soon after the works of Charents were published in Armenia in two editions of 25,000 copies each. Springs and schools were named after the eminent author. The fact is that for 25 seasons Charents had remained buried. After Mikoyan's speech, suddenly Charents blossomed. True that when Mikoyan comes to Armenia the waters do not remain still, but suddenly long interred poets can resurrect."[125]

In the words of Mary Kilbourne Matossian, Soviet Armenian leaders "took their cue" from Mikoyan.[126] Anticipating an increased number of letters, Mikoyan worked closely with them to establish a review commission in the republic in his name on March 18, only one week after the speech. It was to consist of several high-ranking Armenian officials, among them First Secretary Suren Tovmasyan, Chairman of the Council of Ministers Anton Kochinyan, Second Secretary Hrachya (Hrach) Margaryan, Secretary of the Central Committee for Industry Yakov Zarobyan, and First Deputy Chairman of the Council of Ministers Artavazd Buniatyan.[127] On April 3, Tovmasyan sent a letter to Mikoyan's secretariat, headed by Aleksandr Barabanov, indicating the efforts of the committee to forward certain letters to the respective state bodies of the Armenian Republic. These included the Yerevan City Council and the Soviet Armenian Council of

Ministers, Interior Ministry, Prosecutor, and Central Committee. Grievances forwarded to the Interior Ministry dealt with "complaints of improper eviction to the Altai krai," and those to the Prosecutor dealt with "incorrect actions of judicial investigative bodies." Grievances forwarded to the Party Commission of the Central Committee dealt with requests for "reinstatement in the ranks of the CPSU," while Central Committee departments dealt with complaints of "incorrect dismissal and employment" and the department of Party Organs with "refusal of admission to the Party."[128] The commission was not the first instance of Mikoyan forwarding such grievances to Armenian authorities after Stalin's death. On July 13, 1953, shortly after Beria's arrest, Mikoyan forwarded a letter to Armenian First Secretary Arutinov from repressed Armenian satirist Ler Kamsar. In the letter, dated June 3, Kamsar requested his full rehabilitation, noting that it was now "easier to help" after the death of Stalin than it was in the 1930s.[129] The case was eventually resolved with Ler Kamsar's complete rehabilitation on October 1, 1955.[130]

However, appeals to Mikoyan were not limited to questions of political rehabilitations. Soviet Armenian citizens also sent Mikoyan letters regarding socioeconomic concerns, most prominently the shortage in housing.[131] The latter was a major problem in the postwar Soviet Union and one that was not confined to the western parts of the country that were devastated by the war. In his address, Mikoyan announced plans by the Soviet government to increase housing construction to meet the demand not only in Armenia but throughout the union.[132] His words had resonance beyond the Armenian Republic, underscoring the fact that his Yerevan address was widely read across the USSR. In Leningrad, V. A. Golunskaia, chairwoman of the Local Committee of the Saltykov-Shchedrin State Public Library (today the National Library of Russia), wrote to Mikoyan on September 9, 1954, inquiring about the progress of the housing plans that he had announced in his speech:

> Several months have passed since the day of your pre-election address [in Yerevan]. However, contrary to our expectations, we have been unable to find any mention in the press about concrete steps taken toward the realization of your instructions that had brought us so much joy and encouragement. We therefore take the liberty of appealing to you with a request to strengthen, in one way or another, the hopes that arose in us after your speech and to discuss concrete ways to bring these hopes to fruition.
>
> Many employees of the library, and, yes, perhaps, many residents of Leningrad and other large cities are in dire need of living space. Some of our employees have no living space at all. As a result, they are forced to huddle in strange corners.[133]

Back in Armenia, of the 430 letters addressed to Mikoyan from Soviet Armenian citizens, 184 (43%) concerned housing, and 17 (4%) concerned improvements in Yerevan and its vicinity.[134] In his letter, Tovmasyan wrote that it was "also necessary for the secretaries of the [Armenian] Central Committee to consider the acceptance of citizens who have appealed to Comrade Mikoyan with a request to receive him, as well as to consider their complaints regarding the improvement of the city of Yerevan and its surroundings."[135]

Mikoyan likewise forwarded letters to the Soviet Armenian government that were given to him by locals during his Armenia visit. "I am sending you letters from citizens that I received during my trip to Armenia," Mikoyan wrote in a letter to Anton Kochinyan on June 13, 1954. "Please give them direction."[136] Moreover, not only did he forward such appeals to the Armenian leadership, but he also expressed a desire to be actively updated about the findings and outcomes. "I am sending you letters of citizens received in my name," Mikoyan wrote to Kochinyan in May 1954. "I ask you to take charge of, and to consider, these letters and to inform the applicants and me about the results [of these reexaminations]."[137] However, of the appeals that Mikoyan received, he took a much more active interest in those cases relating to rehabilitations than those relating to socioeconomic problems, such as pensions.[138]

One case that Mikoyan followed particularly closely was that of Danush Shahverdyan—the man whom he had attempted to save during the September 1937 intervention in Armenia. On April 20, 1954, one month after the Yerevan speech, Shahverdyan's son Sergei wrote to Mikoyan, appealing to him to have his parents' cases reviewed.[139] He was nine years old at the time of their arrests in 1937. In response, Mikoyan forwarded his request to Soviet Prosecutor General Roman Rudenko that same day. "Please review and inform me about the results," he wrote to Rudenko.[140] The subsequent investigation was, as Colonel of Justice Ivan Maksimov noted on August 24, 1954, "carried out on behalf of Comrade A. I. Mikoyan."[141] Both Danush and Elizaveta Shahverdyan were rehabilitated on September 25, 1954.[142] Mikoyan later played a key role in ensuring Sergei's entry into the prestigious Moscow State Institute of International Relations. Sergei Shahverdyan subsequently went on to enjoy a successful career as a Soviet diplomat, becoming the Soviet consul general in Marseille, France.[143]

Mikoyan similarly played a key role in the rehabilitation of Armenia's former first secretary Aghasi Khanjyan. Soon after his speech in Yerevan, Mikoyan received a personal appeal from Khanjyan's mother, who sought the reevaluation of her son's case and his rehabilitation. Mikoyan followed through and sent her request to the Chief Military Prosecutor's Office in August 1954.[144] After a thorough investigation into Khanjyan's case and the circumstances of his death, Rudenko recommended the official rehabilitation of Khanjyan in a letter to the all-union Central Committee on January 13, 1956. The Presidium of the Central Committee agreed to accept his proposal and posthumously rehabilitated Khanjyan on January 17.[145] This action, in turn, helped facilitate the rehabilitation of other Armenian Party leaders, including Sahak Ter-Gabrielyan, who was rehabilitated on April 26, and Nersik Stepanyan and Drastamat Ter-Simonyan, who were both rehabilitated on June 9.[146] The conclusions of the Khanjyan investigation were later announced publicly at the Twenty-Second Party Congress by KGB Chairman Aleksandr Shelepin, who noted in his speech on October 26, 1961, that Khanjyan was "personally killed by Beria in his office."[147]

In addition to the cases in Armenia, Mikoyan closely followed the statuses of hundreds of other rehabilitation-related cases outside the republic, many sharing a connection with his old Bakuvian/Caucasian revolutionary network. From the numerous lists of individual cases from throughout the USSR, Mikoyan forwarded each one to the respective state bodies and individuals best equipped to resolve them, including Kochinyan, Rudenko, and others.[148] He personally signed off on virtually every single case meticulously in his characteristic blue pencil.[149] "I was astonished," Mikoyan recalled in his memoirs. "There was never an instance in which a case that I sent on was denied rehabilitation."[150] The depth of his involvement in this process, as extensively evidenced by his personal signatures on these lists, stands as a testament to the passion and seriousness with which he approached the de-Stalinization issue. In some instances, victims of the repressions would seek out assistance from Mikoyan personally. In one such case, Veta Gamarnik, the daughter of former commander Ian Gamarnik, went to the Kremlin to seek a direct meeting with the statesman after her return from exile in 1954. In the waiting room, Mikoyan's assistant Barabanov hugged her and announced to the secretary on duty that she was the "daughter of Comrade Gamarnik." Such a warm welcome overwhelmed Veta, so much so that she nearly fainted. In his office, Mikoyan greeted Veta warmly, encouraged her to speak about her ordeal, and then phoned the Moscow City Soviet, requesting that she be granted an apartment as well as money "for moving and furnishing." He then treated her to lunch at his Moscow apartment and later invited her to his family dacha, where she and his wife, Ashkhen, tearfully reminisced about the past.[151]

Mikoyan's speech and his personal review of such cases set the stage for what happened next. A key figure in the subsequent rehabilitation process was Lev Shahumyan, the son of Mikoyan's revolutionary mentor, Stepan Shahumyan. A "courageous and active man" with "a great sense of humor," Lev was regarded by Mikoyan as a "younger brother since 1918." He even shared a prison cell with him in Krasnovodsk that same year.[152] A close friend and confidant, as well as the deputy editor-in-chief of the *Great Soviet Encyclopedia,* he served as the conduit through which many family members of repressed persons contacted Mikoyan.

"Through him [Mikoyan], my father helped many people," recalled Shahumyan's daughter Tatiana, a future orientalist who was a teenager at the time of his rehabilitation efforts.[153] In his eulogy for Shahumyan in 1971, Mikoyan praised him for making "an inestimable contribution to the cause of correcting subjective distortions in the history of the Party and for restoring the memory of those outstanding revolutionaries who fell victim to the cult of personality and who were then completely rehabilitated."[154] "We shared the same views on many questions, and our trust for each other was unlimited," Mikoyan recalled. "I discussed with him the state of affairs with regard to rehabilitations and I told him that all the cases with which I had dealt had been reviewed and that the people turned out to be innocent. And moreover, many of them were members of the Central Committee or People's Commissars." Mikoyan added that such cases were dealt with "at the request of the children and widows of these individuals."[155]

Mikoyan knew that Shahumyan had "an excellent memory" and that he was "himself a living encyclopedia, especially on questions related to the history of our Party."[156] Therefore, six months before the Twentieth Party Congress, Mikoyan requested that he compile information on the number of delegates in attendance at the Seventeenth Party Congress and the number of those who were subsequently repressed. "After all," noted Mikoyan, "this was 1934, when at the congress, there were no longer any anti-Party groupings or disagreements. There was complete unanimity within the Party. Therefore, it was important to see what happened to the delegates of this congress." Mikoyan further asked Shahumyan to compile a list of "members and candidates for membership of the Party's Central Committee who were elected at this congress, and then repressed." Mikoyan recalled decades later that it was important for him to know such information "in order to go to the Twentieth Party Congress with real facts in hand regarding the fate of these two categories of leading individuals."[157]

After researching the subject for about a month, Shahumyan brought his findings to Mikoyan. What Mikoyan saw horrified him. Of the 1,966 elected participants of the Seventeenth Party Congress, 1,108 were arrested, and 848 were shot. Additionally, of the 139 members and candidate members elected to the Central Committee at the Congress, 98 were arrested and shot.[158] As Mikoyan recounted,

> The picture was terrifying. Most of the delegates to the Seventeenth Party Congress and members of the Central Committee had been repressed.
>
> It shocked me. For several days, I could not get the thought of these findings out of my head. All I thought was "How could it have happened? Why did Stalin do this to people whom he knew well?" In short, I made all sorts of guesses, but none of them suited me and all failed to convince me. I thought of the responsibility that we bore and what we needed to do to prevent something similar from happening in the future.[159]

Of course, it must be noted that Mikoyan was obviously not unaware of the Purges, as this quote might imply outside of its context. However, it would be accurate to say that he was shocked by the scale of the repressions, the full murderous extent of which he did not know or comprehend until the 1950s. He expressed the same sense of astonishment when he met privately with rehabilitated Old Bolsheviks during his March 1964 trip to Baku. Significantly, his words at that meeting were echoed in his memoirs years later. "Stalin personally knew many and trusted many, but then proceeded to destroy them," he told the Old Bolsheviks. "It is still difficult to understand how this could have happened."[160] In April 1963, Mikoyan expressed similar sentiments about the fate of the Seventeenth Party Congress delegates in private conversation with Anushavan Arzumanyan, the director of the Institute of World Economy and International Relations and the husband of a sister of Mikoyan's wife, Ashkhen.[161] A native of the city of Ghapan in Armenia's southern Zangezur region, Arzumanyan had himself suffered in the Purges.[162] Similarly, Gulag survivor Aleksandr Mil'chakov, former leader of the all-union Komsomol and an associate of Mikoyan during his Rostov-on-Don years, recounted that Mikoyan raised the issue of the Seventeenth Party Congress delegates during their meeting in the Kremlin in early February 1956.[163]

Mikoyan's sentiments were amplified by the accounts of returning political prisoners who advised him, and eventually Khrushchev, on the details of Stalin's crimes and the horrors of the Gulag. These persons became informally known as "Khrushchev's *zeki*"—*zeki* being the plural form of the abbreviation for the Russian *zakliuchionnyi* ("prisoner"), referring to former political prisoners.[164] Again, it was Shahumyan who played the decisive role. "It was he who also brought to me Olga Shatunovskaia, who I knew since 1917, and Aleksei Snegov, with whom I was acquainted since the 1930s," wrote Mikoyan.[165] At the time, the Kremlin was a "fortified castle," and so Shahumyan's Moscow apartment served as an oasis and a key location where the statesman could meet with Gulag returnees like Snegov and Shatunovskaia. The environment was such that the former prisoners were addressed with the informal "you" (*ty*) by Mikoyan and Shahumyan during their discussions.[166] Snegov was known as "Aliosha," while Shahumyan's daughter Tatiana knew Shatunovskaia as "Aunt Olia."[167]

These meetings at the Shahumyan apartment proved to be revealing for Mikoyan and others who attended them. As Mikoyan recounted,

> They [Shatunovskaia and Snegov] opened my eyes to many things. They told me about their arrests, about the torture employed [by the NKVD] during interrogations, and about the fate of dozens of mutual acquaintances and hundreds of strangers. Olga related one episode to me that helped me realize that the overwhelming majority of those repressed were not guilty of anything. She was sitting in a women's camp. One day, a rumor spread among the prisoners

> that they [the authorities] had brought in a real Japanese spy. Everyone ran over to look at her and began to ask: "Are you really a spy?" She replied angrily: "Yes! And at least I know why I'm here! And you damn communists are dying here for nothing. But I don't feel sorry for you!"[168]

Mikoyan was stunned by such stories. "My father even called over my mother," recalled Sergo Mikoyan. "'Ashkhen, come here, listen to what Olia is saying.'" Sergo recounted that "in the 'House on the Embankment,' the apartment of Lev Stepanovich and his wife Elena Iulianovna, an unusually sincere and wise woman, was easily accessible for the innocent victims."[169] Tatiana Shahumyan likewise recalled the frequent presence of Gulag returnees at the apartment.[170]

It was in 1954, after his father's Yerevan speech, that Sergo Mikoyan first met Snegov at the Shahumyan apartment. He recalled that he "did not look like a broken man at all" and "on the contrary, behaved like a winner. And he was: it was he who defeated his 'torture masters'—the entire repressive system of the Gulag." Indeed, Sergo noted that Snegov "at over 70 years of age, was energetic and mobile, as if he were 30 years younger."[171] Nevertheless, he still bore the physical imprint of the Gulag, as the horrific marks of torture on his back testified.[172] Snegov had long known both Khrushchev and Mikoyan, and Khrushchev's son Sergei later credited him with being the "catalyst" for de-Stalinization.[173] Mikoyan even unsuccessfully attempted to save Snegov during the Purges.[174] During Beria's trial, the government brought him out of exile to testify on Beria's manifold crimes. When Beria saw Snegov in the courtroom, he was stunned. "You're still alive?" he reportedly snarled, to which Snegov simply replied, "It must have been a glitch in your apparatus."[175] Now, after a brief exile in the Komi Republic after the trial, Snegov was free and would play a decisive role in the de-Stalinization process.[176]

After these meetings with Shatunovskaia and Snegov, Mikoyan decided to bring the former political prisoners to Khrushchev to convince him to take action. "I helped arrange for Shatunovskaia and Snegov to meet with Khrushchev," Mikoyan recounted. "He [Khrushchev] knew Olga since his work in Moscow and he knew Snegov even earlier than that."[177] After hearing Snegov and Shatunovskaia, Khrushchev, like Mikoyan, became convinced of the need to act. Sergo stated that both men "learned about many things for the first time, including the scale of the repressions, the 'methods of interrogation', the innocence of almost every convict, the barbaric living conditions of the prisoners, and the mass death of people from hunger, cold, and repression within the camp system."[178] Mikoyan recalled that "these two people [Shatunovskaia and Snegov] undeservedly 'fell out of history,' but they played a major role in our 'enlightenment' in 1954–55 and in our preparations for discussing the question of Stalin at the Twentieth Party Congress in 1956."[179] Snegov in particular saw the Twentieth Party Congress as decisive. "If they should fail to dethrone Stalin at this congress, the first after the death of this tyrant, and if they fail to talk about his crimes, then they will be remembered in history as his willing accomplices," Snegov maintained. "Only by exposing Stalin's role will they convince the Party that they were unwilling accomplices." According to Sergo, Snegov "persistently convinced Khrushchev and Mikoyan of this idea."[180] Shatunovskaia was no less persistent. On the matter of the mass rehabilitation of political prisoners, she implored Khrushchev and Mikoyan that "something urgent had to be done. Otherwise, people would die and perish. If all this were to drag on for years, then they wouldn't survive."[181]

Meanwhile, the rehabilitation commission tasked with reviewing Charents's case took Mikoyan's Yerevan speech into their considerations, emphasizing not only his call to rehabilitate Charents but also his denunciations of national nihilism and his references to Raffi, Patkanyan, and Myasnikyan.[182] The rehabilitation report of another victim of the Purges, Aksel Bakunts, even stated that Mikoyan's speech had already de facto rehabilitated the poet.[183] However, it was only on May 25, 1955, that Charents was officially rehabilitated posthumously by the Soviet government.[184] His rehabilitation was followed by the exoneration of his family. Efforts on the part of the Soviet Armenian government to return Charents's family to his Yerevan home began as early as September 1954. However, although official Yerevan regarded this question as "resolved" by July 1955, his wife, Izabella, remained in exile.[185] In 1959, she attempted to return to Yerevan, but the Armenian authorities declined to grant her an apartment. She tried again in 1961, with the intercession of Leonid Brezhnev, but the Armenian government still denied her request for accommodation.[186] When Mikoyan arrived in Yerevan and met with Charents's daughter, Arpenik, he asked her why her mother "did not settle in a large metropolitan city after her exile." Arpenik recalled that she "burned up and could not restrain" herself. She told him, "You ask me why? Surely you know about the ban on exiles from settling in big cities?"[187] In 1967, Izabella, since remarried and living in Ufa, learned from the magazine *Ogoniok* that Charents's seventieth birthday would be marked in Moscow.[188] She immediately flew to the Soviet capital from distant Bashkiria in the southern Urals.[189] As she later recounted,

> I learned that he was exonerated. And that I was not exonerated. I went to the Writers' House and I told them that I was the wife of the Armenian writer Yeghishe Charents and that I had been living in exile for so many years, and that he [Charents] had been exonerated since 1954 . . . And of course, they said: "We are very glad that you came. You did very well. We will celebrate the anniversary here in twenty days. You will stay for the anniversary. We will give your appeal to your local leadership, and they will do everything for you." And so, it happened.[190]

On the day of the anniversary in Moscow, Mikoyan arrived with Larisa Stepanyan, deputy chairwoman of Armenia's Council of Ministers. "Mikoyan read my appeal," recalled Izabella. "He told Larisa Stepanyan that Charents's wife should go to Yerevan and that you should do everything for her in terms of securing an apartment and pension. Decide on everything. And so, I came to Yerevan. I thank our state for helping me with the apartment and the pension."[191]

Mikoyan's meetings with the Charents family were not isolated cases. He regularly checked in on rehabilitated victims of the Purges in Armenia. For instance, during his 1962 visit to the republic, he met with Vagharshak Norents, who had been arrested on August 10, 1936, and then rehabilitated alongside Vahram Alazan and Gurgen Mahari on July 21, 1954.[192] Mikoyan was concerned not only with the recently rehabilitated but also with those whom he had saved. For example, during the Purges, the statesman had protected the Armenian poet Avetik Isahakyan, who had settled in Armenia after leaving France and had fallen under the suspicion of the local NKVD.[193] Upon learning of Isahakyan's passing on October 17, 1957, Mikoyan penned an emotional letter the next day to the Central Committee of the Armenian Communist Party, expressing his deep bereavement and condolences to the Isahakyan family:

> I ask you to accept my expression of *deep* sorrow over the death of the great son of the Armenian people, Avetik Isahakyan. The beloved of the people, the *varpet* [master] Avetik sacredly preserved the best traditions of the centuries-old culture of old Armenia and, through his tireless creative work, made an invaluable contribution to the construction of a new socialist culture in Armenia. The artistic word of Avetik Isahakyan inspired several generations of people, not only in Armenia, but also far beyond its borders. Many songs and poems of Avetik became popular and entered into everyday life, in the flesh and blood of the workers of the city and the village.
>
> I ask you to convey my sincere condolences to the family of Avetik Isahakyan and the Writers' Union of Armenia regarding this grave, irreparable loss.[194]

Isahakyan's memory remained with Mikoyan for the rest of his life. In 1975, Armenian scholar Khikar Barseghyan presented Mikoyan with a signed copy of his Armenian-language book about his meetings with Isahakyan.[195] Similarly, in July 1971, the sculptor Yervand Kochar (no relation to Hrachya) gifted Mikoyan a personally autographed book of his art in Yerevan.[196] Mikoyan had known Kochar since his Nersisyan School days in Tiflis. Together with the architect Karo Halabyan, the statesman had interceded to secure Kochar's release from imprisonment during the Stalin era.[197] In 1973, during the exhibition of Kochar's works at the Museum of Oriental Art in Moscow, Mikoyan advised Armenian artist Vahram Khachikyan to "take good care of Kochar" (*"K'ocharin lav pahek'"*). He then added, "but why don't you put up his sculpture of [the fifth-century Armenian hero] Vardan Mamikonyan?" Later, at the evening banquet marking the exhibition's closing, Mikoyan gave a toast in which he declared that he was proud to have Kochar as his personal friend.[198]

On the all-union level, at the Twentieth Party Congress, Mikoyan helped set the stage for Khrushchev's denunciation of Stalin by delivering the first attack on the *vozhd'* in his speech of February 16, 1956.[199] American journalist Harrison E. Salisbury, who personally interviewed Mikoyan and gained his respect later, once wrote that "there is no doubt that the wise, battle-scarred Armenian has been the closest man to Khrushchev in the days since Stalin's death. At each step of Khrushchev's rise you could see Mikoyan striking out ahead, testing the ground, as it were, for Khrushchev to follow." Salisbury specifically had in mind Mikoyan's Twentieth Party Congress speech in which he "first openly attacked Stalin—in terms more sharp, in some respects, than used by Khrushchev."[200] After finishing his address, Mikoyan was reproached by his brother Artiom, the famed aircraft designer and a delegate at the congress. "Anastas, you should not have made such speech," he told him. "You were essentially right, but many delegates are not happy with you, and they are reprimanding you. Why did you attack Stalin like that? Why should you take the initiative when others don't speak about it? And Khrushchev said nothing like this." Mikoyan responded to him, "You are wrong. And those comrades who are unhappy with my speech are wrong as well. As for Khrushchev, well, he will be giving a report at the closed session, and he will speak of even worse things."[201]

In the years and months leading to the Twentieth Party Congress, Khrushchev worked closely with Mikoyan to carefully prepare everything, with the guidance of individuals like Snegov, Shatunovskaia, and Shahumyan. "Those speeches [at the Twentieth Party Congress] were no accident," Mikoyan noted in another conversation with Salisbury in the summer of 1967. "They were carefully planned. We fought and fought for that. For three years we carried out a quiet, meticulous investigation—analyzing everything. That's why the Twentieth Party Congress is so important. That is why every party congress since then and, now, the fiftieth-anniversary declaration reiterate the same principle—the Leninist principle of intraparty democracy." As Mikoyan spoke these words, Salisbury noticed a "fire in Mikoyan's eyes."[202] He ascribed this passion to Mikoyan's own realization that he too would have become a victim of a new round of repressions had Stalin lived to initiate them. However, he might have also noted Mikoyan's passion for righting the wrongs of Stalinism and rehabilitating its many victims—including those whom he knew personally. The 1954 Yerevan speech arguably helped set that process in motion.

THE IMPACT ON THE THAW IN ARMENIA

Soviet Armenian statesman Yeghishe Astsatryan recalled that Mikoyan "spoke quite freely on political and national issues" in his 1954 Yerevan address.[203] Indeed, it would be no exaggeration to say that Mikoyan's speech effectively signaled the start of the Thaw in Armenia, an era known among Armenians as *dznhal*, the Armenian equivalent of the Russian *ottepel'*.[204] Armenian writer Ruben Angaladian referred to the address of March 1954 as "the first triumph of justice, ushering [in] 'new times'" for the Armenian Republic.[205] Armenia became one of the first places in the Soviet Union to embrace the liberalization of the era and, as will be seen, even tested its limits in terms of both democratic freedoms and national expression.[206] As historian Benjamin Tromly wrote, "even if it was centered in Moscow, the Thaw was a pan-Soviet rather than ethnically Russian phenomenon. The values proclaimed by its adherents—moral introspection, culture, openness—made it open to participation by non-Russian intellectuals."[207]

The impact of Mikoyan's speech on Soviet Armenian cultural life was immediate. Only a few weeks after the statesman's departure from Yerevan, Armenians were already beginning to taste the nectar of Thaw-era liberalization, with Charents again serving as the symbol of its new freedoms. On April 1, 1954, Hrachya Margaryan ordered the printing of ten thousand copies of the Armenian translation of Mikoyan's speech for public distribution.[208] On April 14, *Kommunist* reported that actor Suren Kocharyan had performed a dramatic reading of Charents's "Lenin and Ali" and part of his "Commander Shavarsh" in Yerevan.[209] That same year, an anthology of Charents's poetry was published in Yerevan for the first time since his arrest in 1937.[210] This publication was followed by a large volume of Charents's works also published in 1954 and assembled by Eduard Topchyan, Soghomon Tarontsi, and Garegin Hovsepyan, with design by renowned artist Hakob Kojoyan.[211] On January 30, 1955, *Kommunist* published a Russian translation of Charents's "Ballad about Vladimir Il'ich, a Peasant, and a Pair of Boots."[212]

The Yerevan address had an impact on those who knew Charents even outside the Armenian context. In May 1954, only two months after the speech, Mikoyan received a letter from Igor Postupal'skii, a Ukrainian-born literary critic and translator, who had also been a former "enemy of the people."[213] In the 1930s, Postupal'skii served as the editor of an anthology of Charents's poetry in Russian translation. In a 1935 letter to Goslitizdat director Nikolai Nakoriakov, Charents personally requested that Postupal'skii oversee the project, which he hoped would become "one of the best books published by Goslitizdat, in terms of quality of translation."[214] Among those translating Charents's poems for the anthology were Anna Akhmatova and Boris Pasternak.[215] In a personal letter to Postupal'skii from 1935, Charents praised him for securing Akhmatova's talents for the project. "For me," Charents wrote, "the translations of this great Russian poetess, who has been well-known to me for quite some time, are an incredible joy, especially since they seem to be very faithful, yes? Please give her my thanks when the occasion arises. I would have written to her myself, but for now it is somewhat uncomfortable. Thank you!"[216] However, in October 1936, one month before Charents faced formal criminal charges, Postupal'skii was arrested by the NKVD, officially due to his flirtations with "Ukrainian nationalism." For his "transgressions," he was sent to the Kolyma Gulag, only to be rehabilitated after the war.[217]

In his letter to Mikoyan, Postupal'skii appealed to the Soviet statesman to intervene to ensure the publication of the long-suppressed Charents anthology. Such a publication, he contended, was the very will of Charents. He wrote to Mikoyan that, in Kolyma, he had met two Armenian prisoners who conveyed the poet's last wishes to him:

> While in Kolyma, needless to say, I also encountered Armenians—prisoners. It so happened that, at different times, I had the opportunity to meet with two Armenians who were sitting in the Yerevan investigative jail with Charents. I do not remember their names, but that is not important. What is important is that these individuals, having recognized my surname, generally informed me together that, while in jail, Charents instructed a number of persons to give me his last wishes if any of them should happen to meet me. The first wish was to speak to *Stalin and Mikoyan* if I have such an opportunity and to inform them that slanderous statements were made against him, Charents. The second wish was to convey to the same two Party and state leaders, that he, Charents, facing death, requests that they rehabilitate him over time—first of all, by publishing his good *Russian* book, after which his memory will no longer be blackened by various envious people, idiots, cowards, etc.
>
> Now you can imagine the feeling of deep satisfaction and genuine excitement that I experienced when I read your remarks about Charents.
>
> Dearest Anastas Ivanovich!
>
> If I did not appeal earlier either to the late Stalin or to you, then it was only due [first of all] to my uncertainty that my letter—the letter of an ordinary man—could ever reach such a high address, and secondly, to my uncertainty as to whether the "time of Charents" had already arrived. Despite a certain sense of discontent among the Soviet Armenian intelligentsia and the wider mass of the Soviet Armenian people, until very recently in Armenia, as you well know, all possible reinsurers and simply fools [*perestrakhovshchiki i prosto gluptsy*] were *silent* about Charents.
>
> But now, with your help, the question of Charents has been resolved in the interests of the people, and I can fulfill my obligation to the late poet in the hope that my message will be heard precisely by those to whom I am addressing.
>
> Dearest Anastas Ivanovich!

> For many years, as you will agree, I was convinced that Charents, whatever his shortcomings, was not, and could not, be an enemy of our Soviet country. I was just as equally convinced that his creative work, that is Charents's work, would not be forgotten. Thus, I kept proofs of his Russian book, which in my time was not released for the reasons stated above.[218]

Then, quoting directly from Mikoyan's speech, Postupal'skii wrote, "In fulfillment of the last will [*predsmertnaia volia*] of the 'talented Armenian poet of the Soviet era,' I appeal to you with a request to assist me in publishing the book of Russian translations of Charents that I have long ago prepared (available in proofs). Naturally, for publication, the text of the book, preserved in the proofs, should be additionally revised and partially updated. Otherwise, the book is essentially *ready*."[219] Signing off on Postupal'skii's letter, Mikoyan endorsed the book's publication and forwarded his request to Goslitizdat director Anatolii Kotov.[220] Mikoyan's endorsement, strengthened by his earlier call to rehabilitate Charents, contributed to the publication process of the work, which had already been underway as early as April 1954. On April 6 of that year, poet Konstantin Simonov, the secretary of the Soviet Writers' Union, also called on Kotov to publish the anthology. Praising Charents's works as "great contributions to multinational Soviet literature," he lamented that they were "little known to the Russian reader" and that they "had not been published in Russian in over twenty years."[221] Goslitizdat would publish the book in 1956.[222]

In January of that same year, *Kommunist* announced the publication of the first two volumes of a ten-volume set of the works of Raffi. The article quoted from Mikoyan's speech about the dangers of "national nihilism" and the importance of Raffi's works to Armenian culture. "The nihilistic attitude of vulgar sociologists toward Raffi's creative works now belongs to the past," wrote the journalist S. Sarinyan. "From the position of a Marxist attitude toward cultural heritage, A. I. Mikoyan condemned this nihilistic view and determined the place of Patkanyan and Raffi in the history of Armenian literature."[223] Behind the scenes, one of the editors of the series, Suren Harutyunyan, even consulted with Mikoyan on the publication. As a result of these consultations, Mikoyan reached out to veteran Soviet diplomat Hamazasp Harutyunyan on December 7, 1956, requesting that he receive the editor to discuss the effort to track down Raffi's archives abroad.[224] In addition to Raffi, an anthology of Bakunts's works was published in 1955, the first printed in Yerevan in almost two decades.[225] Bakunts had been posthumously rehabilitated by the Soviet government on March 2 of that same year, following the posthumous rehabilitation of Vahan Totovents on January 29.[226] In a March 1956 write-up, *Kommunist* noted that, although the Bakunts anthology did not include all of the writer's works, it nevertheless "presented a complete portrait of the creative path of Bakunts as a whole."[227]

Meanwhile, the former "enemy" Charents had not even been officially rehabilitated for one year when the Soviet Armenian government began making him the standard to which young Armenian writers should aspire. Armenian First Secretary Tovmasyan made this point in his official report before the Eighteenth Armenian Party Congress on January 19, 1956, one month before the Twentieth Party Congress of the CPSU:

> The works of our literary scholars and critics published during the reporting period have brought some clarity to the assessment of the literary heritage of many writers. In 1954, the third volume of *The History of Armenian Literature* dedicated to the Soviet period was released. Additionally, the Institute of Literature has prepared and already published books on the works of several Soviet writers. Over time, the writings of Charents, Bakunts, Mahari, Norents, Alazan, and others were published.
>
> The Seventeenth Armenian Party Congress revealed the gross mistakes and distortions in the field of literary criticism that were made in the past and outlined ways to overcome these shortcomings. 1955 saw the beginning of the publication of a ten-volume set of the works of Raffi. The works of Hakob Paronyan, Krikor Zohrab, Daniel Varuzhan, Ruben Sevak, and Rafael Patkanyan were also published.
>
> However, it must be kept in mind that the mere correction of admitted errors cannot solve the large and serious tasks of the continued development of literature and the arts. At the same time, one cannot help but notice that a mood of serenity prevails among our artists, playwrights, composers, and leaders of the Ministry of Culture and the Writers' Union.[228]

Citing one of the "serious shortcomings" in literature and the arts as "a lack of full-fledged works reflecting the life of the working class," Tovmasyan went on to say that "Armenian literature is rich in wonderful traditions celebrating the working class, in particular the traditions established by Hakob Hakobyan and Yeghishe Charents." Moreover, he added, "that was in the early years of the industrialization of our country." Noting Armenia's industrial development and the passage of time, he admonished Armenian writers for "actually consigning to oblivion" the important topic of the workers. "The lack of full-fledged works of art about the working class, the leading force in society, does not honor Armenian writers," he concluded.[229] Tovmasyan continued his praise for Charents in his address before the CPSU Twentieth Party Congress on February 18, between the major speeches of Mikoyan and Khrushchev. Echoing Mikoyan's Yerevan address of two years earlier, Tovmasyan invoked Charents and recalled the poet's quote casting Moscow as the "center of the world."[230] Five years later, Khrushchev himself endorsed the assessments of Tovmasyan and Mikoyan, lauding Charents as an "outstanding representative" of Armenian literature during his trip to Armenia in May 1961.[231]

Following the Twentieth Party Congress, in an April 1956 report to the CPSU Central Committee, Tovmasyan noted that the Twentieth Party Congress and Khrushchev's denunciation of Stalin were generally well received in Armenia. "The workers, kolkhozniks, and intelligentsia," he wrote, "are unanimous in their approval of the decisions of the Twentieth Congress of the CPSU.... Everywhere, in the primary Party organizations [of Armenia], communists unanimously approve of Comrade Khrushchev's report given before the CPSU Twentieth Congress 'On the Cult of Personality and its Consequences.'"[232] In fact, Armenian Party activists not only concurred with Khrushchev's conclusions but went even further by openly voicing scathing denunciations of Stalin. In his earlier report to the Soviet Central Committee from March 23, 1956, Tovmasyan noted that many Party leaders and activists throughout Armenia "dwelled in detail on the issue of the cult of personality and its harmful consequences for the Party and for the Soviet people." They specifically emphasized the necessity of "teaching communists, especially the younger generation, about the gross mistakes of Stalin and the spirit of Leninism." Party activists in Yerevan maintained that Stalin's personality cult did "much harm to the Party, the state, and the people." Many delivered speeches that "were of a harsh character against Stalin." One slammed Stalin as the "executioner of Lenin's cadres" and argued that "for his murder of several thousand people, Stalin did not deserve to lie in Lenin's Mausoleum." "He did not fight for Leninism," the activist said, "and that begs the question: if Lenin's cadres were unable to correct Stalin, and Beria alone made him an enemy, then, apparently, Stalin was not an instrument in the hands of Beria, but Beria was an instrument in the hands of Stalin." Another Armenian comrade stated that for his many misdeeds, Stalin "cannot be a member of the Party" and that "he needs to be posthumously expelled from the ranks of the CPSU."[233]

Taking their cues from Mikoyan's criticism of Stalin's *Short Course* at the Twentieth Party Congress, Party activists in Leninakan likewise criticized Stalin's text for its "incorrect" version of history centered on Stalin and its "undeserved" praise for him. In his report, Tovmasyan highlighted specific questions that Armenian Party activists had raised regarding Khrushchev's denunciation of Stalin. The most frequent included, "How should we treat the ideological legacy of Stalin?" "How should we treat the portraits and monuments of Stalin?" "What is the reaction in Georgia?" and "How can we explain the absence of any delegation from the League of Yugoslav Communists at the Twentieth Party Congress?" Others noted that the Party charter of the CPSU "obligates all communists to report shortcomings to the Party organs" and asked, "Why, then, at the Nineteenth Congress or later during Stalin's life, did the members of the Presidium of the Central Committee not raise the question of his cult of personality?"[234] Recently rehabilitated Party members added to the chorus of Armenian denunciations against Stalin, among them Liparit "Lipo" Barseghyan, a former member of the Armenian Central Committee Secretariat who had been exiled for seventeen years. He argued that Stalin was no different from other "deviationists" like Trotskii, Zinoviev, and Kamenev—top opposition politicians killed on Stalin's orders. "He should have suffered the same punishment as them," he maintained, adding that Stalin "destroyed the best cadres in our country." At the same time, Barseghyan urged caution when dealing with the dismantlement of Stalin's personality cult, noting that "for many years, the cult of Stalin rose before the people and, therefore, the eradication of his name should be carried out gradually."[235] Another recently rehabilitated Party member, the poet Gurgen Haykuni, negatively described Stalin's activities during the civil war period.[236] He called for the dismissal of the "Stalinist bureaucracy."[237]

Conversely, writer Hrachya Kochar was one of the very few public intellectuals in Armenia who criticized Khrushchev's denunciation of Stalin. Expressing his "disagreement" with the Twentieth Party Congress, he alleged that there were "contradictions between the facts that he [Khrushchev] cited and the conclusions that he made."[238] What these "contradictions" were, Kochar did not specify. For his part, the writer Nairi Zaryan criticized members of the Presidium of the Central Committee for not doing enough to stop Stalin. "Who can believe that they have not seen all this?" he asked. "Well, how can one explain the fact that they saw and endured all of this? Out of fear? But truly, does not a coward have the right to act? We cannot forgive cowardice even for an ordinary soldier. An ordinary soldier is shot when he shows cowardice during battle, and when statesmen show cowardice, it leads to a terrible disaster for the people." The Armenian leadership condemned both Kochar's and Zaryan's remarks as "anti-Party" statements.[239]

Later, in his April 1956 report to the Central Committee, Tovmasyan stated that the denunciations of Stalin were almost going too far and were beginning to turn into "anti-Party" manifestations. In response to the outcome of the Party Congress, he noted that "some communists made plainly erroneous statements in their speeches" and that "certain anti-Party elements attempted to use the practice of criticism and self-criticism within Party organizations for their own hostile aims." For example, Tovmasyan wrote that "some members" of Party organizations had "questioned the democratic nature of elections" in the Soviet Union at several educational institutions in the republic, including Yerevan State University, the Institute of History of the Academy of Sciences, School #16 of the Molotov raion, and the Abovyan State Pedagogical Institute. Moreover, they "declared that deputies to the Supreme Soviet are not elected by the people but appointed [by the state]." One Party activist at Yerevan State even suggested "changing the procedure for elections to Party bodies," arguing that the current procedure "allegedly excludes the possibility of free discussion of candidates and the real democratic nature of the elections." Another activist stated that "there is no real freedom of the press in our country," and a member of the Party organization of the Yerevan Medical Institute "displayed liberalism" and "departed from Khrushchev's report" in a published editorial on Khrushchev's condemnation of Stalin. Even the republic's Interior Ministry was not immune to controversy. As Tovmasyan noted, during a meeting of the ministry's primary Party organization, one individual made a "malicious, slanderous statement" against several members of the all-union Central Committee Presidium, proposing to "hold them accountable."[240]

Tovmasyan further charged that others at Yerevan State were creating an "unhealthy environment," which "distracted the attention of some communists" from the "main tasks" of the Twentieth Party Congress.[241] At the Party meeting at Yerevan State on March 29–30, 1956, students and faculty used the discussion on Khrushchev's speech as a springboard for testing the limits of the Thaw. For example, the university's vice rector, Eduard Aghayan, raised the issue of Soviet claims to historical Armenian territories in Turkey.[242] Similarly, one lecturer "proposed the unification of Nagorno-Karabakh with the Armenian SSR." Although several statements during the meeting were "condemned by some communists," Tovmasyan nevertheless noted that those present "did not react [negatively] to the anti-Party fabrications regarding the unification of Nagorno-Karabakh with Soviet Armenia."[243] One graduate student demanded that the Kremlin take more proactive measures in response to the September 1955 Istanbul pogrom in Turkey, in which Greeks, Armenians, and Jews were targeted by organized Turkish nationalist mobs. "The government did not stand up for the rights of the Armenian people persecuted in Turkey," he stressed, adding that France had issued its own condemnation.[244] Later, Mikoyan personally raised this issue in a Moscow meeting with US vice president Richard Nixon in July 1959.[245]

Armenia's newfound Thaw-era freedoms were then tested to the limit by a Yerevan State philosophy professor and member of the University Party Committee who poked fun at the shortcomings of Soviet "democracy" as Armenian Party leaders bristled. "Take, for example, the elections that we just held," the speaker told his audience. "The results were announced as follows: 99.99 percent voted for the Bolshevik bloc of communists and non-Party persons. It was never below 99.99 percent!" His observations were met with howls of laughter from the students in the audience. Other speakers proceeded to openly criticize Tovmasyan, Shmavon Arushanyan, and other Armenian leaders and made "slanderous statements" against them and against the bureau of the Central Committee of the Armenian Party. A June 1956 report further noted that "when some communists tried to talk about shortcomings in the work of the university, they were interrupted, confronted with loud noise, and prevented from speaking, while, conversely, demagogic speeches aroused the approval and applause of those present."[246] Subsequently, the secretary of Yerevan State's Party Committee, A. Adamyan, was dismissed and "severely reprimanded" by the Bureau of the Armenian Central Committee. Meanwhile, "other communists" were disciplined and "held accountable" for their "anti-Party and slanderous statements."[247] Ironically, when Tovmasyan later fell out of favor with Moscow as Armenia's first secretary in November 1960, one of the charges leveled against him by officials in the center was his allegedly relaxed attitude toward "ideological flaws," including the publication of works by writers such as Paruyr Sevak, whom they accused of expressing "nationalist tendencies."[248]

Armenia was not an isolated case. Several Soviet republics were testing the boundaries of acceptable national expression. In Ukraine, writers in L'viv used Khrushchev's condemnation of Stalin as a springboard to "demand greater respect for Ukrainians' language and culture." However, these Ukrainian intellectuals were much more circumspect than their Armenian counterparts and "only joined in this cautious criticism [of Stalin] in 1957."[249] Nevertheless, the flowering of Ukrainian national expression continued apace, and Ukrainian university students, very much like their Armenian peers, likewise began to test the limits of Thaw-era freedoms in the nationality sphere.[250] At the same time, in Latvia, local "national communists" pushed for greater Latvian national expression within the Soviet socialist context.[251] In some cases, rising national sentiments expressed themselves in more violent forms, as seen in the 1956 Tbilisi riots in Georgia, in reaction to Khrushchev's denunciation of Stalin.[252] Throughout the USSR, demands for greater national expression elicited different responses from Moscow, ranging from the coercive to the inclusive, with Mikoyan favoring the latter approach.

3 | Apricot Patronage

In addition to assisting Armenian leaders on rehabilitating national cultural figures such as Charents, Mikoyan worked with them to highlight Armenia as a model of Soviet *dostizhenie* (achievement) in the nationality sphere. It was this endeavor that facilitated the rise of Mikoyan's Armenian patronage network.[1] Indeed, just as Khrushchev had two patronage networks of his own in Moscow and Ukraine, so did Mikoyan, in the cases of Armenia and Baku.[2] In his capacity as a Supreme Soviet deputy for Armenia, the statesman provided crucial assistance to his Armenian network on everything from expanded economic opportunities in Sanahin and Ghapan to support for major projects, such as the Arpa-Sevan and Arzni-Shamiram canals. Mikoyan had served in a consultative role for Yerevan in his Supreme Soviet position since 1937, but it was during the Thaw that he became much more actively involved in developments in the republic. His active involvement during this period reflected not only an increased interest in Armenian affairs but also the changing political dynamics that arose following Stalin's death in 1953. The absence of a single, all-powerful leader created the conditions for the emergence of several networks of power in the USSR.

Patronage networks were by no means unique to the Thaw and played a crucial role in Russian and Soviet life throughout history. An examination of these networks and the ways in which they functioned thus provides us with a window into the world of Soviet politics. As used in this study, the term "patronage network" refers to a "coalition of individuals who share at least one goal and who agree to pool their resources in pursuit of that shared goal." Such a network "requires a sure leader and a group of members who are working toward the common goal."[3] In the case of Thaw-era Armenia, that leader was Mikoyan, and the group of members were the republic's most prominent political figures, among them Yakov

Zarobyan, Anton Kochinyan, and Yeghishe Astsatryan. These leaders worked with Mikoyan collaboratively on various projects in Armenia and came to regard him as the most senior partner in the collective project to "build socialism" in the republic. In this regard, personal connections, always important in the context of the Caucasus, played an especially significant role. Through common bonds of culture, language, and national identity, Mikoyan forged a close bond with these leaders, granting Armenia its own informal conduit to the Kremlin. He likewise rewarded loyalty among members of his network, as reflected in the case of Zarobyan's appointment to the NPNSC Subcommittee.[4] Building on Maike Lehmann's concept of "Apricot socialism" (i.e., a hybrid "Soviet" and "Armenian" identity), one might call Mikoyan's work in Armenia a form of "Apricot patronage." This term refers to the Armenian national fruit, the apricot, whose orange-reddish skin reflects, in Lehmann's words, "yet another variation of the revolutionary red."[5] However, this phrase also alludes to the crucial role that national communities and affinities played in the development of patronage networks in the Soviet Union.

The clients who comprised Mikoyan's Armenian network had varied backgrounds in terms of their positions and origins. Born in Artvin, a provincial town in historical Eastern Armenia annexed by Kemalist Turkey, Yakov Zarobyan served as Armenia's first secretary from 1960 to 1966.[6] Anton Kochinyan, who, like Mikoyan, was a native Loretsi, served as the republic's chairman of the Council of Ministers from 1952 to 1966 before assuming the post of Armenia's first secretary from 1966 to 1974. A native of Nagorno-Karabakh, Yeghishe Astsatryan, who served as deputy chairman of Armenia's Council of Ministers from 1962 to 1966, received crucial support from Mikoyan to pursue his career in Armenia.[7] Born in Baku to a family with Loretsi roots, Aram Piruzyan served as the longtime chief of Soviet Armenia's food industry, weathering the fall of Arutinov in 1953 and eventually ascending to the post of Soviet trade representative to Greece in 1964. Other figures in the network included Suren Tovmasyan, the republic's first secretary from 1953 to 1960, and Georgi Ter-Ghazaryants, second secretary of the Armenian Central Committee in the 1960s and later a veteran Soviet diplomat.

Mikoyan's work with Armenian leaders was guided by his view that the economic development of all Soviet republics and subrepublican autonomies served as an indicator of the successes of the Soviet nationality policy.[8] He therefore saw his contributions to the Armenian Republic as nothing less than the Soviet nationality policy in action. Khrushchev shared this view and articulated it at the Twenty-Second Party Congress in October 1961, stressing that "the greater the contribution of each republic to the common cause of building communism, the wider and more multidimensional the interconnection of the Soviet nations."[9] Perhaps even more significantly, especially given his position as a master international diplomat, Mikoyan attached great value to highlighting his native republic as a model of Soviet achievement in the nationality sphere to foreign observers, specifically in the Armenian diaspora. In his conversations with Armenian leaders, he regularly stressed the importance of the diaspora's awareness of Soviet Armenia's successes.[10] Similarly, Mikoyan greatly valued perceptions of the Armenian Republic from Armenians that he encountered on his trips abroad.[11] At the same time, Mikoyan's work with his Armenian network demonstrated the strength of informal politics within the Soviet Union in the competition for resources among the various parts of the country.[12] Indeed, for Zarobyan, Kochinyan, Astsatryan, Piruzyan, and others, their interest in securing resources for their republic intersected with the general interest, promoted by Mikoyan, in highlighting Armenia as a model of Soviet *dostizhenie*. Unsurprisingly, Zarobyan publicly underscored the link between perceived nationality policy "success" and economic development in his speech before the Twenty-Second Congress of the Armenian Communist Party in September 1961.[13]

Mikoyan took on two roles in his multifarious activities for Armenia, both of which served to cultivate his Armenian network. These roles consisted of (a) the advocate, supporting the Armenian government and lobbying for its interests in Moscow, and (b) the advisor, offering ideas to Armenian leaders and input for improvements in the republic. As he assumed these roles, the official receptions that greeted Mikoyan throughout Armenia highlighted an interplay between the top-down efforts of the Soviet government to project state power and the bottom-up celebrations of Mikoyan as a representative of Armenian national achievement within the Soviet milieu. Despite these celebrations, however, not every issue was so easily resolvable for Mikoyan and his network. The problem of Nagorno-Karabakh specifically revealed the limits of informal politics in the Soviet Union.

MIKOYAN AS ADVOCATE

As an advocate for Armenia and his Armenian network, Mikoyan personally intervened on behalf of Yerevan in Moscow, acting as a lobbyist, especially if the republic needed funds for large-scale infrastructure projects. In these endeavors, he worked closely with the Armenian leadership, constantly consulting with them and forging a collaborative relationship toward the common aim of promoting the economic development of the republic. It was in this context that Mikoyan was able to persuade Kremlin officials to support various projects for which Yerevan needed Moscow's assistance. In most cases, he was successful in securing such support for Yerevan, and his role as an advocate for Armenia in the Kremlin was aided by his close ties with the USSR's highest official, Nikita Khrushchev. "What did Mikoyan do for his homeland? A lot!" recalled Ter-Ghazaryants. "Of course, he could not do this openly. . . . In some cases, on his own initiative, he was the first to speak with Khrushchev, which made our job easier."[14]

Nowhere was Mikoyan's advocacy more apparent than in his efforts to assist Yerevan on major economic projects in his native Lori region, which Ter-Ghazaryants referred to as Mikoyan's "little homeland" (*p'ok'r hayrenik'*).[15] The statesman demonstrated a consistent concern for conditions there and regularly visited his home village of Sanahin and the associated city of Alaverdi, which eventually annexed the village.[16] For instance, Mikoyan played a key role in the "reconstruction, modernization, and expansion" of the large Alaverdi Copper Smelter, a major source of employment for the region's local economy.[17] During his 1954 visit to Armenia, Mikoyan, together with Kochinyan and Tovmasyan, met with the plant's director, Hakob Sargsyan, to discuss its progress and inquire about its needs. Sargsyan requested that Mikoyan appeal to Moscow for support on several issues, including increasing the plan for the plant's production levels; resuming activity at the Lenin Mine (where work had been suspended since 1944) to access ore for the production of black copper; building a processing plant at the Shamlugh deposit, another area rich in ore; constructing gas traps at the Alaverdi plant to reduce gas emissions and prevent sulfur dioxide release into the environment; and finally continued state investment in the plant's cement factory.[18] These concerns were duly noted by Mikoyan and Armenian leaders, with Mikoyan particularly concerned about pollution produced by the plant. "It is necessary to take seriously the issue of sulfur dioxide gas traps in Alaverdi," he stressed.[19] According to Ter-Ghazaryants, Mikoyan used his influence with Khrushchev to facilitate Moscow's approval for the expansion and development of the Copper Smelter in subsequent years.[20] By the time of his 1962 visit to Alaverdi, the plant's production capacity had greatly expanded. Astsatryan recalled that "while Mikoyan was getting acquainted with the combine, the chemical plant, and the city districts in detail, he provided us with a number of tips on improving the surrounding ecological conditions and on enhancing and greening the riverside and hillside areas."[21]

Another Lori project—the large acetate silk plant in Kirovakan—also had Mikoyan's support and patronage. During his 1962 visit, after a short stop in Leninakan, Mikoyan and his entourage arrived in Kirovakan to inspect the ongoing construction of the factory.[22] Supported with modern British equipment, it was proclaimed by *Kommunist* as Armenia's largest contribution to Khrushchev's ambitious Seven-Year Plan (1959–65), intended to bolster economic growth in the USSR.[23] "Another similar factory," recalled Astsatryan, "was under construction in the Russian city of Engels [a suburb of Saratov], where the English side was complaining to the Soviet Foreign Trade Ministry about the slow pace of its operations." At the plant site, Mikoyan and his associates carefully examined the machines and workshops. "Anastas Ivanovich expressed a desire to become acquainted with the construction of the plant on the spot and with many assembly specialists, as well as the English supervisor," noted Astsatryan.[24] The group listened to the explanations of factory director Lazar' Akhnazarov, and Mikoyan chatted with visiting British specialists in the facility's spinning shop, with the aid of an interpreter.[25]

"In Kirovakan," recalled Astsatryan, "Mikoyan became thoroughly acquainted with the pace of many novel manufacturing sites, auxiliary economies, and the assembly of technological equipment. . . . Listening with interest to all parties, Mikoyan was very pleased to hear that the construction assembly work and training of production personnel was proceeding according to the organized, planned schedule." He noted that Mikoyan "did not hide his joy that many large factories with cutting-edge technology were being built and successfully operated in Lori's limited territorial conditions."[26] Mikoyan's active interest in the development of the Kirovakan plant continued after his visit. On August 3, 1962, Viktor Fiodorov, the chairman of the all-union State Committee of the Council of Ministers for Chemistry, informed him that construction was lagging behind schedule and proposed measures to resolve the problems causing the delay in the facility's launch.[27] On the same day, Fiodorov informed Zarobyan that he had also sent him a copy of his letter to Mikoyan.[28] In response, on August 11, Mikoyan forwarded Fiodorov's letter to Kochinyan and representatives of the Soviet Ministry of Construction of Power Plants (Ignatii Novikov), the Council of Ministers of the RSFSR (Mikhail Iasnov), and Gosplan (Semion Vasilenko). "Take action on this matter and report on the results at once," he wrote to them.[29]

Developments in Kirovakan were linked to another project involving Mikoyan in Armenia—the Yerevan Polyvinyl Acetate Plant. The Yerevan plant was one of the first in the Soviet Union that did not use food ethanol in the production of acetic acid, which, as *Kommunist* reported, "made it possible to annually save several million pounds of potatoes or wheat."[30] During his 1962 trip, Mikoyan visited the plant with Zarobyan, Kochinyan, and Astsatryan and was given a "heartfelt welcome" by the workers, including bouquets of flowers from the female employees, shouts of "Ura!" and even Caucasian toasts in honor of their guest.[31] Behind these pleasantries, the real purpose of the visit, as recalled by Astsatryan, was that "one of the raw materials used in the Kirovakan acetate silk plant—acetyl-cellulose—was to be produced at a special production site under construction at the Yerevan Polyvinyl Acetate Plant, the equipment for which we had not yet received from the Gor'kii oblast' and timely receipt was very much in doubt." During the visit, Mikoyan assured Armenian leaders that he would "take measures to ensure the timely preparation of the equipment and its delivery to Yerevan." At the same time, he stressed that "if the equipment was not prepared in a timely manner, then the Soviet government would help the situation for some time by importing the raw material from abroad." In the end, the latter scenario prevailed. "Since the Gor'kii Machine Factory did not manage to produce the technological equipment in a timely manner," noted Astsatryan, "the Kirovakan plant was put into operation on time, but we had to buy acetyl-cellulose from France until we received and finished installing the shop equipment for production of that material at the Polyvinyl Acetate Plant."[32] At the time of Mikoyan's 1962 visit, French advisors were already present at the Yerevan plant. Mikoyan took the opportunity to chat with them, and before his departure, was presented with a parting gift of sample products produced at the factory.[33]

Mikoyan likewise served as Yerevan's patron for the Arzni-Shamiram Canal, another significant part of Armenia's contribution to the Seven-Year Plan. The opening of the first phase of the canal occurred in 1958, and Mikoyan, together with Tovmasyan, Kochinyan, and Shmavon Arushanyan, even inspected the canal site during his visit to the republic in March of that year.[34] Workers at the central Armenian kolkhozes of Yeghvard, Ashtarak, Getamej, Kanaker, and Chatghran toiled to clear stones for the cultivation of the Yeghvard plain. However, they did not have the means to bring the work to completion, and Yerevan needed to turn to Moscow for assistance. Kochinyan appealed to Vasilii Zotov (then deputy chairman of Gosplan), outlined a plan envisioning the cultivation of ten thousand hectares of land, and requested financial support. In response, Zotov dispatched a representative to Armenia to investigate the feasibility of the proposal. Finding the land unsuitable for cultivation, Moscow nearly denied Yerevan the funds it requested.[35]

Undeterred, Kochinyan met with Mikoyan in Moscow and spoke with great enthusiasm about the completion of the first phase of the canal. He showed him a map of the Yeghvard area, highlighting the future cultivation of gardens in its vicinity. Mikoyan studied the map meticulously and expressed skepticism. "You have a surprisingly vivid imagination!" he said. "I see some exaggeration here. I know all of these areas well. When I was there in the 1920s, I could never walk through this land on foot. It is a perfect desert. It will take a long time to master this area and even then, our techniques have still not been perfected. Most importantly of all, it is very difficult to allocate funds for such a project at this time."[36] Kochinyan promised Mikoyan that if funds were allocated to the project, then, during his next trip to Armenia, Mikoyan would observe that the highway between Yerevan and Ashtarak would already be completely green. It was on this condition that Mikoyan agreed to intervene on Yerevan's behalf and speak about the matter to Zotov personally. In his conversation with Mikoyan, Zotov underscored the cost of the undertaking and the stony landscape of the area in question. In response, Mikoyan stressed that there was "no land without stones in Armenia" and that "the fruit grown there is the tastiest of all." After this conversation, Zotov agreed to meet with Kochinyan again. Nevertheless, although Zotov received Kochinyan warmly, Yerevan still had to organize five new sovkhozes in the area before the ministry allocated the necessary funds to complete the project.[37]

Four years later, on the first day of his visit to Armenia in 1962, Mikoyan asked his hosts, "Is it possible to go to Ashtarak? I have not seen it in a long time. Perhaps much has changed." Kochinyan recalled that he "immediately guessed" that Mikoyan wanted to see the progress of the Arzni-Shamiram project.[38] The following day, after a visit to the town of Lusavan (later Charentsavan), Mikoyan and his hosts drove to the orchards cultivated by the Arzni-Shamiram Canal.[39] Mikoyan told the driver to stop the car, and he got out to inspect the lands closely and meet with the students affiliated with the Yerevan Agricultural Institute who were cultivating them. The statesman was genuinely impressed by what he observed. He wished the students "success in their noble cause from the bottom of his heart and said that they can be proud that they have revived lands that were barren for centuries."[40] Back in Yerevan, Mikoyan took Kochinyan aside. "When you told me [about the plan for the Arzni-Shamiram Canal], I did not believe you," he said. "I was always waiting to see everything with my own eyes to make sure. Great work has been accomplished. They are truly wonderful gardens."[41] Later, after Gosplan ceased funding the project, the Armenian leadership appealed to Mikoyan for support of the next phase of the Arzni-Shamiram Canal. "In this respect, very quick and concrete help was provided," Kochinyan recalled. "The magnificent canal was built and about 30,000 hectares of uncultivated, rocky lands became irrigated, and now the best vineyards and orchards in the republic are planted there."[42]

Earlier, at the end of Arutinov's tenure, Mikoyan played a similar role as a patron for the second stage of the Talin Canal, which received water from the Akhuryan Reservoir along the border between Armenia and Turkey. To cultivate the area watered by the canal, Arutinov envisioned the creation of five new sovkhozes in the Talin raion (*shrjan* in Armenian). For this plan, Yerevan needed support from the all-union Food Industry Ministry, and Kochinyan had to go to Moscow to negotiate with Zotov. At first, Kochinyan's meeting with Zotov was very warm and cordial. However, just as Zotov was about to approve the project, the head of the agriculture department handed photos to him showing the dry and stony landscape of the Talin raion. The photographs were the result of an earlier study of Talin after Piruzyan requested funds from Moscow for developing sovkhozes in the area. Although Zotov deemed the project a "senseless" and unprofitable undertaking, he agreed to meet Kochinyan again. Kochinyan then visited Mikoyan, who asked to be apprised of the matter. After discussing the situation with him, Mikoyan smiled and rhetorically asked, "And where in Armenia are there no stones?" He advised Kochinyan to return to Zotov's office the next morning. The next day, Kochinyan met with Zotov, equipped with data and economic justifications from Yerevan. Expecting the worst, Kochinyan was pleasantly surprised when an affable Zotov informed him that the ministry had decided to approve Yerevan's request. "Of course, I immediately realized that Mikoyan had already talked with Zotov," Kochinyan recounted, "but I couldn't wait and asked Zotov if he had spoken to him. Zotov replied that Anastas Ivanovich told him 'And where in Armenia are there no stones? When there is sun and water, the Armenian peasant can work wonders!'"[43]

Armenian officials often took advantage of Mikoyan's trips to Armenia to visibly demonstrate local needs in places like Zangezur and Daralagyaz. According to Kochinyan, Mikoyan had long maintained an interest in these mountainous southern provinces. "Once in a conversation," he recalled, "Mikoyan even expressed a desire to transfer his Supreme Soviet electorate from Yerevan to Zangezur, but such a move was not possible under the conditions at that time."[44] It was not until March 1962 that Mikoyan finally journeyed to Zangezur as part of his Supreme Soviet electoral trip to Armenia.[45] After a meeting with astrophysicist Viktor Hambardzumyan at the Academy of Sciences in Yerevan, Mikoyan, together with Zarobyan, Kochinyan, and Astsatryan, took the overnight train to Zangezur via Nakhichevan', arriving in Agarak, a satellite village of Meghri, on the Iranian border.[46] Later, on the road from Ghapan to Kajaran, Kochinyan suggested that the entourage stop near a series of newly constructed buildings on the Voghji riverbank, not far from the Voghji Hydroelectric Power Station. The buildings housed a boarding school for eighth to tenth graders that would soon serve the whole Ghapan raion. Astsatryan then asked Mikoyan, "Anastas Ivanovich, please be our supreme judge. Which peasant in Armenia would agree to send his child to study at this secondary school, built in these uninhabited valleys, for three years? And this is when there are secondary schools in many neighboring villages!" He suggested transferring the buildings to the jurisdiction of the republic's sovnarkhoz (*zhoghtntkhorh* in Armenian).[47] "Within a short period of time," he added, "we will build additional necessary structures, run a trolleybus line to Ghapan, and set up a modern equipment factory that will employ 2,000–3,000 young Ghapantsi workers." Astsatryan stressed that if such a plan was realized, the locals would "not have to leave the republic in search of work." However, he noted that the all-union Council of Ministers was opposed to the plan. In response, Mikoyan told him, "I fully agree with you, and I will become your state advocate. Look for supporters and devise a positive solution to the matter."[48]

Although it was much more common for Armenian officials like Astsatryan and Kochinyan to speak to Mikoyan informally, there were instances in which they penned formal requests to the statesman about the republic's needs. For example, on July 3, 1958, Kochinyan wrote to Mikoyan, underscoring Armenia's great need for transportation vehicles. The poor state of transportation led to "untimely deliveries of goods to distribution networks in major industrial centers," he wrote. Kochinyan sought the allocation of "200 trucks, 25 specialized vehicles for transporting food products, and 30 Moskvich station wagons." Upon receiving the request on July 14, Mikoyan forwarded it to Gosplan's first deputy chairman, Georgii Perov, for consideration.[49] In another case, on July 12, 1957, physicist Artiom Alikhanyan drafted a letter for Kochinyan to address to Mikoyan requesting that the all-union Ministry of Higher Education increase the number of students admitted to the Physics Department of the Physics and Mathematics Faculty of Yerevan State University. The request was connected to personnel needs in relation to the construction of the Yerevan electron accelerator and the expansion of Alikhanyan's cosmic ray research on Mount Aragats.[50] Mikoyan would later meet with Alikhanyan and inspect the accelerator personally during his 1966 trip to Armenia.[51]

Occasionally, Armenian leaders would appeal to Mikoyan to help resolve disputes among themselves. One such case involved the town of Ijevan in northeastern Armenia. Mikoyan drew "special attention" to the need for development in this town, which Armenian leaders regarded as an important northern "gateway" to the republic. Ijevan was difficult to access via railway, limiting the possibilities for developing heavy industry in its vicinity. "Under such circumstances," recalled Kochinyan, "the best way forward was to develop light industry and our first step in this regard was the construction of a carpet factory." In Moscow, Kochinyan met with Aleksei Kosygin, who was then the Gosplan chairman, to discuss the matter. Kosygin was planning to travel to Leipzig in East Germany as the head of a Soviet delegation. Kochinyan asked if he could explore the possibility of purchasing German equipment to build a carpet factory in Ijevan. "I cannot promise a positive outcome," Kosygin responded, "but send Garnik Darbinyan with our delegation. If there is an opportunity, he will work to formalize the shipment of the equipment in Germany."[52]

Darbinyan served as Armenia's Minister of Light Industry and was trusted by Kosygin. In Germany, he was able to secure agreements for the delivery of the equipment. The plan was approved by First Secretary Tovmasyan. However, at the last minute, Tovmasyan proposed relocating the planned factory from Ijevan to the city of Sevan, on the northern shore of Lake Sevan. Finally, "after a long argument and Mikoyan's intervention, we decided to build the factory in Ijevan, and it is [now] considered to be one of the leading enterprises in our republic," Kochinyan recalled.[53] During a later visit to Ijevan, Mikoyan inspected the carpet factory and spoke to its director, Iu. Yepremyan, as well as the head of Armenia's Light and Textile Industry Department, Armen Tonyan, and the Ijevan Raikom secretary, Vladimir Ghalumyan. In recognition of his efforts, the factory staff presented Mikoyan with "one of the very first examples of an Artsakh [Nagorno-Karabakh] carpet created by the enterprise, at the last hour of a warm farewell." As Astsatryan recounted, Mikoyan "carefully scrutinized the patterns of the beautiful carpet with great interest and expressed his deep gratitude to the factory collective and its leadership. 'It is with great gratitude and love,' he said, 'that I accept this precious gift and pass it on to the Ijevan kindergarten, wishing the children a happy life and good luck!'"[54]

Mikoyan not only received appeals from Armenian leaders but also listened to complaints from local specialists about the need for resources from Moscow. For instance, while visiting a Yerevan watch factory during his 1954 trip, Mikoyan was informed by the director that the all-union Ministry of Medium Mechanical Engineering "was not allocating the necessary investments" for the expansion of the factory and for housing construction for the workers. The factory also produced wooden-framed alarm clocks, but the director bemoaned the fact that "the ministry forbade their distribution, citing a lack of demand in the distribution network." To ensure the distribution of the clocks, Mikoyan instructed Armenian officials "to find ways to correct the situation." Mikoyan similarly inspected a worsted wool factory in Yerevan, where the chief engineer noted that the capacity of the facility could be increased by 30 percent with the installation of additional equipment. He further complained that "the machines that arrived from Leipzig are incomplete, because they were installed at one of the working factories in Leipzig that was bombed [during the war]." He appealed to Mikoyan for assistance. In response, the statesman recommended that Armenian leaders write to Kosygin about the matter.[55]

During the same 1954 visit, in the town of Tumanyan in Lori, Mikoyan proposed increasing the production capacity of the Tumanyan Factory of Refractory Brick Materials to 150,000 tons, based on the comments of that factory's director. The aim would be "to satisfy the full need for metallurgy in the whole of Transcaucasia" and thereby halt the costly shipment of brick materials from faraway Leningrad and Donbass. Moreover, in accordance with the factory director's recommendations, Mikoyan advised Armenian officials to work with the all-union Ministry of Ferrous Metallurgy on the construction of a magnesite brick plant in Sevan, due to the presence of "high-quality" raw materials needed for magnesite brick production.[56] Mikoyan received similar appeals from the director of the Yerevan aluminum plant, who informed the statesman that the facility could produce several times more high-purity aluminum than it did. However, he complained that the all-union Ministry of Non-ferrous Metallurgy planned to produce it in insufficient quantities and therefore sought the statesman's intercession. Mikoyan likewise listened to complaints about poor housing from the factory's workers, who asked him to intervene. One worker complained that he had been "working at the aluminum plant for three years and that he still only lived in a hostel, even though he had a large family, including a wife, child, mother, and father."[57] In addition to housing for workers, Mikoyan stressed to Armenian officials the necessity of "building homes for teachers, doctors, and the intelligentsia."[58] Lieutenant General Grigorii Oriol, deputy commander of the Transcaucasian Military Okrug, similarly reported on the "sharp lack of housing for soldiers" during his meeting with Mikoyan in Kirovakan.[59] Such problems were not unique to Armenia. As historian Steven Harris noted, housing shortages in the postwar USSR were "extreme," and "most urban dwellers continued to live in barracks, dormitories, and communal apartments, as they had before the war."[60]

Mikoyan's trips to Sanahin also afforded locals the opportunity to present their grievances directly to the Soviet statesman. During his 1954 trip to the village, he, together with Tovmasyan and Kochinyan, spoke with local kolkhozniks and workers who complained that "the bathhouse and premises for the cooperative were left unfinished, and that they [the government] had left the apartments for teachers unrepaired." Others apparently discussed the need for local road repairs. In response, the chairman of the local executive committee assured the villagers and Mikoyan that "the construction of the bathhouse and the cooperative would be finished in June," that the teachers' accommodations would be renovated, and that the road would be "put in order."[61] Alert to the need for proper living conditions, Mikoyan stressed to Armenian officials that "a bathhouse must be built at the Sanahin smelter, since the workers of the plant live there." He further advised the construction of additional amenities near the factory, including a store and a school, and alerted Armenian officials to the urgent need to pump water up to the Sanahin Plateau. He also emphasized the necessity of fixing an existing water supply pipe to the village.[62] The water supply issues would be resolved by the time of Mikoyan's 1962 visit to Sanahin, when he returned and drank from the recently completed memorial spring dedicated to Sanahnetsis who served in the Great Patriotic War.[63]

Mikoyan remained an advocate for Armenia even after his retirement from high office in 1965. "For a long time," wrote Kochinyan, "there was much debate over whether we were doing the right thing to create industrial enterprises in rural district centers, even in large settlements. In the central bodies, especially at Gosplan, we were blamed for wasting resources, for not conducting the right policies, and for creating industrial enterprises in remote raions and villages." However, after another visit to Zangezur in the late 1960s, Mikoyan signaled to the Armenian leadership that he would remain a firm voice of support for Yerevan in Moscow. "He said at our meeting in Moscow that we were doing the right thing by creating non-metal factories to provide people with jobs in those localities," recalled Kochinyan. "Additionally, Mikoyan well understood that we were not of the same mind even within our own republic and that many of our leaders echoed the center's mentality and hindered the organization of new initiatives."[64]

In late 1968, in one of his final acts as an advocate for his network, Mikoyan personally assisted the Armenian leadership in organizing the celebrations in honor of the centenary of the Armenian national poet and native Loretsi, Hovhannes Tumanyan. Although the idea of honoring Tumanyan originated with then First Secretary Kochinyan and the Armenian government, Mikoyan served as a key member of the all-union organizing committee for the festivities.[65] Commemorative events were held in Yerevan and Tumanyan's native village, Dsegh, in Lori, on September 20–25, 1969, with Kochinyan and Mikoyan accompanied by Badal Muradyan (then chairman of Armenia's Council of Ministers) and Marshal Hovhannes (Ivan) Baghramyan.[66] In his address on September 24 in Yerevan, Kochinyan publicly acknowledged Mikoyan for his role in realizing the celebrations.[67] For his part, Mikoyan penned a special dedication to Tumanyan, published in the Armenian-language *Grakan T'ert'* on the same day, in which he recounted attending a recitation by the poet with other students of the Nersisyan School.[68] The 1969 Tumanyan festivities marked one of Mikoyan's last visits to his native Lori, and he regarded them not only as a major success but also as a reflection of the achievements of Soviet Armenia and the Soviet nationality policy generally.[69]

MIKOYAN AS ADVISOR

Mikoyan built on his role as an advocate for Armenia with his dual role as an advisor, providing recommendations and guidance to Armenian leaders on various matters. Such input could take the form of consultations in Moscow about large-scale funding proposals, informal conversations about afforestation in Lori, or advocacy for technological advancements in public speeches in Yerevan. In his advisory role, Mikoyan consistently took a collaborative and "democratic" approach toward his Armenian network, acting as if he were only the most senior local official working among other local officials. As a "senior consultant," Mikoyan's deference to Armenian leaders served to strengthen his bonds with them, and they in turn solicited and welcomed his input, viewing it as complementing their work in the republic.

Mikoyan regularly consulted with members of his network in Moscow during their visits to the Soviet capital. In such meetings, Armenian officials like Zarobyan or Kochinyan would update him about the progress on various projects in Armenia and would seek advice on how to frame funding proposals to Soviet central bodies on behalf of Yerevan. Mikoyan would offer not only advice but also insights on the political dynamics within the Politburo and the Council of Ministers. Ter-Ghazaryants has left us with perhaps the most vivid description of such meetings, highlighting the nature of the relationship between Mikoyan and his Armenian network:

> Every time we arrived [in Moscow] for a session of the Supreme Soviet of the USSR, we all met with Anastas Ivanovich beforehand. These were the sessions in which the budget was to be approved and, usually, a few days before then, a plenum of the CPSU Central Committee was also convened. So, the Armenian leadership left in full force. Over the years, its composition changed, but none of these changes had any impact on this case. We all went together to Mikoyan's dacha if it was summertime, or to his city apartment if it was winter. The first thing we did was to tell him about our plans. He listened very attentively and gave advice right from the very beginning. For example, he would say "don't ask that question because it won't work anyway," or "This initiative will be approved if you phrase it properly", or "Why don't you raise the question about . . . ?". This kind of advice was extraordinarily valuable and useful, since Mikoyan knew all the ins and outs of the situation in the Politburo (then known as the Presidium of the Central Committee) and in the Council of Ministers.
>
> For the accuracy of the presentation of our proposals, to make them more "passable," Mikoyan called in Mikhail Sergeevich Smirtiukov. Smirtiukov was the managing director of the all-union Council of Ministers. He was the guy who prepared all the government decrees and thoroughly knew all the subtleties of the Moscow bureaucracy. Mikoyan asked Smirtiukov to receive us and advise us on the best way to formulate our proposals, so that they would go through the "sieve" of Gosplan, Gossnab, the commissions of the Supreme Soviet, and, finally, in serious cases, when it came to the big money, the Presidium of the CPSU Central Committee.
>
> Smirtiukov previously worked as an assistant to Mikoyan and respected him very much. He was on the shores of [Lake] Ladoga during the siege of Leningrad, controlling incoming goods and sending them to the blockaded city. He acted on behalf of State Defense Committee member Mikoyan and reported everything to him by telephone every day. And so, he received us, and for a long time, attentively worked with us. Most often, having familiarized himself with our proposals, and after amendments and additions introduced by Mikoyan, he actually dictated to us the formulation on how to best raise this or that question. Therefore, in fact, we had no misfires. Our proposals almost always passed without problems. And we didn't raise any "impassable" questions.[70]

Although he was the highest-ranking Armenian official in the USSR, Mikoyan was always respectful and deferential toward Armenian leaders and even addressed them formally, as he did with Kochinyan.[71] "One time," Kochinyan recalled, "I asked him, 'Anastas Ivanovich, is it comfortable for you to address someone who is younger than you, in age and in everything, with the formal "you" [*duk'*]?' With a smile, Anastas responded, 'When you are released from the chairmanship of the Council of Ministers of Armenia, I promise to address you with the informal "you" [*du*].'"[72] By addressing members of his Armenian network in this way, Mikoyan was determining the nature of his relationship with them, blurring the lines of official Soviet hierarchy. Mikoyan's rapport with Armenian officials was so close that he was "capable of reading your thoughts from the very first word you uttered and would not let you go on and on explaining," noted Kochinyan. "He would answer almost always accurately and specifically." All parties concerned were invested in Armenia's development and the environment was such that ideas would be discussed and negotiated among them. "It went without saying that Mikoyan loved to talk to people and had a great, one might say exceptional, memory," recalled Kochinyan. "He would talk, ask questions, get acquainted with their moods and conditions of life. If something didn't please him during the conversation, then he would repeat it and reflect on it for some time."[73] Mikoyan also sought to keep his network humble about their accomplishments. On one occasion, he told Kochinyan, "It is true that recently the press of the republic has started to employ very common words, such as 'enormous,' 'globally recognized,' and so on. You don't realize that you've begun to boast, counting small successes as 'enormous' or the completion of a small structure as 'world-class.'"[74]

In his consultations with the Armenian leadership, Mikoyan was keen to ensure that he was receiving accurate information. For instance, during Kochinyan's first meeting with Mikoyan in 1952, Mikoyan's secretary Aleksandr Barabanov recorded all the data that the Armenian official provided about the republic. Mikoyan then checked Kochinyan's data against Moscow's information and met with him again to discuss any discrepancies.[75] For their part, Armenian leaders benefited from using Mikoyan as a sounding board to gauge the political mood in Moscow. Yakov Zarobyan's son, Nikita, recalled that his father discussed "pressing issues for Armenia" with Mikoyan, noting that "the solutions were connected with their consideration by the Presidium of the Central Committee of the CPSU." He added that for his father, "it was important to probe the possible reaction, through Mikoyan, of members of the Presidium to this or that initiative proposed by Armenia."[76] Zarobyan benefited from Mikoyan's insights as a Kremlin insider. For example, as part of his corn campaign, Khrushchev explored the possibility of cultivating corn in Armenia.[77] Although corn was ultimately cultivated in the republic, it amounted to only 2.3 percent of the total area sown by 1960.[78] Despite his political alliance and friendship with Khrushchev, Mikoyan was known to be wary of this campaign and the excessive focus on one crop.[79]

On the eve of Khrushchev's 1961 visit to Armenia, he advised Zarobyan against taking the Soviet premier to the Ararat Valley, out of concern that such a visit might tempt Khrushchev to pursue the mass cultivation of corn there. After raising the issue with Zarobyan, Mikoyan smiled and paused for a moment before remarking, "Can you imagine what it would be like if we had to turn the Ararat Valley into a vast cornfield?"[80] Nevertheless, although Zarobyan greatly valued his consultations with Mikoyan, he also sought to control the information that the statesman received about Armenia.[81]

Some members of Mikoyan's network met with him at his summer home in Pitsunda, Abkhazia, adjacent to Khrushchev's dacha. Meetings here were convenient, given Abkhazia's proximity to Armenia. If Armenian officials happened to be on vacation near Mikoyan's home, they would visit him to discuss developments in the republic. For instance, on July 26, 1964, Kochinyan stopped off for a one-day visit with Mikoyan before heading further north to Sochi.[82] Similarly, while on vacation in Sochi in September 1963, Astsatryan traveled to Pitsunda and stayed with Mikoyan, engaging him in long discussions on Armenian affairs. "After lunch, we went out for a walk along the well-maintained paths of the spacious, peaceful park," recalled Astsatryan. "Anastas Ivanovich listened with interest to my stories about Armenian industry, construction, science, and technology, rejoicing at even the usual successes." Mikoyan likewise complained to Astsatryan that Armenian state radio broadcasts were "poorly heard by the Armenian inhabitants of the Black Sea coast and that it can be assumed that they are not heard at all in foreign countries." Concerned with highlighting Armenia as a model of Soviet achievement to the diaspora, Mikoyan stressed that "it was necessary for foreign Armenians to be fully aware of the successes of [Soviet] Armenia." Astsatryan assured him that Yerevan "would definitely take measures to strengthen the capacity of the [republic's] radio broadcasting stations." He noted that "this task was later accomplished through the efforts of communications specialists."[83]

In fact, when offering advice, Mikoyan frequently consulted with specialists and planners, in response to local needs, demands, and proposals. Moreover, as his son Sergo later recounted, his father put almost too much trust in the word of specialist-engineers who "assured him that there would be no negative consequences" and that "everything was calculated precisely."[84] Many of the statesman's recommendations were oriented toward stimulating economic opportunities, especially in some of Armenia's most popular resorts and spa towns. For instance, in discussions with Kochinyan and Astsatryan, Mikoyan advocated enhancing Dilijan's position as a major spa town within the Soviet Union and encouraged tourism in the city and surrounding region.[85] Similarly, during his 1954 visit, he counseled Armenian officials to build "holiday homes and resorts for factory workers" at both Arzni and Jermuk and recommended organizing a restaurant at Arzni.

Mikoyan made similar suggestions regarding the village of Hankavan, with the aim of enhancing its reputation as a popular Soviet spa town. In 1954, he advised his Armenian colleagues to rename the mineral water brand Marmarik, produced at Hankavan, to the name "Hankavan," and he suggested providing an inscription on the bottles indicating that the water was "recommended by the Ministry of Health of the USSR for medicinal purposes" once that information was confirmed. Mikoyan further proposed splitting Hankavan from the Arzni Mineral Water Plant to make it an "independent factory" geared toward the production of medicinal mineral water.[86] The statesman maintained his interest in Hankavan and returned to inspect it in subsequent years, most notably in 1966.[87]

Mikoyan took a particular interest in assisting his Armenian network in expanding economic opportunities in his native Lori. During his 1954 trip to Alaverdi, he advised Armenian officials to build a dairy plant and a slaughterhouse with a shop for sausage products in the town, and he recommended granting a "personal pension" to Nikolai Kostandyan, the chief accountant of the Alaverdi Brewery.[88] In nearby Uzunlar, Mikoyan suggested the construction of canning and packaging factories and similarly encouraged the building of a "drying and packaging plant for both fresh fruits and dried fruits" at the Shahumyan sovkhoz near Kirovakan. He further urged Armenian officials to appeal to the all-union Food Industry Ministry to restore an adjoining pig-farming sovkhoz that had been dissolved after the war and to "speed-up the design" of a distillery for nearby Spitak.[89] When advising on food-related matters such as these, Mikoyan regularly consulted with Armenia's food industry chief, Aram Piruzyan. "On various occasions, I had to meet with Mikoyan more than once," Piruzyan recalled.[90] During one such meeting, Mikoyan, who was well known for his *Book of Tasty and Healthy Food*, suggested that Piruzyan author a book of his own on Armenian cuisine.[91] The result was Piruzyan's *Armianskaia kulinariia* (*Armenian Cooking*), first published by Gostorgizdat in 1960.[92] According to Piruzyan, the book was so successful that, on his way to Cuba, Mikoyan requested ten copies to give to Fidel Castro and various Cuban scientists and specialists.[93] The Armenian edition of Piruzyan's work, *Haykakan khohanots'*, was published in 1963.[94]

It was not uncommon for Mikoyan to bring shortcomings in northern Armenia to the attention of Armenian leaders. For instance, when he arrived in Armenia at the Ayrum station on the border with Georgia to commence his March 1954 visit, he complained about the glum look of his native land to his Armenian associates. Kochinyan was sent by First Secretary Tovmasyan to greet him, accompanied by Second Secretary Hrachya Margaryan. As Kochinyan recounted,

> The first question that he [Mikoyan] asked us, was "When will the peaceful serenity of the Lori gorge be disturbed by some kind of excitement? It is so lonely and sad here, especially when you drive through it at night." Mikoyan

> turned our attention to the fact that not a single light was visible. It was known that the villages in this area were located on a plateau and their lights were not visible from the railway. It really was a gloomy picture. At that time, the organization of the Noyemberyan sovkhozes had not yet been completed and that plain was like a real desert—dry, almost uninhabited. In short, a rather unpleasant picture. . . . It was under these conditions that this magnificent natural valley in Mikoyan's native Lori left such a negative impression on him.[95]

To illuminate the area, Mikoyan advised Armenian officials "to expedite the completion of the construction of the Ayrum Hydroelectric Power Station for the Ayrum sovkhozes."[96] Yerevan moved quickly to resolve the issue, and within a few years, the look of the local landscape changed dramatically due to the completion of the Ayrum Power Station. "As soon as you reached our border," recalled Kochinyan, "the first lights visible from Ayrum, aside from those of the station, would be the distant lights of the village of Archis, which appear as if they are hanging from the sky, because that village and its neighbors are located on a high mountain plateau, at the edge of a deep gorge." Contrasting this old scene with subsequent developments, he wrote, "When arriving from Tbilisi, you can [now] see new sovkhozes, and, instead of the former deserts, new gardens, new urban-type settlements, and large waterworks structures of which any developed country can boast."[97] Similarly, Piruzyan recounted that the completion of the Ayrum Power Station "transformed this rundown part of the Noyemberyan raion into a flourishing land, of which Armenia is now proud."[98]

In addition to the republic's regions, Mikoyan paid much attention to the development of Yerevan. In his plans for the Armenian capital, the architect Aleksandr Tamanyan originally envisioned the inclusion of a monument to Lenin.[99] However, the idea remained dormant until the late 1930s when, according to Piruzyan, Mikoyan raised the issue and encouraged the Armenian authorities to actively pursue the matter.[100] Tamanyan's vision was finally realized with the installation of Sergei Merkurov's Lenin monument overlooking the city's Lenin Square on the twentieth anniversary of Armenia's Sovietization in 1940.[101] During the Thaw, Mikoyan became more proactive in his advisory role for Yerevan. For instance, while visiting Yerevan's Victory Park in 1954, he inspected the progress on Armenia's Great Patriotic War Museum and suggested adorning the walls of each room with marble quarried in the republic.[102] It was Mikoyan who also proposed the construction of Yerevan's Hrazdan Stadium. The statesman maintained a seasonal residence in the city, overlooking the Hrazdan Gorge.[103] During one of his trips to Yerevan in the 1950s, he suggested using the natural space of the gorge for building a large stadium with a capacity of twenty thousand and nicknamed it "Pishchevik" ("food man"), a reference to his involvement in the Soviet food industry. The stadium was eventually realized in 1970, during Kochinyan's tenure as Armenia's first secretary. The project was supervised by architects Koryun Hakobyan and Gurgen Musheghyan and designer Eduard Tosunyan, working closely under Karen Demirchyan, then first secretary of the Yerevan City Soviet.[104] On December 1, 1970, Mikoyan visited the stadium, just as construction was completed, as part of his trip marking the fiftieth anniversary of Soviet Armenia.[105] He was reportedly very pleased with the finished project and met with its architects and builders in the Hrazdan Gorge. At the meeting, Musheghyan told Mikoyan, "I am aware that the construction of this stadium was your idea. I think that you should be glad that it has now become a reality today."[106]

Mikoyan's role as advisor for Yerevan extended to the city's artistic life, as reflected in his support for cultural figures like the composer Aram Khachaturian. The two men had forged a friendship dating back to the Arutinov years, when the Armenian government held a reception in Mikoyan's honor in the Armenian capital. Khachaturian, who happened to be in Yerevan at the time, learned of the reception, but had not been invited to attend. "Then, at 2:00 a.m., he was woken up and brought to the reception," recalled Mikoyan. "He was in such a hurry that he forgot to take his wife, who was also with him in Yerevan. He recalled that I was surprised that such a great composer, a respected man, was not invited to the reception. For me, there were no convincing arguments to justify such an omission." Khachaturian explained to Mikoyan "that many Yerevantsis considered him to be a Moscow composer, and not a Yerevan composer." For his part, Mikoyan criticized such an attitude as "incorrect," on the basis that Moscow was the Soviet capital and that "one who works in Moscow should not be denied the respect enjoyed by the same workers in Yerevan." He advised the composer to write an "Armenian ballet on a modern theme" for the Decade of Armenian Art in Moscow in 1939.[107] Khachaturian liked the idea and found it to be "very much in tune" with his own ideas. Given the limited time, he had to begin writing it immediately. Mikoyan recommended that he contact Armenian director Gevorg Hovhannisyan, who had already written a ballet libretto, *Happiness*. Composed during an extended stay in Armenia, Khachaturian's resulting ballet, *Happiness*, was well received at its Yerevan premiere in September 1939 and at its Moscow premiere at the Bolshoi Theatre in October that same year. The work would serve as the basis for the composer's ballet *Gayane*.[108]

Yerevan's security was a source of constant concern to Mikoyan, given the city's close proximity to the Soviet-Turkish border. The statesman expressed his disquiet as early as 1937, in a meeting with Armenian officials attended by the architect Mark Grigoryan, at a time when it appeared that Turkey might ally with Nazi Germany in a potential war against the USSR.[109] The context of the Cold War was different, but the threat remained much the same—instead of a potential ally of Nazi Germany, Turkey was now a member of NATO. At the time, as Astsatryan recounted, "more than a third of the [Armenian] republic's human and economic potential was concentrated in Yerevan," and Mikoyan "expressed great concern that it was very dangerous, especially from a military point of view."[110] To remedy the situation, the statesman advised that several small towns between Yerevan and Lake Sevan be built up, becoming "satellites" of the Armenian capital. His Armenian colleagues agreed and moved quickly to spread out the republic's development to communities such as Abovyan, Nor Hachn, Charenshavan, Arzni, Gagarin, Hrazdan, and the city of Sevan.[111] During a later visit, at Mikoyan's request, Zarobyan, Kochinyan, and Astsatryan took him to inspect three of these satellite towns—Abovyan, Charentsavan, and Hrazdan.[112] Of these, Charentsavan had earlier been known as Lusavan, but was renamed in honor of the poet Charents in September 1967, on the advice of Mikoyan.[113]

Mikoyan likewise collaborated with his Armenian network to enhance afforestation throughout the republic. His interest in this issue predated the Thaw and was guided by the specific Armenian context, in which local authorities worked to improve the arid climate conditions of Yerevan and the sunbaked districts of central Armenia through greater afforestation as early as the NEP era.[114] According to Kochinyan, Mikoyan had advocated the expansion of green space in Yerevan since the time of Arutinov's appointment as first secretary in September 1937, when a dust storm swept through the Armenian capital.[115] The Thaw created conditions for a fresh emphasis on environmental reform, which involved the adoption of nature protection legislation by the Armenian Supreme Soviet in 1958.[116] It was in this context that Mikoyan took an even more active role in afforestation initiatives, in tandem with his Armenian network. Thus, during his 1962 trip to Zangezur, he advised local Party officials to enhance green space in Agarak, with the aim of improving local air quality.[117] He offered similar advice during his 1954 trip, when he advocated tree planting not only in Yerevan but also in smaller locales like Arzni, Gyumush, Sanahin, and Shagali.[118] On the highway between Yerevan and Sevan, Mikoyan recommended "increasing the planting of ornamental trees and two to three rows of fruit trees."[119] In the vicinity of Kirovakan, he likewise advised the extensive planting of fruit trees in connection with the development of local fruit farming.[120] Nevertheless, Kochinyan recounted that it could sometimes be "difficult to convince Mikoyan where and in which districts walnut trees could be grown." Moreover, not every afforestation proposal was implemented successfully. In one case, Mikoyan confidently proposed planting walnut trees along the main road to Ijevan. Armenian officials agreed and planted walnut trees along the road, beginning from Uzuntala. However, although the project succeeded in enhancing the beauty of the area, the "envisioned plan was regrettably not fully realized," as Kochinyan recalled.[121]

Mikoyan not only expressed his input privately to Armenian leaders but also openly encouraged improvements and called out shortcomings in his public speeches in Armenia. "There is no need to hide it," Mikoyan told his audience during his March 1954 speech in Yerevan, "but public services in a number of cities and towns are working very poorly." These services included hotels, barber shops, laundries, baths, and more. Calling for improvements, he joked that some heads of these services "should have, as people say, arranged to take a good 'bath' a long time ago." He cited the poor state of baths in Ghapan, Alaverdi, and Artashat, which were in "such a state of disrepair that the population cannot even regularly use them." He also quoted from Hovhannes Tumanyan's "The Dog and the Cat," citing the crafty cat's inability to fulfill the dog's order for a hat as an example of poor customer service and "red tape."[122] Mikoyan echoed similar sentiments in his June 1970 speech in Yerevan. While enumerating the successes that Armenia had achieved over the previous fifty years, he stressed that more improvements had to be made. "The feeling of pride must not cause complacency," he warned. "It must not overshadow the shortcomings and mistakes or those difficulties that must be eliminated in order to enter the second half of the century with even better results. It is necessary to use criticism and self-criticism—Lenin's proven weapon of the Party—to identify and eliminate shortcomings, and to fight bureaucracy and red tape in violation of socialist legality."[123]

Although Mikoyan lauded Armenia's "significant progress in the field of agriculture" in his June 1970 speech, he also criticized local Party bodies, as well as kolkhozes and sovkhozes, for paying "insufficient attention" to the care of the land and stated that, as a result, "planned targets in this area were being unsatisfactorily fulfilled." He added that "if construction in the republic was well organized and capital construction plans were fulfilled, then the results would be even better," with more new houses, schools, and hospitals built in Armenia. Nevertheless, he noted that construction was "reportedly progressing according to plan" and expressed hope that "such momentum would be successfully maintained into the future as well." While praising Armenia's "socialist intelligentsia," Mikoyan bemoaned the fact that there were "large reserves of knowledge" in the republic's technical fields that, "for one reason or other, are not being used" and that needed to be "quickly put into practice." "In an age of technical revolution," he added, "this is absolutely inadmissible." He advised his audience that it was "necessary to not only accelerate the development of scientific knowledge, but also to quickly put it into practice."[124] However, while Mikoyan's public advocacy for such improvements served to augment his position as a patron for Armenia, his personal meetings with Armenian officials did far more to strengthen his bonds with them. Nowhere was this reality more evident than in his role as both an advisor and an advocate for Yerevan in the realization of the Arpa-Sevan Canal.

SAVING THE "ARMENIAN SEA"

Mikoyan's position as both an advocate and an advisor for his network came together in his efforts to help Armenian leaders realize the Arpa-Sevan Canal (also known as the Arpa-Sevan Tunnel), a large-scale project in which the statesman "played a decisive role," in the words of Ter-Ghazaryants.[125] In addition to Mikoyan's advice and influence, the effort would involve a direct meeting of Armenian officials with Khrushchev himself. The aim was to preserve Lake Sevan, the largest freshwater lake in the Caucasus and one of three major lakes of the geographic Armenian Plateau, alongside Lake Van in present-day Turkey and Lake Urmia in present-day Iran. Under Stalin, Sevan's waters were harnessed by the Soviet government for hydroelectric and irrigation projects, based on prerevolutionary proposals advanced by Armenian engineer Sukias Manaseryan in his 1910 pamphlet *The Evaporation of Billions and the Inertia of Russian Capital*.[126] As a result, the turquoise "Armenian Sea" began to experience a dramatic diminution, resulting in a significant ecological crisis. The drop in the lake's water level was so great that the Sevan Island became a peninsula.[127] "Where there was once deep-blue water, there is now only a band of dark, murky stone," lamented Soviet writer Vasilii Grossman in 1962. "The lake is disappearing from its stone basin. Armenia, awash with electric light, grieves for Lake Sevan, which is perishing."[128]

Discussions on potential solutions to the Sevan problem began in the years following Stalin's death in 1953.[129] On May 30, 1958, the all-union Council of Ministers adopted Resolution 585, "On the Energy Base of the National Economy of the Armenian SSR," which favored maintaining the water levels of Sevan at a "mark as close as possible to natural conditions." However, no subsequent measures adequately addressed this aim, and the Armenian leadership agreed that the best way to solve the issue would be to construct a canal to divert water from Armenia's Arpa River into the lake. On January 20, 1961, Zarobyan and Kochinyan submitted the issue for consideration to the CPSU Central Committee and the all-union Council of Ministers in a joint letter.[130] "It is practically possible and economically feasible to preserve Lake Sevan, which holds significance as the only large and unique water basin of the republic," they wrote. "Moreover, it will guarantee normal living conditions for the population of lakefront villages. Thus, such a plan fully follows from the tasks set forth by the Party and the government for the protection of nature, meeting the deep desires of the workers of Soviet Armenia."[131] To their appeal, Zarobyan and Kochinyan attached an accompanying draft resolution on the matter.[132] They also turned to Mikoyan for support and consultation.

Mikoyan had earlier supported the Sevan-Hrazdan Cascade project that led to the drop in Sevan's water levels, but his brother Artiom had changed his mind, underscoring the adverse impact on the lake.[133] Sharing the concerns of Armenian leaders, Mikoyan consequently provided them with crucial advice and assistance. "First of all, he prepared Khrushchev," recalled Ter-Ghazaryants. "Then he examined our proposals and gave us recommendations on ways to make them pass." The aim of Yerevan was to ensure that the "necessary funds would be allocated from the Soviet state budget to the construction of the Arpa-Sevan Canal."[134] As Ter-Ghazaryants noted, the cost was not cheap:

> A lot of funds were needed for constructing a tunnel of this length. Anastas Ivanovich advised us to exclude from our application the costs of the associated work, such as the construction of roads, substations, cable laying, and more. Some of us objected: after all, without this infrastructure, carrying out construction is impossible! "In fact," answered Mikoyan, "these matters will be decided by themselves once a resolution on the construction of the Arpa-Sevan Canal is accepted. After all, you cannot build a tunnel without a road. And then, all the other expenses will have to be approved. Otherwise, the resolution will be impossible to implement. In addition, let the republic take up a portion of the costs, say, 30 percent. This will help achieve the main goal—the adoption of a resolution by the Council of Ministers and the allocation of funds from the union budget. Then it will be possible to solve all other issues."[135]

Mikoyan's advice would prove to be prescient when Armenian officials met with Khrushchev during his state visit to Armenia. Khrushchev arrived in Yerevan on May 5, 1961, to mark the fortieth anniversary of the republic's Sovietization.[136] The commemorative trip was originally scheduled for November 1960 but was delayed at the request of the Soviet leader.[137] Although Khrushchev expressed an interest in having Mikoyan accompany him on the trip, his friend politely declined. "It will also be better for Khrushchev," he said.[138] Nevertheless, the crafty premier managed to sneak in a few references to Mikoyan during his speeches in Armenia, with a mix of playful jest and admiration.[139]

Sevan was to be one of the main items on Khrushchev's itinerary. In Moscow, Gosplan deputy chairman Viktor Khlebnikov and Gosekonomsovet deputy chairman Sergei Tikhomirov had already provided the Council of Ministers with cautious assessments of the Arpa-Sevan proposal based on the Zarobyan-Kochinyan letter from January.[140] Their caution was endorsed by Kosygin.[141] For his part, Zarobyan hoped to use Khrushchev's Armenia visit to better acquaint the Soviet premier with the Sevan problem. On the morning of Soviet Victory Day (May 9), Khrushchev departed from Yerevan to Sevan in an open car with the Armenian leadership.[142] Marshal Baghramyan, a close friend of Mikoyan, joined them.[143] As Mikoyan had warned, budgetary concerns were foremost on Khrushchev's mind, as evidenced by the Soviet leader's negative assessment of a stylized sculpture of a seagull on the road to the lake. "It harmonizes in a very unique and beautiful way with the mountain landscape," Zarobyan stressed. Yet, despite the Armenian leader's enthusiastic endorsement of the modernist marvel, the cantankerous Khrushchev was unimpressed. "And how much did that structure cost?" he asked. "160,000 rubles," responded Zarobyan. "It would have been better to spend that money on something practical, something that people can use," Khrushchev grumbled.[144]

On the way to Sevan, Zarobyan described the magnificence of the lake and, according to Astsatryan, teased out future discussions of its fate by asking Khrushchev what would happen if Ukraine's Dnieper River or Russia's Volga were to dry up. "Yasha, what strange questions you are asking!" the surprised premier responded.[145] Khrushchev was eager to see the blue Sevan, and when the lake finally came into full view, he was not disappointed. "When Khrushchev saw the beauty of the lake," noted Zarobyan's son, Nikita, "he could not cease admiring it."[146] Khrushchev and his hosts first inspected the underground power station of the Sevan Hydroelectric Power Plant of the Sevan-Hrazdan Cascade. Afterward, the jovial premier "lingered in the yard" a bit and chatted with a few workers before he and his entourage departed for the lakeshore, where the boat *Mikoyan* was waiting for them.[147] The Armenian leadership hoped to provide a reception for Khrushchev at Sevan. However, because there were no restaurants or cafés along the shore, they decided to organize a dinner on Mikoyan's boat instead. When Zarobyan informed Khrushchev that they would be dining on the boat, the Soviet premier became very angry. "Why are there are no rest homes, restaurants, and sanatoriums on the shores of such a beautiful lake?" Khrushchev asked incredulously. He called over Kochinyan. "I approached him and said, 'I hear you, Comrade Khrushchev,'" recounted Kochinyan. "It is enough if I say that I almost heard Khrushchev curse when asking why no proper sanatoriums had been built around Sevan. 'No, I will not break bread on the ship *Mikoyan*,' he said. However, I must say that we managed to persuade Khrushchev, and we hosted him on the aforementioned ship. One could say that it was an unforgettable day."[148]

The meeting on the boat lasted for over two hours, and the party dined on barbecued Sevan *ishkhan* (prince) trout, as local boaters greeted them from Sevan's waters.[149] According to Zarobyan, Armenian cognac was supposed to be served as well, but Khrushchev declined the cognac, even though he sampled Armenian wine upon arrival in Yerevan and did not resist the temptation to give at least two toasts of his own in Armenia.[150] In addition to the *ishkhan* feast, Yerevan's case was aided by the lake's natural beauty. As Zarobyan recounted,

> Of course, Khrushchev knew the history of the lake. One should not think that he was so naïve as to simply agree to take a boat ride just to admire Sevan. When we arrived in the center of the lake, he looked at the water endlessly, admired its purity, and was surprised that it was so fresh. He repeatedly remarked

> about how wonderful, clean, and fresh the water was. I lost no time in knowing what I needed to do to enhance the effect. Once, this method had been tried on me too. . . . I pulled out a ten-kopek coin and dropped it into the water. It slowly sank down to the bottom of the lake. We were in the deepest part of Sevan, and we could see the coin sinking clearly. With delight, the Great Secretary exclaimed like a child: "See how clean the water of this mountain lake is! I can see it! I can see the coin!"[151]

Zarobyan seized the moment and spoke to the ebullient Khrushchev respectfully but directly. "The lake is dying," he said, "and, if urgent measures are not taken to save it, then it will dry up by 80 percent and turn into a swamp after only a few years."[152] The Armenian leadership further pointed out a cliff where they noted the previous water level of Sevan.[153] Khrushchev became indignant: "Is it not so that a capitalist would drain such a beautiful, freshwater lake?" Zarobyan responded, "Certainly no communist would tolerate the loss of this lake, but what can we do if the authorities do not allow us to save and preserve it?"[154] Zarobyan outlined the details of the Arpa-Sevan project and emphasized the "extreme importance of building an underground canal for the transfer of water from the Arpa River to Sevan."[155]

Nevertheless, as Mikoyan foresaw, Khrushchev was concerned about the expense of this undertaking, which Tikhomirov estimated to be 480 million rubles (in old price values), with a tunnel spanning "more than fifty kilometers in length."[156] As Ter-Ghazaryants recounted,

> We told him that there was only one way to save the lake: to build the Arpa-Sevan Canal. However, the republic cannot accomplish this task on its own. We need money from the union budget. At first, Khrushchev was horrified by the figures for the tunnel construction costs. Then, when we said, on Mikoyan's advice, that we would incur only a third of the expenses, he calmed down a bit. "Well, then, that's another thing, then we can think about helping you," said Nikita Sergeevich. We explained that if you do not build a canal, then there will be a swamp instead of a lake. And then there will be no water for the irrigation of the valley that harvests grapes, fruits, and vegetables. This convinced him—Anastas Ivanovich warned him about this situation, and here he saw everything with his own eyes. That's how Sevan was saved.[157]

The Soviet premier pledged that Moscow would support the project. Mikoyan later recounted to Zarobyan that, back in Moscow, Khrushchev remarked that he "never imagined that such a heroic and totally loyal people lived in this mountainous, semi-arid country."[158] In March 1962, Mikoyan echoed these comments publicly in Yerevan, noting that Khrushchev was "pleasantly impressed by his meetings" in Armenia and that he "colorfully spoke about the affairs of the republic and the population" and "admired the hard work of the Armenian people."[159]

On August 12, 1961, the all-union Council of Ministers adopted Resolution 726, approving the Arpa-Sevan Canal.[160] On August 29, the Armenian government moved to begin the implementation of the project.[161] The following month, delegates at the Twenty-Second Armenian Party Congress praised Khrushchev "with great satisfaction and gratitude" for the assistance that he "personally provided" in "solving the Sevan problem," among other matters.[162] Zarobyan himself underscored Khrushchev's personal role in his address before the congress. "It is with a feeling of joy," he said, "that we can report to the Party Congress that the issue of transferring the waters of the Arpa River to Lake Sevan has now been finally resolved, thanks to the attention and invaluable help of our dear Nikita Sergeevich Khrushchev." He stressed that Khrushchev, "having visited Lake Sevan," became "personally convinced of the importance and necessity of solving this problem." He went on to "warmly thank our Party Central Committee, our dear Soviet government, and personally Comrade Khrushchev for showing Leninist concern toward the further rapid development of the economy of the republic."[163]

During his 1962 visit to Armenia, Mikoyan likewise lauded Khrushchev for his response to the Sevan issue at the beginning of his March 14 speech at the Yerevan Opera Theatre. Significantly, the drafts of Mikoyan's speech show that he was most concerned with revising and properly preparing the section related to the Sevan question.[164] To make his point directly to his audience, Mikoyan chose to deliver this part of his address in Armenian.[165] "As a result of Comrade Khrushchev's trip to Armenia," he said, "a number of issues raised by your leadership and your scientists concerning economic activity have been resolved. Among them was the issue of measures to maintain the waters of Lake Sevan at a level close to the natural one, a matter of public concern in Armenia." He added, "I bring you greetings from the Central Committee of our Party, from the government of the Soviet Union. It is with great pleasure that I fulfill the instructions of Nikita Sergeevich to convey his heartfelt greetings to all Armenian friends and to all workers of Armenia."[166] Switching to Russian, Mikoyan proceeded to praise "new global-historical victories" and strides that the USSR had made under Khrushchev, including de-Stalinization and the defeat of the "Anti-Party Group." These statements served to bolster the renewed anti-Stalinist campaign, in view of the recent Twenty-Second Party Congress. "Having decisively overcome the harmful consequences of the cult of personality and having routed the Anti-Party Group, the Party carried out a number of revolutionary measures in many spheres of the country's social life, in its economy, science, and culture," Mikoyan said. "Nikita Sergeevich Khrushchev played an outstanding role in these developments."[167]

In subsequent years, Mikoyan regularly encouraged the Armenian leadership to enhance development around Sevan. After Khrushchev's visit to the lake, Kochinyan related to Mikoyan the general secretary's frustrations with the lack of eateries and resorts around its shores. "After listening to this story," Kochinyan recalled, "Mikoyan told me that he was aware of the incident, that Khrushchev had already spoken with him about it, and that he agreed with him. At Mikoyan's suggestion, we divided the lake among various departments and ministries, which quickly commenced construction. In fact, the trade unions and 'Intourist' began construction immediately." Within a few years, the appearance of the Sevan area changed dramatically, with the presence of new "restaurants, vacation homes, and children's sanatoriums." Mikoyan further advised Armenian leaders that Sevan "should be developed to serve more sanatoriums," and that "because there are no prospects for the development of agriculture, it will be necessary to build some industrial enterprises, especially electro-technical or radio-electronic industries. In short, only those that do not produce waste."[168] As with the Alaverdi Copper Smelter, Mikoyan was concerned with the ecological impact of potential overdevelopment of the lake's vicinity, including waste generated from the tourist industry.

During a later trip to Armenia, Mikoyan visited Sevan accompanied by Kochinyan and Astsatryan. At the lake, Kochinyan highlighted the new developments along its shore as well as afforestation efforts in its vicinity. While Mikoyan was pleased with such work, Astsatryan recalled that the statesman was "particularly interested in the work being done to maintain the [water] level of the lake."[169] Mikoyan maintained this interest in the status of Sevan in subsequent years, as reflected in his visits to Armenia in 1966 and 1970, when he personally inspected the building of the Arpa-Sevan Canal. During his 1966 visit, he examined construction work both in Jermuk and in Martuni (i.e., from both the Arpa River and Lake Sevan sides respectively). Accompanied by Kochinyan, Badal Muradyan, and Ter-Ghazaryants, Mikoyan also visited the cities of Sevan and Kamo, took a boat trip on the lake, and visited the Sevan Island (already a peninsula). He would travel to Sevan once more during his trip commemorating the fiftieth anniversary of Armenia's Sovietization on December 1, 1970.[170]

PAGEANTRIES OF NATIONALISM

When Mikoyan arrived by plane in Yerevan at the start of his March 1962 trip to Armenia, he was greeted by a large crowd shouting greetings of "Bari Galust!" and "Welcome, dear Anastas Ivanovich!" At the airfield, Mikoyan, per the traditional Soviet custom, was presented with bouquets of flowers by young Armenian pioneers, whom he then embraced.[171] From there, the statesman and his entourage, which consisted of his son Sergo and Zarobyan and Kochinyan, drove into the

Armenian capital in an open convertible as "thousands" of Yerevantsis "warmly welcomed Mikoyan along the entire route from the airfield to his [city] residence."[172] Massive public receptions such as these greeted Mikoyan everywhere he went in Armenia. Such enthusiastic displays of pomp and pageantry were the result of an interplay in which top-down official receptions arranged by the Soviet state were complemented by bottom-up expressions of national sentiment from the Armenian public. From the top down, the receptions for Mikoyan in Armenia were intended by Soviet authorities to project the power of the state. From the bottom up, the population complemented these official gatherings by turning out en masse, as "tens of thousands" did to wish Mikoyan well when he departed by plane from Yerevan at the end of his 1962 trip.[173] Armenian diasporan writer Antranig Dzarugian witnessed that Mikoyan's 1958 speech at the Yerevan Opera attracted a massive crowd of at least "half-a-million people." "When Mikoyan comes to Armenia," he wrote, "the waters of the Zankou River do not stop flowing but the whole country waits breathlessly." He added that the crowd of "countless thousands, constituting a sea of people . . . surrounded the Opera House extending to the streets further away."[174]

Certainly, to many Soviet Armenians, Mikoyan was the embodiment of Armenian national success within the Soviet system. He was personal proof positive that anyone, even an Armenian from mountainous Sanahin, could rise through the ranks and become, in Kochinyan's words, "the [de jure] president of the multinational Soviet Union" in 1964. "For the first time in our centuries-old history, an Armenian had risen to the Russian throne," Kochinyan wrote, referring to popular Armenian attitudes toward Mikoyan. "Indeed, he made every Armenian proud." He also stressed that it was "through his [Mikoyan's] surname that the Armenian people gained international recognition."[175] It was therefore not uncommon for visitors to see, as Vasilii Grossman did in 1962, "countless portraits" of Mikoyan throughout Yerevan.[176] Khrushchev himself even highlighted Mikoyan and his brother Artiom as examples of Armenian "success" in the USSR during his meeting with representatives of the Armenian diaspora in May 1961.[177] Indeed, the perception of the statesman as a "success story" greatly enhanced his popular national appeal. It held out the promise of mobility, inviting the prospect that the Armenian people could be elevated by the Soviet system as well.

In many ways, Mikoyan represented the embodiment of what Maike Lehmann dubbed "Apricot socialism," bringing together both the "Soviet" and the "national" into a single political figure. His civil-war-era revolutionary credentials and his association with Lenin and the "original promise" of the October Revolution only enhanced his stature in this regard. Consequently, the popular celebrations of Mikoyan functioned as celebrations not only of the Soviet government but also of Armenian nationalism and national achievement within the Soviet system. Moreover, the scale of the popular receptions that Mikoyan received during the Thaw had a lingering impact beyond the Thaw itself. These events enabled the Armenian public to see the potential of mass gatherings, which nationally minded activists would later use to express popular national demands through the lens of loyalty to the Soviet state. This development became apparent as early as 1965 with the demonstrations in Yerevan demanding recognition of the 1915 Genocide and continued with the rise of the Karabakh movement in 1988.[178]

Accounts of the large Mikoyan receptions reflect that some of the republic's remotest regions gave him the most impressive showings, most notably his native Lori in the north and mountainous Zangezur in the south. The receptions illustrate their complementary nature well—functioning as an interplay of the top-down and the bottom-up, the Soviet and the national. For the Soviet state, Mikoyan's presence in distant locales like far-flung Agarak allowed it to make its presence known to even the remotest corners of the USSR.[179] For the Armenian communities hosting these receptions, they were opportunities to celebrate a major Soviet Armenian figure and express a form of Armenian nationalism acceptable to Moscow. Mikoyan was particularly well received in his native Lori region, which he visited during his March 1962 trip, together with Sergo, Zarobyan, Kochinyan, and Astsatryan. In Kirovakan, thousands of Kirovakantsis poured out into the streets to catch a glimpse of the visiting statesman, while the receptions in Alaverdi and Sanahin were just as impressive, if not more intimate.[180] According to Astsatryan, the idea for the Alaverdi-Sanahin visit of 1962 was conceived by Mikoyan himself.[181]

At the Alaverdi train station, tens of thousands of locals gathered to greet their native son and his entourage.[182] As Astsatryan recounted, "Mikoyan's visit to Alaverdi turned into one big festival," and "because the area of the town was so limited, a natural rally was held right there at the train station and it was attended by virtually the entire population of the city."[183] As if to emphasize the festival-like atmosphere, some attendees released white doves into the sky, while still others brought balloons to the gathering.[184] Indeed, although Mikoyan was at the center of the event, its carnivalesque environment, in a very Bakhtinian sense, eroded the hierarchy between him and his fellow Loretsis.[185] In this context, Mikoyan was not so much the high official from Moscow as he was the local boy from Sanahin who made good. His appearance was met with enthusiastic applause from the Alaverdtsis, and, in accordance with Soviet custom, local children presented the high-profile visitor with large bouquets of flowers native to the area.[186] In his address before the gathering, Alaverdi's first secretary A. Stepanyan declared that "today, with boundless joy and enthusiasm, Alaverdtsis host their great compatriot—the outstanding figure of the Communist Party and Soviet state, the storied member of the Leninist guard, our dear Anastas Ivanovich

Mikoyan."[187] Stepanyan then presented the statesman with a gift box on behalf of the people of Alaverdi, with "samples of minerals mined in the area and products manufactured by the copper-chemical combine."[188] "How rich our motherland is!" Mikoyan remarked, as he accepted the gift.[189]

Standing with Zarobyan, Kochinyan, and Astsatryan at the Alaverdi station balcony, the statesman then proceeded to deliver a brief but emotional speech.[190] "Hello to you [*Barev Dzez*], my dear and beloved compatriots," Mikoyan said, addressing the crowd in Armenian. "I am exceptionally happy to be here with you today, in my beloved birthplace. I am amazed by the magnificent transformations that I am now witnessing, and I cannot believe that you have achieved such success within such a short period of time! And how much and how great will be our development prospects in the years ahead?" The local Party newspaper *Dzulogh* reported that the speech was "repeatedly interrupted by thunderous applause" from the animated Alaverdtsis.[191] According to Astsatryan, in this "warm address to his compatriots," Mikoyan likewise "recalled his grandmother and mother and related their kind and clever advice" and became "emotionally moved" as he "thanked all the organizers and participants of the meeting."[192] It was not the only time that Mikoyan became "emotionally moved" by such popular displays. Earlier, during the same trip, he was moved to tears by the storm of lengthy applause from his compatriots just before delivering his speech at the Yerevan Opera Theatre.[193] Kochinyan noted another outburst of sentiment when recounting Mikoyan's trip to Zangezur in the late 1960s. "They say that Mikoyan was a very strong man with nerves," wrote Kochinyan. "Indeed, that was so, but during this trip, he could not restrain himself, wiping his tears with a handkerchief as he shook hands from one person to another. It is impossible to write about such a reception. One had to see and imagine the warmth, joy, and happiness of the people. In Ghapan, many cried out [to Mikoyan] 'let me take your pain' [*ch'ard tanem*]. It was the same with the people in the mountains of this beautiful valley."[194]

The 1962 visit to Alaverdi functioned not only as a popular reception but also as a family reunion, with Mikoyan visiting extended family and relatives in Sanahin. In advance of the stateman's visit, the republic's sovnarkhoz had cleaned up the road to the village, while the Armenian Council of Ministers fixed up Mikoyan's ancestral home. Nevertheless, the sudden arrival of Mikoyan and his hosts via car from Alaverdi proper came as something of a surprise to the locals. "The villagers were happy to see such a large number of high-profile visitors come so unexpectedly to this insignificant village perched on forested, high mountain slopes," Astsatryan recounted.[195] Next to the recently completed memorial spring dedicated to local wartime heroes, Mikoyan, Zarobyan, and Kochinyan each planted one cypress tree in a ceremony attended by a large number of Sanahnetsis. This occasion was followed by another, more solemn ceremony at the Sanahin cemetery, not covered in the Soviet press, in which Mikoyan planted a cypress tree at his father's grave.[196] Following a meeting and conversation with locals at the village school, the guests then attended an extended family dinner.[197] "After the heartwarming reunions," Astsatryan recalled, "Mikoyan's sisters and other friends and relatives invited the guests to their home where they had the table prepared in the old, ancestral form, with traditional dishes."[198] This emphasis on the family connection in Sanahin served to reinforce Mikoyan's connection and commitment both to his native Lori and to Armenia.

The receptions that the locals gave Mikoyan in the southern provinces of Zangezur and Daralagyaz were equally impressive. When Mikoyan visited Ghapan in the late 1960s with then-first secretary Kochinyan and Council of Ministers chairman Badal Muradyan, "the city never seemed more excited," in Kochinyan's words. "Almost all residents of the Ghapan raion—big and small—were gathered at the airport," he recalled, noting that "several tens of thousands of people had come to greet their native son, Mikoyan." From Ghapan, Mikoyan's entourage planned to drive south to the mining town of Kajaran. However, the drive was slowed considerably due to the massive crowd that arrived to greet Mikoyan. "The drive from Ghapan to Kajaran is only a half-hour, but for us, it was two-and-a-half-hours," recalled Kochinyan. "The population of each village considered it their duty to stop the procession of cars, welcome us, kiss the great guest, express good wishes, and only then allow us to continue on our way." Both sides of the road connecting Ghapan to Kajaran were filled with crowds waiting to welcome Mikoyan. "Never before had the Ghapan canyon been so crowded with people," recalled Kochinyan. "It is impossible to describe the joy on display that day in Ghapan. Raikom Secretary Rafael Minasyan was not even given the chance to speak at the meeting. Everyone welcomed and expressed their heartfelt greetings to Mikoyan. The beautiful gorge of Ghapan was made even more beautiful by the slogans and colorful flags."[199] Massive crowd scenes akin to those described by Kochinyan were captured on film by Jergiz Zhamharyan during Mikoyan's trip to Zangezur in 1962, in Agarak, Ghapan, and Kajaran.[200] They were also proudly detailed in the local Party newspapers of Kajaran and Meghri.[201] As Astsatryan recalled of the 1962 trip, "the entire population enjoyed the visit of that high-ranking statesman to their highlands."[202]

Humor added much levity to these visits, "humanizing" the high officials from Moscow and Yerevan. During his late-1960s trip to Zangezur, Mikoyan had one such light interaction with a modest middle-aged woman in traditional Armenian garb in the village of Khndzoresk. Kochinyan recalled that Mikoyan "asked her how many children she had. The woman blushed deeply, and proudly answered 'three!' When Mikoyan said that it was too small, the surprised woman asked,

'How many children did your wife have?' He replied, 'Five boys.' She laughed heartily and said: 'Your wife is a *rashid* [hero]. There is no way that I can top her!'" Back in Goris, Mikoyan and his entourage were treated to lunch in the upper part of the city at the invitation of the jovial sovkhoz director, Suren Bakunts. "I never saw Mikoyan with so much joy and in such high spirits," wrote Kochinyan. "In particular, Bakunts's jokes in the Goris dialect [*Gorisi barbar*] did much to raise his mood." Known for his own quick wit, Mikoyan greatly enjoyed the local humor of the Gorisetsis, and he admired their local stone architecture, which he likened to that of Shushi in Nagorno-Karabakh.[203]

It was not uncommon for locals to greet Mikoyan and his hosts with generous Armenian-style feasts. Near Goris, in the village of Kornidzor, a kolkhoznik modestly treated Mikoyan, Kochinyan, Muradyan, and the other visitors to a small reception of fruits, bread, and cheese at his home. Arriving from Sisian, they encountered even more impressive receptions in Daralagyaz (Vayots Dzor), at Azizbekov, Yeghegnadzor, and Jermuk. "It seemed as though Vayots Dzor had not seen such joy for a long time," recalled Kochinyan. "Residents of distant villages came to the district center with their music, playing our traditional zurna." For the lavish outdoor reception at Azizbekov, the locals "without exception" placed tables on the streets and served "drinks, fruit, bread, meat, and other dishes" to their visiting guests. The structure of the reception at Yeghegnadzor—the "masterpiece of the trip," in the words of Kochinyan—was similar. Every villager had a table from which they invited guests to taste their wares. However, Kochinyan noted that the Yeghegnadzor reception "seemed more intimate, even if, for no other reason, the Yeghegnadzor raion was previously named after Mikoyan."[204]

Mikoyan's visits to Armenia not only functioned as celebrations of the Soviet government and Soviet Armenian achievement. Occasionally, they could also serve as celebrations of the Soviet *druzhba narodov* (friendship of peoples)—that is, the state policy aimed at promoting coexistence among the country's various nationalities. Mikoyan's visits to neighboring Azerbaijani communities were such cases. During his late-1960s trip to Zangezur, he and his Armenian associates briefly stopped at the village of Shurnukh, near Goris, where they were greeted by local Azerbaijanis with gifts of "bread and salt, a sheep slaughtered before his feet, more zurna and dhol music, dancing, and so on."[205] During his 1962 trip, Mikoyan and his hosts took the train from Agarak in Armenia to the Zangelan raion of Soviet Azerbaijan, just south of Nagorno-Karabakh. Arriving at Mindzhevan station, Mikoyan and his associates were greeted by a crowd of Azerbaijani onlookers and received a "warm welcome" from local leaders and Ali Kerimov, deputy chairman of Azerbaijan's Council of Ministers. Mikoyan used the occasion to emphasize peace and brotherhood between Armenians and Azerbaijanis and even delivered a Caucasian toast "in honor of the indestructible *druzhba narodov* of the Soviet Union."[206] Ironically, only a few decades later, the same district became one of the battle fronts in the Armenian-Azerbaijani conflict over Nagorno-Karabakh.[207]

DODGING RAINDROPS IN THE STORM

Soviet anecdotes often poked fun at Mikoyan's ability to seemingly "dodge between the raindrops" during thunderstorms.[208] However, while the statesman was able to assist Armenian leaders on various matters related to the republic's economic development, the ongoing tension surrounding the Nagorno-Karabakh Autonomous Oblast' (NKAO) proved to be less easily resolvable. Citing neglect and discrimination by Baku, the NKAO's majority-Armenian population increasingly called for the incorporation of their native land into Soviet Armenia, something that Azerbaijani authorities were unwilling to accept. The Karabakh quarrel proved to be a significant challenge for Moscow in the nationality sphere, despite Khrushchev's confident proclamation at the Twenty-Second Party Congress that the nationality problem had been "resolved."[209] Ultimately, even Mikoyan and his Armenian network were unable to find a resolution to this problem, in large part due to the limitations of the Soviet state structure itself.

Nestled on the eastern edge of the Armenian Plateau, predominately Christian Armenian Mountainous Karabakh (known as Artsakh among Armenians) was historically distinguished both ethnically and geographically from largely Shia Muslim Tatar (later Azerbaijani) Lowland Karabakh.[210] With the breakdown of Russian Imperial authority in the Caucasus in 1918, the mountainous highland soon became one of the most fiercely contested territories between Armenians and Azerbaijanis. Given his experience as a revolutionary in the region at the time, Mikoyan was all too painfully aware of the ethnic violence occurring between the warring parties. In his memoirs, he wrote about the March 1920 pogrom against Armenians in the city of Shushi by the forces of Musavatist Azerbaijan.[211] Similarly, he referred to the "organized" ethnic cleansing of Muslims in Dashnak-held Armenian territories in his report to Lenin from Baku on the situation in Caucasia from May 22, 1919.[212] As a result of the British intervention in the Caucasus, Mountainous Karabakh came under the rule of Musavatist Azerbaijan.[213] However, this decision was strongly rejected by the region's majority-Armenian population.[214]

In his May 1919 report to Lenin, Mikoyan emphasized the refusal of the Karabakh Armenians to acknowledge the authority of Baku.[215] "The independence [of Musavatist Azerbaijan] is only an illusion, and its authority is unrecognized by several uezds (Karabakh, Mughan, and Lenkoran')," he wrote.[216] He further observed that "Karabakh and Zangezur with a territory of more than three uezds, relies on the armed Armenian peasantry and does not recognize the Azerbaijani government" and that "in some places, the Muslim peasantry also sympathized with, and even supported," the Armenian rebels.[217] At the same time, Mikoyan critiqued the local Armenian Dashnaks (whom he called "agents of the Armenian government") for seeking to "annex" Mountainous Karabakh to the First Republic of Armenia. Noting the population's economic ties to Baku, he claimed that the Fifth Congress of Karabakh Armenians supported the idea of joining a future "Soviet Azerbaijan."[218] However, it is unclear where, or from whom, Mikoyan received such erroneous information, as the Fifth Congress of Karabakh Armenians unequivocally concluded that it considered "unacceptable *any* [emphasis added] administrative program with even the slightest connection to Azerbaijan."[219] Furthermore, as Mikoyan himself personally reported to Lenin in Moscow on November 2 of that year, opposition to Baku continued to "develop most strongly in the Kazakh uezd and in Karabakh."[220]

Nevertheless, despite sustained opposition from the majority-Armenian population, Mountainous Karabakh remained under the formal jurisdiction of Musavatist Azerbaijan by the time that the Bolsheviks arrived in the region. Originally, the Bolsheviks planned to transfer the territory to the administration of Soviet Armenia as an incentive to undermine the Dashnak-led rebellion in neighboring Zangezur. On July 4, 1921, the Kavburo voted to transfer the province to Armenia, an initiative supported by Sergo Ordzhonikidze, Sergei Kirov, and Aleksandr Myasnikyan. However, it reversed its decision the next day, ultimately opting to leave the territory under Azerbaijani control while giving the indigenous Karabakh Armenians the concession of local autonomy. Historians attribute the reversal to political pressure from Azerbaijani Bolshevik leader Nariman Narimanov, combined with the new circumstances arising from the defeat of the Zangezur rebellion.[221] Mikoyan, who was by this time in Nizhnii Novgorod, played no role in this decision.[222] However, Olga Shatunovskaia asserted that Stalin, who was then the commissar of nationalities, provided Narimanov with crucial support in his efforts to influence the Kavburo's decision on the fate of the mountainous province.[223] Just over six months later, in his address before the First Congress of the Armenian Communist Party on January 28, 1922, Myasnikyan revealed that Baku had threatened to halt kerosene supplies to Armenia if Yerevan did not relinquish its claims to Mountainous Karabakh.[224]

The autonomy of the region was formalized as the Nagorno-Karabakh Autonomous Oblast' (NKAO) on July 7, 1923, with its capital at Khankendy, renamed Stepanakert that same year after Stepan Shahumyan.[225] The oblast' became one of only four autonomous entities within the Soviet Union without a titular nationality, the other three being Azerbaijan's Nakhichevan' ASSR, the Russian SFSR's Dagestan ASSR, and Tajikistan's Gorno-Badakhshan AO.[226] The potential tensions in the compromise resolution on Mountainous Karabakh were amplified by political shifts within the Azerbaijan SSR. There were two major factions in the republic's Party leadership—one that viewed Azerbaijan as a nation-state for the Azerbaijani Turks and another, descended from the internationalist revolutionaries of the Baku Commune, that viewed Azerbaijan as a multiethnic republic. The latter faction enjoyed significant influence during NEP but lost much of it during the Stalin era under the republic's first secretary Mir Jafar Bagirov, a close ally of Beria. As the Azerbaijani Party leadership increasingly identified with the titular Turkic Azeri nationality, the pressures to assimilate other national groups in the republic, including the Karabakh Armenians, increased.[227] Mikoyan was apprised of such trends through Armenian officials with roots in Mountainous Karabakh, such as Yeghishe Astsatryan.

During his September 1963 stay in Pitsunda, Mikoyan asked Astsatryan about the quality of life in the NKAO and if he had visited his native province recently. Astsatryan responded that he visited often, and he detailed efforts by Yerevan to assist Karabakh Armenian students who sought to study in Armenia, as well as recent infrastructure improvements in the oblast' led by his native village of Chartar and the head of its kolkhoz, Suren Adamyan. "It is very good," remarked Mikoyan, "the Karabakhtsis are very capable people."[228] However, Astsatryan could not hide the truth. "Yes, it is excellent, but it is a rare reality," he told Mikoyan. "The economy of Karabakh is at its lowest point since the 1930s. There are no roads, and no funds for irrigation, electrification, and mechanization of agricultural work. Despite the over-fulfillment of the Five-Year Plans in the rest of the country, the economic development of Karabakh lags significantly behind that of Azerbaijan. The same is true of education and culture. The youth are being forced to leave the region and move away." When Mikoyan asked about the possibility of the local leadership developing the province's economy, Astsatryan noted that they would need to devise a comprehensive plan for the region. "They need to allocate funds for such a project and to consistently demand its implementation, and the Azerbaijani leadership will not do this because they do not want to do so," he said. "They strive to force the [Armenian] population to leave [Mountainous] Karabakh, just as they did in Nakhichevan'."[229]

Mikoyan took these charges very seriously. In his view, the actions of the Azerbaijani Party leadership were expressions of chauvinism and blatant violations of the Soviet nationality policy as well as the spirit of the *druzhba narodov* that he championed. The situation highlighted the inconsistency between the professed representative and egalitarian ideals of the Soviet state and the lived reality of the Karabakh Armenians. More ominously, Baku's actions seemingly created the explosive potential for a nationalist conflict in the Caucasus. It was in this context that Mikoyan once angrily reprimanded an Azerbaijani Party official over Baku's treatment of the Karabakh Armenians at his dacha in the early 1960s. His son

Sergo recounted that although the official, known by the name Shirali, "seemed to be an energetic and intelligent man without a nationalist leaning," his concern for the Karabakh Armenians appeared less than genuine. Shirali maintained that while "older officials in the government in Baku did not understand the political significance of the matter," he allegedly attached "tremendous importance" to it. Referring to allegations of neglect and national discrimination in the administration of Mountainous Karabakh, the official conceded that "the authorities in Baku may have made mistakes," but he "guaranteed that all shortcomings would be eliminated."[230]

Such remarks incensed the normally calm Anastas Ivanovich, who angrily said "that the authorities in Baku themselves are to blame for everything." He added "that they failed to create jobs and higher and technical educational institutions and that, in general, they appeared to be doing everything in their power to push the Armenians out of Karabakh, just as they had pushed them out of the Nakhichevan' Autonomous Republic." He further stressed that "it is very bad, if you have such a goal in Baku. In that case, [the demands of] the Karabakh Armenians can be easily understood." Shirali attempted to assuage Mikoyan and assure him that Baku had no such goal and that the "obkom secretary of the NKAO was an indecisive man who, like all the other local secretaries, was unable to solve all the issues." As Sergo recalled, "the mendacity of such explanations was evident. I distinctly remember my father being angry and dissatisfied." Shirali then invited Sergo to fly with him to Baku that same day. "It was early autumn, the 'velvet season' in Azerbaijan," Sergo recounted. "After all, your father is very revered by us. You will be my personal guest," Shirali offered. As Sergo remembered, "without giving me time to think, my father answered for me, saying that I don't have the time, and that, in general, I have other plans. The obvious sycophancy [of Shirali] clearly did not work. The envoy [from Baku] was not a stupid man and in fact, was smart, educated, knew what to say, and knew how to dodge the answers to difficult questions. He was full of empty promises about how well and freely the Armenians would live in Karabakh."[231]

Given the poor treatment of the Karabakh Armenians by Baku, the idea of transferring the NKAO to Soviet Armenia began to be periodically raised by both Karabakh Armenian representatives and the Armenian leadership. As early as November 1945, Armenian First Secretary Arutinov had personally addressed an appeal to Stalin, advocating the transfer of the NKAO to Armenian jurisdiction and the restoration of the city of Shushi.[232] However, his appeal was vetoed by Azerbaijan's Bagirov, who in turn asserted Azerbaijani counterclaims on Armenian territory.[233] This pattern repeated itself throughout the Soviet era. Initiatives to alter the status of the NKAO from Stepanakert or Yerevan were consistently opposed by Baku, which exercised its veto enshrined in Article 18 of the

Soviet constitution, mandating that "the territory of the union republics cannot be changed without their consent."[234] Even though Khrushchev's 1954 transfer of the Crimea to Soviet Ukraine served as a powerful reminder that internal border adjustments were possible, the Crimean case was ultimately based on the mutual agreement of Moscow and Kiev. By contrast, any initiative to transfer the NKAO to Armenia was always met by vigorous opposition from Baku, on the basis of the province's cultural and economic importance for Azerbaijan. Yet, Karabakh Armenian grievances continued to remain inadequately addressed by Azerbaijani authorities, leaving the issue perpetually unresolved.

The liberalized atmosphere of the Thaw presented new opportunities for raising the Karabakh question. After Khrushchev's denunciation of Stalin in 1956, at least one lecturer at Yerevan State University and one member of the Armenian Writers' Union proposed transferring the NKAO to Armenian jurisdiction.[235] In a letter to Nikolai Bulganin on May 12 of that same year, Armenian Catholicos Vazgen I likewise raised the issue of Mountainous Karabakh, following a three-month pastoral trip to Armenian communities in the diaspora.[236] During Khrushchev's visit to Armenia in May 1961, diasporan representatives similarly inquired about both the NKAO and the Nakhichevan' ASSR in their meeting with the Soviet premier.[237] As Astsatryan noted years later, Zarobyan had organized the meeting with the expressed intention of raising the Armenian territorial question with Khrushchev.[238] At least one speaker, the French Armenian cartographer Zadig Khanzadian, also asked about the fate of the historical Western Armenian lands in Turkey. On the latter, Khrushchev stressed that it would be impossible for the USSR to assert any claim to Turkish territory without provoking a larger war with NATO.[239] Nevertheless, he confidently predicted that the peaceful reunification of the Armenian lands would inevitably take place, with the triumph of Soviet communism in the Cold War.[240] Khrushchev did not, however, address the fates of Mountainous Karabakh or Nakhichevan'.[241] Instead, he reportedly remarked that both regions, as part of Soviet Azerbaijan, "are Soviet territories" and that "we are a united country with a single indivisible border."[242] Astsatryan later related this episode to Mikoyan in their Pitsunda discussion.[243]

The following year, in 1962, representatives of the NKAO and adjoining majority-Armenian raions appealed directly to Khrushchev, enumerating their grievances with official Baku and requesting the transfer of their territories from the jurisdiction of Soviet Azerbaijan to that of either Soviet Armenia or the Russian SFSR.[244] The issue was raised again by participants in the 1965 demonstrations in Yerevan.[245] In 1966, continued Karabakh Armenian appeals received a boost from prominent intellectual, scientific, and cultural figures of Soviet Armenia, among them the celebrated painter Martiros Saryan, the sculptor Yervand Kochar, and the poets Hamo Sahyan and Paruyr Sevak. Addressing a petition to Moscow with

1,906 signatures, they requested the unification of the NKAO with the Armenian SSR and proposed that it coincide with the anniversary of Armenia's Sovietization.[246] On August 9, Moscow decided to instruct Baku and Yerevan to consider the request advanced in the appeal.[247] After "carefully studying all aspects" of the issue, Kochinyan, by then Armenia's first secretary, penned a joint letter with Badal Muradyan to the CPSU Central Committee on September 30, endorsing the proposed initiative on the NKAO and potential discussion on the status of the Nakhichevan' ASSR. Referring to numerous appeals addressed to the Armenian and all-union Central Committees, the authors underscored that popular support for unification between Soviet Armenia and the NKAO was "widespread," in both the Armenian Republic and the NKAO itself.[248] Kochinyan was even more proactive behind the scenes and secured the "warm support" of the recently retired Mikoyan for finding a "positive resolution to the issue."[249] The Armenian first secretary also sought a meeting with Azerbaijan's Vali Akhundov to discuss the matter personally. However, Baku again vetoed the initiative, reportedly with backstage support from Mikhail Suslov, the rising "grey cardinal" of the Politburo, known for his opposition to such dramatic changes.[250]

Despite his support for such initiatives, Mikoyan nevertheless fully understood that no resolution on the matter could be realized without Baku's consent. He expressed this sentiment when Astsatryan inquired about the possibility of having Moscow manage the NKAO's economy directly during their 1963 Pitsunda meeting. Implicitly referring to Baku's opposition in accordance with Article 18 of the Soviet constitution, Mikoyan told Astsatryan that "the Azerbaijani leadership does not want such a scenario, the Karabakh leadership cannot ask for it, and Armenia has no right to interfere in the sovereign affairs of another republic." "The question is fundamentally incorrect," Mikoyan stressed. "The Armenian-populated area of this Armenian territory must be connected with Armenia in order to plan and implement the economic, scientific-technical, cultural-educational development of the province within the framework of national planning." Astsatryan then asked Mikoyan about his decision to sign the decree to transfer the Crimea to Ukraine. Mikoyan smiled and replied, "I did not sign the decision on the Crimea. Khrushchev suggested that I sign it, but I explained to him that it was Russia's territory and that I had no right to sign such a decree."[251]

In the end, no resolution materialized on Mountainous Karabakh, and even Mikoyan was unable to influence the situation, regardless of his high position in the Kremlin. The statesman's personal inability to contribute to a resolution was partially due to his own political constraints. "As an Armenian, my father understood that he should be alert and understand the limits of his abilities," recalled Sergo. "And he always remembered this during different negotiations. That is why he could not appeal to Khrushchev to hand over Nagorno-Karabakh to Armenia, as many naïvely believe, especially those unfamiliar with the behaviors and habits of Kremlin leaders."[252] Ultimately, however, the limitation of the Soviet state structure was a much more significant factor. In an era of renewed emphasis on "socialist legality" (*sotsialisticheskaia zakonnost'*), the Karabakh imbroglio presented a considerable dilemma for Moscow.[253] Baku was well within its legal right to veto any proposed accession of the NKAO to Armenian jurisdiction. However, it did not have the right to deny the cultural or ethnic rights of the Karabakh Armenians or other indigenous nationalities, like the Talysh or Lezgins. The lack of a veto mechanism on the part of the NKAO highlighted a serious shortcoming of the Soviet nationality policy and state structure, something that Mikoyan and his reformers might have been able to fix had the constitutional reforms of the 1960s been realized. However, the tension remained unresolved. The frustrations of the Karabakh Armenians continued to simmer, eventually exploding during Mikhail Gorbachev's perestroika. Perhaps unsurprisingly, at that time, one of the earliest and most vocal advocates for unification between Nagorno-Karabakh and Armenia was Sergo Mikoyan.[254]

CONCLUSIONS

At the end of Mikoyan's 1962 trip to the Armenian Republic, *Kommunist* noted that the statesman's visits to various Armenian regions and cities would "forever remain in the memory of the working people of Armenia."[255] Similarly, the local Party newspaper of Kajaran stressed that the Kajarantsis would "never forget the day" of Mikoyan's visit to their town on March 13, 1962.[256] Nevertheless, as time passed, the memory of Mikoyan's visits and his patronage for Soviet Armenia faded from popular Armenian memory. While in office and even in retirement, Mikoyan himself spoke and wrote little of his Armenian activities. Others, however, were less reticent. In the late 1970s, at his suburban Moscow dacha, Mikoyan's close associate Marshal Baghramyan held a dinner in honor of his friend, attended by such guests as Marshal Hamazasp Babajanyan and Armenian First Secretary Karen Demirchyan. At the start of the meal, in the presence of Mikoyan and the other distinguished invitees, Baghramyan pointed out "that the Armenian people mistakenly believed that Mikoyan did little in his capacity for Armenia, but that the facts told a different story."[257] Diasporan observer Dzarugian echoed Baghramyan's sentiments when recounting Mikoyan's 1958 visit to Armenia:

> The man [Mikoyan] who came to the podium accompanied by thundering applause and who cracked a few witty jokes in Armenian is also Armenian. . . . This man who is one of the very highest-placed officials in the Soviet Union. What has he done for Armenia? I ponder. At first glance the answer is nothing.

> But once you dwell further and after having been in contact with the people of Armenia, you realize that they, in their unmistakable instincts, see in Mikoyan a compatriot who cares for them but does not articulate, protects but does not show. If the style is the essence of writing, so it is in politics.[258]

It was in this subtle and cautious way that Mikoyan sought to highlight Armenia as a model of Soviet *dostizhenie* for audiences foreign and domestic, underscoring the successes of the republic as successes of the Soviet nationality policy. Through his role as a both an advocate and advisor for Yerevan, he cultivated a patronage network of officials who shared a common interest in Armenia's economic and cultural development. However, despite Mikoyan's position as patron, not every issue was easily fixable. As evidenced by the challenge of Nagorno-Karabakh, even informal politics could not resolve fundamental contradictions within the Soviet state structure, a reality that underscored the necessity of political reform. Nevertheless, whether using his contacts with Khrushchev to lobby on Yerevan's behalf or offering advice on framing proposals to Gosplan, Mikoyan's work with his Armenian network serves as a vivid testament to the indispensability of informal politics in the Soviet Union, especially in the Caucasus. Even in retirement, Mikoyan continued to travel to Armenia, where he continued to offer advice and assistance. On one such visit, Ter-Ghazaryants recalled that Mikoyan "shared his thoughts on what else could be done and wondered why something hadn't been done." "In general," he recounted, "what began as a vacation turned into a business trip. Mikoyan just couldn't relax. He was accustomed to working, even on vacation. Moreover, once he found himself in Armenia, he simply couldn't be a 'tourist.' His soul ached for everything [in Armenia]. He was very happy about our successes—but they were . . . also to a great extent, thanks to him."[259]

Anastas Mikoyan delivering his speech in Yerevan for the Supreme Soviet elections, March 14, 1962. Courtesy of the National Archives of Armenia, Yerevan.

Mikoyan and Soviet Armenian leaders at the welcoming ceremony in Alaverdi, Lori, Armenia, March 15, 1962. *From left to right:* Anton Kochinyan, Anastas Mikoyan, Yakov Zarobyan, and Yeghishe Astsatryan. Courtesy of the National Archives of Armenia, Yerevan.

Zarobyan, Mikoyan, and Kochinyan greeted by admirers at the performance of Aram Khachaturian's *Spartacus* at the Spendiarov Opera Theatre, Yerevan, March 11, 1962. Courtesy of the National Archives of Armenia, Yerevan.

Mikoyan greeted by youth in Ghapan, Zangezur, Armenia, March 13, 1962. Courtesy of the National Archives of Armenia, Yerevan.

Mikoyan and Kochinyan greeted with traditional offerings of lavash and salt at the Karchevan Railway Station in Agarak, near Meghri, Zangezur, Armenia, March 13, 1962. Courtesy of the National Archives of Armenia, Yerevan.

Mikoyan, with Zarobyan and Kochinyan in Sanahin, Alaverdi, Lori, Armenia, March 15, 1962. GARF R-5446/120/1723/17.

Zarobyan and Mikoyan meet with Viktor Hambardzumyan at the Armenian Academy of Sciences, Yerevan, March 12, 1962. Courtesy of the National Archives of Armenia, Yerevan.

Left to right: Marietta Shahinyan, Artiom Mikoyan, Marshal Hovhannes (Ivan) Baghramyan, and Anastas Mikoyan, Moscow, mid-1960s. Courtesy of Vladimir Mikoyan.

Mikoyan at the Yerevan Institute of Physics with physicist Artiom Alikhanyan, May 23, 1966. Courtesy of the National Archives of Armenia, Yerevan.

During all his visits to Armenia, Mikoyan was greeted by capacity crowds, especially in the provincial centers of the republic. In this photograph from Kirovakan during Mikoyan's March 1962 visit, the crowd extends for miles to the outskirts of the city (the largest in the Lori region and the third largest in the Armenian Republic). Courtesy of the National Archives of Armenia, Yerevan.

The Mikoyan family on vacation in the Crimea, at Mukhalatka, north of Beregovoe, 1956. *Left to right, back row:* Alla Mikoyan (née Kuznetsova), Ashkhen Mikoyan (née Tumanyan), Stepan Mikoyan, Sergo Mikoyan, Eleonora Mikoyan (née Lozovskaia), and Anastas Mikoyan; *front row:* Svetlana and Vladimir Mikoyan (children of Alla and Sergo); Aleksandr, "Bolshoi" Vladimir, and Ashkhen Mikoyan (children of Eleonora and Stepan); and Olga (daughter of Vano Mikoyan). Courtesy of Vladimir Mikoyan.

Mikoyan and his son Sergo with Armenian officials in Yerevan, March 16, 1962. On Mikoyan's left is First Secretary Yakov Zarobyan, and on his right is Anton Kochinyan, then chairman of the Council of Ministers. Standing between Mikoyan and Zarobyan is Yeghishe Astsatryan, and standing between Mikoyan and Kochinyan is Badal Muradyan. GARF R-5446/120/1723/27.

Mikoyan and his son Sergo at the tree planting ceremony during his visit to Sanahin, March 15, 1962. GARF R-5446/120/1723/11.

Mikoyan receiving flowers from a young woman, with Zarobyan in Leninakan, Armenia, March 15, 1962. GARF R-5446/120/1723/21.

Nikita Khrushchev and the Soviet Armenian leadership departing Mikoyan's boat on Lake Sevan, May 9, 1961. Courtesy of the National Archives of Armenia, Yerevan.

Mikoyan meets with Abkhaz elders at the Lykhny kolkhoz in the Gudauta raion of Soviet Abkhazia during his vacation in Pitsunda of September–October 1960. GARF R-5446/120/1552/13.

Mikoyan dancing, Caucasian style, at the Lykhny kolkhoz in Abkhazia during his vacation in Pitsunda of September–October 1960. GARF R-5446/120/1552/14.

Anastas Mikoyan—an Armenian hero in Baku, Azerbaijan SSR, March 1964. GARF R-5446/120/1847/52.

Mikoyan at the home of the family of Mashadi Azizbekov during his March 1964 trip to Baku. GARF R-5446/120/1844/69.

Mikoyan in Baku, together with Azerbaijani First Secretary Vali Akhundov, laying a wreath at the 26 Baku Commissars memorial, March 27, 1964. The ribbon is inscribed, "To the Fierce Fighters for the Cause of Communism, the Twenty-six Baku Commissars, from Anastas Mikoyan." GARF R-5446/120/1847/40.

Mikoyan and Vali Akhundov meet with workers in Baku, March 27, 1964.
GARF R-5446/120/1847/21.

Mikoyan at the reception at the Chemists' Palace of Culture in Sumgait, Soviet Azerbaijan, March 28, 1964. GARF R-5446/120/1847/42.

Rehabilitated Old Bolsheviks meet with Mikoyan and Vali Akhundov in Baku, March 30, 1964. GARF R-5446/120/1847/53.

Eternity: The Final Path of Charents, by Regina Ghazaryan, 1996–98. Ghazaryan's painting honors Mikoyan's speech of March 11, 1954, in Yerevan, in which he called for the rehabilitation of the poet Yeghishe Charents. In her work, Ghazaryan contrasts the repressions of 1937 with 1954 as a "release," symbolizing the beginning of the Thaw in Soviet Armenia. Courtesy of the Yeghishe Charents House-Museum, Yerevan.

4 | *Druzhba* Defended

The environment of the Thaw created the conditions for increased national expression across the Soviet Union. In some cases, such sentiments manifested themselves in complex national disputes, as Mikoyan observed in the growing tension over Nagorno-Karabakh. These developments prompted different responses from the center. One response took a coercive line toward nationalism, as evidenced by the purge of Party leaderships in republics like Latvia and Azerbaijan. Another response, favored by Mikoyan, took a more inclusive approach. In pursuing the latter option, the Armenian statesman drew on historical narratives that underscored the benefits of Soviet socialism for national republics while also highlighting the possibilities for cooperation and coexistence among the different national communities of the USSR. The narratives that Mikoyan promoted among audiences in the Caucasus focused on the period of the 1918–20 civil war. His authority to speak to this history was enhanced by the fact that he was a personal eyewitness of and participant in the revolutionary events that swept up Caucasia in those fateful years. In this context, Mikoyan's focus on both national identities and national coexistence reflected his long-standing commitment to the preservation of the Russian multiethnic state, which dated back to his initial decision to join the Bolsheviks.

For Mikoyan, the preservation of the state meant geopolitical security for his native Armenia as well as the potential for peaceful relations among the nationalities of the Caucasus. For that reason, as sociologist Liliana Riga noted, the statesman "consistently supported Russian reoccupation, not Armenian independence."[1] However, while Mikoyan's writings attest to the great importance that he personally attached to the geopolitical integrity of the Soviet Union, they also indicate that his Marxist political convictions were no less important. Just as he believed in the necessity of preserving the multiethnic, *rossiiskii* state, so too did he believe in the revolutionary promise of Marxism and the Soviet socialist experiment. Nowhere were these views better expressed than in Mikoyan's discussions of Armenian history. The narratives on Armenia that he espoused underscored that national identities (i.e., a sense of belonging to a specific ethnic or national community) were not mutually exclusive to a larger all-union Soviet identity (i.e., a sense of identification with the Soviet state and socialist ideology). As Maike Lehmann stressed, these identities came together in the Soviet era to form a "very Soviet hybrid of national and socialist elements," a phenomenon that she calls "Apricot socialism."[2]

During the Thaw and even beyond, Mikoyan actively promoted this hybrid identity to Soviet Armenian audiences, aiming to bring them "into the revolution" and to "secure their active involvement in the great socialist experiment," in the words of historian Francine Hirsch.[3] He drew on the lived experiences of Armenians during the traumatic period of the 1915 Armenian Genocide and the First Armenian Republic of 1918–20. He specifically singled out the foreign policy orientation of the latter toward the West, as determined by the Armenian Revolutionary Federation (ARF-D, also known as the Dashnaktsutyun or the Dashnaks). Mikoyan contended that this policy did not produce the peace and security that the Armenian people needed, and he frequently contrasted it with the security and material benefits that were associated with the USSR. He also stressed the benefits of the mutual cultural enrichment derived from the interaction between the Russian and Armenian peoples and revolutionary movements. At the same time, Mikoyan did not seek to personally rewrite history himself, something for which he had criticized Stalin at the Twentieth Party Congress.[4] Nevertheless, inspired by the increased freedoms in Soviet historical sciences during the Thaw, Armenian historians frequently sought out his counsel as an eyewitness to the events of the civil war in the Caucasus.[5] Although Mikoyan consented to answering their questions, he consistently insisted that only they, as professional historians, could do the work of critical historical scholarship.

The historical narratives that Mikoyan invoked served to bolster the Soviet policy known as the *druzhba narodov* or "friendship of peoples" (*zhoghovurdneri barekamut'yun* in Mikoyan's native Armenian). This policy sought to promote harmonious coexistence and peaceful relations among the different national and ethnic groups of the USSR. Naturally, the lived reality of relations among these groups was much more complex than this concept suggested, encompassing an array of personal and individual relationships, such as genuine friendship, conflict, and intermarriage. Due to this same nuanced reality, it would be equally inaccurate to dismiss the *druzhba narodov* as entirely "Soviet myth." The concept was first introduced by Stalin in 1935 to emphasize a sense of identification among the USSR's various nationalities with the Soviet state.[6] It succeeded the earlier NEP-era concept of the *bratsvo narodov* ("brotherhood of peoples"), which, although stressing "proletarian unity," played only a "minor role in state efforts to promote Soviet unity." By the end of the 1930s, the *druzhba narodov* had evolved into an "officially state sanctioned metaphor of an imagined multinational community."[7]

In his use of the phrase during the Thaw, Mikoyan employed the *druzhba narodov* concept more in the way that Josip Broz Tito employed the concept of "brotherhood and unity" in Yugoslavia—that is, to emphasize the importance and necessity of peaceful relations among the state's various national groups as a means of promoting state unity.[8] For Mikoyan, the stress on such unity was especially important at a time of rising national sentiment throughout the USSR and in the Caucasus in particular. From his experience of the civil war in Transcaucasia, Mikoyan knew well the explosive potential of ethnic strife between the region's various national groups, especially Armenians and Azerbaijanis. He therefore regarded the issue of interethnic relations as a delicate question and, above all, a question of national security. Indeed, years later Mikoyan stressed that opponents of the Soviet government used "any, even the most trivial, facts that may be interpreted as national injustice" against the geopolitical integrity of the state.[9] It was not without reason that the statesman, while on a visit to the frontier village of Firiuza in Turkmenia in January 1957, wrote that the *druzhba narodov* "serves as the basis for the invincibility of the Soviet system."[10]

In the Yugoslav context, Belgrade could turn to the World War II–era sacrifices of the multiethnic Yugoslav Partisans as lived examples of "brotherhood and unity."[11] Similarly, when invoking the *druzhba narodov,* Mikoyan frequently turned to the example of the twenty-six Baku commissars. Stepan Shahumyan, Mashadi Azizbekov, Aliosha Japaridze, and Ivan Fioletov were not only Mikoyan's comrades in arms but also symbols of self-sacrificing revolutionaries who eschewed national differences in the service of common revolutionary aims. Mikoyan's efforts to uphold the memory of the Baku 26 further alluded to contemporary political struggles over de-Stalinization. In his meeting with rehabilitated Old Bolsheviks in Baku in March 1964, Mikoyan stressed the shared kinship between victims of Stalinism and the commissars, framing both as victims of "antirevolutionary" tyranny. Thus, alongside the Soviet victory in the Great Patriotic War, the story of the Baku 26 served as a powerful legitimizing narrative for the *druzhba narodov,* enhanced by Mikoyan's status as a personal participant in the Baku revolutionary movement. The statesman's use of such narratives not only underscored his commitment to the multiethnic Soviet state but also reflected the basic contours of the Thaw-era nationality policy that he played a key role in developing, stressing state unity while embracing cultural diversity.

NARRATIVES OF ARMENIA

During the Thaw and even after his retirement in 1965, Mikoyan actively promoted a hybrid "national" and "Soviet" identity among Soviet Armenians by emphasizing historical narratives that combined Armenian national concerns with socialist ideology and anti-imperialism. In promoting this hybrid identity, Mikoyan focused on the continuity between Soviet Armenia and the historical Armenian revolutionary movement. This link reflected the larger Soviet narrative emphasizing continuity between the Russian revolutionary movement and the Bolshevik Party. The narratives that Mikoyan invoked also underscored the failure of the Dashnaks to provide material benefits to the Armenian people in the short-lived Armenian Republic of 1918–20 and targeted their "naïve" dependence on their Western "imperialist" allies. Mikoyan's writings, both public and private, further reveal that he strongly believed that Russia was crucial to the survival of the Armenian people, especially in the aftermath of the 1915 Armenian Genocide. Therefore, the narratives of Armenian history that he espoused stressed the importance of relations with Russia as a guarantor of Armenian security, material well-being, and national survival, reflecting his broader commitment to the geopolitical unity of the USSR.

Mikoyan strongly emphasized such narratives in the separate overview on Armenian national issues that he prepared in early 1954 for his Yerevan address that year. In that text, he highlighted the significance of the "unification of Armenia with Russia" as "a turning point in the fate of the Armenian people." "During their long period under the yoke of the Turkish Sultan and the Iranian Shah," Mikoyan wrote, "the Armenian people were not only deprived of their independence and statehood and were not only subjected to barbaric feudal-serf exploitation and extortions, but also faced the threat of final physical annihilation." Referring to the Genocide of 1915, Mikoyan wrote that "the tragic fate of the Western Armenians, who remained under the yoke of Sultanist Turkey, unequivocally showed what awaited the Armenian people if Armenia did not unite with Russia."[12] Mikoyan framed Armenia's situation as a historical choice: "Either to be finally physically annihilated [by Turkey], or to join Russia, be drawn into a higher order of economic development than feudalism, to experience the beneficial influence of advanced Russian culture, to go forever together with the Russian people, to fight together with them against foreign invaders, against tsarism, and then against capitalism under the leadership of the Russian working class, and to secure Armenian statehood and social and national renewal on the path of socialist revolution. That is how history posed the question to the Armenian people."[13] Although Mikoyan never included this text in his final speech, it would have had a strong emotional resonance among Armenians if he had. The 1915 Genocide, committed by the Young Turk authorities of the Ottoman Empire, claimed the lives of 1.5 million Armenians and forever fundamentally shaped the way in which the Armenian people conceived their past and present.[14] As historian Razmik Panossian wrote, the Genocide is "the cornerstone of modern Armenian identity" and a "defining moment, which on the one hand acts as a fundamental break with the past and the historic homeland, while on the other serves as a prism through which national identity is seen, politics interpreted, and culture redefined."[15]

In the 1954 overview text, Mikoyan emphasized that "for the Armenian people, joining Russia was not a 'lesser evil'" but "the greatest progressive historical act, responding to the fundamental hopes and aspirations of the Armenian people and its working masses." He framed this act of unification within the broader trajectory of a dialectical Marxian view of history. In his view, the path for Eastern Armenia's unification with Russia was laid by "an entire course of prior developments in economic and cultural ties between Russia and Armenia." Mikoyan wrote that "ordinary Armenian people, like the Georgians and the Azerbaijanis, enthusiastically greeted the Russian army [when they entered the Caucasus] and provided it with all possible assistance." He added that the Eastern Armenian "possessing classes" and "above all the bourgeoisie" were also positively predisposed toward the Russian orientation because "unification with Russia opened up more favorable prospects for economic development and enrichment for them." At the same time, Mikoyan strongly criticized the "cruel colonialist policy of tsarism," in reference to the more oppressive policies pursued by Alexander III toward the Armenians of the Russian Empire. He was likewise critical of the Eastern Armenian "possessing classes" in their attempt to use Russian tsarism to "pursue narrow selfish class interests" and to "intensify the exploitation of the working Armenians."[16]

However, in the final analysis, Mikoyan emphasized that the unification of Eastern Armenia with Russia was overall beneficial for the Armenian people.[17] In his 1954 overview, Mikoyan even quoted from Khachatur Abovyan's novel *Verk' Hayastani* (*Wounds of Armenia*) to emphasize this point.[18] Abovyan's words, wrote Mikoyan, "reflect a deep historical truth. From those days [of the early nineteenth century] onward, the fate of the Armenian people was forever linked to the fate of the Russian people. The closeness to the Russian people, the beneficial influence of Russian culture on the culture of the Armenian people, the joint struggle with the Russian workers against tsarism, and the communication with progressive, revolutionary representatives of the Russian nation raised the material and spiritual culture of the Armenian people."[19] He added that "the Russian working class and the Bolshevik Party saved the Armenian people from imminent threat" and that "the victory of socialism turned Armenia into a flourishing republic on the doorstep of the East."[20]

In his memoirs, Mikoyan echoed these same sentiments, but he was even more explicit in his discussions of the events of 1915, expressly using the term "genocide" (*genotsid*) twice to describe them.[21] "For several centuries," he wrote, "Armenia had been subjected to multiple conquests by foreign invaders, who destroyed and plundered the wealth of material and spiritual culture accumulated by the Armenian people." Many were "forced to flee from their homes to foreign lands," while others were "forcibly taken to the countries occupying Armenia." Still others "died in an unequal battle with the invaders." Mikoyan added that "hundreds of thousands of Armenians were subjected to direct physical extermination more than once," culminating in the "unprecedented genocide by Turkey in April 1915."[22] He further stressed that "every decent Armenian understands that an inextricable link with Russia is a guarantee for the physical existence of the Armenian people and the preservation of their national statehood. And it is no accident that during the civil war, when Armenia was cut off from Soviet Russia, many Armenians fought selflessly in the ranks of the Red Army." On Soviet Armenia, Mikoyan wrote that "the Soviet Republic, having gone through the most difficult trials, survived. That was the main result of the path traveled. This path did not merely represent another respite, but a whole historical period of peaceful development [for the Armenian nation]."[23] In this context, Mikoyan again framed Armenia's union with Soviet Russia as an existential question on the fate of the Armenian people. In his view, it was the best possible outcome for their survival. At that moment, he argued, Armenia "decided on a question of life or death."[24]

Mikoyan also emphasized the connections between the nineteenth-century Armenian national movement and the radical Russian revolutionary movement of the same period.[25] In his 1954 overview, the statesman stressed that "after joining Russia, the Armenian people immediately experienced all the beneficial influences of the great Russian culture." This influence included exposure to "the revolutionary-democratic thought of Russia," which, he noted, "gave proper direction to Armenian social thought and contributed to its development." He further added that "under the beneficial influence of Russian culture and the ideas of Belinskii, Herzen, Chernyshevskii, and Dobroliubov, two great sons emerged from the masses of the Armenian people—the educator-democrat Khachatur Abovyan and the revolutionary democrat Mikael Nalbandyan." Mikoyan noted that "it was they who led the revolutionary democratic direction in the framework of the Armenian reality. During this period, the revolutionary democratic movement, headed by Nalbandyan, connected [Armenia's] liberation with the revolutionary democratic movement in Russia and struggled for the victory of the peasant revolution. It was most logical in that era to form, with the support of the Armenian masses, an alliance with Russia's revolutionary democratic circles, devoted entirely to the Russian people."[26] In this way, Mikoyan was able to tie the aims of the Russian revolutionary movement—and eventually the Bolsheviks—to the aims of the major Armenian national figures of the era. Moreover, he criticized historical narratives that obscured the links between the Armenian and Russian revolutionary movements and that stressed a "second link" of the Armenian national liberation struggle to the "Western European bourgeoisie." "Needless to say," he noted, "this is idle fiction of a nationalist sort."[27] Mikoyan's position is reflected in the final version of his 1954 Yerevan speech, when he underscored the fact that Raffi "devoted his first work with admiration to Mikael Nalbandyan, an associate of Chernyshevskii," referring to the revolutionary Russian author of the 1863 novel *What Is to Be Done?*[28]

In his assessments of Armenian history, Mikoyan was, perhaps unsurprisingly, highly critical of the Dashnaks. An Armenian socialist-nationalist political party, the Dashnaktsutyun had governed the short-lived independent Armenian Republic in the Caucasus (also known as the First Republic of Armenia) from 1918 to 1920.[29] Mikoyan's criticisms of their policies served to demonstrate to Soviet Armenians (1) the folly and even danger of relying on Western powers to protect Armenia and (2) the demonstrated benefits of Soviet rule compared to the misery of the civil war years, as well as the failure of the Dashnak leadership to provide socioeconomic material benefits to the population. Naturally, these narratives were rooted in Mikoyan's firm commitment to the integrity of the multiethnic Soviet state, as well as his equally firm conviction that the protective umbrella of Russia, especially in its Soviet form, represented the ideal path for the peaceful development of the Armenian people. Such narratives not only legitimized Soviet authority in Armenia but even popularized it. The bitter memories of the 1915 Genocide and the poverty, violence, and instability of the First Republic served as unique experiences for the Armenian people, and they resonated strongly among the population, as did the perception of Western betrayal.[30] To many Soviet Armenians, the successes of their republic therefore came to represent successes not only of the Soviet state and the revolutionary vision of the Bolsheviks but also of Armenian survival.[31] Consequently, these *dostizheniia* became instrumental in promoting the hybrid Soviet Armenian identity among the population by Soviet Armenian authorities and scholars as well as Mikoyan.

Mikoyan's sentiments about the Dashnaks were informed not only by political and ideological disagreements but also by his personal history with them, dating back to his youth at the Nersisyan School in Tiflis.[32] At school, Mikoyan was a radical student leader who encouraged rebellious political activity against faculty and staff who were sympathetic to the Dashnaks. "The youth were largely against the teachers since many of the teachers were Dashnaks," recalled Mikoyan in a private March 1958 reunion with his former Nersisyan classmates in Yerevan. "Well, if everyone were communists, then we would be confused," he added to laughter from his classmates. "The fact that some teachers were Dashnaks helped us," Mikoyan noted. "We had a desire to act. . . . We wanted to fight."[33] Accounts from former classmates reflected on Mikoyan's position as a charismatic organizer who had the ability to captivate others with his ideas. One credited him with "lighting the revolutionary fire in our hearts already from a young age.[34] Another recalled a meeting at the Tiflis City Duma in which a young Mikoyan was to speak, but the son of a prominent Dashnak attempted to prevent him from doing so. His fellow comrades in the class chased the provocateur away. In a line evocative of future remarks by Armenian statesman Hovhannes Kajaznuni, one even stated that "since the Dashnaks behave so rudely and defiantly, they will not be able to do anything. They think that they are the saviors of the nation."[35] In addition to such early episodes, Mikoyan later recounted his experience of personal "betrayal" by the Dashnaks during the period of the Baku Commune, accusing Dashnak leader Hamazasp Srvandztyan of surrendering the front to the Turks during the Ottoman invasion of Transcaucasia.[36]

There was certainly no love lost on the part of the Dashnaks toward Mikoyan either.[37] In his account of the Sovietization of Armenia in 1920, the First Armenian Republic's last prime minister, Simon Vratsyan, accused Mikoyan and other Armenian Bolsheviks of "betraying" Armenia to Moscow.[38] In a 1929 summary of a conversation with an anonymous Soviet official in Vienna, a correspondent for the official ARF organ *Droshak*, then based in Paris, dismissively referred to Mikoyan as "clearly a nothing." He added that Mikoyan was promoted within the Soviet leadership "only by being faithful to Stalin" and that it would be "naïve to attribute any national identity to him," noting that "he is as much Armenian as he is Chinese."[39] In 1959, the Dashnak Armenian American newspaper *Hairenik Weekly* echoed this sentiment while lambasting the statesman as a "symbol of [Soviet] dictatorship." "When a man becomes a Communist, he loses his nationality," wrote the paper's longtime editor James Tashjian. "Mikoyan is as much an Armenian as is Khrushchev today, or as was Beria or Stalin yesterday; that is, he is a Communist, and a Communist cannot be an Armenian; nor can he be Hungarian, American, French, Irish, or anything other than a Communist." Tashjian further maintained that, "rather than being the great practicing Armenian," Mikoyan only brought "terror and hardship to his people" and that he "helped actively to destroy the Independent Republic of Armenia, of 1918–20, by his behind-the-scene [*sic*] maneuverings in Moscow."[40] Therefore, in an inverse of Dashnak narratives that framed Mikoyan as a "Bolshevik traitor" working against Armenia in the service of Soviet Russia, Mikoyan framed the Dashnaks as "traitors" against Armenia working hand-in-glove in the service of Western imperialism.

In the final version of his 1954 Yerevan speech, Mikoyan made only passing mention of the Dashnaks, in the context of general condemnations of all the ruling parties of the civil war–era Caucasus republics (e.g., "the struggle against Musavatist-Dashnak-Menshevik counter-revolution").[41] However, in his earlier draft overview on Armenian issues, Mikoyan devoted significantly more attention to their activities, describing their "treachery" in harsh terms, stressing that the party had "earned itself the deep contempt of the Armenian people" for their reliance on Western powers. He even went so far as to call them "literally the executioners of the Armenian people in their attempt to tear Armenia away from Russia and to expose the Armenian nation to extermination by Turkey." However, Mikoyan apparently felt this criticism of his political opponents to be excessively harsh and therefore heavily edited these passages with blue pencil before deciding to remove them entirely.[42] Nevertheless, his words reflected themes that would emerge in his later speeches, such as the one that he delivered in Yerevan in June 1970, on the eve of the anniversary of Armenia's Sovietization. "Having been subjected to many difficult trials and tribulations," Mikoyan said, "the Armenian people were brought to impoverishment, ruin, and hunger, and to the verge of death, by the Dashnak government. The Dashnaks, having tied the fate of the Armenian nation to the chariot of Anglo-American imperialism, relying on its help and deceiving the people, turned their back on Soviet Russia, the only force that could—and eventually later did—save Armenia."[43] At the same time, in his meeting with Armenian historians in Yerevan in 1962, Mikoyan emphasized the correctness of the decision of the Armenian Bolsheviks to co-opt "left Dashnaks" into the Soviet Armenian government "to establish Soviet power in Armenia without bloodshed." "I personally think that such a tactical approach toward the Dashnaks was correct," Mikoyan stressed, despite the fact that some Soviet Armenians blamed this step for enabling the anti-Bolshevik uprising of 1921.[44]

Mikoyan contrasted his harsh criticisms of the Dashnaks with praise for the successes of the Soviet Armenian republic, later known among historians as the Second Republic of Armenia. The changes and achievements that occurred in Armenia from the NEP era to the Thaw were indeed genuinely monumental, and, as historian George Bournoutian stressed, "Soviet rule, for the first time, transformed Armenia from a primarily agricultural land into an urban and industrial society."[45] Significantly, in his June 1970 speech in Yerevan, Mikoyan underscored these *dostizheniia* as being those of the Armenian people first and foremost:

> During its half-century of existence, Soviet Armenia has achieved astonishingly great successes, especially if you keep in mind the terrible situation in which the Soviet government found Armenia and the Armenian people. Poor, destitute Armenia has become industrialized, and public education is at a high stage of development. The pride of the republic is its working class, its leading

> force, and the kolkhoz peasantry, its loyal ally. And there is a large detachment of socialist intelligentsia—scientists, engineers and technicians, agronomists, doctors, teachers, writers, and artists who make a great contribution to the high rates of development of the republic's economy and culture. . . .
>
> Under the Dashnak government, most of Armenia's 700,000 inhabitants starved and suffered from unemployment. Now the population in the republic has more than tripled and stands at 2.5 million people. Moreover, not only is there now zero unemployment, but, as they say, many enterprises do not have enough workers![46]

However, Mikoyan was also quick to stress the important role of the Communist Party and the Soviet government under Lenin in providing "generous military, political, and economic assistance" to Armenia in the early NEP years. He maintained that this aid "opened a new era in the history of the Armenian people" as well as "close ties and friendship with the Russian people, neighboring peoples, and all peoples of the Soviet Union."[47] Mikoyan stressed a similar point in his 1958 meeting with his Nersisyan School classmates, underscoring that "all peoples of our country are pleased by the great successes of Armenia."[48]

Although Mikoyan frequently invoked historical narratives, he was not involved in the process of writing Soviet Armenian history, a matter that he left to the republic's professional historians. In fact, while writing his memoirs, Mikoyan consulted with these scholars about those historical episodes of the Sovietization of the Caucasus that he did not personally witness. For example, in 1967, he met in Moscow with Ashot Hovhannisyan, who told him about an unpublished manuscript on events in Nagorno-Karabakh in 1917–20 written by the Karabakhtsi Armenian historian Harutyun Tumyan. Mikoyan became intrigued, and Hovhannisyan pledged to send him the full text directly from Yerevan. On November 29, 1967, he sent the complete 330-page Armenian-language manuscript to Mikoyan, along with a detailed map of the Nagorno-Karabakh AO and testimonies from the first prime minister of Musavatist Azerbaijan, Fatali Khan Khoiskii, from the Armenian Archives.[49] In an accompanying letter, Hovhannisyan stressed that, despite Tumyan's former Dashnak affiliations, he presented events in an "impartial manner" (*anach'ar vochov*) and drew on materials held in the Armenian Archives extensively. "In all cases," he wrote to Mikoyan, "the historical information that he imparts will give you the opportunity to restore the forgotten course of events and connections as you write your memoirs." Hovhannisyan emphasized that Tumyan's epilogue (*verjaban*) contained a "document worthy of special attention"—the Armenian translation of the 1962 Karabakh Armenian appeal to Khrushchev.[50] He concluded the letter by expressing gratitude to Mikoyan for his input on his latest academic study. "I wrote that prologue for my new work, an idea that you suggested to me," Hovhannisyan wrote. "I think that your advice will insure me against attacks from those insidious critics. For this, I thank you very, very much."[51]

Mikoyan's counsel to Hovhannisyan was not an isolated case. Although the statesman refused to participate in the writing of Armenian history, he was frequently sought out by Soviet Armenian historians who wanted to clarify important historiographical questions on various Armenian issues. Mikoyan's position as a participant in and eyewitness of the civil war in the Caucasus, combined with his very public attack on Stalin's *Short Course* at the Twentieth Party Congress, lent him credibility and authority among Armenian scholars.[52] The desire on the part of professional Armenian historians to seek Mikoyan's input on major historical questions also came amid monumental shifts occurring within Soviet historical sciences generally, ushered in by Khrushchev's denunciation of Stalin at the Twentieth Party Congress. Under Stalin, the science of history had been "reduced to little more than a 'handmaiden' to party policy," in the words of historian Roger Markwick.[53] The advent of de-Stalinization served to "embolden professional historians to critique historical writing" and led to the rise of revisionist Soviet scholars, who rejected Stalinist approaches to history.[54] Soviet Armenian historians were no exception to these larger trends. In this regard, they sought Mikoyan's counsel as they explored the extent of the new freedoms, especially on sensitive questions, such as Stalin's Purges or the Bolshevik collaboration with the forces of Mustafa Kemal Atatürk (the Kemalists) of Turkey.

During his March 1962 visit to Armenia, Mikoyan consented to meet with historians from the Armenian branch of the Institute of Marxism-Leninism at their request at the Armenian Central Committee building in Yerevan. The timing of the visit was significant—only a few months after the Twenty-Second Party Congress of October 1961, which gave a fresh impetus to both de-Stalinization and Soviet historical revisionism.[55] Mikoyan's discussion with the historians commenced immediately after his hour-long meeting with a delegation of Armenian writers, including the recently rehabilitated Vagharshak Norents.[56] The historians sought Mikoyan's input on a number of historiographical questions for the writing of the *Sketches of the History of the Communist Party of Armenia*.[57] The meeting was attended by very prominent Soviet Armenian figures, including First Secretary Yakov Zarobyan. The discussion was guided by the eminent Armenian historian Tsatur Aghayan, the head of the Armenian branch of the Institute of Marxism-Leninism.[58] Mikoyan's son Sergo was in attendance as well.[59]

The first question that Aghayan posed to Mikoyan concerned the proper Soviet historical interpretation of the Armenian volunteer movement of the First World War. He noted that some Armenian historians characterized the Armenian volunteers as "patriots" who "set themselves to the task of going to help the Armenian people oppressed under the yoke of Turkey." This group characterized them as a "national liberation movement" representing a "progressive phenomenon in the history of the liberation struggle of the Armenian people." He contrasted this view with that of other Armenian scholars who argued "that this movement contributed to the implementation of the aggressive designs of the tsarist autocracy, and that the Turks used this moment to destroy the Armenian people." In response, Mikoyan stressed that although World War I was an imperialist war, the Caucasian Front and the Armenian struggle for Ottoman Armenia constituted a war of national liberation for the Armenians. "Of course, Russian tsarism wanted to use this movement [the Armenian volunteer movement] for its own interests," Mikoyan told Aghayan. "However," he insisted, "that does not change its character. And naturally, the nationalist parties also wanted to use this movement for their own reactionary ends. Nevertheless, this movement was progressive." He proceeded to liken it to the Bulgarian volunteer movement and stressed its inclusion of workers and peasants. Even more importantly, Mikoyan maintained that "although the war of 1914–18 was generally an imperialist war, the advance of the Russian army on the Turkish front objectively played a progressive role in the struggle of the Armenian people against the Turkish enslavers."[60]

Although Mikoyan's response extended logically from his 1954 writings, it would have been surprising to a younger Mikoyan in 1919. During World War I, the future statesman volunteered to fight against Ottoman forces in northern Iran as part of the First Armenian battalion commanded by General Andranik Torosi Ozanyan. "Among Armenians, the name of Andranik was surrounded by an aura of glory," Mikoyan recalled. "As we later observed, he enjoyed unquestioned authority among our fighters."[61] At that time, Mikoyan's political ideas, like those of other Armenians of his generation, constituted a mix of socialism and Armenian nationalism. He saw the war over Ottoman Armenia as a war of national liberation. However, after becoming a Bolshevik, Mikoyan embraced internationalism and renounced his earlier nationalist views on the Western Armenian lands, following a trend among Party leaders favoring collaboration with the Kemalists.[62] In a December 1919 letter to Lenin, Mikoyan endorsed the idea of renouncing Bolshevik claims to Ottoman Armenia, given that the region had become majority Muslim Kurdish and Turkish as a result of the 1915 Genocide.[63] Mikoyan strongly condemned the Turkish government for "tirelessly pursuing a policy of physical annihilation and total destruction of the Armenians on the territory of Turkish Armenia, subjecting over a million people to fire and sword."[64] However, he condemned in equally strong terms the idea of annexing Ottoman Armenia, which he claimed was a "reactionary chimera" that reflected the "chauvinist" designs of the Dashnaks, supported by Western "imperialists." Moreover, he contended that this idea threatened to alienate the "Muslim masses" against the Bolsheviks.[65] Mikoyan conceded that the Russo-Turkish theater of World War I represented an objectively revolutionary "national liberation struggle" in favor of the Western Armenians. However, even here he was equivocal, despite the fact that he had served on that same front under the command of General Andranik.[66]

Nevertheless, by the time of the Thaw, Mikoyan's views on such issues had changed significantly. In his 1962 meeting with the Armenian historians, he criticized his own youthful naïveté and "national nihilist" attitudes. Speaking of his positions on nationality issues at the time of the civil war, a contrite Mikoyan told those present, "In this matter, we communists, myself included, have shown nihilism."[67] In his 1919 letter to Lenin, the younger Mikoyan wrote that the main aim of the Bolsheviks "should not be the establishment of this or that state border, or the creation of this or that national state, but the development of the revolutionary movement and the class solidarity of the working masses of all nationalities."[68] By contrast, at the 1962 Yerevan meeting, the elder statesman Mikoyan underscored the value and importance of national statehood, as articulated by his mentor, Stepan Shahumyan, who favored an equal federal union of national autonomous regions. At the Bolshevik all-Caucasus Congress of October 1917 in Tiflis, Shahumyan had proposed granting broad home rule to the peoples of Transcaucasia by dividing the area into three autonomous units, approximately corresponding to the future Soviet republics of Georgia, Armenia, and Azerbaijan.[69] However, as Mikoyan stressed to the historians, the majority of the congress delegates, himself included, opposed this idea, and Shahumyan "remained in the minority" at the time. "This was a mistake," Mikoyan said.[70] Regarding similar opposition to the formation of specific nationality-based branches of the Communist Party, Mikoyan added, "I too thought it was nationalism. Moreover, we proceeded from the assumption that there would be no need for separate nation-states after the victory of Soviet power in Transcaucasia. Our understanding did not make it possible to use the form of national statehood for the success of the socialist revolution."[71]

Another key issue on which the Armenian historians sought Mikoyan's clarification was the founding date of the Communist Party of Armenia. This matter proved to be particularly contentious for Soviet leaders in both Yerevan and Moscow, especially given the recent fortieth anniversary of Armenia's Sovietization. The confusion originated from the fact that, in 1918, the Armenian poet and political leader Gurgen Haykuni founded an Armenian Communist Party in Tiflis with the aim of promoting the Bolshevik cause among Ottoman Armenian refugees who had fled the 1915 Genocide.[72] However, Yerevan argued that the Communist Party of Armenia that governed the Armenian SSR was descended not from the party established by Haykuni but from the party established in 1920, on the eve of the Sovietization of the First Armenian Republic. Although Party leaders in Moscow initially favored Haykuni's position, they ultimately endorsed the one espoused by Yerevan, with the caveat that the important role of Haykuni must not be dismissed.[73] Nevertheless, the matter remained contentious in Armenia, as historian Khikar Barseghyan emphasized in a letter to Mikoyan on December 16, 1960.[74]

In his 1962 meeting with the historians, Mikoyan stressed the official Party position. He argued that, although the official founding year of the ruling Armenian Communist Party was 1920, there was "no need to deny the positive role of the 'Communist Party of Armenia' headed by Comrade Haykuni" and that "history must be written as it really was." Mikoyan added that "we assumed that Armenia [i.e., both Eastern and Western] would be completely liberated and that this would play a big role for the entire international revolutionary movement."[75] At the same time, he highlighted Haykuni's shortcomings, in particular his refusal to join the Transcaucasian Kraikom of the larger Russian Communist Party. Additionally, Mikoyan frankly discussed his own "sharp speech" against Haykuni over this issue.[76] He noted to the historians that an article clarifying the Haykuni question would soon be published in the journal *Kommunist*.[77] Behind the scenes, Mikoyan not only was well aware of the article but even acted as a consultant on it at the request of the journal's editor-in-chief, Fiodor Konstantinov.[78] The finished text, coauthored by Gennadii Obichkin, Gazanfer Shanshiev, and Lev Shahumyan, was published one month later and included quotes from Mikoyan from archival documents regarding his position on Haykuni's Armenian Communist Party at the time.[79] Moreover, despite past disagreements, Haykuni, who was a victim of Stalin's repressions, maintained a correspondence with Mikoyan in the early 1960s.[80]

The Armenian historians also inquired about the Armenian Bolshevik uprising of May 1920. Known as the May Uprising, this event constituted a popular Bolshevik revolt that swept up much of northern Armenia, with Aleksandropol' (later Leninakan, today Gyumri) serving as its revolutionary center.[81] The uprising was ultimately crushed by the Dashnak-dominated government of the First Armenian Republic.[82] Reflecting his historical interpretation of the uprising, Mikoyan wrote in his memoirs that "although the May Uprising of the working people of Armenia ended in defeat, it laid the groundwork for the victorious uprising in November of that same year throughout Armenia."[83] He made the same case in his meeting with the Armenian historians. "Not every uprising has to immediately end in victory," Mikoyan argued. "If every rebel were to stop rebelling after defeat, then he wouldn't be a revolutionary. This business is fraught with great difficulties. But is it really possible to blame the revolutionaries for the fact that the uprising did not end successfully? The May Uprising of 1920 in Armenia undoubtedly played a positive role. The masses learned political struggle from these difficulties."[84]

Influenced by his focus on Cuban affairs, Mikoyan even drew parallels between Armenia's ill-fated May Uprising and Fidel Castro's ill-fated attack on the Moncada Barracks in Cuba.[85] The statesman argued that just as "history had absolved" Castro, so had history absolved the Armenian Bolsheviks. "Proper decisions are drawn up in the course of the revolutionary struggle," Mikoyan maintained. "In Cuba, for instance, some communists did not support Fidel Castro at the beginning. And now the Cuban communists recognize Fidel Castro as their god. This man developed together with the people and entered Marxism-Leninism fighting."[86] Mikoyan further articulated the reasons for the defeat of the May Uprising, including "the fact that the Russian army at that moment could not come to the rescue" and that "the Armenian Committee of the Bolshevik Party (Armenkom) was poorly organized and did not receive support." He remarked that the uprising itself was "poorly prepared" and noted that "just as the revolt began in one place, it ended in another." Nevertheless, Mikoyan's overall verdict was that the "uprising was a heroic page in the history of the revolutionary struggle of the Armenian people and a great lesson."[87] He later reiterated this conclusion in his June 1970 speech in Yerevan, stressing that the May Uprising was "a mass popular movement" that "spoke to the growth of the socialist revolution in Armenia, and to the continuation of the October Revolution on Armenian territory."[88]

Mikoyan's 1962 discussion with the historians also touched on sensitive subjects, such as Stalin's Purges, the mistakes of previous Soviet Armenian governments, and the Bolshevik collaboration with Turkey's Kemalists in 1920–21. In this respect, the historians sought Mikoyan's opinion as a way to determine the extent of the freedoms of the Thaw. The subject of the Kemalists was especially sensitive for Armenians because it resulted in the loss of certain territories that had been part of Russian Armenia and that held major cultural and historical significance for the Armenian people.[89] These included the Surmalu uezd with Mount Ararat, and the Kars oblast' with the cities of Kars and Ardahan as well as the ruins of the medieval Armenian capital of Ani. The Bolsheviks ceded these territories to Kemalist Turkey at the end of the Russian Civil War in the treaties of Moscow and Kars in March and October 1921, respectively.[90] During the talks for the Kars treaty, Soviet negotiators attempted to retain at least Ani and a concession on the salt-mining town of Koghb, in Surmalu, for Soviet Armenia. However, the Kemalists rejected any amendments to the agreed border, much to the disappointment of the Soviet side.[91] In addition to these painful territorial losses, the atrocities committed by Kemalist forces against Armenian civilians only added to the sensitivity surrounding the issue for Armenians in the Soviet Union.[92] The fact that Mikoyan was so willing to address such a controversial subject so openly was significant in the context of the broader thaw within Soviet historical sciences, especially because the Bolshevik-Kemalist issue had the potential to throw into question the Party's standing among Armenians. Although more conservative Soviet officials might have balked at such questions, Mikoyan addressed them openly and candidly and even used the occasion to further criticize Stalin. In all cases, he advised the historians to cover events "objectively" but "within a Marxist-Leninist framework," based on Lenin's position that Marxist theory represented objective social science, albeit open to ongoing revision and amendment.[93]

Aghayan posed the question on Kemalism frankly. "It is known that the Soviet government had a positive attitude toward the Kemalist movement and supported it in every possible way," he said. However, he pointed to the reality that "the Kemalists acted as ardent nationalists [*iarye natsionalisty*], enslaving and exterminating other peoples—Greeks, Armenians, etc." Specifically, he cited the "great devastation and suffering" that they brought to the Armenian people, including "the seizure of Armenian territories and the destruction of the civilian population." "How should we treat these facts?" he inquired. In his response, Mikoyan addressed both the negative and positive aspects of the Kemalist phenomenon and of the early Bolshevik support for it as an "anti-imperialist" movement from Asia that could inspire similar uprisings. "We assumed that the other countries of the East would rise against the [Western] imperialists in a chain reaction," Mikoyan said. "Inside the country, the Kemalists opposed the Sultanist regime and the feudal order. In that sense, the Kemalist movement should be considered progressive." However, he emphasized that this was only "one side of the phenomenon." "The other side," Mikoyan stressed, "was that the Kemalist movement was directed against small peoples" and that this aspect "led to aggressive actions on the part of the Turks and resulted in the Armenian people suffering significant casualties and losses of territory." Mikoyan concluded that this aggression was a "manifestation of the reactionary tendency of the Kemalist movement." He advised the Armenian historians to approach the matter by highlighting these two sides of Kemalism. "When characterizing the Kemalist movement," he told them, "it is necessary to stress its anti-imperialist character, but at the same time, it is impossible to ignore its reactionary side—its aggressive actions towards other peoples."[94] When Artashes Karinyan responded by assessing Lenin's decision to collaborate with the Kemalists as "correct" given that the movement was "anti-imperialist," Mikoyan pushed back. Again, he insisted that both sides had to be represented. "Historical facts and phenomena must be elucidated objectively, just as they took place in reality," he maintained.[95]

For the Armenian historians present at the meeting with Mikoyan, the process of de-Stalinization presented new issues that needed to be addressed, including the wholesale reinterpretation of historical figures and events. "In some cases,"

Aghayan told Mikoyan, "the decisions of the plenums and congresses of the Armenian Communist Party during the period of the cult of personality contain erroneous characterizations of individual events." As an example, he cited the efforts by the Armenian Party leadership to associate "individual shortcomings and the failure to fulfill industrial plans in Alaverdi" with the Shakhty Trial at the Sixth Armenian Party Congress of 1929. He asked if such "mistakes" should be criticized in the *Sketches on the History of the Communist Party of Armenia*.[96] Mikoyan answered affirmatively but once again advised the Armenian historians to cover all aspects of the history—both negative and positive.[97] Moreover, in his response Mikoyan used the occasion to critique Stalin on collectivization, advising the historians to "also discuss leftist mistakes" on the issue. "At one time," he told the historians, "like everywhere else [*kak i vsiudu*], Stalin pressed to immediately cover 100 percent of Armenia with kolkhozes. Because of this, I remember that two Armenian villages wanted to go to Turkey. These were extremes. It should be noted that collectivization was often carried out without any clear preparation, that we often ran ahead of ourselves, and that everything had to be subsequently corrected." In addition, Mikoyan discussed the adverse impact of the Purges on the economic development and productivity of Armenia. "During the period of the cult of personality," he said, "your growth and development slowed down, just as it did throughout the country, due to the fact that a significant number of cadres were arrested in 1937–38."[98]

Mikoyan further advised the historians to cover all of Soviet Armenia's leaders "objectively," in accordance with Marxism-Leninism. "In your *Sketches*," he told them, "you should write about the leaders of the Council of Ministers and the Central Committee of Armenia, such as Kasyan, Ter-Gabrielyan, Myasnikyan, Hambardzumyan, and others. History must know its people. There is no need to praise them. Just write it as it was." Ashot Hovhannisyan inquired about Mikoyan's opinion of Sargis Lukashin, Hovhannisyan's predecessor as Armenia's first secretary in 1921–22 and later a victim of the Purges. "You know that I didn't have any particular sentiment toward him," Mikoyan said. "But what difference does that make? He was a good, knowledgeable worker and you should write about him." He also advised those in attendance to write about Grigorii Arutinov, Armenia's longtime Party boss who was appointed in 1937 and later ousted by Moscow as first secretary in 1953. This advice was significant, given the circumstances of Arutinov's removal from office. "He was not a wrecker," Mikoyan said. "After Stalin's death, Beria wanted to remove him and put [someone else] in his place. But he didn't have time to do it." He conceded Arutinov's shortcomings as a leader, noting that he was "bureaucratic" and "haughty" and that he "did not study Armenian" and therefore "communicated little with the people" due to his poor knowledge of the language. Nevertheless, Mikoyan emphasized that Arutinov was an "intelligent man" and a "good organizer." "After his death," Mikoyan said, "Tovmasyan and Arushanyan demanded that he be expelled from the Party. It was wrong. Here the Armenian vengefulness manifested itself, going from one extreme to another. If they beat a man, then they want to finish him off to the end." To these remarks, Zarobyan added, "Correct. Arutinov died as a member of the Party." Karinyan raised the issue of Arutinov's mistakes. "That is correct," responded Mikoyan. "You need to write about the errors too."[99]

Mikoyan similarly called for an objective assessment of the recently ousted first secretary Suren Tovmasyan. This advice held significance as well, given that Tovmasyan had been one of the republican leaders ousted by Moscow in part due to his allegedly relaxed attitude toward "ideological flaws" and "nationalist tendencies" in Armenia.[100] However, Mikoyan took a more charitable view. "Comrade Tovmasyan should also not be mixed with dirt," he said. "He did a lot of stupid things, which were intolerable. But you need to approach the issue objectively. He did not have sufficient political training, but he tried to do his best. It's good that he was dismissed without any commotion." Ultimately, though, Mikoyan maintained that it was up to the historians to examine the history judiciously in an "objective Marxist way" and to "analyze negative and positive facts and draw the corresponding conclusions."[101]

The Armenian historians later sent the official transcript of the Yerevan meeting to Mikoyan for verification. However, Mikoyan once again encouraged them to instead use his comments only as starting points for deeper historical investigations. "I understand them in the sense that they want ready-made answers from me on a number of the most pressing questions about the history of the Communist Party of Armenia," Mikoyan wrote to Zarobyan on October 19, 1962. Nevertheless, he added that it was "up to the comrades themselves" to examine these deep historical questions. "I cannot in any way replace them in this area," he said. "It is easier for them than it is for me because I must use the data of my memory and it cannot always be a reliable source of judgment." He added that "they [as historians] also have documents and other evidence, as well the necessary time for study and evaluation." However, Mikoyan stressed, "I do not exclude my participation when the book on the history of the Armenian Communist Party is finished and if it is discussed in the Central Committee and my consultation is required." He asked Zarobyan to convey his message to the historians.[102]

Yet, even after this exchange, Armenian historians continued to seek Mikoyan's counsel in clarifying details on the history of the revolution in the Caucasus. To these matters, Mikoyan acquiesced, albeit with reservations and always stressing their role as professional historians.[103] For instance, a popular belief among Armenians held that, in early 1918, Stepan Shahumyan traveled from Baku to Tiflis and back at his own risk, "without proper protection and without the knowledge of the leading Party bodies." Armenian historians turned to Mikoyan for clarification on this matter, and he publicly refuted such assertions in a letter cited by the scholar Karapet Mamikonyan in an article entitled "A Page from the Chronicle of the Life of Stepan Shahumyan." The work was published in the *Bulletin of the Armenian Archives* in October 1968, coinciding with the ninetieth birthday of Shahumyan and complementing Mikoyan's own efforts to preserve the memory of the fallen twenty-six Baku commissars.[104]

IN THE FOOTSTEPS OF THE COMMISSARS

Mikoyan firmly believed that the security and success of the Soviet Union was strongly contingent on the ethnic and national harmony within it. The memory of the Baku Commune of 1918 played an essential role in his promotion of such harmony, through the concept of the *druzhba narodov*. A significant episode in the history of the Russian Revolution, the Baku Commune was established by a group of Caucasian revolutionaries in Baku, then one of Imperial Russia's leading industrial cities and home to an ethnically and religiously diverse population. Led by Armenian Bolshevik Stepan Shahumyan (also known as the "Caucasian Lenin"), the commune pursued power democratically and nonviolently. Mikoyan, who looked to Shahumyan as a mentor, was one of the young revolutionaries involved in this ill-fated experiment, which lasted only between April and July 1918.[105] After its fall, twenty-six of its leaders—the mostly Bolshevik Baku commissars—met a tragic fate with their execution on September 20, 1918, by British-allied Socialist Revolutionary (SR) forces in the sands of Turkmenia.[106]

Known as the Baku 26, the commissars hailed from a range of ethnic backgrounds—Armenian, Azeri, Georgian, Russian, Jewish—but all overlooked their national differences in the face of major goals or challenges, such as the aim to build a more egalitarian society and the need to repel interventionist forces in the region. Consequently, in Mikoyan's view, the Baku 26 embodied the essence of the *druzhba narodov*, providing a vivid example of unity across national lines in the pursuit of common aims in the service of the revolution and, ultimately, the Soviet state. Mikoyan highlighted the significance of this aspect of the twenty-six commissars in his 1954 Yerevan address, when he called on his audience to "preserve and fully develop" the "wonderful traditions of internationalism" of the Bolshevik revolutionaries of the Caucasus.[107] In the same speech, Mikoyan proclaimed that the heroism of the Baku 26 would "never be eradicated from the memory of the people." "Alongside Stepan Shahumyan," he said, "the Russian Ivan Fioletov, Georgian Aliosha Japaridze, Azerbaijani Mashadi Azizbekov, Jewish Iakov Zevin and others faced death as well."[108]

For Mikoyan as a participant in the revolution in Baku, the memory of the commissars was sacred. In 1980, American journalist Harrison Salisbury wrote that their execution "never left Mikoyan" and that the statesman had feelings of guilt about the fact that he had, by chance, survived and escaped the fate of his fallen comrades.[109] The largely SR authorities of Transcaspia excluded Mikoyan from the list of the twenty-six, along with Shahumyan's two sons Suren and Lev and six others.[110] "By that simple accident," recalled Salisbury, "Mikoyan escaped and Shaumian did not. All his life Mikoyan was to wonder over this accident, feeling somehow at fault that he had lived while his beloved leader Shaumian and his other comrades had died."[111] Although Mikoyan appealed to stay with the twenty-six, the SR authorities in Krasnovodsk denied his request.[112] As Mikoyan recounted, Shahumyan advised him not to fight the decision:

> Taking me aside, Shahumyan said: "It's no problem that your request was denied. You will be released—you, together with Surik and Leva. Try to make your way to Astrakhan, and from there, to Moscow. Meet with Lenin and tell him about everything that happened to us here. On my behalf, make a proposal to arrest several prominent Right SRs and Mensheviks, declare them hostage, and offer them to the [SR] Transcaspian government in exchange for us."
>
> I replied that, of course, I would do all of this. Then Shahumyan walked up to his sons Surik and Leva, put his hands on their shoulders, and said: "You need to go together with Anastas to Astrakhan, then to Moscow, to Lenin. Tell your mother not to worry. Soon we will be together."
>
> Like brothers, we all began to say our warm farewells. In those minutes, we had no doubt that we would all be released. The thought that our comrades would no longer be alive the next day did not even enter into our minds. It was only in Shahumyan's gaze, when he said farewell to me, that I felt some kind of hidden anxiety.[113]

As it happened, the commissars were never released and instead met the fate of revolutionary martyrs. When Mikoyan personally related their story to Salisbury more than forty years later, the details were so vivid that "it sounded as though it had occurred only yesterday, so fresh were the details in his memory, so keen his emotion." For him, it was "the most dramatic episode of a life that was crowded with dramatic episodes." As for Shahumyan, Salisbury recounted that Mikoyan "never tired" of talking about him, "nor of singing his praises as a remarkable revolutionary leader." "He was dedicated to Shaumian's family and children," he wrote, "and in later years treated them as if they were his own."[114]

However, Mikoyan's commitment to preserving the memory of the commissars was not limited to his personal desire to keep their memory alive. By the mere fact of their multiethnic composition, Mikoyan saw the commissars as a microcosm of the USSR itself. Just as the Soviet Union was a vast multiethnic state whose peoples had to work together to "achieve communism," so did the

Baku Commune unite individuals across ethnic and national lines in the service of the revolution. The moral of the story was that, if different peoples can work together to achieve common revolutionary aims, then they can also come together for the common development of the Soviet state. Mikoyan regularly drew attention to the multiethnic character of the Baku Commune in this manner, in public speeches, writings, and even meetings with workers. In one such instance, during his March 1964 visit to Baku, Mikoyan chatted with the oil workers (*neftianiki*) on Oil Rocks, off the Caspian coast, and inquired about their living and working conditions. "How do you live? Amicably? [*Druzhno?*]" he asked. "Amicably, Anastas Ivanovich," they responded. Highlighting the multiethnic composition of their group, they proudly boasted that "our brigade is international, we live like one big family." Immediately drawing the association with the commissars, Mikoyan warmly replied, "The Baku proletariat has always been renowned for its internationalist traditions."[115]

Mikoyan stressed the necessity of reteaching the story of the Baku 26, not only in the Caucasus but throughout the USSR. In his criticism of Stalin's *Short Course* at the Twentieth Party Congress, he called for "showing the entire multifaceted life of our Soviet Fatherland, instead of its lacquered façade." "Indeed, until recently," Mikoyan remarked, "we had books in circulation on the history of our major Party organizations, such as those of Transcaucasia and Baku, which were even regarded as indisputable standards. Yet, in those works, facts were manipulated, with some people [e.g., Stalin] arbitrarily exalted and others not even mentioned at all."[116] Party activists in Armenia "seconded" Mikoyan's sentiments. In a report to the Soviet Central Committee from March 23, 1956, Armenian First Secretary Suren Tovmasyan noted that in Leninakan, Party activists criticized the "incorrect" interpretation of history in the *Short Course*. In their view, the text "failed to cover the activities of progressive Caucasian revolutionaries such as Comrades Shahumyan, Japaridze and other Party leaders" and instead "spoke only of Stalin." They criticized the fact that the book "undeservedly credited him [Stalin] as the organizer of the Red Army, while ignoring the role of Lenin." Furthermore, they noted that "all theoretical developments on the national question were unjustly attributed to Stalin." The Party activists further stressed that Soviet secondary school textbooks, "which say little about the role of the Party and the people," needed to have more coverage on the role of non-Russian nationalities in the history of the country. "Along with presenting the history of the Russian people," they concluded, "it is also necessary to present the history of the other peoples of the USSR more fully than that which is currently given in the textbook."[117] Although it is unclear how these Party activists envisioned the presentation of such a history, their sentiments were in full accord with Mikoyan's efforts to promote the memory of the Baku 26.

Mikoyan was especially committed to keeping Shahumyan's memory alive. In his earliest known dedication to Shahumyan from March 19, 1919, he wrote the following:

> In the personality of Comrade Shahumyan, our Party has lost an irreplaceable and talented leader in the Caucasus. The Baku proletariat has lost its old and most-tested leader in the revolutionary struggle for communism.
>
> The vile executioners of this great fighter and martyr for the workers' cause, raising their dirty hands over his bright life, knew very well what a bright star was fading from their treacherous blow on the red horizon of the international proletarian revolution. In their newspapers, they were raving about their heinous misdeeds. Comrade Shahumyan was called the "Caucasian Lenin" . . . And they were right.[118]

Forty-nine years later, Mikoyan revisited his old fallen comrade in an article published in *Pravda* in commemoration of Shahumyan's ninetieth birthday in October 1968. "He [Shahumyan] had not yet reached the age of forty when he was killed in the Transcaspian sands among the twenty-six fiery Baku commissars, at the hands of SR executioners, mercenaries of English imperialism," Mikoyan wrote. He added that Shahumyan and his associates "met death heroically, with proud exclamations: 'We are dying for communism!', 'Long live communism!'"[119] Such text hardly represented an "objective" telling of history, as Mikoyan had advised the Armenian historians in Yerevan, but it nevertheless stressed the place of the Baku 26 in the Soviet pantheon of Old Bolshevik revolutionaries.

Mikoyan also used his 1968 article to underscore Shahumyan's important contributions to the Soviet nationality policy, especially his exchanges with Lenin on the national question. "As early as 1906," he wrote, "he [Shahumyan] published a pamphlet entitled *The National Question and Social Democracy*, and in 1914 he wrote another pamphlet *On National Cultural Autonomy*, where he exposed those nationalist Social Democrats who promoted the idea of splitting workers of different nationalities." Mikoyan stressed that Lenin sought Shahumyan's counsel on nationality issues, asking him "to prepare a statement about [his] pamphlet for publication in the Bolshevik magazine *Prosveshchenie*." He further emphasized Shahumyan's efforts to translate Marxist literature into Armenian and Georgian under Lenin's leadership in Geneva, where the Armenian revolutionary "struck up an enduring friendship with Vladimir Il'ich that lasted throughout his life." Mikoyan likewise highlighted Shahumyan's cofounding of the Union of Armenian Social Democrats (later part of the RSDRP) with Bogdan Knunyants. As he noted, it was Shahumyan who penned the union's manifesto, which was praised by Lenin in *Iskra* for its "excellent endeavor to provide a correct formulation on the national question." Underscoring the growing interest in Shahumyan and his work, Mikoyan wrote that "half a century has passed since the death of Shahumyan, but his memory does not fade."[120] He would have been well aware of such interest, given that he wrote introductions to two books dedicated to Shahumyan by scholars Khikar Barseghyan and Grigori Hakobyan.[121] Nor was Mikoyan's 1968 article his last dedication to the revolutionary. In 1977, one year before his own passing, Mikoyan penned yet another article in honor of the centenary of Shahumyan.[122]

During Mikoyan's travels throughout the Soviet Union, the memory of the Baku commissars was never far behind. In January 1957, he flew to Soviet Turkmenia for a five-day trip to award that republic the Order of Lenin for its successful cotton harvest for 1956.[123] However, Mikoyan also used the occasion to draw attention to the legacy of the Baku commissars and to familiarize himself more deeply with a part of the Soviet Union that played such prominent role in their story.[124] After inspecting two kolkhozes specializing in cotton production near the city of Mary, Mikoyan arrived in Ashkhabad.[125] It was there in the Turkmen capital that he delivered an address invoking the memory of the commissars:

> This is my third time in Ashkhabad, but each time I come here, it is in a completely different way. I was in Turkmenia for the first time during the difficult days of the English occupation. I was a prisoner, in Krasnovodsk, Kizyl-Arvat, and then in the city of Ashkhabad, and, from there, I was deported in orderly fashion back to Baku. And so, I was deprived of the opportunity to get to know your city, and I did not see it. My second visit was already in 1920, in early April, together with Comrade [Mikhail] Frunze, when the first train from Tashkent arrived in Ashkhabad, after the city was liberated from the English occupiers and the Whites. At that time, I also did not have a chance to see the city—I was in a rush to get to Baku for underground work in preparation for the revolution in Azerbaijan. Now, on my third visit, I hope to get acquainted with Ashkhabad.[126]

Tying the history of the revolution in Baku to Cold War politics, Mikoyan proceeded to liken Ashkhabad's occupation by the British army and White forces during the civil war to Britain's role in the Suez Crisis against Egypt. He reminded his audience that just as they had freed themselves from the British and the Whites, "with the help of the Russian proletariat," so had the Egyptian people "now succeeded in cutting the tail off the English colonial lion and freed themselves from the English yoke, as Comrade Khrushchev wittily remarked."[127]

Much more significant was Mikoyan's trip to Baku of March 25–30, 1964. The official purpose of the visit was to deliver a marathon speech at a Plenum of the Central Committee of Azerbaijan's Communist Party, entitled "The Struggle of the CPSU for the Unity of the International Communist Movement."[128]

Although the title alluded to the ongoing Sino-Soviet split, the address itself was not transcribed, let alone published, and, in the manner of Mikoyan's revolutionary days, it was largely improvised.[129] Its extraordinary duration—an astonishing four hours—not only was highly unusual for Mikoyan but also called to mind the fiery addresses of the passionate Fidel Castro, whose Cuban Revolution reminded the statesman of his own youthful experiences in the Baku Commune.[130] More generally, the visit appeared to be aimed at bolstering Khrushchev and his anti-Stalinist policies at a politically critical moment in the Kremlin. Naturally, Mikoyan likewise used the occasion to honor the memory of the Baku 26, as well as Baku Bolsheviks who had survived both the civil war and Stalin's Purges. On March 27, the third day of his visit, he went to the memorial commemorating his fallen comrades at Twenty-six Baku Commissars Square, accompanied by Azerbaijan's first secretary Vali Akhundov, chairman of Azerbaijan's Council of Ministers Enver Alikhanov, and many other Azerbaijani officials as well as Bakuvian Old Bolsheviks. At the solemn ceremony, Mikoyan laid a wreath at the graves of the commissars with a ribbon featuring the inscription, "To the Fierce Fighters for the Cause of Communism, the Twenty-six Baku Commissars, from Anastas Mikoyan." He also inspected the monument dedicated to their memory sculpted by Sergei Merkurov.[131]

Mikoyan and Akhundov's entourage then traveled to inspect Oil Rocks, the first offshore oil drilling site in the world. Khrushchev's earlier visit there in April 1960 was still fondly remembered by the workers. At an impromptu gathering in front of the Palace of Culture, Akhundov introduced Mikoyan as "one of the leaders of the Baku revolutionary proletariat, an outstanding Soviet Party and state figure, and the closest ally [*blizhaishii soratnik*] of Comrade Khrushchev."[132] Those present listened attentively to Mikoyan's lively speech, in which he invoked the Bakuvian revolutionary past, including his own efforts to organize oil workers:

> I had to work with Baku oil workers in the pre-revolutionary years when we organized them in order to prepare them to seize power. In those days, the *tartal'shiki* worked in the oil fields. Many of you probably have no idea what this word means today. The life of the workers was hard. Penury and illiteracy were their lot. At that time, many political parties fought for influence among the working masses, posing as defenders of the interests of the people. But the dark, illiterate Baku oil workers unmistakably identified their true friend and followed the Bolsheviks. The working class of Baku has always been a citadel of Bolshevism.[133]

Mikoyan went on to cast the Baku oil workers as "the vanguard of the working class." The workers in turn presented the statesman with a model of an offshore drilling rig in appreciation of his visit.[134] By highlighting his audience as the heirs of the Baku 26 and the traditions of Bakuvian internationalism, Mikoyan was making a seemingly distant past appear not so distant. Once again, he was stressing the relevance of the commissars to contemporary Soviet life.

The following day, accompanied by Akhundov and Alikhanov, Mikoyan visited nearby Sumgait. Decades later, the town would become infamous for the violent anti-Armenian pogrom that intensified the conflict over Nagorno-Karabakh and seemingly set the *druzhba narodov* on the pathway to being "empirically falsified," in the words of scholar Artyom Tonoyan.[135] However, at the time of Mikoyan's visit, the prospect of such ethnically inspired bloodshed was far from anyone's mind. If anything, it was only a distant memory of the nightmarish ethnic upheavals that engulfed the Caucasus in the final years of the Russian Empire. Mikoyan contrasted the memory of such violence with the internationalism of the commissars, whose efforts to work together across ethnic lines continued to live on in the then-model Soviet community of Sumgait. Boasting of the city's apparent reputation for tolerance, Sumgait Party committee secretary Nadir Balakishiev even proudly called Sumgait "the city of the *druzhba narodov,* in which representatives of over forty nationalities live and work as one big family."[136]

In the era of the *druzhba narodov,* the Armenian Mikoyan was "warmly greeted" by the majority Azerbaijani residents of Sumgait.[137] A citywide rally for Mikoyan was organized by the Soviet Azerbaijani government at the city's Chemists' Palace of Culture, where Mikoyan received a standing ovation and a reception by local pioneers.[138] The proceedings commenced with various speakers again boasting of the town's tolerance and multiculturalism. Whether their words reflected genuine expressions of tolerance, performances with an eye to personal elevation in the Communist Party, or both remains an open question. Balakishiev lauded Mikoyan as an "outstanding Party and state figure," an "old Bakuvian," and a "great friend of the Azerbaijani people."[139] In his speech, the Old Bolshevik D. N. Tel'zner reflected on his personal memories of Mikoyan and added that "the fraternal *druzhba narodov* is growing and strengthening" in Azerbaijan. "This development is especially evident in our enterprises, in our city, where Azerbaijanis, Armenians, Russians, and many representatives of other nationalities live and work side by side," he said. "We will celebrate the one hundred and fiftieth anniversary of Azerbaijan's incorporation into Russia as a great holiday of the *druzhba narodov.*"[140] These sentiments were echoed by T. Nabiev of the Lenin Azerbaijan Pipe-Rolling Plant and B. Galustyan of the Sumgait Synthetic Rubber Plant.[141] In his remarks, Veniamin Agamoglanov, first secretary of the Sumgait Komsomol Gorkom, went so far as to tell Mikoyan that "starting from today, please consider yourself a Sumgait citizen, a citizen of the city of youth and spring, where you are so welcome!"[142] He further stressed that Mikoyan's revolutionary activities "do not fade in the memory of the Old Bolsheviks, who carry their stories to us, the youth."[143]

Second only to Baku as one of Azerbaijan's leading industrial centers, Sumgait was still a relatively new Soviet town at the time. Therefore, for Mikoyan and other Party officials, it was a showpiece of Soviet achievement since the period of the Baku Commune. Sumgait English teacher Solmaz Ibrahimova underscored this point in her speech, highlighting the significant changes in Azerbaijan since 1917 as the realization of everything for which Mikoyan and the Baku 26 had fought. "Once our republic was 90 percent illiterate," she said in her speech at the Chemists' Palace, "and now we have become a republic of complete literacy. Now every fourth citizen of our republic is covered by some sort of education. There are far more students in schools in Azerbaijan than in schools in Iran and Turkey combined, although the population of these countries is thirteen times larger than the population of our republic."[144] In his speech, Mikoyan matched Ibrahimova's words with plaudits for her as a symbol of the revolutionary progress achieved, referencing the unveiling campaign in traditionally Shia Muslim Azerbaijan and associating it with women's emancipation.[145] He lauded her ability to speak "perfectly and purely in Russian," while adding, to the laughter of the audience, "and here I am, a man who, despite speaking Russian for many years, still has an [Armenian] accent!" The astonished Mikoyan added, "And as it turns out, she teaches English! An Azerbaijani woman who has a perfect command of Russian and teaches English! It speaks of great education, it speaks of culture."[146] The statesman highlighted Sumgait itself as a reflection of revolutionary *dostizhenie*, recalling that the city did not even exist in 1918 and that its rapid growth made it "not the brother of Baku, but rather the son of Baku." He likewise marveled at its rubber industry, stressing that rubber production had been earlier focused on "Karabakh and other places."[147]

Mikoyan reminded his audience that such progress would have been impossible without the revolutionary sacrifices of the Baku 26 and other Caucasian Bolsheviks. "I am pleased," he said, "that at all meetings of the communists and workers of Azerbaijan . . . they consider it their duty to mention the names of Shahumyan, Azizbekov, Japaridze, and Fioletov, as well as Narimanov, Ordzhonikidze, and Kirov, who were here [in Sumgait]." Mikoyan highlighted these figures and "all those not yet named heroes and ordinary revolutionaries" as having "demonstrated their high integrity and determination in serving the cause of the revolution." He advised his audience that these revolutionary Bolshevik traditions "must be kept scared" and that they must be kept fresh to incorporate "new methods of struggle, until communism is fully built." He further underscored the importance of following the example of the revolutionaries by working across ethnic lines and opposing national chauvinism. Gratified to see that the Baku working class had "preserved their revolutionary traditions," Mikoyan emphasized their role as the "bearers of the ideas of class cohesion, the ideas of internationalism and the *druzhba narodov*, and not of national disunity." He stressed that the "working class encompasses workers of all nations who are brothers" and that "the capitalists of all nations are their enemies." He added that this dichotomy was something that the "working class understood decades ago, when they were beat and oppressed under the tsarist boot." Mikoyan contrasted this history with that of contemporary Soviet Sumgait, which he cited as a "good example" of a city that embodied the *druzhba narodov*, with "workers, toilers, and intelligentsia imbued with the ideas of internationalism." He perceived Sumgait as a city building a "strong friendship among all peoples" with "nationalities from all corners of our country."[148] The Armenian statesman concluded his address with a toast in honor of "the glorious Azerbaijani people," the local Azerbaijani authorities, and "the friendship of all peoples."[149]

The next day, Mikoyan went on an excursion to Lenkoran' and Astara in Azerbaijan's southern Talysh region on the border with Iran. There he visited kolkhozes and sovkhozes, inspected tea plantations, spoke with schoolchildren, met with one of the border detachments, and even attended a town meeting in Astara.[150] This trip too carried revolutionary symbolism, given the importance that Mikoyan attached to the experience of the short-lived Lenkoran' Mughan Soviet Republic from the civil war era.[151] Even more significant was Mikoyan's private meeting with a group of Bakuvian Old Bolsheviks that occurred the following day, on March 30, the final day of his visit.[152] The gathering was arranged by Akhundov in the republic's Central Committee building in Baku.[153] Praising the Azerbaijani first secretary for organizing the meeting, Mikoyan stressed that "Azerbaijan has not forgotten its leaders." "This is such a concordance of generations, a spirit of generations," he added. "It is necessary and useful for us to have this meeting." Once again, he expressed astonishment at Baku's achievements since 1918, adding, "Allow me to say, comrades, that I cannot even find words to express my joy about meeting with you and about how I found Baku. In fact, my perception of Baku lagged behind the reality. It was ahead of all our fantasies and expectations. . . . We never expected then that we would have built so much."[154]

Mikoyan underscored the position of the surviving Bakuvian Old Bolsheviks as carriers of the revolutionary legacy of the twenty-six commissars. "It took great courage not only to remain a communist, but also to defend your ideas," he said. "And I must frankly say, perhaps you too remember the difficulties with great sweetness. Although the conditions were seemingly difficult, isn't it much more rewarding to devote your youth to a cause? After all, isn't it pleasant to remember? Especially when you consider that these years will not be repeated. An interesting story that happened once and will never happen again. Our generation, which took part in the revolution, in the struggle to establish Soviet power, was a lucky generation."[155] Mikoyan's stress on the "courage" to "remain a communist" arguably applied just as much to the experiences of the Old Bolsheviks as victims of Stalinism as it did to their experiences in the Baku revolutionary movement. He further emphasized that Baku had special conditions for producing revolutionaries "capable of enduring all the difficulties in the struggle of the working class." "Leningrad aside," he added, "there were few cities with such conditions."[156] While recounting episodes from the revolution in Baku, Mikoyan noted that the "death of the leaders of the Baku Commune sobered up those workers who had been mistaken before" and that they had become "new people," who were "more confident, who experienced both life and practice, and who found the answer to their words not in books, but in life."[157] He underscored the historical legacy of the Baku revolutionaries and their internationalist ideals as speaking "to the strength of the working class and to the strength of Lenin's ideas."[158]

Mikoyan was not the only one invoking the memory of the revolution in Baku. Those present did so as well, reminding Mikoyan of his own role in the Party organization. Old Bolshevik Ivan Gandiurin recalled his escape with Mikoyan from a Musavatist jail. "Cement floor, water, and millet—those were the conditions in which we were kept there," he recalled of the jailing. "They said, 'We will send you to [Anton] Denikin,' and Denikin at that time was eager to get to Baku."[159] He also recounted his role in the burial of the Baku 26. "How many tears there were, what a funeral it was," he said. "They were killed for the workers' cause. They said that we are dying, but the youth who are now growing up will remember us and follow our path."[160] Gandiurin was not alone. The other Old Bolsheviks also reflected on their memories of their revolutionary years in Baku. Natalia Abramova remembered an episode in 1920 at the Baku workers' club on the location of the city's Sabir Square. This de facto Party headquarters was frequented by all of Baku's most prominent Bolshevik leaders—Mirzoyan, Pleshakov, Mikoyan, Shatunovskaia, and others. It was in a secret room at this club where Abramova recalled speaking at a clandestine Baku Party meeting. "Comrade Mikoyan asked which districts were ready to fight the Musavatist government, how many Party cells were organized, and what reserves were in each district," she recounted. "I was young then, and I spoke very timidly. This was my first speech at such a responsible meeting."[161] Similarly, Mamed Veisov recalled Mikoyan's ability to deliver speeches on the fly and fondly remembered the telegram that Mikoyan sent to Lenin in 1919 referring to Baku as "the hotbed of future socialist revolution in Azerbaijan" and "a boiling cauldron of Bolshevik enthusiasm." "These lines are always read by us with excitement, and we direct this excitement precisely to your address," he said. Reflecting on the revolutionary dynamism of the period, Veisov recalled reading an article by an English general in a magazine in Iran in 1920, describing the Baku 26 as "much stronger dead than alive."[162]

Mikoyan was pleased when Akhundov informed him that the Azerbaijani government was dispatching the Bakuvian Old Bolsheviks to factories and plants to meet the workers and give speeches recounting the city's revolutionary past. "It is necessary! It is necessary!" Mikoyan insisted. "It is very useful. The youth think that all this was easy—that the decision was made, approved, and that was all. Such is what they think, and they think that all this went according to plan, that we foresaw everything in advance, when to retreat, when to win. Life most often does not go according to plan." Gandiurin fully concurred. "The youth think that the doors were opened, and that Soviet power just walked right in," he said.[163] Both he and Abramova emphasized that the Old Bolsheviks were working actively to impart the memory of the Baku revolutionary movement to the youth. "I wanted to say that Soviet power won, but certainly not easily," Abramova said. "And this is what we relate to our youth. Victory did not just happen by itself. It was won by the working class, and, in our recollections, we relate how our Party led the victory of the revolution."[164] For her part, Frida Shlemova, the widow of purged Azerbaijani revolutionary Ruhulla Akhundov, spoke about her efforts to preserve the legacy of her husband. "When I returned here [to Baku]," she said to Mikoyan, "I worked on all of Ruhulla's documents for some time. His autobiography is at the Institute of Party History. Now he cannot convey his words of love to you. I know how much he cherished his meeting with you. He wrote: 'In 1917, I met Mikoyan, and in 1918, I worked at *Izvestiia* of the Baku Soviet. I owe my Party spirit [*partiinost'*] to Comrade Mikoyan.' Anastas Ivanovich, on my own behalf and on behalf of Ruhulla, thank you for everything you have done."[165]

The meeting with the Baku Old Bolsheviks was also significant for the fact that Mikoyan used the occasion to tie the fate of the twenty-six commissars with the fate of the victims of Stalinism, both of which Mikoyan framed as martyrs for the socialist revolutionary cause. Half of the Old Bolsheviks present at the meeting were victims of the repressions, including all of those who spoke.[166] All had been rehabilitated by the Soviet government after Stalin's death, and, as was customary, all praised Khrushchev and Mikoyan for their efforts in rehabilitating former political prisoners and dismantling Stalin's cult of personality. The meeting offered a rare and candid glimpse of Mikoyan's views on de-Stalinization in a private setting during the Thaw. The statesman had already implicitly referred to the Stalin issue in his earlier Sumgait speech, discussing "mistakes" made by the Party and the need for "Leninist self-criticism." In his meeting with the Old Bolsheviks, Mikoyan would voice his thoughts much more openly, often using the same language but specifically mentioning Stalin and his crimes. However, in the presence of public company in Sumgait, he chose to take a more cautious and diplomatic line, an approach undoubtedly informed by the recent pro-Stalinist disturbances that shook the town on November 7, 1963.[167] As Mikoyan stated,

> Comrades, our Party had difficulties in building a socialist state. There were many mistakes and defeats. However, without these, nothing can happen. Do not think that everything went smoothly, that we only went forward and forward. No, there have been defeats and mistakes, but in the end, everything ended with the victory of Bolshevism, the victory of Lenin's ideas. We won in October, and we won the civil war. . . .
>
> We have very good people, but there are also very bad people. There are few, but they spoil the blood of many and many. In that regard, a lot of work needs to be done.
>
> We have had, and will have, miscalculations and mistakes, but the Central Committee is certain that we are not afraid to admit them. We do not hide them before the people, and this helps the people to understand and mobilize themselves.
>
> Lenin said that you need to have the courage to tell the people the truth and to say it no matter what the truth may be. He knew that only in this way could the Party gain support from the people, eliminate all shortcomings, and attain success. And this is done by our Central Committee, and in this Central Committee of our Party, Nikita Sergeevich Khrushchev plays a big role in developing self-criticism, revealing shortcomings, and highlighting achievements.[168]

At his meeting with the Old Bolsheviks, Mikoyan went much further, by directly associating the tragic fate of the Baku 26 with the fate of the victims of the Purges. "We must surround with love those who were fortunate enough to stay alive and see the fruits of the victory of the working class throughout the country and here in Azerbaijan," he began. "In addition, we must honor the memory of those who died, including the 26 Baku commissars and the brutally tortured Nariman Narimanov . . . as well as others." From this point, Mikoyan shifted to the impact of Stalinism on the Baku Bolsheviks. He advised those present to "not forget those who died as a result of the arbitrariness of Stalin's cult of personality" and to "honor their memory" as well. The cautious Mikoyan tempered his criticism of Stalin by calling him a "good manager" who "defended the Zinovievites and Trotskiites" but who also made "rash decisions on collectivization" that "could have been avoided" and "where there would have been fewer casualties." However, Mikoyan told his audience that although "we scored a victory on collectivization and it went very quickly," Stalin changed dramatically soon afterward. "He did all of this, and then suddenly Stalin became different," he claimed.[169]

Mikoyan proceeded to chronicle the tragic fate of several prominent Baku and Azerbaijani Bolshevik leaders who were killed in the Stalinist repressions. "You see how many people were killed," Mikoyan told those present. "Stalin knew [Mirza Davud] Huseinov well. When Huseinov came [to Moscow] once or twice a year, he met and talked with him. Then Stalin withdrew and did not meet with anyone. He only accepted [Mir Jafar] Bagirov and did not accept others." Mikoyan continued, "Stalin killed Huseinov, as well as [Gazanfar] Musabekov, who was a very good man and a communist. I met him when he came to Moscow from Baku. I also met him back in 1919 in Astrakhan. I came to Baku with him and [Habib] Jabiev from there. Musabekov was an honest man who fell victim and was killed [by Stalin]. For what?"[170] Mikoyan began naming the names of other Old Bolsheviks from Azerbaijan who became victims of the Purges, including Dadash Bunyadzade, Hamid Sultanov, Viktor Naneishvili, and, in a nod to Shlemova, Ruhulla Akhundov. He lauded the latter as "a well-trained Marxist and a principled man from the Azerbaijani Party intelligentsia." "He was an outstanding individual," Mikoyan recalled. "He too became a victim of [Stalin's] arbitrariness. Did anyone ever think that it would be like this? Everyone could expect that they would die for the ideas of Marxism. But death by the hands of one of their own? No one thought this, and many other comrades were killed."[171] Mikoyan also raised the case of Armenian Old Bolshevik Levon Mirzoyan, another victim of the Purges who served as the first secretary of Azerbaijan during the late 1920s and later as the first secretary of Kazakhstan during the 1930s. "We arrived with him from prison across the Caspian. He was young and competent and played a big role here [in Azerbaijan]. To this day, he is remembered in Kazakhstan as the best raikom secretary. Mirzoyan too was killed. It is simply not clear why Stalin began to destroy the best cadres of the Soviet government, who trusted him and never opposed him. They fought for the Party and were ready to die for it at any time."[172]

Mikoyan's calls to remember the victims of Stalinism in Azerbaijan were accompanied by praise for the key role that Khrushchev played in de-Stalinization. In his words about Khrushchev, Mikoyan invoked his full name, including patronymic, to emphasize his respect for his ally and his great historical act. "We remember this so as not to forget our fallen comrades, in order to highly appreciate the great work that our Central Committee has done in the struggle against the cult of personality," he said. "Nikita Sergeevich Khrushchev played a particularly important role here. And if not for him, if the struggle against the cult of personality had never been launched, then the atmosphere of Party spirit would not have been created as it is now." Following these words, the room erupted in applause, after which Mikoyan added, "Because the fact is that if the leader had been Beria, then it is completely unknown how it would have ended."[173] He continued,

> Therefore, Nikita Sergeevich Khrushchev played a particularly important role [in dismantling Stalin's personality cult] and it is difficult to find words to evaluate this moment. As for the others—Molotov, Kaganovich—they,

> of course, are not Beria. Together with Nikita Sergeevich Khrushchev, they participated in the liquidation of Beria. However, they too were carriers of the ideas of the cult. They were very supportive of Stalin and tried to have more [of the cult of personality]. And moreover, Stalin would not have refused to correct such moves. What Nikita Sergeevich said then at the Twentieth Congress, when he told the truth to the Party about what happened, we did not want to speak out about, because the enemies were in front of us. It was Nikita Sergeevich who made such a report.
>
> We recall the heavy sacrifices suffered by our Party at the hands of our own Party in order to appreciate the high significance of the turning point made by the Twentieth Party Congress, and [to ensure] that nothing like that could happen in the Party again. That is why, comrades, we, in reviewing the past of our Party, must say that this path traveled was not so smooth without a bump. Therefore, we highly appreciate the fact that our Party and our working class were so strong both internally and ideologically that even such things as leaving behind Stalin and his personality cult could not lead the Party off the right path. We thank our Party for having stood the tests of history so well, and now it has become the center of world events.[174]

Mikoyan's plaudits were motivated not only by admiration for Khrushchev's historic deed but also by high Kremlin politics. His apparent political aim was to bolster Khrushchev's anti-Stalinist initiatives, especially in the aftermath of the Twenty-Second Party Congress. Given Mikoyan's long-standing ties to the Baku Party organization, the city seemed a natural place to rally support for the anti-Stalinist cause, especially given that so many Baku Old Bolsheviks had been decimated by the Purges. Moreover, Mikoyan's Bakuvian circle comprised one of his major patronage networks, a fact emphasized at the Baku meeting by Suren Badamyan of Nagorno-Karabakh, a victim of Bagirov's repressions.[175] In this context, Mikoyan could count on a warm reception from his old Bakuvian comrades. Thus, the Baku meeting served to strengthen support for Khrushchev among Old Bolsheviks and former political prisoners during a time when the position of the Soviet leader was becoming increasingly tenuous in the Kremlin.[176] After all, "Khrushchev's *zeki*" served as an important bloc of supporters, both for his leadership and for de-Stalinization.[177] Mikoyan's emphasis on Khrushchev's denunciation of Stalin, as well as his work on rehabilitating Gulag survivors, was therefore especially significant. The meeting in general once again highlighted the reality that the struggle within the Soviet Union over Stalin's legacy was just as much a political issue as it was a moral and historical one. Mikoyan's unfavorable references to Beria, Molotov, and Kaganovich as the "carriers" of Stalin's cult underscored this political significance.

In response to Mikoyan's words, many Old Bolsheviks spoke. These Gulag survivors and former "enemies" thanked Khrushchev and Mikoyan for their roles in de-Stalinization and emphasized the importance of preserving the memory of the victims of Stalinism, just as they had with preserving the memory of the Baku 26. Frida Shlemova expressed her joy at being able to see Mikoyan again. "In 1955, when I was being rehabilitated, I was at your dacha," she said. "But at that time, I was so overwhelmed by what had happened that I could not say everything I wanted to say." She proceeded to remind Mikoyan about his role in her upbringing and education as a young Party member. "You were young, and I was just a girl," she said. "I really wanted to be a good Party member. That was everybody's dream. And so, I remember in 1921 or at the beginning of 1922, when Ruhulla and I were in Moscow, we met with you, and we discussed what it takes to be a real Bolshevik."[178] She emphasized her loyalty to the Party and its principles even after that same party under Stalin had condemned her to the Gulag and her husband to execution. She recounted one episode when a rumor spread among the prisoners that the German communist Ernst Thälmann had been released. "The whole prison began to shout: Long live Stalin!" she said. "Although we were in prison, although we were accused of the devil knows what, the whole prison shouted: Long live Stalin! Because we believed that Stalin knew nothing about this. Only afterwards did I understand the whole reality."[179]

Jeyran Bairamova, widow of Azerbaijani Bolshevik revolutionary Ali Bairamov and a survivor of the Purges, also expressed her gratitude to both Khrushchev and Mikoyan for their role in the rehabilitation of political prisoners:

> Comrade Mikoyan, when I was elected a delegate, our women, both rehabilitated and non-rehabilitated, very much asked to convey our sincere greetings to our Central Committee of the Party, and personally to Comrade Khrushchev. We are very grateful to him for giving us a second life after rehabilitation, returning to us the freedom that was given to us by the October Revolution and the Party of Lenin.
>
> I beg you, Comrade Mikoyan, to convey our sincere regards and even a kiss from all women to Comrade Khrushchev for releasing us. We wish you, Comrade Mikoyan, good health and that this will not be your first or second visit, but that you will visit us several more times. Do not forget our Azerbaijan. Come more often. We wish you good health and many years of life.
>
> Although we are old, Comrade Mikoyan, you feel that the more we age, the more our soul becomes younger. Long live our Communist Party, led by Comrade Khrushchev![180]

Bairamova was followed by Suren Badamyan, the former chairman of the Executive Committee of the Nagorno-Karabakh AO, who was arrested during

Bagirov's reign in Azerbaijan in 1937. Another former "enemy," Badamyan thanked Mikoyan and Khrushchev for their roles in rehabilitating victims of the Purges:

> There is one thing that I must ask you to convey to Comrade Khrushchev. 50 percent of us sitting here are victims. These are comrades who somehow brought their bones to their homeland in the city of Baku. We owe all of this to Comrade Khrushchev. If not for him, no one would have taken the liberty to bring these cadres back, to restore those Leninist norms that are dear to our Party. On behalf of the entire Baku Party organization, especially on behalf of the victims, I ask you to convey to Comrade Khrushchev that we are grateful to him for giving us the opportunity to return and work honestly in our Party organization.[181]

Badamyan added that "we have now begun to forget those years [of Stalin's Purges]," stressing that the Party organization of Azerbaijan had received rehabilitated political prisoners "exceptionally well." "We have no complaints," he said, adding that Akhundov and the Azerbaijani leadership, as well as the Presidium of the Central Committee, had fulfilled all their requests. With a touch of humor, he added, "You know, the older you get, the more whimsical you become and sometimes these comrades just have to babysit us." However, he noted that many Old Bolsheviks continued to work, regardless of old age. "In particular, I will soon turn seventy, and I still work," he said. "Many people, who are able to work, do work, and those who cannot work are constantly supported [by the state]." Stressing his commitment to the Party, despite his imprisonment, Badamyan concluded, "We believe in the Party organization, we have always been with it, and we will continue to be with it."[182] His statement was more than just a pledge of Party loyalty—it also signaled to Mikoyan that he and the former political prisoners remained loyal to Khrushchev in the larger struggle over de-Stalinization.

CONCLUSIONS

Amid rising national sentiments during the Thaw, Mikoyan's invocation of historical narratives through the foci of Armenia and the Baku 26 presented an inclusive response that promoted hybrid "national" and "Soviet" identities as well as cooperation and coexistence among national groups. In the context of Armenia, Mikoyan invoked narratives that stressed the hybrid "Apricot socialist" identity, fusing together Armenian national sentiments with Soviet socialist ideology. Through these narratives, Mikoyan stressed to Soviet Armenian audiences that the Soviet and the national were complementary, mutually constitutive, and actively in conversation with each other. Nevertheless, although he regularly invoked historical narratives in his public speeches and writings, Mikoyan always deferred to professional historians when it came to the writing of history itself.

As an eyewitness to and later memoirist of the revolution in the Caucasus, he was frequently sought out by Soviet Armenian scholars to answer the most burning historical questions and to help them determine the parameters of the Thaw in Soviet historical sciences. However, while he often engaged with them, he ultimately preferred to leave the science of history to the historians.

In the context of Azerbaijan and Baku, the narratives on the fate of the Baku 26, invoked by Mikoyan and kept alive by the surviving Old Bolsheviks, provided a useful metaphor for state unity by highlighting a group of committed revolutionaries who overlooked ethnic and national differences in the pursuit of common revolutionary aims. Mikoyan specifically sought to highlight the Baku 26 as realizations of the Soviet notion of the *druzhba narodov* and therefore to promote their memory in order to strengthen peaceful relations among the various national groups within the Soviet state. However, Mikoyan went beyond employing such narratives in the context of nationality policy and placed them in dialogue with the ongoing political struggles over de-Stalinization. Thus, the story of the Baku 26 served to promote not only notions of national coexistence and state unity but also the kinship shared between the commissars and the victims and survivors of Stalinism.

When taken together, these narratives reflected both Mikoyan's long-standing commitment to the geopolitical integrity of the Soviet state and an alternative to more coercive policies in response to the growing national sentiments across the Soviet Union. They highlight the reality that, in the struggle between Moscow and the republics to define the extent of acceptable national expression, there were different possible approaches and options at the center's disposal. Mikoyan's use of historical narratives to promote "Apricot socialist" identities and the Soviet *druzhba narodov* thus constituted one such response, amid Khrushchev's broader reform agenda of reversing Stalinist dictatorship.

5 | The Peoples' Return

Mikoyan's contributions to the development of Thaw-era Soviet nationality reforms reflected his inclusive attitude toward difference throughout his long career.[1] This association was particularly apparent in his advocacy for the rehabilitation and return of the Chechens and the Ingush, both victims of wartime Stalinist deportations. Although the rehabilitation of the deported nationalities was a hallmark of de-Stalinization, opposition to the return of these groups was considerable among Soviet security officials, in particular KGB chief Ivan Serov.[2] When the Soviet government finally authorized the return of the Chechens and the Ingush, it was confronted with new challenges in the form of territorial and property disputes. In these instances, the Stalinist legacy complicated the efforts by Khrushchev, Mikoyan, and other Soviet officials to forge a new path for the USSR in the nationality sphere. This history demonstrates that the Khrushchev government's adoption of a policy favoring greater national expression was contested within the Soviet leadership and that the return of the deported peoples was fraught with antagonisms and practical difficulties.

Although Mikoyan demonstrated a broad concern for the peoples of the North Caucasus, he took a particular interest in the fate of the Chechen and the Ingush peoples. During the era of Lenin's New Economic Policy (NEP) in the 1920s, it was Mikoyan who played a leading role in the establishment of Chechnia and Ingushetia as autonomous entities, and in the process, he developed a personal connection with the local elites of these republics. In 1944, Mikoyan was the sole voice of objection to Stalin and Beria's proposal to deport the Chechens and the Ingush to Central Asia. During the Thaw, Mikoyan met with Chechen and Ingush representatives and oversaw the restoration of the Checheno-Ingush ASSR as well as the return and rehabilitation of these peoples to their native lands. In these events, the role of the Chechen and Ingush peoples merits special attention, given their leading position in the movement for the return of deported Soviet nationalities more broadly. Furthermore, the conflicts that were associated with the return of these peoples provide the opportunity to examine the response of the Soviet state in the context of Thaw-era cases of nationality-related unrest.

This chapter commences by contextualizing Mikoyan's efforts on the rehabilitation of the Chechen and Ingush peoples in his earlier work as the first secretary of the North Caucasus krai during the 1920s. Mikoyan's governorship of this region provided him with his first practical experience in managing difference and promoting autonomy, literacy, and cultural and national expression among indigenous ethnic groups, in line with the Soviet policy of *korenizatsiia* (nativization).[3] As Sergo Mikoyan later wrote, it was in the North Caucasus that his father "formed his habitual practice of honoring different nations, beliefs, traditions, and customs that he encountered in his political work."[4] This experience had a lasting impact on Mikoyan and later proved invaluable to his contributions on the rehabilitation of the deported North Caucasus nationalities during the Thaw. The statesman's work in this sphere was complemented by bottom-up initiatives from representatives of these groups to return to their native lands and achieve the restoration of their autonomous republics. Most significant in this regard was Mikoyan's May 1956 meeting with a Checheno-Ingush delegation at the Kremlin, led by Chechen linguist Iunus Desheriev and Ingush writer Idris Bazorkin. Two months later, Mikoyan played a central role in the effort to manage the return of these groups with the formation of the Mikoyan Commission in July 1956.

Yet, as this chapter also highlights, efforts to return the deported nationalities were met with significant opposition by state security officials, underscoring that even the return of groups like the Chechens and the Ingush was highly contested. Ultimately, developments on the ground, most notably the unauthorized return of the deportees, forced the security officials to drop their opposition to the restoration of Checheno-Ingushetia. Nevertheless, while Khrushchev's government oversaw the return of the Chechens, Ingush, and other deported nationalities, the exclusion of certain groups, notably the Crimean Tatars and Volga Germans, highlighted the limitations of this process. Additionally, the return process itself was not without challenges, as evidenced by the Ingush-Ossetian dispute over the Prigorodnyi raion and the tensions between the local Slavic inhabitants and the Checheno-Ingush returnees.

MIKOYAN AND THE BIRTH OF CHECHNIA

At the beginning of the 1920s, after four years of violence and civil war, the Soviet state needed to establish stability and authority in the North Caucasus, a region of the Russian SFSR initially known as the "Southeastern krai" in the early NEP era.[5] In his post as first secretary of the region, Mikoyan's task was to lead the effort in rebuilding the area and bringing together its various groups, particularly the Cossacks and the North Caucasian highlanders. To that end, he actively promoted the idea of partitioning the large Gorskaia, or Mountain, ASSR into individual autonomous entities for the peoples of the region. The Gorskaia ASSR was "not a national republic, but a republic of nationalities," as Mikoyan wrote in 1922.[6] It encompassed "a large group of North Caucasian mountain peoples: Chechens, Ingush, Kabardins, Ossetians, Balkars, Karachai, and part of the villages of the Terek Cossacks." As Mikoyan recalled, "These peoples were very different and among some of them, ethnic tensions still remained."[7]

As a result of the gradual dissolution of this large entity, the Soviet government effectively "fathered" several national republics that form the contemporary Russian North Caucasus. This is not to say that the Soviet state merely created nations ex nihilo, on the whim of officials like Mikoyan. There were cultural, historical, and linguistic bases for the creation of these entities, and local North Caucasian elites actively assisted the state in the effort to consolidate these groups into "imagined" national communities.[8] Mikoyan acknowledged this reality in a speech that he delivered in Rostov-on-Don, capital of the North Caucasus krai, in June 1925. In his address, he declared that in contrast to Transcaucasia, with its three dominant nations—Armenians, Georgians, and Azerbaijanis—the North Caucasus lacked fully "formed nations" (*oformlennye natsii*) and that national identities were "only just beginning to take shape." "It is most interesting that Soviet power creates nations," he observed, adding that it "helps individual tribes take shape as nations." In the North Caucasus, he said, "we have tribes, not nations—we do not have a national self-consciousness, as such."[9] Significantly, Karachai scholar and Bolshevik revolutionary Umar Aliev endorsed Mikoyan's speech and used it as the preface of his 1926 book on the national question in the North Caucasus.[10]

The dissolution of the Gorskaia ASSR was already underway even before Mikoyan's arrival in the region. Throughout 1922, the Soviet government carved out new national entities for the Kabardins, Balkars, Karachai, and Cherkess from the Gorskaia ASSR.[11] By the end of 1922, Mikoyan believed that the situation in Chechnia warranted its separation from the Gorskaia ASSR as well. "The situation in Chechnia was very tense at that time," he recalled in his memoirs. "The remnants of anti-Soviet elements were operating throughout the area, and they encouraged Chechens to oppose Soviet power. They also organized bandits who attacked the outskirts of Groznyi as well as oil fields, railway stations, and trains. There were cases of killings of Soviet workers in Chechen villages. Many of these bands continued operating in Chechnia, even after banditry in our territory was largely eliminated."[12] In a report to the Central Committee on the Gorskaia ASSR from October 1, 1922, Mikoyan wrote that the situation in Chechnia and Ingushetia was "becoming progressively worse every day" and "inspires great concern." He stressed that the situation was so bad that representatives of the government could not even set foot in Chechnia "without risk to their own lives."[13] Citing the first chairman of the Chechen Revkom, Tashtemir El'derkhanov, Mikoyan wrote years later, "Not only was there no solid power throughout Chechnia, but there was no Soviet power at all."[14]

To the Armenian Mikoyan, the solution to these persistent problems seemed obvious. In order to firmly establish Soviet authority in Chechnia, he reasoned that the Chechens should feel that they had a stake in the system. To that end, he concluded, they must be granted political and cultural autonomy, independent of the Gorskaia ASSR. "It became impossible to tolerate such a situation anymore," Mikoyan later recalled. "Even in Chechnia itself, there were more and more urgent requests from the region's most active Party and non-Party comrades, especially from the Komsomol members. They wanted us to strengthen their power and grant them autonomy."[15] In fact, within the administration of the Gorskaia ASSR, there was scant Party representation among the Chechens and the Ingush. While the organs of governance were dominated by Ossetians and Russians, "not a single Chechen or Ingush sat on the local *sovnarkom*, and not a single Chechen was enrolled in the local party schools."[16] In his October 1922 report, Mikoyan noted that, in such an arrangement, "the Chechens and the Ingush do not feel themselves to be empowered. Instead, they feel themselves to be powerless and resentful in a republic ruled by Ossetians and Russians—representatives of numerically smaller peoples."[17] Mikoyan raised the autonomy question with Feliks Dzerzhinskii. "I told him that the reason for the tense situation in Chechnia was due to the lack of any real Soviet work there," he recounted. "The Mountain Republic cannot cope with this. It was necessary to establish a Chechen national autonomy, led by the Chechens themselves, and only then would the situation in Chechnia be somewhat defused. Dzerzhinskii supported us."[18] In Moscow, Mikoyan subsequently discussed his proposal with Stalin. "He reacted approvingly to the idea," Mikoyan recalled, "but warned of the necessity to exercise caution and to ascertain the true mood of the population."[19]

The next step came on October 9, 1922, when the Orgburo of the Central Committee established a commission to explore the possibility of granting autonomy to Chechnia, "in view of the new question put forth by Comrade Stalin" on the matter. The commission, which included Mikoyan, Kliment Voroshilov, and Sergei Kirov, was tasked "within ten days" to submit "concrete proposals to the Central Committee on measures to improve the situation in Chechnia" and to discuss "the advisability of separating Chechnia into an autonomous oblast'."[20] "The commission worked in Vladikavkaz and traveled to the area in order to become acquainted with the actual state of affairs," recalled Mikoyan. "The leading workers of the Gorskaia Republic took part in its work."[21] Once the commission completed its evaluation of the situation, it formally submitted a proposal to the Central Committee on October 22, 1922, to "separate Chechnia from the Gorskaia Republic into an autonomous oblast' with residence in the city of Groznyi, while excluding Groznyi from autonomous Chechnia." The commission further proposed establishing a Chechen Revkom, composed of seven Party members and six non-Party representatives, all of whom were ethnic Chechens, except for two Russian Party members.[22] The proposal for the creation of the Chechen AO was accepted by the Soviet government and realized on November 30, 1922, by the Presidium of the All-Russian Central Executive Committee.[23] As historian Alex Marshall observed, the establishment of an autonomous Chechnia "ironically also made these profoundly Soviet political figures [i.e., Mikoyan and his colleagues] the true founding fathers of the modern Chechen state."[24]

However, problems continued to persist. Although the Soviet government established Groznyi as the administrative center of Chechnia, it initially decided to maintain the predominately Russian city as a separate, self-governing entity.[25] Yet, the lack of a strong regional center left the new Chechen autonomy poor and Groznyi insecure. The Chechen Revkom did not have sufficient funds to support the construction of schools and vital infrastructure, and it received no funds from Groznyi's industrial production. The North Caucasus regional budget allocated some funds to the Chechen Revkom, but according to Mikoyan, "they were not great." Even worse, given that Groznyi was surrounded geographically by Chechnia, it was subject to frequent raids by Chechen bandits. El'derkhanov and other Chechen Revkom members brought these grievances to the attention of Mikoyan, who, in turn, raised these issues with Moscow:

> In Moscow, I told the Central Committee of the Party and the government that many Chechens regard Groznyi as an alien city. Therefore, the raids launched by the bandits on the city were not condemned by the Chechens. In fact, many of the bandits were well-known to everybody. They freely strutted around the villages like dashing heroes and the population viewed their banditry as a form of daring. Nothing will change until the Chechen people and the Chechen Soviet authorities begin to fight this banditry themselves. I told them that it was necessary to somehow interest the Chechens financially and to make the Chechen budget contingent on the success of the Groznyi oil industry. It was necessary for Groznyi to become part of autonomous Chechnia.[26]

Groznyi was eventually incorporated directly into the Chechen AO in November 1928, followed by much of the Cossack Sunzha okrug in April 1929.[27] The

1928 addition of Groznyi would strengthen the Chechen autonomy financially with its oil industry. However, until that time, Chechnia and Groznyi reached an agreement whereby a portion of the revenue from Groznyi's oil production would be allocated to the Chechen Revkom. The amount received from oil revenues would be tied to the damages that the bandits inflicted on Groznyi, thereby allowing Chechen leaders to blame the bandits for "robbing the budget of the autonomous oblast'" and thus depriving their compatriots of a valuable source of "income and funds necessary for the construction of schools, roads, hospitals, and more." This approach began to achieve results, as Revkom members traveled throughout Chechnia, talking to locals to underscore the damage that the bandits had inflicted on the oblast's economy. "This had a major impact," recalled Mikoyan. "The revenues of the Revkom increased, its influence strengthened, and the Chechen population became attracted to the fight against the bandits. The robberies in Groznyi almost stopped. This was a great achievement in improving the situation in Chechnia and Groznyi."[28]

Banditry (i.e., robbery or outlaw activity) persisted against local railway networks. The problem was resolved when Mikoyan, together with the Chechen Revkom and a prominent former bandit leader, worked to thwart the robbers. "By the end of 1924 and the beginning of 1925, calm came to Chechnia," Mikoyan recalled. However, although Chechnia was at peace, the fact that many Chechens remained armed was a concern to the Soviet government. In his memoirs, Mikoyan recollected a meeting with Dzerzhinskii in which he expressed concern that foreign powers—specifically Poland's Marshal Józef Piłsudski—would attempt to use Chechnia to destabilize the Soviet Union. "In order to be completely calm," Dzerzhinskii told Mikoyan, "it is necessary to disarm Chechnia." After securing the support of Stalin, Aleksei Rykov, and the Politburo, Mikoyan, together with the military and the OGPU, organized a plan to disarm Chechnia in the spring of 1925. Once executed, the operation went smoothly, with relatively few casualties on both sides.[29] According to Mikoyan's grandson Vladimir, the disarmament was a "dramatic event which demanded from my grandfather not only wisdom, a cool-head, and diplomacy, but personal bravery as well." Vladimir recounted the following from his grandfather's vivid retelling of this episode years later:

> [In] this unprecedented operation, Mikoyan rode horseback into the mountains in front of the military orchestra, while keeping the major military units far behind. In every village, he was meeting the respected elders, had long and calm discussions with them, and kept on launching something of a feast with dancing and music, displaying a friendly attitude. A lot of armaments and ammunition were surrendered voluntarily as a result. The elders even supplied Mikoyan with the information on the hiding place of Imam [Nazhmudin]

> Gotsinskii—the moral and military leader of the local bandits who allegedly was in contact with the British. He was surrounded and taken prisoner. That is when—in an almost bloodless but dangerous military operation, my grandfather's inborn diplomatic skills showed up![30]

In the process of securing Soviet authority in traditionally Sunni Muslim Chechnia, Mikoyan offered both "carrots" and "sticks" to the local population. While working with the military and security forces to disarm the bandits, he concurrently offered a generous position toward Chechen national and cultural expression, in line with the policy of *korenizatsiia*. Of his father's approach, Sergo Mikoyan later recalled that "rather than issue dry orders, he used persuasion, economic stimuli, appeals to century-old traditions and consideration for these traditions in his work."[31] In other circumstances and contexts, the extent of Mikoyan's generosity would be unthinkable. As Marshall noted, in February 1924, Mikoyan called attention to the fact that in Chechnia, "the Bolsheviks had departed further from 'pure' Soviet principles of governance than anywhere else in the country, up to and including the radical step of inviting representatives of the Islamic clergy into government."[32] Indeed, although a nonbeliever, Mikoyan was much more tolerant of religion than other Soviet leaders, a perspective influenced by his education in the Armenian Church and by the religiosity of his mother.[33]

The implementation of *korenizatsiia* in the Chechen milieu often followed practical needs. In the Chechnia of the NEP-era USSR, very few people knew Russian or any other language aside from their native Chechen. Therefore, to quickly organize new Party cadres to occupy administrative posts, the Soviet government placed greater stress on learning and perfecting Chechen. Mikoyan later recounted in 1925 that, although it was easier for Chechnia's religious leaders to oppose Russian in favor of Arabic, it was more difficult for them to oppose instruction in their national tongue. "When I was in Chechnia," Mikoyan recalled, "I said that you need to write in Chechen instead of Arabic. Not a single mullah could object, although almost all were supportive of Arabic and opposed the use of Chechen. However, if I said that we do not want Arabic, but we need Russian, then he would find something to say."[34] In the end, the efforts by the Soviet government "to publish textbooks in Chechen and to organize courses for teaching the Chechen script" ultimately "paid off," in Mikoyan's words.[35] Indeed, they did. *Korenizatsiia* in Chechnia, including the deferential approach toward the local language, contributed to the growth of Party cadres. As Marshall notes, by 1924, "61 per cent of workers in [Chechnia's] central apparatus [were] now of Chechen nationality," which was a striking contrast to its North Caucasus neighbors.[36]

In the years following Mikoyan's departure from the North Caucasus, the Soviet government merged the autonomous oblast' of the Chechens with that of their Nakh (Vainakh) cousins, the Ingush, into the Checheno-Ingush AO in 1934. By 1936, the combined Checheno-Ingush autonomy was elevated to the status of a full ASSR.[37] For his part, Mikoyan never forgot the region and never forgot his own advocacy for promoting the autonomy of the Chechens, the Ingush, and other national groups. At the risk of his own standing within the Soviet leadership, he even attempted to defend them, albeit to no avail, during their tragic deportation to Central Asia by Soviet authorities in 1944. The architect of the mass expulsion of Chechens, Ingush, and other peoples was Lavrentii Beria, Stalin's feared head of the NKVD. Beria proposed the wholesale internal deportation of these nationalities on the flimsy charge that the entire population was complicit in collaboration with the Germans. Although it was true that a handful of Chechens and Ingush collaborated with the Nazi invaders, it was likewise true that the majority of them were either supportive of or at least ambivalent toward the Soviet war effort. In fact, as the scholar Pavel Polian reminds us, Checheno-Ingushetia "virtually avoided occupation completely."[38] Such facts mattered little to the sadistic and ruthless Beria, whose "Bolshevism" masked his Georgian chauvinism. Beria himself demonstrated a desire to directly participate in the operation and traveled to Groznyi on February 20, 1944, to oversee the implementation of the deportations personally.[39] In the aftermath of the operation, the mountainous portions of Checheno-Ingushetia were gifted to Soviet Georgia, along with Mount Elbrus from the Balkars and the Karachai, exiled victims of another vicious deportation devised by Beria.[40]

Mikoyan recounted how the eviction of "entire nations from their ancestral lands" left a "depressing impression" on him.[41] In the Politburo, he alone dissented on the deportation plan, albeit on the grounds that it would harm the international reputation of the USSR.[42] He detailed his position in his memoirs:

> I objected to it. But Stalin explained that these peoples were disloyal to Soviet power and that they sympathized with the German fascists. I did not understand how it was possible to blame entire nations for almost treason, because there are Party organizations, communists, the mass of peasants, the Soviet intelligentsia! Finally, many were mobilized into the army and fought at the front. Several representatives of these peoples received the title of Hero of the Soviet Union!
>
> But Stalin was stubborn. And he insisted on the eviction of every single one of these peoples from their settled places.
>
> This was incredible, especially on the part of a man who was famous as the expert authority on the national question, a conductor of Leninist nationality policy. This was a departure from the class approach in the resolution of the national question. You cannot blame a whole nation for treason. Perhaps there were some reactionary elements who decided to collaborate with the Germans, as there were among the Russians, Ukrainians, Armenians, and others. However, these were only just a few cases, and they could be easily identified, tracked down, and investigated.[43]

Mikoyan's cautious objections were not limited to the Chechens and the Ingush. According to Dmitrii Koroliov and Mikoyan's son Sergo, the statesman opposed a similar proposal advanced by Beria to deport the peoples of Dagestan. In that case, he successfully "managed to convince Stalin to exclude Dagestan from the list of liquidated and banished republics."[44] However, such objections ultimately proved to be costly for Mikoyan and contributed to his demotion within Stalin's inner circle. Nor did it make a difference to the fate of the Chechens, the Ingush, and other peoples, beyond its symbolic significance.

The entire Chechen and Ingush population was ultimately uprooted and exiled to the distant lands of Kazakhstan and Kirgizia. The operation, devised by Beria and approved by Stalin, was known as *chechevitsa* (lentil), a phonetic play on the word "Chechen" in Russian.[45] To Chechens, it was known as the *aardakh* (exodus, literally "lead out").[46] The deportees were crammed into trains and shipped to various parts of Soviet Central Asia. Many died along the way from hunger, disease, and cold. Others who lived in remote villages and who could not be easily evacuated were simply murdered outright by Beria's men, in order to finish the job within eight days. The wholesale burning of these villages and the people within them was "their barbaric method of choice," in the words of Polian.[47] Much of the core territory of the former Checheno-Ingush ASSR became part of a new province stripped entirely of any Chechen or Ingush identity, known simply as the Groznyi oblast'. The former republic's remaining areas were divided among neighboring Georgia, North Ossetia, and Dagestan.[48]

In the end, over one-third of the Chechen and Ingush deportees perished.[49] Beria's NKVD officers were given wartime honors by the Soviet state for their "services." In the Checheno-Ingush lands, all Nakh toponyms were changed by Soviet authorities.[50] Officially, Checheno-Ingushetia, like the autonomous entities of the Karachai, Balkars, and Kalmyks, was completely wiped off the map by Stalin and Beria. In their places of destination, the deported peoples were forced to live in restricted "special settlements." Worse, at the end of the war, banishment in exile became defined by the state as "eternal, without the right to return to their native places" in the decrees of the Presidium of the Supreme Soviet of November 26, 1948, and October 9, 1951. Any escape was to be punished by "20 years of penal servitude."[51] The trauma and violence of this period deeply impacted the peoples of the North Caucasus and continues to impact them to this day.

A MEETING WITH MIKOYAN

The circumstances created by the deaths of Stalin and Beria in 1953 presented new opportunities to redress the deportation of the North Caucasus nationalities. As early as July 18, 1953, following Beria's arrest, a group of Ingush representatives sent an appeal to Malenkov and Voroshilov from Frunze, Kirgizia. In it, they applauded the Soviet government's actions against Beria and requested their "return to the fraternal family of peoples of the USSR, with equal rights," and the removal of "all restrictions against us."[52] By the beginning of 1954, Soviet officials were discussing the possibilities of lifting certain restrictions on "special settlers," such as the exiled Ingush.[53] Then, on July 5, 1954, the all-union Council of Ministers adopted the resolution "On the Removal of Certain Restrictions on the Legal Status of Special Settlers." The act provided for the "right of freedom of movement to any point of the country on a general basis" and for the cancellation of punishments imposed on special settlers "for violations of the regime in their places of settlement." It also provided for the deregistration of special settler children sixteen years of age or younger, and it allowed children older than sixteen to attend educational institutions in any part of the country.[54] However, the resolution was not applicable to certain deported groups, specifically Western Ukrainian nationalists, "Andersovtsy," Jehovah's Witnesses, and "nationalists" and "kulaks" from the Baltic republics, Western Belorussia, and the Pskov oblast'. Moreover, the special settlers were still required to register with the Interior Ministry once every year.[55] A subsequent decree of the Presidium of the Supreme Soviet on July 13 officially canceled the infamous decree of November 26, 1948, that defined the exile of the deported groups as "eternal," without the right to return. It further noted that unauthorized departure (or escape) from the special settlements would still be punished, but in accordance with the laws of the union republics and not all-union law.[56] Both the July 5 resolution and the July 13 decree were confirmed in an order issued by the Soviet Interior Ministry on July 16.[57]

These steps were followed by more resolutions issued by the Presidium of the Central Committee throughout 1955. Among the special settlers, registration restrictions were lifted on March 23 for military conscripts; on May 9, for members and candidate members of the CPSU; and in November, for participants in the Great Patriotic War and women married to local residents, among other groups.[58] June 29 of that same year saw the adoption of the consequential resolution on "measures to strengthen mass political work among the special settlers." As this act noted, it was built on the foundations established by the July 1954 resolution, which "significantly expanded the civil rights of the special settlers" and "created the necessary conditions for the further improvement of their material and living conditions, as well as their cultural development, advancing their engagement in active social-political life." The text described the political distrust and discrimination that the deported peoples faced from the local authorities, as well as their exclusion from local Party politics. It argued that such attitudes "run counter to the Party line and do great harm to the cause of the communist education of the working people."[59] It also detailed the "unsatisfactory" efforts to carry out political education and cultural work among the deported peoples. To remedy these problems, the Central Committee instructed the local authorities hosting the deported populations to correct all shortcomings, detailing ways to improve ideological work and education. It called on officials to "condemn and abandon" the "wrong and harmful" view of these peoples as "second class citizens."[60] Finally, on December 13, 1955, the Presidium of the Supreme Soviet passed one more major resolution—the decree lifting restrictions on the deported Germans. The latter marked the first major decree specifically concerning a deported nationality, although the Germans would not be compensated for their property losses and would not be permitted to return to their original places of settlement.[61]

These legislative acts set the stage for February 1956, when Khrushchev, in his condemnation of Stalin at the CPSU Twentieth Party Congress, signaled a major change in policy by strongly denouncing the deportations:

> Comrades, let us now turn to some other facts. The Soviet Union is rightfully considered to be a model multiethnic state because we have in practice secured the equality and friendship of all the peoples living in our great motherland.
>
> That makes all the more monstrous those acts initiated by Stalin that constituted gross violations of the basic Leninist principles of the national policy of the Soviet state. Here we have in mind the mass expulsions of entire nations from their native places, together with communists and Komsomol members, without any exception. These expulsions were not dictated by any military considerations.[62]

Khrushchev specifically singled out the liquidation of the homelands of the Karachai, Kalmyks, and Balkars, as well as the Chechens and the Ingush, all of whom were "expelled to remote areas," even as "constant breakthroughs on the fronts of the Great Patriotic War determined the outcome of the war in favor of the Soviet Union." The jovial Ukrainian-born first secretary then jested that "the Ukrainians avoided this fate only because there were too many of them and there was no place to send them. Otherwise, he [Stalin] would have expelled them too."[63] Behind the scenes, Mikoyan strongly encouraged Khrushchev's discussion of the wartime expulsions. On the eve of the congress, he stressed that the condemnation of Stalin had to include discussion not only of Lenin's Testament but also of Stalin's violations of the nationality policy, an implicit reference to the deportations. Referring to opposition from Molotov on the matter, Mikoyan inquired, "Why doesn't Viacheslav want to publicize [Stalin's abuses of] the nationality issue?"[64]

Khrushchev's open condemnation was followed by the gradual implementation of resolutions by the Presidiums of the Central Committee and the Supreme Soviet on the lifting of special settlement restrictions on the Kalmyks,

Crimean Tatars, Balkars, Turks, Kurds, and Hemshin Armenians.[65] These moves prompted hope and action from the representatives of other repressed nationalities. In March 1956, only a few weeks after his address before the Twentieth Party Congress, Khrushchev had already received a letter from nine Ingush writers and intellectuals, lauding his speech. Their intent was to express the "thoughts, feelings, and hopes of the entire Ingush people" for redress and return to their homeland. After highlighting the Ingush contribution to the October Revolution, the authors of the letter strongly condemned the "slander against the Ingush people" by Beria and lamented their deportation to Central Asia, for which they also held the "monster Beria" directly responsible.[66] Yet, despite these "savage actions," the authors maintained that Beria and the former Stalinist authorities were only "temporarily successful" in their intentions. "It is now clear where truth and justice stand," they wrote. Significantly, although advocating for the return of the Ingush, the authors voiced opposition to displacing those who had moved to the former Ingush territories since 1944. "We know, just as our nation knows," they wrote, "that now people live on our lands and that it would be unjust to bring ruin to them and to drive them out of the places where they have settled. But we also realize, as our entire nation does, that there will be enough space in our native land both for our people and for those who live there now." As a resolution, they advocated allowing the settlers to retain the properties that they held. "Our people will not quarrel over homes and property," the authors pledged. "Let all that remain with those who now own them. We will build new homes, better than those that we had. Through honest work, we will acquire everything that a Soviet person needs for a prosperous and cultural life."[67]

As deliberations continued behind the scenes, Chechen and Ingush leaders appealed to Mikoyan. Party member and former raikom Party secretary Sultan Nalaev and the doctor Sultan Khamiev penned a joint letter to the statesman, which they sent on March 30. "The expulsion of the Chechens and the Ingush was accompanied by monstrous terror, humiliation, and looting," they wrote. "These are just a few of the dark acts and hostile deeds of the fascist-plunderer bands of Beria and his accomplices. The atrocities of these sworn, despicable bandits of Beria and his like-minded associates [Bogdan] Kobulov, [Shalva] Tsereteli, and others, will remain in memory for many years."[68] After detailing these crimes and highlighting the service of the Chechens and the Ingush to the USSR in the Great Patriotic War, Nalaev and Khamiev directly appealed to Mikoyan for the restoration of their autonomous republic:

> For a long time, moral oppression and mockery have caused immense damage to the collective psyche of our people. Therefore, colossal propaganda and organizational work is needed among the Chechens and the

> Ingush to eliminate this moral trauma once and for all, and such effective work can only be accomplished by the restoration of the Checheno-Ingush Republic.
>
> At the present time, having destroyed Beria's gang and the theory of the cult of personality, the Communist Party and the Soviet government have created the conditions for the further strengthening of the *druzhba narodov* of the USSR. It seems that it is the right time to ask the Presidium of the CPSU Central Committee and the Soviet government to restore our lawful Checheno-Ingush Republic on its former territory.[69]

Nalaev and Khamiev expressed hope that their request would be soon satisfied by the Soviet leadership. "People dream of the places where their grandfathers and great-grandfathers were born, raised, and worked," they wrote. "The restoration of the Checheno-Ingush Republic is the cherished dream of the Chechens and the Ingush. The restoration of the republic will open broad possibilities for the Chechen and Ingush peoples for intensive progress in the economy, in culture, and in politics. Furthermore, it will finally eliminate the moral trauma that Beria and his conspiratorial group inflicted on them."[70]

Nalaev and Khamiev likewise took the opportunity to praise Khrushchev's denunciation of the deportations and his condemnation of the abolition of Checheno-Ingushetia. "The Checheno-Ingush people were waiting for the truth and they finally received it," they said. "Recently, in institutions and enterprises, we acquainted ourselves with the letter of the Central Committee of the CPSU. Then, when we heard the truthful words of Comrade Khrushchev, feeling fraternal sympathy in those words, we, the Chechens and the Ingush, filled with joy, could not control ourselves at that moment. Tears of happiness and joy flowed from us." They concluded by expressing confidence that the Chechen and Ingush peoples "would return to their homeland in the near future and stand under the common Leninist banner of the multinational peoples of the USSR and go forth toward the shining heights of communism."[71]

Internally, the letters to Khrushchev and Mikoyan prompted an immediate reaction from the state. On April 9, 1956, Head of the Department of Party Bodies Evgenii Gromov, Head of the Department of Science and Higher Education Vladimir Kirillin, and Head of the Department of Culture Dmitrii Polikarpov issued a letter to the Central Committee of the CPSU on the Ingush appeal to Khrushchev. It underscored the work that had been accomplished in the educational and cultural spheres of the deported peoples since the July 1954 and June 1955 resolutions. These included the publication of newspapers and political literature in the Chechen and Ingush languages. Moreover, Gromov, Kirillin, and Polikarpov recommended the formation of Chechen and Ingush dance ensembles and the publication of works of Chechen and Ingush national literature in their native tongues.[72]

However, despite the March 17 letter and Khrushchev's strong words at the Twentieth Party Congress, the authors noted opposition from state officials on the lifting of restrictions on the Chechen and Ingush deportees to return to their former places of residence. "With regard to lifting the restrictions on the Ingush and the Chechens," the authors wrote, "Prosecutor General Comrade Rudenko, Chairman of the KGB Comrade Serov, Minister of Internal Affairs Comrade [Nikolai] Dudorov, and Minister of Justice Comrade [Konstantin] Gorshenin consider it best to temporarily refrain from making a decision on this matter." They noted that their position was informed by the "improper behavior of some part of the Ingush and the Chechens in their places of settlement, including the disruption of public order on their part, up to factual manifestation of banditry." They further stressed that it "must be kept in mind that in all cases of lifting restrictions on citizens of other nationalities, evicted by the respective decisions, it was specifically indicated that they have no right to return to their former places of residence." Therefore, they concluded, "it would be inappropriate to make an exception for the Ingush and Chechens in this respect."[73]

However, this position began to change as early as the following month. On May 17, Gromov, together with Valentin Zolotukhin, then deputy head of the Department of Administrative Bodies, issued a joint note to the CPSU Central Committee on the deported nationalities. The authors wrote that the Departments of Party and Administrative Bodies of the Central Committee had received "121 letters, which were signed by 6,565 citizens" of Chechen, Ingush, Karachai, Balkar, and Crimean Tatar background. "These letters," they wrote, "articulate requests for the return of the evicted citizens to their former places of residence and the restoration of their formerly existing autonomous republics and oblasts." Gromov and Zolotukhin further noted that "as of now, restrictions on special settlements have been lifted for the Kalmyks, Balkars, and Crimean Tatars, and a draft has been presented for lifting restrictions for the Karachai as well." Consequently, they wrote that restrictions remained in place for only the Ingush and the Chechens. "We would consider it appropriate," they maintained, "to charge a commission consisting of Comrades Rudenko, Serov, Dudorov, Gorshenin, and Zolotukhin with considering this issue, keeping in mind the possibility of lifting the restrictions on these nationalities." Their recommendations on the restoration of the autonomous republics and oblasts remained very conservative. Rather than restoring these entities within the boundaries of the Russian SFSR, they advised consulting the Central Committees of the Central Asian republics on this matter, "taking into account that, if the question arose of restoring one or more autonomous oblasts, then this should be done within the above-mentioned union republics."[74]

Then, in May, one of the signatories of the March 17 letter to Khrushchev, Ingush writer Idris Bazorkin, joined with Chechen linguist Iunus Desheriev to organize a delegation of the deported peoples to meet with high officials in Moscow.

Unfortunately, they were unable to find representatives from every deported nationality, despite Desheriev's best efforts. "The idea of organizing a delegation of representatives of all repressed peoples was not successful," he recalled. "In Moscow, I turned to one Balkar. He categorically objected to the organization of such a delegation and told me that 'this is none of our business.' One Crimean Tatar essentially said the same thing." Desheriev wrote that they feared "new repressions." He likewise recounted meeting with the retired Kalmyk Colonel-General Oka Gorodovikov, who "regularly relaxed" at Nikolai Tomskii's monument to Nikolai Gogol facing Arbat Square. When Desheriev offered Gorodovikov the position of leader of the delegation to the Kremlin, he cautiously declined "due to poor health."[75] Therefore, Desheriev, Bazorkin, and others decided to express their grievances as an exclusively Nakh (i.e., Checheno-Ingush) delegation.[76]

Alongside Bazorkin, Desheriev worked to carefully select the members of the group, paying particular attention to the "social composition of the delegation, as well as to the coverage of all the major areas of their settlement." The delegation was technically unofficial, as an official delegation would need to be composed of elected representatives. As Desheriev stressed, "We did not dare organize such an 'elected' delegation, as the local [i.e., republican] authorities would impede the holding of such elections, and appeal to higher authorities, requiring official permission."[77] The final Checheno-Ingush delegation consisted of fourteen representatives.[78] The group was "careful and endeavored not to advertise everything that it aspired to achieve." One month later, on June 9, 1956, the delegation arrived at the Spasskii Gate to meet with Mikoyan at the Kremlin and request the restoration their autonomous republic.[79] They originally sought an audience with Khrushchev, but the first secretary was busy attending to Yugoslavia's Josip Broz Tito, who then visiting the USSR for the first time since the Tito-Stalin split.[80] It was therefore left to Mikoyan to meet with the group. After a thorough inspection by the guard, the delegation arrived at the Soviet House of Government at 3:20 p.m.[81] At 5:00 p.m., they were invited to enter and meet Mikoyan in his office. After shaking hands with the delegates, Mikoyan gestured for them to sit at a large table. Mullah Abbas Gaisumov spoke first. He began to outline the goals of the delegation and expressed gratitude for the reception and for the political rehabilitation of their peoples, with Desheriev acting as interpreter. Sitting at the head of the table, Mikoyan listened carefully, while an assistant, Romanenko, took notes at a nearby desk. Bazorkin recounted that after Gaisumov had finished, Mikoyan "immediately replied that Stalin was to blame for our tragedy and that there was no need to thank the Party, as the Party was obliged to correct its mistakes."[82]

Gaisumov then gave the floor to Bazorkin, who read the letter of the delegation to Mikoyan. "I was agitated in certain places and stopped three times for a few seconds, but no one interrupted me or interfered," Bazorkin recounted. He added that he "finished firmly and confidently read this document, which could have been better or worse, but spoke firmly enough to the representative of the authorities that we are alive, that we want to live, and that, sooner or later, we will live like everyone else."[83] Then Desheriev spoke, outlining the essence of the delegation's demands to the Soviet government, which consisted of "a condemnation of the repression against the deported peoples, their return to their original homelands, and the restoration of their national autonomies."[84] To emphasize the tragedy of the Chechens and the Ingush, he further spoke about "the misfortune of the people, about his own misfortune, about how even here, in Moscow, he was poorly treated because of his nationality, just like it was for those who lived in Central Asia."[85] After the speech, Desheriev presented Mikoyan with the letter and the appeal of the delegation, to be given to Khrushchev. Taking the two documents, Mikoyan told Desheriev and the others, "You did well to explain all your proposals in detail. I will hand them over to Comrade Khrushchev and, of course, I will support you."[86]

According to Desheriev, Mikoyan inquired about the fate of Idris Ziazikov, the first leader of the short-lived Ingush AO and a victim of Stalin's repressions. "His widow Zhanetta is with us," responded Desheriev. Zhanetta came forward and "spoke about the tragic fate of her late husband."[87] Magomed Shataev and Dzhabrail El'murziev also spoke at the meeting. Zhanetta acted as an interpreter for El'murziev, who "expressed resentment for what had been done to us and hope that everything would be corrected, asking the question: 'What should we say to the people?'" She posed the same question to Mikoyan in her own remarks.[88] All the speakers dwelled on "the difficult material situation and the moral-psychological suffering of the repressed peoples." Amid these statements, Mikoyan's phone suddenly rang. He picked it up and told the caller that he could not be bothered. "I am accepting the Checheno-Ingush delegation now." Gaisumov leaned over to Desheriev and quietly told him in Chechen, "So now we have become the Checheno-Ingush delegation!" "Before that," recalled Desheriev, "we never dared call ourselves the 'Checheno-Ingush delegation.' We could be asked: who directed you, who authorized you? This was entirely our own initiative, which was subsequently warmly and gratefully supported not only by the Chechen and Ingush peoples, but also by the Balkar, Kalmyk, and Karachai peoples."[89]

The accounts of the meeting by Desheriev and Bazorkin differ in their impressions of Mikoyan's reception of the delegation. Desheriev, who recorded his memories of the meeting decades later, wrote that Mikoyan greeted the visiting delegation "warmly."[90] By contrast, in a letter to his daughter Aza from June 23, 1956, Bazorkin recounted that Mikoyan, although sympathetic to his guests, was guarded and cautious, maintaining his composure throughout the meeting and careful not to express his own sentiments overtly. The statesman would have been well aware of the behind-the-scenes efforts to remedy the issue, as well as the disagreements over the matter within the Soviet leadership. The Ingush author recounted that Mikoyan "sat almost motionless" and "listened calmly, but not indifferently." "He showed none of his disposition toward us, nor did he show any unfriendliness," Bazorkin wrote. "There was neither one, nor the other." He added that Mikoyan was "dry, but not impolite" with "not a single smile" and "not a drop of warmth." In fact, he recalled that Mikoyan "did not utter a single human word," nor did he "allow himself to speak to a people who had to endure and suffer so much over the years." Overall, Bazorkin felt that Mikoyan's cautious diplomatic demeanor was intended "not to leave us any impression of his personal attitude on this issue."[91]

The meeting with Mikoyan lasted one hour.[92] At the conclusion of the meeting at 6:00 p.m., Mikoyan called the director of the Kremlin Armory Chamber and "asked him to retain the chamber staff in order to give the Checheno-Ingush delegation the opportunity to visit the Armory." The delegation was "moved by such attention," given the uncertainty about their potential return and the lingering sense of stigma felt among deported nationalities.[93] However, they left the meeting with mixed sentiments. Desheriev felt confident that the meeting had firmly secured the restoration of the Checheno-Ingush ASSR. However, Bazorkin was more pessimistic and much less certain about Mikoyan's ability to influence the final decision on the matter. In his 1956 letter to his daughter Aza, he wrote,

> I don't know how it will all end. I have no confidence in anything, but I do know one thing: that this man [Mikoyan] . . . can now, after our meeting, say in his soul to himself, "But still, the Ingush and the Chechens live, they have pride, they have patriotism, they are small, but not so small, they have people."
>
> And that's enough. If the outcome is not destined to be good, then at least we let them know that we are certainly not fools and that we understand everything.[94]

Once the delegation reached the Armory, Desheriev, who had already visited the museum, left the group to organize a dinner reception to assess the outcome of the meeting.[95] Meanwhile, a member of the Armory staff took the rest of the group on a tour of the chamber for two hours.[96] Afterward, Desheriev invited the group to conclude the day, perhaps fittingly, at the legendary Armenian restaurant Ararat in Moscow to discuss the meeting. The dinner commenced with a prayer led by Gaisumov and Ingush Mullah Aki Mataev. Desheriev recounted that all those present were in a "wonderful mood."[97] Bazorkin, however, was more reflective, stressing to Aza that "this was not a drinking party or a revelry after a victory won." "It seemed to us that we did not make any outstanding missteps in this enterprise," he recalled. "We agreed right there—to tell the people only what we heard from Mikoyan. For this, we decided to record all circumstances and answers fresh from our memories."[98]

Meanwhile, Desheriev concluded that the meeting was a success. In his memoirs, written many years later, he wrote,

> These days will forever remain in the memory of the members of the first Checheno-Ingush delegation, in our memory, in the memory of the people. It was essentially the first delegation of repressed peoples.
>
> After several telephone calls by members of the delegation from Moscow to their places of residence in Central Asia and Kazakhstan, word spread about the meeting of the delegation of repressed peoples in the Kremlin and the attention shown to it. Even the members of the delegation who did not have time to return already joyfully greeted one another and organized meetings and rallies, expressing their gratitude to Khrushchev, Mikoyan, the Soviet government, and the Twentieth Party Congress of the CPSU for exposing the cult of personality and condemning repressions.
>
> Returning from Moscow, the members of the delegation were received solemnly. The "appeal" to the Presidium of the Supreme Soviet, the Central Committee of the CPSU, and the Council of Ministers was propagated and distributed throughout almost all the places of residence of the representatives of the repressed peoples.[99]

Desheriev subsequently met with representatives of other deported nationalities to tell them about the outcome of the Kremlin reception in the days after the meeting. Returning to Arbat Square, he met again with Colonel-General Gorodovikov, who "became immediately interested" in the results of the meeting and inquired about who had received the representatives. "I told him about the reception of our delegation by Mikoyan, about the materials that we delivered to him, and about Mikoyan's promise to support us," recalled Desheriev. Gorodovikov was stunned. "Mikoyan promised to support your delegation?" he asked pointedly. Desheriev repeated his "words about Mikoyan's support" and immediately urged Gorodovikov to organize a Kalmyk delegation to arrange an official Kremlin reception, with the same mission. "Gorodovikov was thrilled," he recalled. "He thanked me for the information and stood up. 'I will go and see how it turns out. So long.' A few days later, the Kalmyk delegation arrived in Moscow. Then a Balkar delegation, then a Karachai one."[100] The news of the successful meeting was well received not only by other repressed peoples but also by other Soviet nationalities more generally. "All the peoples of the Soviet Union (that is, the overwhelming majority) approved and welcomed the condemnation of the brutal and historically unprecedented repressions against entire nations," Desheriev wrote. "My business trips to Central Asia, the Caucasus, the Baltic states, Ukraine, and Moldavia convinced me of this. Such was the time of the so-called 'Khrushchev Thaw.'"[101]

In terms of the deported nationalities, the Karachai had appealed to Mikoyan directly even before their in-person meeting. Like the Chechens and the Ingush, they too had a long-standing relationship with the statesman. In his capacity as the first secretary of the North Caucasus, Mikoyan consistently maintained a "special concern for the cultural and holistic development" of the Karachai, in the words of his son Sergo. He actively backed the creation of the Karachai capital city, Karachaevsk, and when he left the region to assume the post of Soviet trade minister in Moscow, the local leadership officially named the town Mikoyan-Shakhar in gratitude for his support.[102] During the Thaw, Karachai leaders once again turned to Mikoyan for assistance. On May 21, a group of 1,163 exiled Karachai addressed a letter to him, requesting the restoration of their homeland and expressing their hope for a swift return. After briefly enumerating the benefits of Soviet power for their people, the Karachai representatives raised the issue of their ill-treatment at the hands of Beria. "All these successes and achievements of the Karachai people," the authors wrote, "were eliminated by the hostile activities of the despicable gang of Beria and other enemies. As a result, we were subjected to political, economic, and national humiliation. We were considered criminals only because we are Karachai by nationality. This created a situation in which one would assume a Karachai to be a bandit and so on. All of this artificially incited national strife."[103]

However, the signatories to the letter "confidently expected that our Communist Party would give weighty words to this unheard-of indiscriminate eviction of an entire people under the conditions of Soviet power, because in the country of Soviets, the country of Lenin, such a situation could not exist for long." As with the Chechens and the Ingush, the Karachai were likewise "looking forward to the Twentieth Party Congress" and were not disappointed by its results. Khrushchev's condemnation of the deportations and of the abolition of autonomous republics elicited "boundless joy and enthusiasm" from the Karachai, who expressed "gratitude to the Presidium of the Central Committee and our entire Party." The signatories were confident of an imminent resolution, expressing hope for the restoration of their homeland in the North Caucasus, "thereby rehabilitating our nation as an equal member of the family of the peoples of the USSR." Referring to Mikoyan's tenure as the first secretary of the North Caucasus during NEP, they added, "Dear Anastas Ivanovich! Many of us know you personally, and we all know you as the former secretary of our Party kraikom. We appeal to you, as a member of the Presidium of the CPSU Central Committee who knows us, so that you can objectively and justly assist in resolving our request, i.e., to return us to the North Caucasus."[104]

Such appeals would have a cumulative impact on the Soviet leadership's decision to act. Indeed, the May 21 letter was not to be the last appeal that Mikoyan received from the Karachai. Only a week later, on May 28, a group of Karachai communists sent a similar letter, addressed not only to Mikoyan but also to Voroshilov, Malenkov, Brezhnev, and Nikolai Beliaev.[105] This letter and another appeal from a group of Kalmyk deportees were both reviewed by members of the CPSU Central Committee Presidium on June 21. The resulting resolution led to the establishment of a commission of the Presidium of the CPSU Central Committee, under the chairmanship of Mikoyan, tasked with "studying questions related to the rehabilitation of the repressed peoples."[106] "After the death of Stalin," Mikoyan recounted, "we organized a commission under my chairmanship on the return of unjustly evicted nationalities to their homelands, to their native lands, for the restoration of their statehood."[107] It would become informally known as the "Mikoyan Commission."[108]

THE MIKOYAN COMMISSION

The Mikoyan commission intensified efforts to remedy the plight of most of the deported nationalities in the wake of the meetings and appeals. The task was well suited for Mikoyan, especially given his experience in the North Caucasus and his role in determining the original boundaries of the region's autonomous entities during the NEP era. On July 5–6, the Presidium of the Central Committee met again in Moscow to discuss the report of the commission on the appeals of the deported peoples. In the end, it resolved (a) that the Mikoyan commission "continue its work and prepare specific proposals" and (b) to "remove special settlement restrictions on the Chechens, Ingush, and Karachai on the same grounds as was done with the Germans, Kalmyks, Balkars, and Crimean Tatars."[109] However, as the work of the commission proceeded, it soon became apparent that the potential return of the Chechens, Ingush, and Karachai was highly contested within the Soviet government. In particular, the security forces opposed the return of these peoples to their indigenous lands. One week after the July 5–6 Presidium meeting, the CPSU Central Committee Secretariat solicited recommendations from Gromov, Iosif Shikin, Viktor Churaev, Zolotukhin, Rudenko, Serov, and Dudorov on the appeals of the Chechen, Ingush, Balkar, Karachai, Kalmyk, and German deportees. It included the March letter from Nalaev and Khamiev to Mikoyan as a reference.[110] However, their recommendations were apparently much more conservative than Mikoyan and others had hoped. A resulting decree, issued on the following Monday (July 16) by the Presidium of the Supreme Soviet and signed by Voroshilov and Nikolai Pegov, lifted the special settlement restrictions on the Chechens, Ingush, and Karachai. However, it still prohibited these deportees from formally returning to their former places of residence.[111]

The July 16 decree effectively met the deportees halfway by removing restrictions but stopping short of restoring their autonomous republics and allowing their return to their homelands. This compromise decision likely originated from internal disagreements on the matter, with Mikoyan favoring the return of the deportees but encountering resistance from Serov and other security officials. The reasons for their opposition remain unclear, although available evidence indicates that they primarily feared potential destabilization in the North Caucasus, which they claimed would have resulted from the "improper behavior" on the part of "some" Chechen and Ingush returnees.[112] Moreover, many security officials had played key roles in the wartime deportations, most prominently Serov, who served as Beria's deputy. Mikoyan even went so far as to propose the idea of revoking the awards that Serov had bestowed on those officers and military personnel who participated in the deportations during the war. They were subsequently stripped of their honors.[113]

Predictably, the July 16 decision proved too little for the deportees, who continued to challenge the restrictions from below. Chechen, Ingush, and Karachai exiles in Kazakhstan and Kirgizia made clear their strong disagreement with the decision as soon as it was officially announced by the Soviet Interior Ministry on July 18.[114] A flurry of additional letters from Chechen, Ingush, Karachai, and Kalmyk deportees requesting return to their original places of residence and the restoration of their autonomous republics prompted further action from the government. On September 7, officials tasked with reviewing these letters sent a report to the CPSU Central Committee's Mikhail Pervukhin in which they revealed the determination of the deportees to return to their former residences anyway, regardless of official decree.[115] The sheer volume of the return was such that "by October–November 1956, 80–100 [train] tickets were sold to Caucasians in Akmolinsk *each day*."[116] Arriving from Kazakhstan and Kirgizia, the unofficial returnees encountered open hostility from local officials in the Dagestan ASSR and the Groznyi oblast'. Letters were sent to Soviet high officials from Russians as well as Avars and other Dagestanis complaining about the unauthorized return of the Chechens and the Ingush. The authors of the report to Pervukhin noted that, according to local officials, six to seven hundred Chechen and Ingush families (2,500 people) arrived in the Dagestan ASSR, while thirty to forty families arrived in the Groznyi oblast'.[117] The strong opposition to their return from different national communities anticipated the territorial and property disputes and conflicts to come.

In response to the unofficial return of Chechens and Ingush and the growing tension with neighboring national groups, Pervukhin called for a discussion on the issue at the Presidium of the Central Committee in a September 8 resolution. "I consider it necessary to discuss the questions raised in these letters at the

Central Committee Presidium," he said.[118] The situation was very serious, and it quickly became apparent that the July decree was not enough to resolve this issue, which threatened to destabilize the North Caucasus. Therefore, the Central Committee decided to change tack and instead began to explore the possibility of restoring the autonomous republics of the deported peoples and officializing their return to their former places of residence. On September 15, exactly one week after Pervukhin's resolution, Gromov sent a report to the Mikoyan commission on the feasibility of officially returning the deportees and restoring their republics. The report was based on the findings of a group of employees of the Central Committee apparatus, the Presidium of the Supreme Soviet, and the Ministry of Internal Affairs.[119] Overall, the study concluded that return and restoration were indeed feasible and that the former homelands of the deportees were underpopulated and unevenly developed. In the case of the former Kalmyk, Karachai, and Balkar territories, Gromov noted that "as a rule, the local population has a positive attitude toward the arrival of these peoples." However, in the former Checheno-Ingush lands, he stressed that "Party and Soviet bodies, as well as many residents in the Groznyi oblast', the Dagestan ASSR, and the North Ossetian ASSR, categorically object to the return of the Chechens and the Ingush." Gromov further added that, although Soviet Kirgizia was open to allowing the deportees to return to their native lands, other republics with deportees, such as Kazakhstan, were reluctant to let them go "due to the lack of labor force."[120] Proposals by the Central Committee representatives to establish autonomous units for the Chechens, Ingush, Kalmyks, Karachai, and Balkars in their places of exile received an "extremely negative" reaction from these nationalities.[121]

Deliberations continued until finally, on October 16, 1956, Averkii Aristov, Aleksandr Gorkin, and Supreme Soviet employees P. Pigalev, M. Ponomarev, and A. Fomenko presented a draft resolution to Mikoyan on "the restoration of the national autonomy of the Kalmyks, Karachai, Balkars, Chechens, and Ingush." This draft strongly condemned the deportations as a "gross violation of the basic principles" of the Soviet nationality policy and "one of the manifestations of the cult of personality alien to Marxism-Leninism." Even more significantly, the draft underscored that earlier rehabilitation measures for the deportees "cannot be considered sufficient." Such measures, the authors stressed, "do not resolve the issue of the complete rehabilitation of unjustly evicted peoples, as well as the restoration of their equality among other nations. Furthermore, they do not resolve the lack of conditions for the development of these peoples and the return and restoration of their autonomies." With that, the draft resolution proclaimed the decision of the CPSU Central Committee and the Council of Ministers to restore the autonomous units of the Kalmyks, Karachai, Balkars, Chechens, and Ingush "within the next three to four years." Regarding the Chechens and the Ingush, the resolution noted the presence of the new populations in their native territory that had arrived there since 1944. It called for the formation of a government commission, including Soviet state and Party officials as well as Chechen and Ingush representatives, to determine the boundaries of the restored Checheno-Ingush ASSR.[122]

The draft formed the basis for the official resolution on the rehabilitation of the repressed peoples adopted by the Presidium of the CPSU Central Committee on November 24, 1956.[123] In addition to the creation of the commission to determine the boundaries, the resolution called for the organized return of all those deported and for the active participation of representatives of the repressed nationalities to assist with the restoration of their autonomous republics. These representatives were organized by the Soviet government into "organizing committees" (*orkomitety*).[124] "During the period of the restoration of the [Checheno-Ingush] republic," recalled committee member Dziiaudin Mal'sagov, "the orgkom was to assume the functions of the government and the Supreme Soviet. Muslim Gairbekovich Gairbekov became the chairman, and they appointed me to be his deputy. Abdul-Hamid Tangiev was likewise included in the orgkom in order to be nominated to the post of the Chairman of the Supreme Soviet of the republic in the future."[125] In the specific case of Checheno-Ingushetia, the decision to officially restore the autonomous republic was accompanied by efforts by the Soviet Interior Ministry to slow down the mass flow of unofficial returnees and to organize a more orderly return of the Chechens and the Ingush that would minimize the potential for conflict as much as possible.[126]

However, not all deported nations were given the opportunity to be rehabilitated. Significant exceptions were made for the Crimean Tatars and the Volga Germans.[127] Although the civil rights of these groups and the restrictions on their movements were restored by the Soviet authorities, they were "not granted a legally formulated right of return to their homelands."[128] In its official explanation, the government noted that both peoples already had "homelands" outside of their respective regions—the Tatar ASSR in the case of the Crimean Tatars and Germany in the case of the Volga Germans, with the latter already having a scattered presence throughout the USSR. The November 1956 resolution stated that it was "inappropriate to grant national autonomy to the Tatars who previously lived in the Crimea, given that the former Crimean ASSR was not an autonomous republic for the Tatars alone, but rather a multinational republic in which the Tatars made up less than one fifth of the total population." The resolution further maintained that "within the composition of the Russian SFSR, a Tatar autonomous entity already exists—the Tatar ASSR" and that the "territory of the Crimea is presently a populated oblast' of the Ukrainian SSR." Consequently, the resolution emphasized that the Crimean Tatars had the full right to freely settle in the Tatar ASSR and that the Tatar Council of Ministers and the Tatar Obkom would "render the necessary assistance for the economic and work arrangements of the Tatar population, which will arrive for permanent residence in the republic."[129] Nevertheless, the efforts by the authorities to accommodate the Crimean Tatars did not stop their determination to return to the Crimean peninsula for the entire duration of the Soviet era.[130]

According to Mikoyan, Khrushchev believed that both groups adapted well to their new locations. In the case of the Tatars, the Soviet authorities felt that they had "settled down well in the new areas [of Central Asia] and Khrushchev saw no reason to resettle them again, especially since the Crimea had become part of Ukraine." Similarly, Khrushchev believed that the Volga Germans had become "well accustomed to the Virgin Lands of Kazakhstan and worked there well." He therefore concluded that "there was little point in resettling them, except to return them to the places where their ancestors lived." As Mikoyan noted, the Presidium of the Central Committee agreed with this decision. "Much was corrected after Stalin's death, but not everything was possible to fix," he recalled, in a statement that implied a certain sympathy on his part toward these groups.[131] Historian Michaela Pohl likewise noted that the Germans were needed by the Soviet authorities "as the basic permanent workforce in the *tselina* [of Kazakhstan], especially considering the substantial seasonal migration of Virgin Lands workers." Moreover, she noted that "the Germans were more committed to fitting into the Soviet collective," making it "possible to keep them in the Virgin Lands."[132] Additionally, Pavel Polian has argued that the use of state resources to resettle both groups in their original lands did not seem feasible to Soviet leaders and that they were "extremely wary of any disturbances to the status quo that may have developed with the absence of these peoples."[133] In other words, the Soviet government feared not only the potential cost of returning these nationalities but also potential conflict between the returnees and the settled population. This explanation certainly forms part of the story but given that voices within the Soviet leadership shared similar concerns about the return of other deported peoples, such the Chechens and the Ingush, other factors undoubtedly contributed to this decision. These factors would have included (in the specific case of the Crimean Tatars) the 1954 incorporation of the Crimea into Soviet Ukraine, or, more significantly, political conflict within the Soviet leadership over the return of these peoples.

Mikoyan alluded to the Polian explanation when he received a delegation of Volga Germans on June 7, 1965. Much like the Checheno-Ingush delegation ten years earlier, the group arrived in Moscow and met with Mikoyan and Deputy Premier Aleksandr Shelepin in the hope that the Soviet government would restore their autonomous republic and allow them to return to their former homeland.[134] Mikoyan listened carefully to their demands and responded to them:

> You raise the question of reestablishing the republic. We understand very well that that would be the best solution to the problem. But that is impossible, because we would have to take half a million people [from the Volga (Povolzh'e) region] and resettle them. There is no reason to think that the Germans cannot live without a republic. After all, before the war, two-thirds of the Germans lived outside the boundaries of the republic. At this time, we cannot reestablish the republic. That would involve great difficulties. Not everything that has been done in history is correctable. No one confuses you with the West Germans. You are Soviet citizens and have the right to newspapers, schools, and so on. In the present situation, we cannot move toward reestablishing the republic, because that would entail enormous economic losses. But as far as cultural needs are concerned, we can meet you halfway.[135]

Mikoyan's response is noteworthy, at once expressing his personal support for the restoration of the Volga German ASSR while also saying that it was not feasible. Although sympathetic and apologetic, he was effectively admitting that he alone could not influence the outcome, but he nevertheless attempted to assuage the concerns of his guests by proposing to meet them "halfway."[136] His frank response further alluded to the likelihood that the outcomes for the Crimean Tatars and the Volga Germans were the result of internal political struggles, akin to those over the return of the Chechens and the Ingush. In the case of the Volga Germans, Mikoyan's grandson Vladimir noted that limited funding, internal disagreements, and a desire to keep the Germans on the Virgin Lands contributed to a lack of action on the issue.[137] Polian likewise alluded to the factor of internal political disagreement, noting the reluctance on the part of the security services to allow for the return of these groups. For instance, upon learning that the Volga Germans were scattered throughout the USSR and numbered sixty to eighty thousand "only in nine regions," Soviet Interior Minister Dudorov concluded that the restoration of their autonomous republic was "pointless." Similarly, Polian wrote that in 1956, Dudorov "found it most logical to create an autonomous republic for [the] Crimean Tatars in Uzbekistan" because its climatic conditions were "approximate [to] the conditions in their previous place of residence."[138]

OLD DISPUTES, NEW CONFLICTS

The Checheno-Ingush ASSR was officially restored by the decrees of the Presidiums of the Supreme Soviets of the USSR and the Russian SFSR on January 9, 1957.[139] The newly reconstituted republic would receive the core territory of the former Groznyi oblast' without the Kizliar area, which was to be divided between the Stavropol' krai and Dagestan.[140] In connection with the Groznyi oblast' forming the "core" of the restored republic, the Groznyi Obkom became the Checheno-Ingush Obkom.[141] Moreover, the restored Checheno-Ingushetia retained control over the Cossack Naurskii, Shelkovskii, and Kargalinskii raions located north of the Terek River, all of which were not part of the autonomous republic before 1944.[142] The restoration further entailed the return of certain territories that the Soviet government had transferred to neighboring Georgia, Dagestan, and North Ossetia, a process that was not without dispute, especially regarding the status of the Prigorodnyi raion.[143]

Years later, Mal'sagov recalled that an initial plan for the borders of the restored Checheno-Ingush ASSR envisioned Dagestan, Georgia, and North Ossetia retaining the territories that Moscow had granted to them in 1944. Central Committee Department head Viktor Churaev reportedly devised this proposal and presented it at a meeting of the Mikoyan commission attended by the Checheno-Ingush Orgkom. Predictably, the orgkom "sharply opposed" this plan. Mal'sagov recounted asking Mikoyan, "Anastas Ivanovich, how are you going to restore the republic by giving five raions to Dagestan, three to Georgia, and one to [North] Ossetia?" Mikoyan sought to assuage his concerns by indicating that parts of the Groznyi oblast' that were not part of Checheno-Ingushetia before 1944 would be given to the republic instead. "This will not correct the situation, Anastas Ivanovich," Mal'sagov insisted. "The people will oppose it. You are essentially depriving us of our homeland. In this way, there will be no republic." His colleague, Tangiev, strongly backed him up. Moscow's work was made easier when the leaders of the neighboring republics voluntarily ceded most of the areas in dispute back to Checheno-Ingushetia, thus largely restoring the autonomous republic to its original boundaries. "After us, the first secretary of the Dagestan Party Obkom spoke," recalled Mal'sagov. "He said that he would relinquish the five raions of Checheno-Ingushetia and would relocate his people from there to Dagestan. Then the secretary of the Communist Party of Georgia rose and said: 'We also relinquish the mountainous raions of Checheno-Ingushetia.'"[144] From Georgia, the autonomous republic received the parts of the Dusheti and Kazbegi raions located north of the Greater Caucasus range, thus "restoring the border that existed between the Russian SFSR and the Georgian SSR before March 7, 1944."[145] From Dagestan, the Andalalskii, Vedenskii, Ritliabskii, and Suragatskii raions were restored to the reconstituted Checheno-Ingush ASSR, in addition to the "western portions of the Botlikhskii and Tsumadinskii raions."[146]

However, the process of determining the new boundary between Checheno-Ingushetia and North Ossetia proved to be much more contentious. The years of forced exile of the Ingush had created new realities on the ground with which the Soviet authorities had to contend, specifically Ossetian control of certain territories that were Ingush before the deportations. With the restoration of Ingushetia, the local leadership of North Ossetia was open to returning most of these territories, but with significant exceptions. To its restored neighbor, it ceded the town of Malgobek and its surrounding area, as well as the "Kosta-Khetagurovskii raion and the northeastern part of the Pravoberezhnyi raion."[147] However, it retained a narrow corridor connecting the republic with the northern town of Mozdok, and, even more significantly, it retained the Prigorodnyi raion, which surrounded the North Ossetian capital of Ordzhonikidze and was economically tied to the city.[148] The retention of Prigorodnyi was incomprehensible to the Checheno-Ingush Orgkom, which regarded the district as "the heart of Ingushetia" given that it was "the location of the village of Angusht, from which the very name of the Ingush is derived."[149] As Polian noted, the new political boundaries "contained ominous omissions and land deletions that foreshadowed the bloody conflicts of the future," most prominently the Ingush-Ossetian conflict of the early 1990s.[150] There were also echoes of the past, as the city of Ordzhonikidze itself had earlier been the object of Ossetian-Ingush dispute during NEP.[151]

Vladimir Agkatsev, the first secretary of the North Ossetian Party Obkom, was opposed to ceding Prigorodnyi and argued that the raion had become "populated mainly by Ossetians and that it would be impractical to return it."[152] In defending the decision to retain the raion, he stated that he sought to "create a center of friendship between the Ingush and the Ossetians" in the district. He further emphasized that North Ossetia "would accept all Ingush who were evicted from the area and resettle them in the raion and in Ordzhonikidze city."[153] According to Caucasus scholar Arthur Tsutsiev, many observers believe that the cession of the three northern Cossack raions of Naurskii, Shelkovskii, and Kargalinskii to Checheno-Ingushetia was intended to serve as form of compensation for the loss of Prigorodnyi, although the "available historical record offers no evidence" of such an intention.[154] A desire on the part of the Soviet government, and in particular Mikoyan, to find a "compromise" solution to the problem certainly forms part of the explanation. However, a report on Checheno-Ingushetia from the Presidium of the CPSU Central Committee from December 22, 1956, offers another key reason for the decision on the three northern Cossack districts. The report, signed by Mikoyan, Voroshilov, Malenkov, Brezhnev, and Beliaev, indicates that the Soviet authorities decided to include Naurskii, Shelkovskii, and Kargalinskii within Checheno-Ingushetia to provide the republic with more space to accommodate the returning Chechen and Ingush populations.[155]

Regardless, the best efforts of Moscow and North Ossetia did little to soothe the loss of the Prigorodnyi raion for the Ingush. "In all other respects," recalled Desheriev, "they [the members of the Checheno-Ingush Orgkom] were very pleased with the results achieved in Moscow."[156] However, with regard to the fate of Prigorodnyi, the orgkom felt betrayed. To them, it seemed as though the Soviet government had imposed the decision on them, despite their strong objections. "It was felt that Mikoyan and others were ready to satisfy this [Agkatsev's] request," recalled Mal'sagov. "We realized—they were giving them the raion.

I think that there was a preliminary agreement [between Moscow and North Ossetia]."[157] However, according to Desheriev, the cession of Prigorodnyi to North Ossetia was not a conspiracy between Moscow and the Ossetians but an accident that led to the creation of a tragic and complicated ethnic conflict. At a meeting on the restoration of the Checheno-Ingush ASSR attended by Mikoyan and Voroshilov, the Soviet government presented a letter to the Checheno-Ingush Orgkom from Agkatsev. As Desheriev recalled,

> He [Agkatsev] requested the retention of the Prigorodnyi raion as part of the North Ossetian ASSR. The commission wanted to know the opinion of the members of the orgkom on this letter. But at that moment they were in a state of euphoria over the decision to return the Chechens and the Ingush to their native homeland and to restore the Checheno-Ingush ASSR. The jubilation of the members of the orgkom turned their heads away from the issue and they forgot to react to the letter from the secretary of the North Ossetian Obkom. The government commission perceived the lack of reaction to this letter by the orgkom members as their agreement with its contents.[158]

The Checheno-Ingush Orgkom eventually "came to their senses" and "urgently wrote a letter addressed to the government commission on the necessity of returning the Prigorodnyi raion to the Ingush people."[159] They consulted with Desheriev on the composition. "There [with Desheriev], until morning, we prepared a note to the Presidium of the Central Committee," recalled Mal'sagov. "In the morning, we arrived at the hotel with this document, gathered our delegation, and having familiarized everyone with the situation, asked them to sign it. It was signed by Gairbekov and all members of the delegation without exception. It was a protest against the transfer of the Prigorodnyi raion to North Ossetia."[160] The letter read,

> Now, when discussing the return of the Checheno-Ingush people to their former place of residence and the restoration of their national autonomy, it seems completely inconvenient to raise the question of tearing away a raion from this autonomous republic, as some Ossetian comrades propose. Their brotherly neighbors have endured so much suffering and are [now] returning to their native land by the will of the Party and the government. However, at this most solemn moment, instead of sympathizing with, and supporting, their neighbors and helping them in every conceivable way, they raise the question of excluding the Prigorodnyi raion from Checheno-Ingushetia, an ancestral Ingush territory, saturated with the blood and sweat of the Ingush people.[161]

The letter also raised the claim to the village of Angusht, as the origin of the Ingush ethnonym, and argued against the Prigorodnyi raion's economic ties to

North Ossetia and its ethnographic composition as reasons for its inclusion in the republic. "The raion's entry into the composition of the Checheno-Ingush ASSR in no way disrupts supply to the city of Ordzhonikidze," the document stressed. "Prigorodnyi will continue to supply the city of Ordzhonikidze with everything it can." The letter likewise dismissed arguments regarding the changing ethnic composition of Prigorodnyi, adding that the cession of the raion to North Ossetia was "an unfair solution to this issue" that could cause "completely undesirable phenomena in the relations between the Checheno-Ingush and Ossetian peoples." It further attacked North Ossetian politicians who accused Chechens and Ingush of atrocities and banditry against Ossetians. "We are talking about this matter only to emphasize the necessity, especially at this moment, to be more sensitive than ever to offended feelings," the authors wrote.[162]

Gairbekov, Tangiev, and Mal'sagov went to the Central Committee, where they gave a copy of the letter to Khrushchev's assistant and "asked him to organize a meeting with Nikita Sergeevich."[163] However, although the letter reached Khrushchev, the Soviet authorities were reluctant to make additional border modifications. As Desheriev recounted years later, "They were told: 'You should have raised this at the meeting of the government commission. Your silence could be understood as agreement with the contents of the letter of the secretary of the [North Ossetian] obkom. The commission has already completed its work.' And thus, the complex inter-ethnic problem of the Prigorodnyi raion arose. The members of the orgkom were greatly upset by their mistake, foreseeing possible complications in Ossetian-Ingush relations due to the Prigorodnyi raion."[164] Stalin's legacy of violent deportations had left Khrushchev and Mikoyan with a potentially explosive situation. To them, the best solution was to accept the circumstances that had evolved on the ground rather than risk a greater regional destabilization. Further border modifications in favor of the Ingush would have undoubtedly incurred accusations from the Ossetians of favoritism toward Checheno-Ingushetia on the part of Moscow. To avoid a potential Pandora's box of conflicting ethno-territorial claims and counterclaims, the best solution from Moscow's view was to simply retain the newly established status quo, while encouraging coexistence between the neighboring peoples. However, that arrangement was never fully accepted by the Ingush, and tensions over Prigorodnyi persisted quietly until they boiled over with the end of the USSR in 1991 and the explosion of the Ossetian-Ingush conflict in 1992.

The dispute over the Prigorodnyi raion was only a preview of the much more dramatic violence that was to come, in connection with the physical return of the Chechens and the Ingush to their historical homeland. Overall, the repatriation of the repressed nationalities was a smooth process, with only a few sporadic cases of violence.[165] However, of those cases of violence, the majority involved the return of the Chechens and the Ingush. Even before the official return of the two groups, many Slavic settlers who arrived after 1944 were already considering a return to central Russia as "tense competition for resources and living space arose." Friction quickly emerged between the returnees, who wanted their old homes immediately, and the new residents who "could not, even if they desired, give up their household overnight." As the Chechens returned and concern grew among the newer, mostly Slavic residents, the local authorities of the Groznyi oblast' "feared either possible counter-aggression from the Russian settlers or an uncontrollable exodus of Russians from the North Caucasus."[166] The speed and scale with which the Chechens and the Ingush were returning further exacerbated tensions. The situation finally reached a boiling point with the clashes in Groznyi of August 1958, which were ultimately put down forcefully by the Soviet central government.[167] Significantly, historian Roy Medvedev once claimed that Mikoyan played a role in defusing tensions between the Chechen returnees and the newer Slavic residents. However, no evidence exists to substantiate this claim, and Medvedev's source is unclear.[168] Nevertheless, given Mikoyan's experience in the North Caucasus and his advocacy for the rehabilitation of repressed nationalities, it would certainly not be outside the realm of possibility.

CONCLUSIONS

During the years of the Thaw, Mikoyan played an indispensable role in supervising the return and rehabilitation of the deported peoples, as well as the restoration of their autonomous republics. This substantial undertaking not only legally and politically exonerated whole nations but effectively saved them from assimilation and disappearance entirely. It was due to this effort that the returning nationalities were able to preserve their languages, cultures, and identities for generations to come. It cemented Mikoyan's central role as Khrushchev's point man on nationality affairs and became one of the major hallmarks of de-Stalinization in the sphere of nationality policy, serving as a clear rejection not only of assimilation but also of Stalinist "arbitrariness" and the legacy of the "cult of personality."

Nevertheless, this process was not without challenges. The effort to manage the return of these groups underscored the reality that Mikoyan's approach toward the nationality issue did not find unanimous approval within the Soviet leadership. Although the statesman had long-standing experience with many of the deported peoples in the context of the North Caucasus, not all Soviet officials deferred to his experience and ideas. From the outset, although reform-minded figures like Mikoyan favored the return of the repressed nationalities, Soviet state security officials were reluctant to allow any return to proceed, stemming from concerns over regional destabilization. This conflict echoed the broader struggle within the Soviet leadership on how to proceed on the development of nationality policy after Stalin's death, between those who favored expanding the space for national expression and those who favored a more assimilationist approach. Even when the state did allow most deported nationalities to return, the Khrushchev government still made exceptions for certain groups, denying the Crimean Tatars and Volga Germans the right to return to their homelands.

The process of restoring Checheno-Ingushetia specifically presented another set of challenges for the Soviet state. The return of most of the deported nationalities was a largely peaceful process. However, the return of the Chechens and the Ingush and the restoration of their republic proved to be a more taxing undertaking, encompassing a complex thicket of property and territorial disputes, as the conflict over the Prigorodnyi raion demonstrated. Looming large above these dilemmas stood the long shadow of the Stalinist legacy, as manifested by the aftershocks of the deportations and the redrawing of boundaries in the region. As Chechen historian Abdullah Bugaev wrote, "If Stalin and Beria managed to deport hundreds of thousands of people—entire nations—to distant exile with lightning speed, in a matter of days during a difficult war, then it was not easy to return them to the land of their ancestors. And this was in peace time!"[169] Nevertheless, despite all challenges, the restoration of Checheno-Ingushetia and the homelands of other repressed nationalities served as a defining element of de-Stalinization in the nationality sphere. In this major undertaking, Mikoyan's role was essential.

6 | Toward a More Perfect Union?

The struggle to define the Soviet Union's post-Stalin nationality policy was manifested in several ways, most notably in the tensions between Moscow and the union republics over the level of local autonomy but also within the Soviet leadership at the highest levels. Mikoyan was well placed to influence the latter struggle. Having articulated a framework for the post-Stalin nationality policy in his 1954 Yerevan address and playing a key role in the rehabilitation of the deported nationalities, he emerged as a leading authority on the nationality question during the Thaw. However, his involvement in the practical development of a central approach toward nationalities truly commenced with his contributions to the Third Soviet Communist Party Program of 1961 and his subsequent leadership of the constitutional Subcommittee on Nationality Policy and National-State Construction (NPNSC). Together, these reform efforts represented an official rejection of assimilationist approaches and Stalinist centralization by the Party, and they were embraced by Khrushchev as part of his broader reform agenda of "democratizing" the Soviet system and realizing his vision of "socialist democracy" in the USSR. Indeed, although the Khrushchev era was initially characterized by alternating trends between centralization and devolution, ultimately the overall prevailing trend was toward greater devolution to the union republics and national autonomous entities.

To better comprehend Khrushchevian nationality policy, several Western scholars initially arrived at the conclusion that Khrushchev's 1958 education reform and the purge of nationally minded leaderships in republics like Latvia represented a trend toward "Russification."[1] However, these steps from Moscow came amid a broader struggle to define the parameters of permissible national expression and therefore represented only temporary policy trends. In fact, the overall trend was toward more, not less, decentralization, as reflected in the nationality platform of the CPSU's Third Party Program that Mikoyan played a significant role in developing. Especially noteworthy was the Soviet leadership's decisive rejection of the concept of the merger (*sliianie*) of smaller nations into larger ones, due to Mikoyan's influence. The constitutional reform initiative took such decentralizing tendencies a step further. The consensus among the members of the NPNSC Subcommittee, led by Mikoyan, was that the 1936 Stalin constitution represented a form of "extreme centralization" (*krainiaia tsentralizatsiia*), as Mikoyan would later write in his memoirs.[2] Therefore, discussions around state reform focused on granting republics and autonomous entities more rights in relation to the center, effectively "undoing" key aspects of the 1936 constitution. Of the positions discussed by the subcommittee, one in particular stands out—Mikoyan's stance on the nature of the Soviet state structure itself. He contended that the USSR was more than a federation, and that it was, in fact, a union of states, a difference that he stressed was important. If implemented, the model that he envisioned and described would have turned the USSR into something closer to a confederation, with much greater self-governance for the republics in relation to the central government in Moscow. His vision was not realized, but his articulation of it illustrates that support for decentralizing the state was strong at the highest levels within Khrushchev's government, well into 1964.

Several Western scholars of federalism have argued that the Soviet federal model represented a form of "sham federalism"—that is, representative on paper but not in practice, due to the Communist Party's monopoly on political power.[3] However, the evidence from the Thaw highlights that the internal discussions surrounding Soviet federalism, nationality policy, and political representation were far from rigid. In fact, they were often lively, as Mikoyan's July 1962 meeting with Soviet legal experts illustrates. Indeed, Soviet reformers, including Mikoyan, were aware of Western criticisms of Soviet federalism, including the "sham" thesis, which they understood as a reflection of the excessively centralized Soviet constitution adopted by Stalin in 1936.[4] The NPNSC Subcommittee actively studied such criticisms, with an eye toward finding ways to "de-Stalinize" the Soviet federal model and make it more representative for republics and autonomous entities. The subcommittee also reflected the national diversity of the Soviet state, encompassing the first secretaries of Armenia, Georgia, Kazakhstan, and Uzbekistan as well as representatives of other republics and autonomies. In the end, it grappled with centuries-old questions regarding the ways in which Russia as a multiethnic state should be governed, most notably regarding self-governance versus centralization, the extent of benefits and obligations to national communities, and ultimately the structure of the state itself.

NATIONALITY AND THE 1961 PARTY PROGRAM

Mikoyan's role in shaping the nationality policy for the CPSU's 1961 Party Program signaled his direct involvement in developing a new official policy for Soviet nationalities. The 1961 Party Program served as the opening act for Khrushchev's broader reform agenda, which was to be concluded with the completion of a new Soviet constitution. At the time that Khrushchev launched the process to develop the new Party Program in 1958, no new program had been adopted by the CPSU since 1919, although Stalin made attempts to introduce a new program in the 1930s and again in the 1940s.[5] Khrushchev saw his recent success in defeating the "Anti-Party Group" as an opportune time to introduce a new program. Such an action would also allow him "to claim an ideological continuity with Lenin's legacy" and to eliminate Stalinist deviations. Historian Alexander Titov noted that "the new Programme represented a revivalist vision of the Soviet communist project" that was "free from negative aspects" of Stalinism. "In this way," Titov concluded, "the adoption of the new Party Programme was to become a high point of Khrushchev's ideological and political revolution."[6] Moreover, Khrushchev expressed the hope that the program would serve as the first step toward greater "democratization" (*demokratizatsiia*) not only within the Party but also "among the people, in the country." The idea would be to have a constant "update" (*obnovlenie*) of the political elite and the bureaucracy through popular elections, with the aim of moving "toward the realization of the position of Lenin that every cook should be able to govern her own state."[7] Khrushchev directly associated this aspiration with de-Stalinization and the reversal of Stalinist "arbitrariness."[8]

Work on the new Party Program commenced in 1958 with the formation of a commission tasked with developing a draft of the text. It was headed by Khrushchev and consisted of Mikoyan, Otto Kuusinen, Mikhail Suslov, Piotr Pospelov, Boris Ponomarev, Mark Mitin, and Pavel Iudin, with Khrushchev delegating the main work of drafting the program to Kuusinen and especially Ponomarev.[9] Mikoyan was to play a key role in shaping the nationality section of the program, entitled "Tasks of the Party in the Sphere of Nationality Relations" ("*Zadachi partii v oblasti natsional'nyh otnoshenii*").[10] Informed by his intimate understanding of the issue as someone of non-Russian background with experience managing difference, Mikoyan worked to tone down the "internationalist" orientation of the text and the more utopian instincts of Khrushchev, making it more palatable to the concerns of the non-Russian nationalities. His suggested revisions were virtually all accepted into the final program, with only minor changes. Due to Mikoyan's input, the final version of the text was not only deferential to nationality concerns but often generous to them, most significantly by rejecting the assimilationist idea of the *sliianie* concept. In striking a balance between sensitivity toward national cultures and the struggle against national chauvinism, the section was strongly evocative of the position articulated by Mikoyan in his 1954 Yerevan speech.

While virtually all of Mikoyan's ideas were accepted by the commission, the victory of his positions was not inevitable. This reality reflected a larger debate within the Soviet leadership over the direction of the post-Stalin nationality policy. The dynamics of this debate were raised by Ivan Tsameryan of the Soviet Academy of Sciences at Mikoyan's July 1962 meeting with Soviet legal scholars as chairman of the NPNSC Subcommittee. In the meeting, Tsameryan noted that "even before the publication of the draft Party Program," there were disputes over the future direction of the nationality issue.[11] He maintained that there were "two expressed positions"—the *sliianie* (merger) position and the *sblizhenie* (rapprochement) position. Tsameryan warned that the *sliianie* position "adhered to the point of view that the rapprochement of nations is, essentially, the beginning of the process of the merger of nations, and therefore the question of improving national statehood should not even be considered, that the line should go toward the eventual dissolution of the republics, etc." He stressed that the "publication of the draft Party Program dealt a strong blow to views such as these, that preached the merging of nations."[12] The *sblizhenie* concept itself was not necessarily new in the context of Soviet nationality policy. Stalin invoked the term in his *Marxism and Questions of Linguistics*, but only as part of the larger *sliianie* vision.[13] However, in the context of Thaw-era debates, *sblizhenie* became opposed to *sliianie*. Although the reasons for the victory of the *sblizhenie* position are unclear, Mikoyan's proximity to Khrushchev and his authority to speak on nationality issues as a non-Russian from the Caucasus offer some potential clues and explanations.

Mikoyan made clear his thoughts on the nationality issue in the formative stages of the Party Program project. In the program's original draft plan from August 25, 1958, he took exception to the wording that called for the voluntary merger (*sliianie*) of "smaller nations and ethnic groups into the larger socialist nations close to them" as part of the "process of the consolidation of nationalities into socialist nations." At this proposed text, the Armenian Mikoyan bristled, objecting that such a process should not be the job of the government or the Party but could only occur naturally, if the smaller nations favored such an approach. "This is a natural [*estestvennyi*] process," Mikoyan wrote, "not a Party task."[14] Mikoyan's criticism of the concept of the "merger of nations" (*sliianie natsii*) became even more direct in his review of the initial draft of the Party Program in early 1961. The original draft stated that the "expanded communist construction within the USSR opens a new period in the development of national relations, characterized by a further rapprochement [*sblizhenie*] of nations, and the preparation for the conditions of their future merger." Mikoyan heavily struck out the ominous-sounding latter portion of this sentence with his thick blue pencil and underlined it in red.[15] He articulated his opposition to Ponomarev in the subsequent draft that he reviewed in April 24–26, 1961. "The program does not talk about the merger of nations," he wrote. "In connection with this, exclude the words 'and the preparation for the conditions of their future merger.'"[16] Significantly, Mikoyan's position on the *sliianie* issue was supported by Kuusinen in his letter to Khrushchev on the Party Program from March 29, 1961.[17]

In his review of the earlier 1961 draft, Mikoyan also crossed out an entire subsequent paragraph that dealt with the *sliianie* concept. "With the victory of communism," the paragraph read, "the economic and moral-political community of the Soviet nations will grow even more, and the common communist features of their spiritual appearance will develop. Erasing national differences, especially linguistic differences, is a significantly longer process than erasing class boundaries. The merger of nations will occur not in the form of a one-time act, but as a result of a gradual and prolonged close communication of peoples after the victory of communism in all countries."[18] The wording of this paragraph was slightly modified in the subsequent draft reviewed by Mikoyan in April 1961. However, he continued to strongly oppose its inclusion entirely, especially the final portion regarding the timeline of the eventual merger. From the paragraph, he recommended saving only the phrase "the development of common communist features of their spiritual appearance" and merging that line into an earlier paragraph.[19] The commission accepted Mikoyan's suggestions with minor revisions for the final version of the program. Nevertheless, it decided to retain the acknowledgment from the deleted paragraph that "erasing national differences, especially linguistic differences, is a significantly longer process than erasing class boundaries."[20] Similarly, in opposition to the *sliianie* idea, Mikoyan entirely struck out section D in the early 1961 draft, which called for "completing the overcoming of the remnants of the former backwardness of individual peoples of the USSR." This section further called on the Party "to assist the objectively ongoing process of consolidating formerly backward small peoples into socialist nations." It noted that the Party would accomplish this task "both by merging small ethnic groups close to each other into a single nation on the basis of a common, voluntarily adopted language, and by voluntarily merging smaller peoples and ethnic groups with the [larger] socialist nations close to them."[21]

Another issue that Mikoyan raised in his revisions was the place of the Russian language in the Soviet nationality policy.[22] As he emphasized in his 1954 Yerevan address, Mikoyan strongly believed that although knowledge of Russian was essential as a language of interethnic communication, its diffusion among non-Russian nationalities had to be voluntary. In the early 1961 draft, Mikoyan heavily struck out a passage arguing that "national parochialism [*natsional'naia ogranichennost'*] in the sphere of language impedes cultural communication among the peoples of the USSR, as well as the use of their experiences and achievements in the economic and cultural construction of all Soviet peoples." He especially took aim at the phrase "national parochialism in the sphere of language," which he underlined in red.[23] In the next draft that Mikoyan reviewed, in April 1961, the language portion of the nationality platform advised the Party "to assist the ongoing process of voluntarily learning the Russian language, alongside the native language." Emphasizing the importance of learning Russian voluntarily, Mikoyan circled the word "*sodeistvovat'*" (to assist) and noted to Ponomarev "do not talk about the Party's *assistance* in the process of learning Russian alongside native languages." Although the "national parochialism" passage remained in a slightly modified form, it was still strongly opposed by Mikoyan, who advised Ponomarev to remove it, which he did.[24]

In the end, not only did the commission accept Mikoyan's recommendations on language, it even enhanced them. The new wording that appeared in the final version of the program was significantly more generous to non-Russian nationalities. The text now called on the Party "to henceforth ensure the free development of the languages of the peoples of the USSR, as well as the complete freedom for every Soviet citizen to speak, raise, and educate their children in any language they wish, without allowing any privileges, restrictions, or coercions in the use of certain languages." The final version also underscored that "the ongoing process of voluntarily learning the Russian language, alongside the native language, holds positive significance, as it facilitates the mutual exchange of experiences, and the familiarization of each nation and nationality with the cultural achievements of all other peoples of the USSR and with world culture." It concluded that, "in fact, the Russian language has become the common language of interethnic communication and cooperation for all the peoples of the Soviet Union."[25]

Mikoyan was likewise deferential to the distinctive national cultures of the republics and defended them in his comments on the drafts of the Party Program. For example, in the draft of early 1961, Mikoyan crossed out a reference to the development of "new, international forms of culture" that would supplant the particular and well-established national cultures of the Soviet republics and autonomies.[26] He elaborated his thoughts on the matter further in his review of the April 1961 draft. One section of this text noted that "new, international forms of Soviet culture, common to all Soviet nations, are arising and developing" and that "the cultural treasury of each nation [*natsiia*] is increasingly enriched by creations that transcend the boundaries of its national form." To this statement, Mikoyan objected. "It is wrong to speak of a culture that is 'international in form', of a culture 'transcending the boundaries of its national form,'" he wrote to Ponomarev. Instead, he suggested editing the end of the paragraph to read, "A common international culture is developing for all Soviet nations. The cultural treasury of each nation is increasingly enriched by creations that are acquiring international significance."[27] Mikoyan's suggested wording was used almost exactly in the final version of the program, with only the word "significance" changed to "character."[28] Another phrase of the early 1961 draft referred to the future vision of a communist society with a "universal human culture" that would be "unified in form and content." Again, in a nod to national cultures, Mikoyan crossed out the "unified in form" part and suggested changing it only to "unified in content."[29] Then, in the April 1961 draft, Mikoyan suggested the removal of the phrase "form and content" entirely, and once again, this edit was accepted in the final version of the program.[30]

Mikoyan's proposed revisions for the Party Program further suggest that he viewed the Soviet nationality policy as one that encompassed not only the rights of republics and autonomies but also the rights of individual Soviet citizens of different national backgrounds. In the early 1961 draft and again in the April 1961 draft, Mikoyan struck out the adjective "territorial" (*territorial'nyi*) in reference to the Soviet "community of nations and nationalities."[31] In the initial 1961 draft, Mikoyan noted that the word "territorial" was *otpalo*—that is, not the best option or no longer needed, suggesting that the issue had already been discussed. He also added a question mark next to the term and underlined it.[32] In the end, his suggestion to remove this adjective was accepted by the Party, and the final published version of the Party Program did not define the Soviet "community of nations" as "territorial." In fact, even the adjective "political," used to describe the "community of nations" in the earlier drafts, was replaced by the term "ideological" in the final version, given that "political" could also imply "republican."[33] Nevertheless, although the extraterritorial aspect of the Soviet nationality policy was evidently in Mikoyan's thoughts, he did not go so far as to explicitly articulate nationality policy as encompassing the personal rights of, for example, Georgians in Leningrad, Armenians in Krasnodar, Jews in Odessa, or Russians in Riga. Although Mikoyan did not elaborate on such matters in the context of the Party Program, the preliminary draft of the 1964 constitution brought his ideas to their natural conclusion. Specifically, Article 58 noted that legal equality among Soviet citizens, regardless of nationality, would ensure the "attainment of actual equality among nations in economic and cultural life," the "education of citizens in the spirit of socialist internationalism," and the "opportunity to maintain one's native language and national culture" regardless of one's location in the USSR. Article 58 further enshrined the principles of the Soviet *druzhba narodov*, underscoring that legal equality encompassed efforts to "eliminate the causes for mistrust between nations" and to "strengthen cooperation and friendship among nations."[34]

Almost all of Mikoyan's editorial suggestions were included in the final text of the Party Program's platform on nationality policy. There was, however, one notable exception—his recommendation on both 1961 drafts to remove a passage that called for a "further exchange of cadres between nations." This section likewise strongly condemned "any manifestation of national detachment [*natsional'naia obosoblennost'*] in the training and use of cadres" as "especially inadmissible."[35] The retention of this passage was hardly a surprise. As Titov reminds us, "the idea of rotation of cadres was Khrushchev's favourite," so it would have been highly unlikely for Mikoyan to secure the removal of any passage related to that issue.[36] In fact, the text not only was retained in the final program but became conspicuously more Khrushchevian, with the phrase "further [*dal'neishii*] exchange of cadres" changed to "constant [*postoiannyi*] exchange of cadres." At the same time, "especially inadmissible" was toned down to simply "inadmissible."[37] Overall, the fact that Mikoyan was unable to secure the removal of this text reminds us that not all of his proposals on nationality policy found acceptance within the Soviet leadership and that some of his ideas could even be challenged by Khrushchev himself.

The essence of the Party Program's position on nationalities now closely followed the framework that Mikoyan had articulated in his March 1954 address in Yerevan. Moreover, it foreshadowed his work on the nationality issue as part of Khrushchev's major constitutional reform effort. In his address on the Party Program before the Twenty-Second Party Congress on October 18, 1961, Khrushchev summarized the revisions to the nationality platform and emphasized their importance. In the section of his speech entitled "Rapprochement of Nations and the Strengthening of the Friendship of Peoples" ("*Sblizhenie natsii i uprochenie druzhby narodov*"), the Soviet premier stressed that "two interconnected progressive tendencies in the national question" were occurring under socialism. The first tendency that Khrushchev identified was the "rapid and all-round development of each nation" and the "expansion of the rights of the union and autonomous republics." In this respect, he underscored the economic development of the union republics and autonomous entities as an indicator of the successes of the Soviet nationality policy. At the same time, he stressed the need to enhance their national sovereignty, noting that it was "necessary to make full use of all possibilities laid down in the Soviet principles of federation and autonomy." Khrushchev further noted the importance of the "free development" of languages "without any restrictions, privileges, and coercions," stressing that "we have no brakes on the development of national languages." Echoing Mikoyan's earlier editorial comments, he underscored the "voluntary study" of the Russian language as a means of "interethnic communication" and "interethnic cooperation."[38]

The second tendency identified by Khrushchev was the *sblizhenie* process, which, as he noted, was characterized by the "intensification of the mutual influence and mutual enrichment" of the Soviet nationalities.[39] Here Khrushchev conceded that "even after communism is essentially built, it will be premature to declare a merger of nations [*sliianii natsii*]." He noted that even Lenin "underscored that state and national differences will continue to exist long after the victory of socialism in all countries." Although Khrushchev strongly asserted that "communists will not conserve and perpetuate national differences," he nevertheless conceded that the *sblizhenie* of nations was an "objective process"—that is, a natural process developing without state or Party intervention. He further maintained that this process was "occurring in the conditions of communist construction on the basis of voluntariness and democracy."[40] In his speech at the Party Congress on October 20, Mikoyan was even more direct on this point, noting that the Party Program "unambiguously and very correctly states that artificially pushing for the rapprochement of nations, as well as deterring it, can only do harm." Concurring with Khrushchev, he emphasized that the "development of national cultures and the economies of the national republics, in combination with the policy of their rapprochement, is one of the greatest driving forces on our path toward communism."[41]

KHRUSHCHEV'S CONSTITUTIONAL DREAMS

Through his recommendations for the 1961 Party Program, Mikoyan established himself as the Kremlin's leading authority on the nationality issue. Khrushchev recognized his friend's expertise in his next major reform initiative—the drafting of a new Soviet constitution to supplant the Stalin constitution of 1936. Immediately following the completion of the Party Program, Khrushchev turned his attention to laying the groundwork for a new constitution. The idea was already on his mind as early as the summer of 1961.[42] His motives for initiating this undertaking were similar to those behind the new Party Program. These included restoring the "principles of Leninism" in the aftermath of Stalinist "arbitrariness," realizing "socialist democracy" (*sotsialisticheskaia demokratiia*) both within the CPSU and in broader Soviet society, and reflecting the changes in Soviet life that had taken shape since the adoption of the 1936 constitution, most notably the growing urbanization of the country. The realization of the new constitution was to be the crowning achievement of Khrushchev's major reform agenda, and the wily first secretary made no secret of his plans to the delegates at the Twenty-Second Party Congress in his address on October 17, 1961. "The Soviet Union has entered a new stage in its development and socialist democracy has risen to a higher level," he told those present. "A new constitution for the USSR, which we are starting to develop, must reflect the new features in the life of Soviet society during the period of expanded communist construction."[43] Mikoyan very much shared Khrushchev's "democratic" visions. In his speech before the congress, he expressed the hope that the Soviet "all-people's state" (*obshchenarodnoe gosudarstvo*) would elevate "socialist democracy to an even higher level, when more and more millions of members of society [would] join in the participation and administration of the state and social affairs."[44]

Behind the scenes, in the autumn of 1961, Khrushchev oversaw the establishment of a "Working Group for the Preparation of Materials on Constitutional Questions" under the CPSU Central Committee. On February 5, 1962, this group presented Khrushchev with a very rough draft of a new constitution as well as additional materials, including a memorandum that "theoretically substantiated the need to adopt a new Basic Law." The memorandum (*pamiatnaia zapiska*) was a highly significant document that provided theoretical guidance for the reform effort. It would be used by all the subcommittees of the future Constitutional Commission.[45] Among other points, the memorandum echoed Khrushchev's remarks on the need for the new constitution to reflect the "enormous changes" that had occurred in Soviet society and international affairs since 1936. Following the Party Program and the philosophy of socialist legality, it also stressed the need for legislative guarantees against "any recurrence of the cult of personality." However, the fundamental question that the memorandum underscored was the place of political power in the reformed Soviet state. Rather than the "dictatorship of the proletariat," the new constitution was to provide the legal basis for the transformation of the USSR into the "all-people's state" that Mikoyan referenced.[46] The latter concept was first developed by Finnish-born Party veteran and theoretician Otto Kuusinen.[47] Central to the "all-people's state" was the idea of popular democracy (*narodovlastie*)—that the citizen would have a direct say in the governing process.[48] Although the 1962 memorandum still defined the CPSU as playing the "vanguard" role in the system, the new constitution would combine this role with popular sovereignty, providing Soviet citizens with the ability to participate directly in the governance of the state through legislative initiative via public organizations and other means.[49] A subsequent memorandum in January 1963 elaborated on these ideas and included a proposal to introduce a section in the constitution entitled "On the Power of the People" ("*O vlasti naroda*").[50]

The aims of the February 1962 memorandum were articulated publicly by Khrushchev in his speech on the new constitution before the first session of the sixth convocation of the Supreme Soviet on April 25. "Why is it necessary," he asked, "to create a new constitution and not limit ourselves to the introduction of individual amendments and additions to the current constitution?" As in his remarks before the Twenty-Second Party Congress, he explained that the 1936 constitution was "already outdated in its main provisions" and that it "fails to reflect the changes that have taken place in the life of society for over a quarter of a century and does not correspond to its current state."[51] "Socialism has won a complete and final victory in our country," Khrushchev insisted, "and that is the essence behind the changes that have occurred in the Soviet Union since the adoption of the present constitution. The USSR has entered into a period of expanded communist construction. At this new stage of our development, the state of the dictatorship of the proletariat has grown into an all-people's socialist state, and proletarian democracy—into an all-people's democracy [*obshchenarodnaia demokratiia*]."[52] The premier further called attention to the fact that the international situation had changed dramatically since 1936. "Our state has emerged from capitalist encirclement," he said, "and a great community of socialist countries [around our state] has been formed and strengthened." With the external situation under control, Khrushchev reasoned, now was the time to place greater emphasis on domestic reform and to fully realize what he called "socialist democracy." He stressed the necessity that "the new constitution should be the constitution of the all-people's socialist state, the constitution of communism under construction. It must correspond to this new historical period in the life of our country."[53]

Khrushchev went on to sketch the main aims of the future constitution. The first would be "to reflect the new stage of development of the Soviet society and state." The second would be to "raise socialist democracy to an even higher level." To achieve the latter, Khrushchev maintained that it would be necessary "to devise even stronger guarantees of the democratic rights and freedoms of the workers," guarantees that would "strictly adhere to socialist legality," in order to prevent any return of the "cult of personality." Likewise, it would be of the utmost importance "to prepare the conditions for the transition to public communist self-governance"—that is, to expand the role of the citizenry in the political processes of the state.[54] Khrushchev argued that the enhancement of democratic rights fully corresponded with the aim of restoring the Leninist principles of the Party and the Soviet state.[55] He concluded by underscoring the "enormous, truly historical significance" of developing a new Soviet constitution, declaring that "the Soviet people will be acting as the pioneers of new forms of state and social organization, corresponding to the period of expanded communist construction."[56]

Shortly after Khrushchev's address, the Supreme Soviet formally established a Constitutional Commission consisting of ninety-seven members, with Khrushchev serving as chairman.[57] The commission's first meeting, held on June 15, was very brief, and the main thrust was to announce the organization of the reform effort. Party ideologist Leonid Il'ichev outlined the nine subcommittees that comprised the commission. Il'ichev himself was to head the Editorial Subcommittee, while Khrushchev would chair the main Subcommittee on General Political and Theoretical Questions. The latter focused on the overall development of the constitution and brought together most of the subcommittee chairmen (including Mikoyan), as well as members of the Central Committee Presidium.[58] In his opening remarks, Khrushchev summed up the style that was to characterize the commission. "Let us follow the most democratic direction, and exchange opinions," he said. "The subcommittees will get together and discuss. Let them articulate their own understanding on how they think things should be done regarding the issue or section on which that subcommittee must present its considerations. Then we shall meet and bring this all together into a single document." The next step, as Khrushchev saw it, would be to send the finished draft to all members of the commission for their feedback.[59]

Having earlier demonstrated his expertise on nationality matters with the Party Program, Mikoyan was appointed by Khrushchev to chair the Subcommittee on Nationality Policy and National-State Construction (NPNSC). The subcommittee's name perfectly encapsulated its main task—to overhaul the Soviet nationality policy by reforming the union state and revamping the relationship between Moscow and the republics within a new political framework, in the spirit of the ideals articulated by Khrushchev.[60] In addition to Mikoyan, the subcommittee consisted of thirteen individuals, representing various parts of the USSR, including the first secretaries of four union republics—Yakov Zarobyan of Armenia, Vasilii Mzhavanadze of Georgia, Dinmukhamed Kunaev of Kazakhstan, and Sharaf Rashidov of Uzbekistan. It also included the chairman of the Soviet of the Union—Ivan Spiridonov of Leningrad—and the chairman of the Soviet of Nationalities—Jānis Peive of Latvia. Aleksandr Korneichuk of Ukraine, a close Khrushchev ally, was likewise a member of the subcommittee, as were two Supreme Soviet deputies—Tursunoi Akhunova of Uzbekistan and Vladimir Svetlichnyi of Krasnodar—both of whom were Heroes of Socialist Labor. Akhunova was the only woman who served on the subcommittee and one of the few women involved in the Constitutional Commission overall. Other subcommittee members included Vasilii Kozlov (chairman of the Presidium of the Supreme Soviet of Belorussia), Turabai Kulatov (chairman of the Presidium of the Supreme Soviet of Kirgizia), Ziia Nuriev (first secretary of the Obkom of Bashkiria), and Nikolai Organov (chairman of the Presidium of the Supreme Soviet of the Russian SFSR).[61] Ukrainian first secretary and Khrushchev protégé Nikolai Podgornyi was originally a member of the subcommittee but left after Khrushchev granted him the chairmanship of the Subcommittee on Public and State Organization, a position originally held by Frol Kozlov.[62]

In his opening address at the June 15 meeting, Khrushchev initially insisted twice that there was "no need to rush" the process of developing a new constitution. However, Khrushchev, being Khrushchev, could not help himself and named an approximate deadline anyway. "Perhaps we will finish our work by the end of this year [1962] and maybe next year, we will present the draft of the constitution," he said. However, he concluded by reiterating twice more that there was no need to rush and no need to set a firm deadline for the completion of the constitutional reform. "Agree, comrades?" he asked. "Agree," responded those present.[63] Following the meeting, the NPNSC Subcommittee commenced its work almost immediately. First, in line with Khrushchev's call to base the development of the new constitution on Leninist principles, Mikoyan requested that his assistant, Vasilii Chistov, compile a report comparing the wording on the nationality issue in the 1936 Stalin constitution with that of the 1918 Russian SFSR and 1924 all-union constitutions. A trained historian with knowledge of German, Chistov was a "laconic, calm, thoughtful, highly intelligent, and decent man," in the words of Mikoyan's son, Sergo.[64] His completed report, which he presented to Mikoyan on June 22, closely scrutinized the texts of the 1918 and 1924 constitutions. His comparative study underscored the ways in which these earlier constitutions favored greater self-governance over the centralization characteristic of the 1936 constitution, especially regarding the right of secession and the competencies of the republics in relation to Moscow.[65] This issue would become fundamental to the subsequent work of the NPNSC Subcommittee—that is, developing ways to undo the excessive centralization that defined the constitution of 1936.

THE JULY MEETING

A few days after receiving Chistov's report, Mikoyan arranged a Moscow meeting with Soviet legal scholars on July 28. The aim was to discuss various aspects of the nationality issue and Soviet state structure, setting the stage for a future working meeting of the subcommittee, then scheduled for October.[66] From the outset, Mikoyan identified five items for discussion. These included building on the nationality platform of the 1961 Party Program; selecting "those elements of the first Russian constitution and the first constitution of the USSR to which it would be advisable to return"; determining which "Leninist formulations and statements on the national question should be used" in the constitution; discussing Stalin's distortions of the nationality policy, especially in the last period of his rule, and corrections to be reflected in the new constitution; and expressing opinions on ways to improve state mechanisms in the sphere of nationality policy, "as socialist democracy develops."[67] Overall, the July meeting proved to be a productive and lively discussion, highlighting fundamental questions related to the rights of the union republics, the structure of the state, and the position of national autonomous entities.

A central issue that Mikoyan and the legal scholars sought to address was the need to enhance the rights of the republics in relation to the central government in Moscow. This matter was especially relevant, not only because of the legacy of the 1936 constitution but also because the Stalin-era effort to implement an all-union legal code, thus invalidating the law codes of the republics and imposing the will of the center over them. Mikoyan argued that such a step constituted a "great encroachment on the sovereign rights of the republics and a completely injudicious act." The vision of a unified law code was expressed in the 1936 constitution, and Mikoyan later claimed that it was devised either by Andrei Vyshinskii or by Stalin himself.[68] Nevertheless, the idea remained dormant for much of the Stalin era, and it was not until after Stalin's death in 1953 that the CPSU Central Committee established a commission to develop unified Criminal and Criminal Procedural Codes, chaired by Konstantin Gorshenin.[69]

By May 24, 1955, draft codes were approved by the Presidium of the Supreme Soviet, then chaired by Kliment Voroshilov. Further edits were made by a commission that included Gorshenin, Roman Rudenko, and others, and on June 21, Voroshilov submitted the revised drafts to the CPSU Central Committee for approval.[70] However, the Central Committee rejected both draft codes, first on December 1, 1955, and then again on April 5, 1956.[71] The opposition to the initiative was led by Mikoyan. "Is it really necessary to centralize?" he inquired in the December 1955 meeting.[72] His position was supported by Khrushchev and Nikolai Bulganin. At the meeting of the Presidium of the Central Committee of April 5, Khrushchev sharply reprimanded Voroshilov. "Why is it necessary to screw with, and limit, the republics?" he openly inquired. For his part, Bulganin noted that Voroshilov's proposal was "politically harmful."[73] In place of the all-union code, Mikoyan instead advocated for a new legal formulation, stressing that the all-union Supreme Soviet should only establish the basis for the laws enacted by the republics, which would in turn be devised by the republics themselves.[74]

At the July 1962 meeting, the legal scholars not only agreed with Mikoyan's position but advocated expanding and clarifying it even further. They also criticized the excessive centralization of the Soviet state under the 1936 constitution. In particular, David Zlatopol'skii of Moscow State University took aim at Article 15, which declared the sovereignty of the union republics to be "restricted within certain limits." "But sovereignty cannot be restricted," he insisted.[75] Another scholar from Moscow State University, Aleksei Lepioshkin, pointed to Article 14, which articulated the duties of the Soviet central government. He believed that power was excessively concentrated in the hands of the central authorities and that more of it needed to be delegated out to the union republics.[76] In terms of republican rights, one that garnered particular attention among the legal scholars was the right of secession. Although it is unclear what the actual process of secession entailed, the scholars regarded it as "one of the most vivid expressions of sovereignty" for the union republics and that it "testified to the voluntary nature of the unification of the republics into the USSR."[77] In the 1924 Soviet constitution, the right of secession was guaranteed in Article 4 and, according to Article 6, could be amended only with the consent of all union republics. The 1936 constitution dropped the latter point, but the scholars favored restoring it. Zlatopol'skii went even further, proposing the radical idea that such a right should not be subject to any constitutional amendment at all.[78]

A major point of discussion at the meeting was the criteria for what constituted a union republic as opposed to an autonomous republic, autonomous oblast', or national okrug.[79] Moreover, what criteria would an autonomous republic need to meet to be elevated to the rank of a full union republic? Piotr Romashkin of the Academy of Sciences noted that Stalin's criteria included (1) sharing a border with a foreign state, (2) having a compact ethnic majority of the titular group, and (3) having a relatively large population, comprising at least one million people. However, he noted that "such criteria are no longer suitable for defining a union republic." He specifically highlighted the ways in which the Soviet-backed Warsaw Pact states had changed conditions for "borderland" (*okrainnyi*) union republics like Ukraine and Belorussia. Instead of bordering "hostile" capitalist countries, they now bordered "friendly" allied socialist states like Poland, Czechoslovakia, and Hungary.[80] The other legal scholars likewise spoke in favor of updating these criteria, although they expressed differences on the specifics.[81] Romashkin also raised an earlier proposal, rejected by Stalin, to elevate the Tatar and Bashkir ASSRs to union republic status.[82] Lepioshkin agreed with the idea of elevating the Tatar ASSR, noting that it was in "no way inferior to a whole number of union republics." Although he expressed the point of view that "not all autonomous republics needed to be elevated to the union republic category," he believed that the issue nevertheless merited discussion. Moreover, he spoke in favor of promoting national okrugs to the rank of autonomous oblasts and of elevating autonomous oblasts to the rank of autonomous republics, citing the Adyghe AO as an example.[83] Conversely, Hatik Azizyan of *Pravda* made the case that some autonomous republics could be downgraded in status due to changes in national self-identification. He emphasized his point by highlighting the decline of the "Adjarian" identity in the Adjarian ASSR of Soviet Georgia.[84]

One of the fundamental issues addressed at the meeting was the nature of the Soviet state structure. Following "from Lenin's experience in constitutional construction," Viktor Kotok of the Academy of Sciences stressed that the new constitution should open with a preamble that articulated the "essence of the state and the position of the individual in society." He turned to the 1918 Russian SFSR constitution, underscoring that it began with the "Declaration of the Rights of the Laboring and Exploited People" and that a similar declaration should appear in the new constitution.[85] His idea would later be endorsed by subcommittee members Kunaev and Kozlov.[86] Some of the legal scholars, in particular

Zlatopol'skii, also advocated unambiguously defining the USSR as a federal state in the constitution, given that the lack of such a definition was causing arguments within the Soviet legal community.[87] However, Mikoyan took a broader view and argued that the Soviet state, from its inception, was intended to be something *more* than a federation, with much greater sovereignty devolved to the republics. He believed that the USSR was intended to be a free union of states, on the order of a confederation. Mikoyan expressed this point of view earlier in his speech at the Twenty-Second Party Congress, when he underscored Lenin's original vision of a "union of equal and sovereign national republics" and Lenin's rejection of the view that "proposed only their inclusion into the Russian SFSR with the rights of autonomy." Mikoyan further stressed that Lenin recognized the Russian SFSR as "equal in rights with the Ukrainian SSR and others, and that together, and on an equal footing with them, they entered into a new union, a new federation, the Union of Soviet Republics."[88]

Years later, Mikoyan emphasized this same point in his memoirs when recalling the adoption of the first Soviet constitution in 1924, referring to it as being "based on the Leninist principles of a voluntary state union of equal peoples."[89] His perspective was undoubtedly influenced by his revolutionary mentor, Stepan Shahumyan, who had earlier advocated for an equal union of national republics in the Caucasus context.[90] Mikoyan's view likewise reflected the great value that he personally attached to the realization of Armenian statehood within the USSR, as expressed in his memoirs and the draft material that he prepared for his 1954 Yerevan speech.[91] He was therefore very sensitive to maintaining and even expanding the rights of the union republics and autonomous entities. Perhaps unsurprisingly, "the development of national statehood" later became one of the legal guarantees of the equality of Soviet citizens, regardless of nationality, as enshrined in Article 58 of the 1964 draft constitution.[92]

At his meeting with the legal scholars, Mikoyan emphasized the importance of differentiating the concept of a union (*soiuz*) from that of a federation (*federatsiia*). He insisted that "each word acquires a specific meaning" and that the matter had to be considered by the subcommittee "thoroughly."[93] The distinction of wording did indeed matter because the use of the term "union state" rather than "federal state" implied, at least in theory, that much greater powers should be devolved to the local administrative units in relation to the central government. Mikoyan conceded that a union state was a *type* of federation, but of a higher form than a federal state. He remarked that the federal state, confederation, and autonomy were "all forms of a federation, but with different content." However, he emphasized that a union was a "federation of a different kind, formed on the basis of sovereign states and their unity." He argued that there were two types of federation within the Soviet Union. One type was the federative union republic, like the Russian SFSR or the short-lived Transcaucasian SFSR. The other was the union state itself, encompassing the fifteen Soviet socialist republics. "This word [*soiuz*] is Russian," said Mikoyan, "but a different concept is already embedded within it, even though theoretically a union and a federation are one and the same." He stressed that "this [*soiuz*] is the form [of state] that has developed in our country historically and is most suitable for us."[94]

Mikoyan's emphasis on the idea that a union implied more than a federal state also implied that the USSR, although theoretically a union, did not function as such under the conditions of the Stalin constitution of 1936. Anushavan Arzumanyan, a close associate of Mikoyan, raised this point at the meeting. "We have a lot of centralization," he said. "Even the USA, which is also a federal state, has less centralization."[95] Mikoyan responded that the US was a "united state" that combined elements of a union and a federal state. By contrast, he stressed that the USSR was (at least theoretically) a "union of national, sovereign republics." "There is a nuance here to which you are not attaching importance, and therefore you insist on introducing the term 'federation.' We need to think about this," he said. However, Mikoyan did not directly address Arzumanyan's point on the disparity between the theory of the USSR as a union and the reality of the centralized state as it existed.[96]

Another point that Mikoyan did not address was the status of autonomous entities in such an arrangement. The existing evidence indicates that, both within the NPNSC Subcommittee and outside of it, Mikoyan favored devolving greater powers to these entities, especially autonomous republics. For instance, in his consultations with the working group on autonomous entities for the subcommittee, he expressed opposition to having union republics approve the constitutions of autonomous republics.[97] He similarly opposed the idea put forth by subcommittee member Kozlov to downgrade all autonomous republics to the status of autonomous oblasts.[98] Furthermore, at the meeting with the legal scholars, Mikoyan reacted negatively to a proposal to abolish the Soviet of Nationalities advanced by Dmitrii Gaidukov of the Institute of Law of the Academy of Sciences.[99] The body comprised one of two chambers of the all-union Supreme Soviet, the other being the Soviet of the Union. The Soviet of the Union was composed of representatives of electoral districts, with each deputy representing three hundred thousand people. The Soviet of Nationalities represented Soviet citizens from the country's many national-territorial subdivisions, including not only the union republics but also the various autonomous republics, autonomous oblasts, and national okrugs.[100]

Mikoyan's sensitivity toward autonomous entities was undoubtedly informed, to a considerable extent, by his administrative experience in the North Caucasus and his sympathetic yet cautious position toward the Armenians of

Nagorno-Karabakh. However, it is unclear how he could reconcile his sympathetic position with his vision for a significantly more devolved union state. If Moscow's powers were to be greatly diminished in favor of the union republics, would it not weaken the ability of autonomies like Abkhazia and South Ossetia to influence their position vis-à-vis the union republic to which they were subordinated (in this case, Georgia)? Did Mikoyan and his constitutional framers envision some sort of veto in case their autonomy would be threatened by Tbilisi? Would there be instances in which the central government in Moscow might be compelled to intervene? On these matters, they have left today's historians without answers, although the need for a veto was already evidenced by the ongoing tension between Azerbaijan and majority-Armenian Nagorno-Karabakh, of which Mikoyan was well aware.

The picture becomes even less clear when dealing with numerically smaller nontitular nationalities, such as the Talysh, Lezgins, or Udi of Azerbaijan.[101] In his contributions to the Third Party Program, Mikoyan rejected the assimilation of smaller nations into larger ones and favored mutual respect for different national cultures. Moreover, in his later writings, the statesman praised the cultural achievements of nontitular groups, like the Avars of Dagestan.[102] During his trip to Azerbaijan in March 1964, Mikoyan paid a visit to Lenkoran' and Astara in the southern Talysh region and even attended a local town meeting in Astara, although it is uncertain if any specific Talysh-related questions were raised.[103] Overall, it is unclear how Mikoyan could reconcile his rejection of assimilation with a much more devolved union state in which nontitular groups might face such a threat from titular republican leaderships. If Mikoyan and his framers sought to base their vision for reform on the new Party Program and the rejection of the *sliianie* concept, then did they envision certain "federal protections" for the preservation of the languages and cultures of these indigenous groups? Did they see their reform efforts as an initial step toward these more specific issues? For a subcommittee whose remit was nationality policy, in addition to national-state reform, such a path would seem logical, but on this matter, we are also left without answers.

SEEKING INPUT AT HOME AND ABROAD

At the July meeting, the legal scholars, most notably Lepioshkin and Zlatopol'skii, raised the matter of criticisms of Soviet federalism from "bourgeois" Western observers, especially as they related to the excessive centralization of the 1936 constitution. In response, Mikoyan told his colleagues that "the Institute of Law [of the Academy of Sciences] needs to collect all the bourgeois criticism of our constitution in relation to questions on nationality policy." He stressed the necessity of selecting "all statements, without hesitation, without sanitizing, but with annotations," and to highlight "the most vivid places where they criticize us, our weaknesses, without concealing anything, especially criticism hostile to us."[104] Mikoyan's call was realized on September 13, 1962, when Romashkin sent him a thorough overview of Western views of the Soviet constitution in the area of nationality policy and state structure, focusing exclusively on criticisms and negative assessments.[105] The report was prepared by Vladimir Tumanov of the Academy of Sciences' Institute of State and Law, a man who would later become better known for his chairmanship of the Constitutional Court of post-Soviet Russia. As Mikoyan requested, Tumanov's report stressed that it excluded statements from Western observers that "recognized the successes of [nationality] policies and national-state construction in the USSR." Instead, it focused exclusively on "the main theses of reactionary propaganda aimed at discrediting Soviet nationality policy and socialist federalism."[106]

The report covered everything from broad anti-Soviet propaganda (e.g., that the USSR was a "prison house of nations") to academic legal criticism of the Soviet federal system.[107] Naturally, Mikoyan and his associates were most interested in the latter criticism, which focused on the shortcomings of the 1936 constitution and the limits that it imposed on the sovereignty of the union republics. Overall, Tumanov identified five criticisms of Soviet federalism prevalent in Western literature. These criticisms included the arguments (1) that the Soviet nationality policy was "nothing more than a form of colonialism"; (2) that Soviet federalism was a "fiction," given the centralized nature of the Soviet state and the CPSU; (3) that the "rights of the union republics were limited and insufficient"; (4) that "Soviet federalism lacks legal guarantees"; and (5) that the "main purpose" of Soviet federalism was to serve "external political aims and external propaganda."[108] The second point of criticism, which characterized Soviet federalism as being effectively a "dead letter" (albeit representative on paper), was considered by Tumanov to be the "leitmotif of criticism of socialist federalism."[109] He meticulously documented examples of each of these criticisms, drawing on various works by authors in the US, the UK, France, and West Germany, and quoting from articles published in Western journals, such as the *Slavic Review, Soviet Studies* (today *Europe-Asia Studies*), and the *American Journal of Comparative Law.*[110]

The fact that Western authors pointed to excessive centralization in the 1936 constitution as being the cause for the limits on the sovereignty of the union republics was of particular interest to Mikoyan, who underlined such sections in his copy of the report. One section that he highlighted openly acknowledged that "until 1936, the union republics enjoyed greater rights." Tumanov noted that "in general, Western literature quite often emphasizes that the 1936 constitution was characterized by the diminution of the rights of the republics when compared to earlier effective legislation." Mikoyan specifically highlighted Western criticisms rooted in Article 14 of the 1936 constitution, which concentrated disproportionate power within the central government.[111] He was also very interested in Western commentary comparing the 1924 and 1936 constitutions on the matter of the right of secession from the union. "Bourgeois authors," wrote Tumanov in a section of particular interest to Mikoyan, "emphasize in every way that Article 4 of the 1924 Soviet constitution, which guaranteed the right of secession, could be 'changed, restricted, or abolished' only with the agreement of 'all republics included in the USSR' (Article 6)." By contrast, he wrote that the 1936 constitution "does not include such a guarantee and, therefore, the right to withdraw can be annulled by a simple constitutional amendment." He further noted that "bourgeois authors contend that this change is no coincidence, and that it expresses a certain consistent line toward the elimination of the legal guarantees of federalism." In another section highlighted by Mikoyan, Tumanov emphasized that "bourgeois authors also see the absence of legal guarantees for Soviet federalism in the fact that the [1936] constitution does not have in place any procedure by which the Soviet republics could defend their rights in case of a conflict with the federal government."[112]

In addition to studying Western criticisms of Soviet federalism, Mikoyan and his colleagues, under the leadership of Khrushchev, examined constitutional models in other countries for comparison. The Constitutional Commission reviewed the constitutions of both Western states and Eastern Bloc countries.[113] However, the model that interested Mikoyan and other reformers the most was that of Josip Broz Tito's nonaligned Socialist Yugoslavia and its 1963 constitutional reforms. This specific federal arrangement was of particular interest to them, as it brought together a more representative federal system with a more devolved political-economic model.[114] On the theoretical level, the Yugoslavs had similar debates on the future development of their constituent national republics under socialism, with Tito, Edvard Kardelj, and Vladimir Bakarić playing particularly important roles. In the end, they too rejected assimilationist approaches in favor of their own form of rapprochement (*zbližavanje*) and the equal and independent development of nations within a single Yugoslav federation.[115] On November 28, 1962, Mikoyan received an extensive twenty-eight-page report on the preliminary draft of the new Yugoslav constitution, as prepared by Il'ichev.[116] In accompanying notes on the Yugoslav reforms, Mikoyan strongly underlined passages dealing with the nationality issue that mirrored those of the Soviet experience. These included passages on demands from the Yugoslav republics for greater economic autonomy and on the preservation and strengthening of the Yugoslav Council of Nationalities, both of which mirrored Soviet discussions on expanding the rights of the union republics and on preserving the Soviet of Nationalities.[117]

The reformers also sought the input of the Soviet public in the constitutional reform process, in line with Khrushchev's larger vision of "democratizing" the system and expanding the participation of society in the governance of the "all-people's state." From July 1962 to December 1964, the Constitutional Commission received letters from numerous citizens across the USSR in which they gave their input on the development of the new constitution.[118] Summaries of these letters were prepared by the Legal Department of the all-union Supreme Soviet and were then sent by Il'ichev to the subcommittees.[119] Citizens' recommendations on matters related to the nationality issue are particularly noteworthy. Some of them underscored the historical tension within the Soviet Union regarding the state's identity and self-perception—was it a primarily Russian (*russkii*) state or a more inclusive, multiethnic (*sovetskii*, or *rossiiskii*) state? Some members of the public contended that, although it was a multiethnic state, the USSR was, at the end of the day, essentially Russian at its core. Hence, one citizen from Moscow suggested renaming the country from the Union of Soviet Socialist Republics (USSR) to the *Russian* Union of Soviet Republics (RUSR), with "Russian" rendered as "*rossiiskii*." The Muscovite contended that the word "socialist" was redundant and unnecessary because "it goes without saying that if a republic is Soviet, it is also socialist."[120] More to the point, a citizen from Leningrad advised that the constitution directly state that "Russia *is* the Union of Soviet Socialist Republics."[121] In a similar vein, a letter writer from a village near Kurgan called for the Soviet government to "safeguard the full way of life of all citizens of the USSR," and to "specifically provide for the protection of the national dignity of Russians," due to the fact that, in his view, "under the guise of equality, there is currently an infringement on [the rights of] the Russian people."[122]

Taking a more internationalist line, a large number of citizens proposed removing the "nationality" column (*grafa*) from Soviet internal passports and other documents, with most arguing that the inclusion of such a category was simply unnecessary in contemporary Soviet conditions. As an alternative, many suggested adding the option of "Soviet" as a form of self-identification or "Citizen of the USSR."[123] Other letters reflected themes familiar to Mikoyan and his associates—such as proposals to elevate autonomous Bashkiria and Tataria to the status of union republics. Others went even further and suggested the promotion of not only Bashkiria and Tataria to union status but also Dagestan, Udmurtia, Mordovia, Chuvashia, Iakutia, and the Komi Republic.[124] Several citizens suggested consolidating republics into larger federations, including proposals to revive the Transcaucasian SFSR and to consolidate the Central Asian republics into a single Turkestan SFSR and the three Baltic republics and Kaliningrad oblast' into a single Baltic Soviet Socialist Republic.[125] Alternatively, Party member P. G. Ena of Krasnodar proposed transferring the Kaliningrad oblast' to the Belorussian SSR "as a symbol to the great merits of the Belorussian people before the entire Soviet people in the fight against the German invaders."[126] One citizen from Moscow floated the idea of creating a separate federative union republic for Siberia—the Siberian SFSR—from the territory of the Russian SFSR.[127] By contrast, a more far-sighted citizen from the town of Novomoskovsk, near Tula, proposed denying the right of republican secession to the Russian SFSR, underscoring the central role of Russia as the basis for the USSR.[128]

One anonymous letter received by the commission, described as a "treatise" (*traktat*) by the summary report, requested that Nagorno-Karabakh and Nakhichevan' be transferred from the jurisdiction of Soviet Azerbaijan to Soviet Armenia. The authors of the letter referred to the administration of these territories by Azerbaijan as a "historical injustice" that was a "consequence of the personality cult of Stalin and the pernicious activities of Beria and Bagirov." The summary of this letter was thickly and heavily underlined by Mikoyan.[129] Similarly, a citizen from Yerevan likewise requested the transfer of Nagorno-Karabakh to Armenia.[130] The idea was also endorsed by several non-Armenian Soviet citizens. For example, Ena recommended that majority-Armenian Nagorno-Karabakh be transferred to Armenia, while majority-Azeri Nakhichevan' be abolished entirely as an ASSR and administered directly by Baku. As he bluntly put it, "There are no such nationalities as 'Nakhichevanians' or 'Karabakhians'. There are Armenians and Azerbaijanis. So why do we need these autonomies?" In compensation for Azerbaijan's loss of Nagorno-Karabakh, he recommended transferring the Dagestan ASSR to Baku's jurisdiction.[131] O. K. Larin of Nukus in Uzbekistan's Karakalpak ASSR advocated a similar solution but also proposed upgrading Nagorno-Karabakh to the status of an autonomous republic, while downgrading Nakhichevan' to the status of an autonomous oblast'.[132] Both Ena and Larin similarly proposed unifying North and South Ossetia into a single autonomous republic, under the jurisdiction of either the Russian SFSR or Soviet Georgia, a point that Mikoyan underlined.[133] Mikoyan remained most impressed by Larin's proposals and even took some of them into consideration. Among them was the idea of elevating all autonomous oblasts to autonomous republics and then abolishing autonomous oblasts as an administrative class entirely. Mikoyan likewise considered Larin's proposal to list the Russian SFSR—"the first among equals"—as first on the list of union republics in the constitution.[134]

THE WORK OF THE SUBCOMMITTEE

With the foundation laid for the constitutional reform, Mikoyan and his team in the NPNSC Subcommittee proceeded to develop a new framework for the Soviet nationality policy and union state structure. However, it was already clear that they needed much more time to devise their potential proposals and that they would not be able to submit any formal recommendations to the commission in early 1963. Originally planned for October, the first subcommittee meeting was delayed by two months, to December 14, with a second meeting planned for June 9, 1964.[135] In this respect, the NPNSC Subcommittee was not alone. Almost all of the subcommittees did not present their recommendations to Khrushchev and the Constitutional Commission until 1964. The sole exception was Kosygin's Subcommittee on Economic Questions and National Economic Management. The Kosygin subcommittee was the only one to submit its proposal on time, in early 1963, following Khrushchev's originally proposed schedule.[136] As for the NPNSC Subcommittee, the extended time frame provided its members with greater space to develop their ideas. In advance of the December meeting, Mikoyan received recommendations from two subcommittee members—Kozlov of Belorussia and Kulatov of Kirgizia—together on November 30. Their recommendations built on the earlier ideas put forth by the legal scholars to Mikoyan and provided an outline for the December meeting.[137] Significantly, both also argued against granting union republics the right to establish their own military formations, an idea that Kozlov dubbed "inconsistent with reality."[138] Mikoyan and the rest of the subcommittee agreed and ultimately decided against including this provision in the final recommendations that they sent to Khrushchev in June 1964.[139]

After reviewing the proposals of Kozlov and Kulatov, Mikoyan and the subcommittee met on December 14. Those in attendance included only seven of the thirteen subcommittee members—Kozlov, Kulatov, Nuriev, Organov, Peive, Rashidov, and Svetlichnyi. Outside the subcommittee, legal scholars Viktor Chkhikvadze, Piotr Romashkin, and Aleksei Orlov likewise attended the discussion.[140] There was no transcript of the meeting, but debate over potential proposals continued into the next year. Approximately one month later, on January 10, 1963, subcommittee member Kunaev, who had recently been demoted from the post of Kazakhstan's first secretary by Khrushchev, sent additional feedback to Mikoyan from Alma-Ata.[141] His letter proved to be the last significant activity of the subcommittee until February 1964. During that yearlong hiatus, Mikoyan developed a fourteen-point list of recommendations that the subcommittee would present formally to the Constitutional Commission. The fourteen points, which Mikoyan sent to the subcommittee with a brief introductory letter dated February 28, were as follows:

1. In principle, the position on nationality policy and national-state construction, as articulated in the preexisting constitution, is generally correct and warrants no change.
2. The new constitution must have a preamble, articulating the essence of the state and stressing the voluntary nature of the union. The formation of the USSR in 1922 would be characterized as an expression of "the right of nations to self-determination up to,

and including, secession, as proclaimed by the Party and by Lenin." For this point, Mikoyan also included a preamble draft text.

3. The original wording from the 1924 constitution on the right of republican secession must be restored in the new constitution. Thus, the article on secession could be amended only with the approval of all union republics. Alternatively, following the suggestion of Zlatopol'skii, Mikoyan proposed an "even more radical" option: to prevent the article from being amended at all.
4. The new constitution must emphasize that the union republics exercised their sovereignty through the union state on matters within all-union jurisdiction and that, "in all other respects, they exercise their power independently as sovereign states."
5. The rights of the union republics must be articulated in the new constitution. These rights included the right "to call for the convocation of a session of the all-union Supreme Soviet; to call for a national referendum; to call for a report on the work of the highest authorities up to the all-union Supreme Soviet and Council of Ministers; and to challenge decisions made by union (and union-republic) ministries and institutions."
6. The new constitution must stress that in "areas of activity where the basis of legislation is established by the union government (e.g., education, healthcare, etc.), the government of the union republic also legislates in these spheres."
7. In the section on the rights of the union republics, the representatives of the republics in all-union bodies should be articulated.
8. Consideration should be given to the possibility of establishing an all-union Constitutional Court that would serve as an arbiter of potential conflicts between the union government and the republics, or among the republics. This idea had another important objective—providing a legal check against government bodies to prevent any recurrence of the "cult of personality."
9. The new constitution should provide legislative initiative not only to the two chambers of the Supreme Soviet and "the commissions created by them" but also to "the all-union Council of Ministers and the Supreme Soviets of the union republics." Mikoyan further recommended discussing "the question of granting the right of legislative initiative to public organizations on issues affecting their interests as well." This suggested step would provide Soviet citizens with an avenue for direct participation in the governing process, in keeping with the vision of "democratization" and the "all-people's state."

10. The enumeration of the union republic ministries and the state structure of republican bodies should not be included in the new constitution. Instead, there should be "several fundamental provisions, on the basis of which union and autonomous republics can determine their own state structure apparatus specific to each republic." Moreover, Mikoyan added that there should be "certain fundamental provisions defining the place of national autonomies within the system of Soviet statehood."
11. State security should be carried out jointly by both the union government and the governments of the union republics.
12. Articles 16 and 92 of the 1936 constitution state that the constitutions of union (and autonomous) republics must be structured in "full accordance" with the all-union Soviet constitution. In the new constitution, the phrase "full accordance" should be revised to simply "accordance," given the specific characteristics of each republic and the fact that the phrase "full accordance" was "politically harmful" and unnecessarily restricted republican rights. This point was raised earlier by the legal scholar Viktor Kotok.
13. Per the advice of Kozlov, prosecutors should be elected by the Supreme Soviets of the republics rather than appointed by the USSR prosecutor general. At the same time, they should be subordinate to both the all-union prosecutor general and the local Supreme Soviets. In terms of judicial authority, it must be established that courts under the jurisdiction of the union include the Supreme Court of the USSR and military tribunals, while courts under republican jurisdiction include the Supreme Court of the union republic, district (city) people's courts, and courts for oblasts, krais, autonomous oblasts, and national okrugs.
14. Following the advice of Kulatov, the state anthem of the USSR and the anthems of the union republics should be enshrined in the all-union and republican constitutions, respectively, as "one of the expressions of state sovereignty."[142]

On February 29, 1964, Mikoyan sent copies of his recommendations to all subcommittee members, as well as Il'ichev and the legal scholar Chkhikvadze.[143] On March 3, Mikoyan sent two additional points to the subcommittee, based on Kunaev's remarks:

1. To add a line to the draft preamble noting the realization of Lenin's position on the "possibilities of backward nations and nationalities making the transition to socialism, bypassing the capitalist stage of development."

2. To form interrepublican economic bodies to promote cooperation among republics, "while respecting their sovereignty and equality."[144] The essence of this idea was to help establish horizontal relations among the republics to deepen integration within the union. It had been earlier floated by Khrushchev in his speech on the Third Party Program before the Twenty-Second Party Congress.[145]

Collectively, the fourteen draft points, along with the two additions, comprised a rough portrait of a reformed Soviet state structure that favored greater decentralization for the republics in relation to Moscow. In developing these points, Mikoyan attempted to incorporate the various perspectives of his constitutional framers as well as the legal experts. It was to be the basis for the finalization of the state reform package that he would eventually present to Khrushchev on behalf of the subcommittee at the meeting of the Constitutional Commission on July 16.

The response to Mikoyan's draft points varied among his constitutional framers. Uzbekistan's Rashidov sent Mikoyan letters of general agreement with all recommendations.[146] Armenia's Zarobyan, a member of Mikoyan's Armenian network who regularly consulted with him on Armenian affairs, likely communicated his approval informally. Six members of the subcommittee—Kunaev, Kozlov, Kulatov, Korneichuk, Peive, and Nuriev—provided Mikoyan with more specific feedback in letters.[147] Taking their remarks into consideration, Mikoyan sent invitations to the subcommittee on June 3 for its second major meeting, scheduled for June 9, 1964, at 10:30 a.m. in Moscow.[148] The next day, he followed up by sending summaries of the respective recommendations to all subcommittee members, as a foundation for discussion.[149] The June 9 meeting was attended by a majority of the subcommittee membership—Akhunova, Zarobyan, Kulatov, Kunaev, Mzhavanadze, Nuriev, Peive, Rashidov, and Svetlichnyi. The legal scholars Chkhikvadze and Orlov were also in attendance, as was the Ukrainian Party official Skoba. Korneichuk declined to attend due to health reasons but was later updated about the meeting by Mikoyan.[150] At the meeting, of which there was no transcript, Mikoyan and his framers developed a final version of their recommendations for the Constitutional Commission. The subcommittee members then gave their approval to Mikoyan to send their recommendations to Khrushchev. He did so six days later, on June 15, 1964.[151]

The new list of recommendations was essentially the same as the earlier one that Mikoyan sent out to the subcommittee, with revisions according to the input of the subcommittee members. There were some important additions. Instead of fourteen points, there were now seventeen. The first of these new points (point 5) stressed the significance of the bicameral system of the Supreme Soviet and reflected a proposal by Bashkiria's Nuriev to increase representation for autonomous entities in the Soviet of Nationalities, making it equal to the Soviet of the Union.[152] The second new point (point 15) raised the possibility of relisting the union republics in alphabetical order, based on input from Kunaev and Nuriev.[153] A third new point (point 17) called for the preservation of the right of the union republics to enter into "direct relations with foreign states," an idea introduced by amendment to the 1936 constitution in 1944 and strongly favored by Kunaev and Korneichuk.[154] The revised list further recommended extending legislative initiative to the Soviet Supreme Court and to the republican Councils of Ministers, following advice from Korneichuk and Kozlov. Mikoyan's proposal to extend legislative initiative to public organizations was excluded from the new list, although the idea itself later became a prominent feature of the 1964 draft constitution.[155] Finally, Kunaev's proposal to create interrepublican cooperative bodies did not find support among the subcommittee, which deemed the idea "inexpedient" and therefore opposed its inclusion in the final text.[156]

Proceeding from the suggestion of Kulatov, the subcommittee also tasked a working group with developing draft articles for the new Soviet constitution to legally define autonomous republics, autonomous oblasts, and national okrugs.[157] The working group consisted of Kulatov, Nuriev, and Chkhikvadze, as well as the obkom secretaries of several autonomous republics, including Mikhail Bgazhba of Abkhazia, Abdurakhman Daniialov of Dagestan, Fikriat Tabiev of Tataria, Kallibek Kamalov of Karakalpakstan, Bilar Kabaloev of North Ossetia, and Salchak Toka of Tuva.[158] On July 6, Kulatov and Daniialov sent their input on the draft articles to Mikoyan.[159] The final draft articles were submitted to Mikoyan by Nuriev on July 15.[160] These articles not only articulated the legal status of autonomous entities in relation to union republics but also stressed their representation in the all-union Supreme Soviet with the direct election of deputies in the Soviet of Nationalities.[161] Significantly, in the article defining the Soviet state, Mikoyan crossed out the word "federation" and replaced it with "union" (*soiuz*).[162] He further struck out a passage stating that an autonomous republic's constitution had to be approved by the union republic, thereby enhancing the rights of these autonomies.[163] The latter idea was earlier suggested to Mikoyan by Dagestan's Daniialov. However, the final text did not include Daniialov's proposal to provide an autonomous republic with the right to "transfer itself from [the jurisdiction of] one union republic to another" and "to elevate itself to the status of a union republic, under the appropriate conditions."[164] Such rights would have provided significant political clout for an autonomous republic like Abkhazia vis-à-vis Soviet Georgia and, if applied to autonomous oblasts, would have undoubtedly found favor with the Armenians of Nagorno-Karabakh in their desire to join the Armenian SSR or the Russian SFSR. In fact, the Karabakh Armenians would eventually take such a step in practice during perestroika, with their adoption of the resolution to unify the NKAO with Soviet Armenia on February 20, 1988.[165]

After receiving the draft articles on autonomies from Nuriev, Mikoyan formally presented the subcommittee's recommendations at the second meeting of the Constitutional Commission on July 16. In his address, the statesman began by revisiting Khrushchev's call to base the work of the new constitution on the "great ideological heritage" of Lenin. "Proceeding from that point of view," Mikoyan said, "we began to develop the constitutional provisions related to the national question, largely focusing on the first constitution." Mikoyan proceeded to put forth the subcommittee's idea for restoring the preamble of the 1924 Soviet constitution, outlining the structure of the state. He argued that the lack of such a preamble in the 1936 constitution "politically impoverished and schematized" the text. He stressed that the constitutional reform presented an opportunity not only to correct this issue but also to develop an enhanced preamble, reflecting the developments in Soviet society since the first constitution. "Now the preamble can be very rich, since it will reflect the development of the Soviet system, the socialist republics, the growth of national culture, economy, and the whole society," Mikoyan said. He added that the subcommittee envisioned that the preamble should "not be long" but that it should "provide precise formulations."[166]

In his speech before the Constitutional Commission, Mikoyan further discussed the points raised by the legal scholars regarding the definition of the Soviet state. However, citing examples of other federal states, Mikoyan again stressed that the USSR was something more than a federation, and that it was in fact a union of sovereign states. "The legal scholars are tossing up the idea of defining the union state as a federation," he said. "We proceed from the fact that there have been many different federal states throughout history, but that the content of each federation is distinctive. The name is the same—federation—but once you sort it out, the essence is different. For example, take the United States, West Germany, and Austria—they are different things." He noted that the Russian SFSR was also a federation and that "if we speak of our union federation, then we need to indicate all the differences." Mikoyan argued that it was "no coincidence" that "neither the first nor the second Soviet constitutions use the term 'federation.'" "We need to choose a definition [of the Soviet state] that really fits," he said. "I do not consider it necessary to analyze the difference, and we see no grounds for changing the article, which directly says 'union state.' This [definition] was established by our revolution."[167]

Mikoyan likewise raised the secession issue, stressing the subcommittee's recommendation to return to the original formulation on the matter as articulated in the 1924 constitution. He also outlined the subcommittee's position on the issue of the sovereignty of the union republics, exercising sovereignty through all-union bodies and all other rights through republican bodies. Referring to foreign perceptions of Soviet federalism, Mikoyan noted that such a formulation "would be very beneficial, especially from a foreign policy point of view." Following the newly added point 5, Mikoyan emphasized the importance of the bicameral structure of the Supreme Soviet and the need to preserve the Soviet of Nationalities. He also presented the subcommittee's proposal to increase the number of deputies in the Soviet of Nationalities to make it equal with the number of deputies in the Soviet of the Union. Given the projected increase of deputies of the Soviet of the Union with the rise of the population, Mikoyan stressed that an increase in the number of deputies of the Soviet of Nationalities was necessary to prevent "an inequality of chambers." Toward the latter aim, he put forth the subcommittee's idea of permitting votes in the Supreme Soviet to be made by the two chambers separately rather than as a joint vote. Khrushchev was intrigued by this proposal and, in response, suggested making the number of deputies for both chambers stable, regardless of the growth in population. "Therefore, whatever the growth, the representation will be the same," he maintained. "This is something that is necessary to think about. Then, in that way, it will obviously limit the number." Mikoyan not only agreed with Khrushchev but added that his proposal was "even better" than that of the subcommittee.[168]

Mikoyan proceeded to discuss the subcommittee's remaining proposals. He specifically pointed out the necessity of outlining and enhancing the explicit rights of the union republics, including the need to preserve local republican law codes. He further detailed the subcommittee's proposal for formally making chairmen of the Presidiums of the Supreme Soviets of the republics deputy chairmen of the all-union Supreme Soviet Presidium. He stressed this idea as "theoretically, practically, and politically important," as it would allow the republics to directly take part in the work of the all-union Presidium of the Supreme Soviet. He deemed the preexisting system to be "awkward" and "politically wrong."[169] However, as Mikoyan articulated this proposal and others, Khrushchev alerted him to the fact that he was short on time. "I have a question for the Chairman of the Presidium of the Supreme Soviet," Khrushchev said, cheekily alluding to the new state position of his friend. "Does he obey the general regulations or not?" "He obeys," responded Mikoyan, "but I didn't look at my watch."[170] Mikoyan then summarized the subcommittee's proposals to create a Constitutional Court, to allow for the election of republican prosecutors by local Supreme Soviets, and to establish that state security is provided by both the union government and the republics jointly. He concluded his report by discussing the subcommittee's positions on the order of the union republics, the importance of constitutionally enshrining republican state anthems, and the necessity to drop the term "full" when speaking of the "full accordance" of the republican constitutions with the all-union constitution.[171] Subsequently, in the aftermath of the Constitutional Commission meeting, Mikoyan sent the draft articles defining the legal status of national autonomies to both Khrushchev and Il'ichev on July 24.[172]

EPILOGUE

The work of the Constitutional Commission proceeded with the development of two full draft constitutions in 1964—a preliminary version introduced in the summer and a second, final version completed by the autumn. In the words of legal scholar Svetlana Zgorzhel'skaia, the "most complete and democratic" of these two draft constitutions was the summer draft, which included 276 articles. Although the NPNSC Subcommittee's articles on national autonomies were not yet received by the commission at the time of the completion of this initial summer text, they were incorporated into the final version.[173] The proposal for a Constitutional Court, as articulated by Mikoyan, was also included in the final draft.[174] Overall, the finished constitution appeared to be ready for formal adoption by December of that year, promising a radical overhaul of the Soviet political system and state structure.[175] If implemented, the new basic law would have dramatically reshaped power dynamics between the Soviet state and Soviet citizens, between Moscow and the union republics, and even between the union republics and autonomous entities. However, the dream of realizing the democratic "all-people's state" was ultimately dashed with Khrushchev's ouster from office in October 1964.[176] Although Mikoyan had been a staunch supporter of Khrushchev to the very end, Brezhnev retained him in his post until Mikoyan's resignation in December 1965.[177] Only two months later, in February 1966, the trial of Andrei Siniavskii and Iulii Daniel' signaled the definitive end of the Thaw.[178] Mikoyan had been opposed to putting the two anti-Stalinist writers on trial and even attempted to convince Brezhnev not to proceed with the criminal case, but to no avail.[179] Although embittered by these experiences, Mikoyan left office less isolated than Khrushchev and remained in the public eye, often to the annoyance of Brezhnev.[180]

In retirement, Mikoyan remained preoccupied with the nationality question and attached particular importance to communicating his ideas to Armenian audiences. In June 1966, during his Supreme Soviet electoral trip to Armenia, Mikoyan devoted a significant portion of his Yerevan speech to nationality matters. With the memory of the 1965 Yerevan demonstrations still fresh, the statesman emphasized the same philosophy that he first articulated in 1954, warning against the dangers of both "great power chauvinism" and "local nationalism."[181] Mikoyan later expanded this section of his 1966 speech into a full essay on the nationality issue, published as a booklet to mark the fiftieth anniversary of the formation of the USSR in 1972, with corresponding Armenian and English translations.[182] In his memoirs, Mikoyan also touched on the issue of centralization and devolution and, despite his friendship with Khrushchev, strongly criticized the creation of new all-union bureaucracies during the Thaw, which he saw as infringing on the rights of the republics. "It is impossible and unnecessary to manage everything from the center, to command thoughtlessly," he wrote.[183] Pro-devolutionist sentiment continued to strongly resonate in Armenia itself, where it found expression in cultural works like Henrik Malyan's film *We and Our Mountains* (1969). The latter was based on a story authored by Armenian writer Hrant Matevossian in 1962, at the height of constitutional reform initiative.[184]

Meanwhile, the process of developing a new constitution continued, eventually culminating in the adoption of the Soviet constitution of 1977. Significantly, the 1977 constitution did include some of the innovations articulated by Khrushchev, Mikoyan, and the Constitutional Commission, albeit in a dramatically watered-down form.[185] Among those ideas that found their way into the constitution were the clear delineation of the rights of the union republics and the right of republican secession from the USSR. However, no restrictions were placed on the potential amendment of the article on secession (Article 72), unlike the version proposed by the subcommittee.[186] More fundamentally, the 1977 constitution did not signal a dramatic shift in the structure of the Soviet state or the distribution of political power, as envisioned by Khrushchev, Mikoyan, and others. Much more significant state reforms, echoing the democratic idealism of the Thaw, would be realized only in the constitutional changes of another era—that of glasnost' and perestroika. Mikhail Gorbachev's New Union Treaty of 1991 seemingly promised the realization of the real free union of republics that Mikoyan and the NPNSC Subcommittee had envisioned and proposed in the 1960s.

Overall, the history of Mikoyan's role in the 1960s Soviet constitutional reform and the 1961 Party Program demonstrates that the tendency of the Khrushchev government in the early 1960s was toward greater decentralization to the union republics and autonomous entities. In Mikoyan's formulation, the aim of the Soviet government would be the realization of the USSR as a genuine union of sovereign states. Although such promises ultimately went unrealized in the 1960s, they nevertheless underscore Khrushchev's reform initiatives as an ambitious and admirable effort to reject the long shadow of Stalinism in favor of a more inclusive, representative, and democratic model of Soviet socialism.

Conclusions

How does one manage difference in a multinational, multiethnic state? In the context of the Thaw-era Soviet Union, Anastas Mikoyan offered an answer proceeding from the premise that the diversity of the state should be embraced. This fundamental idea guided the evolution of the Soviet nationality policy during the Khrushchev years, with Mikoyan playing a key role in the articulation and development of the new policy approach. This approach constituted a rejection of Stalinist state violence and centralization. It was structured on the basis of the principles of state unity and a respect for cultural diversity, ideas that, although not new in the history of the Soviet nationality policy, were nevertheless given new life by Mikoyan during the Thaw. Under Mikoyan's guidance, Moscow rejected policies that advocated assimilation in favor of those that promoted ethnic diversity within the framework of the unified state, as well as greater decentralization and self-governance for national entities. The Soviet state likewise rejected mass repression in the nationality sphere by implementing the rehabilitation of national cultural figures, as well as the return of deported nationalities. However, the aim of state unity also led to political struggles between Moscow and republican elites to define the limits of acceptable national expression. Moreover, the new approach toward national policy, as articulated by Mikoyan, had its limits and did not go unchallenged within the Soviet leadership.

All of these different aspects of the Khrushchev-era nationality policy, as guided by Mikoyan, have been explored in detail throughout this study. Chapter 1 argues for the significance of the 1937 Yerevan intervention in setting the stage for Mikoyan's later reform efforts during the Thaw. The intervention exemplified Stalin's disregard for the autonomy of national republics, while Mikoyan's participation in the repressions in Armenia left him with a guilt that guided his later reform initiatives on de-Stalinization and nationality policy. Chapter 2 contends that Mikoyan articulated the framework for Thaw-era nationality policy reform in his March 1954 speech in Yerevan, an address that doubled in significance as setting the stage for Khrushchev's denunciation of Stalin and enabling the process of the mass rehabilitation of political prisoners. The matter of articulation is particularly noteworthy in the historical context of the post-Stalin USSR. After Stalin's death, Beria and Khrushchev moved to employ a series of reforms aimed at expanding the space for national expression in the context of their competition for the Soviet leadership. Both men sought to use the issue to solidify their respective power bases. However, Mikoyan was the first Soviet political figure to articulate a concrete framework toward a post-Stalin nationality policy in his 1954 Yerevan speech. His expressed approach of waging a dual struggle against both "national nihilism" and "national chauvinism" provided the foundation for the struggle that would characterize Moscow's relations with the republics during the Khrushchev years. Mikoyan also used the 1954 speech to connect the question of nationality policy reform directly with de-Stalinization in his call for the rehabilitation of the poet Yeghishe Charents. By invoking the name "Charents," Mikoyan tied a greater sensitivity toward national expression with the dismantling of Stalin's personality cult, the rehabilitation of Gulag victims, and the advancement of what he and Khrushchev called "socialist democracy" within the CPSU and Soviet society generally. In this respect, the speech underscored another important aspect of Khrushchev-era nationality policy—the rehabilitation of repressed national cultural figures.

As Chapters 3, 4, and 5 underscore, Mikoyan pursued reforms throughout the Thaw that reflected the spirit of the nationality policy framework that he outlined in Yerevan. As chapter 3 demonstrates, Mikoyan was actively invested in highlighting his native Armenia as a successful model of Soviet nationality policy achievement to both foreign and domestic audiences. He assisted Armenian leaders on projects large and small, from the Arpa-Sevan Canal to the development of Sanahin's village economy. In the process, he fostered a patronage network through his dual role as an advocate and an advisor for the republic. By eschewing official hierarchies in his deferential approach toward Armenian leaders, he became the most senior partner in the project to "build socialism" in Armenia with the aim of projecting it as the model realization of the nationality policy in action. Meanwhile, across the various regions of Armenia, from Alaverdi to Agarak, state receptions for Mikoyan functioned as popular festivals of Armenian national achievement in the Soviet context. Nevertheless, despite the achievements of Mikoyan and his Armenian network, they were unable to find a resolution to the ongoing conflict over Nagorno-Karabakh favorable to the Karabakh Armenians. The Karabakh quandary ultimately demonstrated the serious limitations of the

Soviet nationality policy and state structure generally, underscoring the necessity of political reform.

As chapter 4 contends, Mikoyan invoked his personal experiences as a Bolshevik revolutionary during the civil war years as a response to growing national sentiments in the USSR, especially in the Caucasus. In the context of Armenia, he frequently contrasted the lived experiences of many Armenians during the First Armenian Republic of 1918–20 with the accomplishments and benefits of Soviet Armenia. The lesson that he emphasized was that the First Republic's dependence on the Western Allies failed to deliver any promised good for the Armenian people. In this context, Mikoyan underscored his identity as both a committed Bolshevik revolutionary and an Armenian patriot. The two, as he regarded it, were not mutually exclusive but rather mutually reinforcing and constitutive, a decidedly "Apricot socialist" view that informed his commitment to the geopolitical integrity of the multiethnic Soviet state. Within the Caucasus context, Mikoyan also worked tirelessly to preserve the memory of the twenty-six Baku commissars and frequently invoked them in his public speeches, especially his comrade and revolutionary mentor Stepan Shahumyan. By highlighting the example of the Baku 26, Mikoyan sought to promote the idea of the Soviet *druzhba narodov*, of national coexistence and cooperation in the pursuit of common aims in the service of the revolution and Soviet state building. Moreover, by tying the fate of the Baku 26 to the victims of Stalinism, he underscored the relevance of the commissars to contemporary political struggles over de-Stalinization.

As chapter 5 argues, Mikoyan followed his philosophy on the nationality question through his actions in the North Caucasus. As with his 1954 Yerevan speech, Mikoyan tied reform of the nationality policy to de-Stalinization, which, in the North Caucasian context, found its expression in the rehabilitation of deported peoples. In working to right the wrongs of Stalinism, Mikoyan's personal experiences again influenced his views on this issue. During his time as governor of the North Caucasus during the NEP period, Mikoyan pursued an inclusive and deferential approach toward the nationalities of the region and played a key role in promoting political autonomy for Chechnia and Ingushetia. From the time of Stalin's death, he actively began working behind the scenes with Khrushchev to rehabilitate the deported North Caucasian nationalities, encountering resistance from state security officials. In 1956, Mikoyan met with Chechen and Ingush representatives and subsequently led the Mikoyan Commission to ensure the return of deported nationalities to their homelands and the restoration of their autonomous republics. However, as Mikoyan, Khrushchev, and other high officials soon discovered, this process was far from easy or clear-cut. The restoration of Checheno-Ingushetia raised new challenges for the Soviet government. Among the most pressing of these was the delimitation of new borders among the North

Caucasus republics, which prompted the rise of new territorial disputes, most notably the protracted conflict over the Prigorodnyi raion. Managing tensions between the established Slavic settlers and Chechen and Ingush returnees presented additional challenges, eventually erupting in the 1958 Groznyi riots. These realities once again served as a reminder of the manifold dilemmas of governing such a vast multiethnic state. In such cases, pragmatic policies trumped ideological considerations. Moreover, the process of the rehabilitation of repressed nationalities had its limits. While the Khrushchev government favored the return of most of these groups (e.g., the Chechens, Ingush, Balkars, and Kalmyks), others (e.g., the Crimean Tatars and Volga Germans) were less fortunate.

Chapter 6 highlights Mikoyan's efforts to realize nationality policy reform, both in the CPSU's 1961 Party Program and in the initiative to develop a new Soviet constitution in the early 1960s. As part of his endeavor to break with Stalinism and move the country toward a form of "democratization," Khrushchev began to develop a new Party Program, and for that project, Mikoyan's input on the nationality question became essential. Mikoyan's rejection of the *sliianie* concept represented an official defeat for assimilationist approaches within the CPSU. It further spoke to the reality that, despite the struggle between Moscow and the union republics during the 1950s, the overall orientation of Khrushchev's government was toward greater decentralization within the union. Similarly, Mikoyan rejected the characterization of the Soviet nationality policy as "territorial," leaving open the possibility that it could also encompass questions of individual citizenship and personal extraterritorial nationality rights. The reasons for the acceptance of such proposals remain unknown, although both Mikoyan's proximity to Khrushchev and his position as a non-Russian from the Caucasus, with experience in managing difference, offer potential clues in this regard. Ultimately, the statesman's recommendations, as articulated in the drafts of the Party Program, were largely adopted by the Khrushchev government. Enshrined in the nationality platform of the final version published in 1961, they strongly echoed the ideas that Mikoyan first articulated in Yerevan in 1954.

Impressed by Mikoyan's arguments and ideas, Khrushchev deferred to him as his chief reformer on the nationality question and appointed him chairman of the NPNSC Subcommittee of his constitutional reform commission. It was through this position that Mikoyan worked with others to reform the Soviet state structure by enhancing the rights of the union republics and autonomous entities at the expense of the central government. Encompassing a variety of views, the subcommittee worked to reverse the centralization of the 1936 Stalin constitution and return to the "democratic" spirit of the Lenin constitutions of 1918 and 1924. In particular, Mikoyan stressed that the USSR was more than a federal state and that it was in fact a union state—a free association of individual republics, more on the order of a confederation. Such a formulation implied a much more devolved Soviet state, with significantly greater self-governance for the republics in relation to the central government in Moscow. Moreover, it was fully consistent with Khrushchev's stated aim of democratization, to expand the role of the citizen in the governance of the "all-people's state." Nevertheless, Mikoyan did not articulate the specifics of this union vision, leaving today's historian with more questions than answers. One area requiring particular clarification would be the status of national autonomous republics, oblasts, and okrugs. Although Mikoyan supported enhancing the rights of these entities, he did not specify how he could reconcile that support with his vision for a greatly devolved union, which could threaten the status and position of national autonomies.

The role of Anastas Mikoyan is essential to our understanding of the development of the post-Stalin nationality policy. His reforms represented a significant departure from Stalinist dictatorship, centralization, and mass violence. They came to define the nationality policy during the Thaw and beyond, representing a crucial part of Khrushchev's wide-ranging reform effort to reject the Stalinist legacy. At the same time, these ideas did not go unchallenged within the Soviet leadership. Mikoyan often struggled to have them adopted, and some of his ideas on nationality policy and state structure were ultimately unrealized. These ideas, such as his vision for a decentralized union state, were not only evidently ambitious but also vague on concrete details, leaving one to ponder how they might have evolved if Khrushchev and Mikoyan had remained in office. Ultimately, the end of the Thaw cut short what might have been a consequential reform effort for the Soviet state. What is clear is that Mikoyan's favored approach for an inclusive model of managing difference has universal significance, beyond Russia and the former Soviet Union, recognizing diversity as an asset and an opportunity. It is an approach toward governance from which societies the world over can still learn.

GLOSSARY OF PLACE NAMES

Throughout the twentieth century, and especially since the dissolution of the USSR in 1991, many of the place names mentioned in this study have changed. The older names are used in the text within their respective historical contexts. This glossary serves as a guide to readers, allowing them to match the former name with its contemporary equivalent. The historical names are listed below on the left, while the present names are listed on the right. This glossary does not include easily recognizable variants, such as Ashkhabad/Ashgabat, Ghapan/Kapan, Kiev/Kyiv, Lenkoran'/Lankaran, and Shamkhor/Shamkir.

Historical Name	*Present Name*
Akmolinsk	Astana, Kazakhstan
Aleksandropol'	Gyumri, Armenia
Alma-Ata	Almaty, Kazakhstan
Azizbekov	Vayk, Armenia
Bashkiria	Republic of Bashkortostan, Russia
Belorussia	Belarus'
Chatghran	Nor Geghi, Armenia
Daralagyaz	Vayots Dzor marz, Armenia
Elar	Abovyan, Armenia
Firiuza	Archabil, Ashgabat, Turkmenistan
Frunze	Bishkek, Kyrgyzstan
Ghamarlu	Artashat, Armenia
Gor'kii	Nizhnii Novgorod, Russia
Gyumush	Karenis, Armenia
Iakutia	Republic of Sakha (Iakutia), Russia

Kamo	Gavar, Armenia
Khanlar	Goygol, Azerbaijan
Kirgizia	Kyrgyzstan (Kyrgyz Republic)
Kirovakan	Vanadzor, Armenia
Koghb	Tuzluca, Turkey
Krasnovodsk	Turkmenbashy, Turkmenistan
Lenin Square, Yerevan	Republic Square, Yerevan
Leninakan	Gyumri, Armenia
Leningrad	St. Petersburg, Russia
Lusavan	Charentsavan, Armenia
Moldavia	Moldova
Mikoyan	Yeghegnadzor, Armenia
Nor Bayazet	Gavar, Armenia
Ordzhonikidze	Vladikavkaz, Republic of North Ossetia-Alania, Russia
Sardarabad	Armavir, Armenia
Shagali	Vahagni, Armenia
Shahumyan	Ashaghy Aghjakend, Azerbaijan
Stalingrad	Volgograd, Russia
Tataria	Republic of Tatarstan, Russia
Tiflis	Tbilisi, Georgia
Turkmenia	Turkmenistan
Uzunlar	Odzun, Armenia
Uzuntala	Aygehovit, Armenia
Zangezur	Syunik marz, Armenia*
Zankou (Zangu) River	Hrazdan River, Armenia

* Historically, the larger region of Zangezur/Syunik could also encompass several adjoining territories, especially Vayots Dzor (Daralagyaz) but also much of Gegharkunik (centered on Lake Sevan), as well as parts of Nagorno-Karabakh and Azerbaijan's Nakhichevan' exclave. On the historical Armenian principality of Syunik, see Hewsen, *Armenia*, 121–123.

NOTES

INTRODUCTION

1. The full expression in Russian is "*Ot Il'icha do Il'icha bez infarkta i paralicha*," referring to Mikoyan's tenure in high office from Vladimir Il'ich Lenin to Leonid Il'ich Brezhnev.

2. On Mikoyan's role in the Soviet food industry, see Glushchenko, *Obshchepit*.

3. On Mikoyan's role in Soviet-Cuban relations, see Sergo Mikoyan, *Anatomiia Karibskogo Krizisa* and *Soviet Cuban Missile Crisis*.

4. The term "de-Stalinization" is of Western origin, whereas Soviet leaders officially referred to the rejection of the Stalinist legacy as the "overcoming" or "exposing" of the "cult of personality" (*preodolenie/razoblachenie kul'ta lichnosti*). For further information, see Jones, *Dilemmas of De-Stalinization*; Jones, *Myth, Memory, Trauma*; Bittner, *Many Lives of Khrushchev's Thaw*; and Bohn, Einax, and Abeßer, *De-Stalinisation Reconsidered*.

5. Denis Kozlov and Eleonory Gilburd, "The Thaw as an Event in Russian History," in D. Kozlov and Gilburd, *Thaw*, 18, 25.

6. A. Mikoyan, *Rech' na sobranii izbiratelei*, 42–43.

7. On Mikoyan's support for Khrushchev in the events of 1957, see A. Mikoyan, *Tak bylo*, 644–645. On the case of the "Anti-Party Group," see Taubman, *Khrushchev*, 310–324.

8. Hirsch, *Empire of Nations*, 9.

9. In addition to the 1960s constitutional reform effort, Khrushchev's government experimented with economic devolution in the sovnarkhoz reform. Although the outcome of the reform was mixed, Mikoyan praised the initiative as a "very good idea of Khrushchev's, based on the experience of the 1920s," since it "delegated power to the localities and, most importantly, to the republics." (A. Mikoyan, *Tak bylo*, 648.) On the history of the reform, see Kibita, *Soviet Economic Management under Khrushchev*.

10. Suny and Kivelson, *Russia's Empires*, 330.

11. Burbank and Cooper, *Empires in World History*, 12.

12. Although 301 is the traditional date for the Christianization of Armenia, historians have cited a range of other dates, with 313 or 314 being the most favored. For further information, see Hacikyan et al., *Heritage of Armenian Literature*, 1:75–81.

13. Abraham Terian, "Introduction," in Terian, *Life of Mashtots'*, 3–4. See also Hacikyan et al., *Heritage of Armenian Literature*, 1:83–91.

14. A. Mikoyan, *Tak bylo*, 30–31. On the Sanahin monastery, see Khalpakhchian and Alpago-Novello, *Documents of Armenian Architecture* 3.

15. Riga, *Bolsheviks and the Russian Empire*, 4. For a related argument, see Gerasimov, "Great Imperial Revolution," 21–44.

16. Riga, *Bolsheviks and the Russian Empire*, 218–221.

17. Richard Simeon, "Introduction," in Basta, McGarry, and Simeon, *Territorial Pluralism*, 1.

18. John McGarry and Brendan O'Leary, "Territorial Pluralism," in Basta, McGarry, and Simeon, *Territorial Pluralism*, 34.

19. A. Mikoyan, *Rech' na sobranii izbiratelei*, 42–43.

20. For examples of such works, see Hirsch, *Empire of Nations*; Martin, *Affirmative Action Empire*; Suny and Martin, *State of Nations*; Slezkine, "USSR as a Communal Apartment," 414–452; Blitstein, "Stalin's Nations"; Edgar, *Tribal Nation*; and Khalid, *Making Uzbekistan*.

21. Blitstein, "Researching Stalin's Nationality Policy," 126–127.

22. On Buriatia, see Chakars, *Socialist Way of Life*. On Ukraine, see Risch, *Ukrainian West*; and Tromly, "Unlikely National Revival," 607–622. On Latvia, see Prigge, *Bearslayers*; and Loader, "Stalinist Purge," 244–282. On Georgia, see Kaiser, *Georgian and Soviet*; Blauvelt and Smith, *Georgia after Stalin*; and Scott, *Familiar Strangers*. On Azerbaijan, see Goff, *Nested Nationalism*.

23. Loader, "Beria and Khrushchev," 1759–1792.

24. See Risch, *Ukrainian West*, 20; Amar, *Paradox of Ukrainian Lviv*, 15–16; and Chernyshova, "De-Stalinisation and Insubordination," 387–409.

25. For examples, see Connor, *National Question*, 398–399; Goff, *Nested Nationalism*, 150; Risch, *Ukrainian West*, 22; Simon, *Nationalism and Policy*, 245–258; and Michael Loader, "The Centre-Periphery Relationship during Khrushchev's Thaw: The View from Latvia," *Peripheral Histories*, January 7, 2017, https://www.peripheralhistories.co.uk/post/the-centre-periphery-relationship-during-khrushchev-s-thaw-the-view-from-latvia.

26. Conquest, *Russia after Khrushchev*, 207.

27. Risch, *Ukrainian West*, 22.

28. Suny and Kivelson, *Russia's Empires*, 330.

29. Lehmann, "Apricot Socialism," 13. Claire Kaiser advances a similar argument in Kaiser, *Georgian and Soviet*. For Anderson's arguments, see Anderson, *Imagined Communities*.

30. Khalid, *Making Uzbekistan*, 9–10.

31. A. Mikoyan, *Tak bylo*, 27–28.

32. Mikoyan published parts of his memoirs in several installments in *Iunost'* from late 1966 to early 1969. The first installment (his memories of Sergo Ordzhonikidze) appeared in the October 1966 issue of the magazine. Additional installments followed, beginning with the issue of March 1967 and then the issues from November 1967 to February 1968, from May to June 1968, and finally from September 1968 to April 1969. For the two volumes published by Politizdat, see A. Mikoyan, *Dorogoi bor'by* and *V nachale dvadtsatykh. . . .*

33. As Sergo Mikoyan noted in his introduction to the post-Soviet edition of his father's memoirs, "It needs to be said that the second volume carried the visible imprint of the heavy hand of the editors and censors of the CPSU Central Committee." (Sergo Mikoyan, "Zhizn', otdannaia narodu," in A. Mikoyan, *Tak bylo*, 10.) On Mikoyan's personal experiences with censorship of his memoirs, see A. Mikoyan, *Tak bylo*, 685.

34. Sergo Mikoyan, "Zhizn', otdannaia narodu," 12.

35. For the Armenian translations, see A. Mikoyan, *Payk'ari ughiov* and *K'sanakan t'vakanneri skzbin.*

36. For example, an Armenian reader in Paris, P. Muradyan, penned a letter to Mikoyan on July 10, 1973, expressing his "exceptional happiness in reading your superb book *The Path of Struggle*." "I can modestly say," he wrote, "that through your memoirs, I became much better acquainted with the events of 1915–23 than through the many histories that I read." (RGASPI 84/3/105/32.)

37. The Parisian diasporan wrote the following to Mikoyan on October 10, 1972: "How happy we diasporan Armenians would be if your charming, as well as educational, memoirs were published in the beautiful and wonderful Armenian orthography of Hovhannes Tumanyan, Avetik Isahakyan, Ashot Hovhannisyan, and Vahan Teryan." In his letter, the author addressed Mikoyan with the traditional (and very respectful) honorific Armenian title *tiar*, rendered in the corresponding Russian translation as *mnogouvazhaemyi* (highly respected) by the translator A. Ohanyan. (RGASPI 84/3/105/5–6ob.) On the Armenian orthography issue in relations between Soviet Armenia and the Armenian diaspora, see Panossian, *Armenians*, 344–345.

38. For the English translation of the first volume, see A. Mikoyan, *Memoirs of Anastas Mikoyan.*

39. See Stepan Mikoyan, *Vospominaniia voennogo liotchika-ispytatelia*. For the English translation, see Stepan Mikoyan, *Memoirs of Military Test-Flying.*

40. The question of why the Soviet Union dissolved—the "question of questions" (*vopros voprosov*)—continues to elicit, even provoke, intense debate and discussion throughout the post-Soviet space, especially in Russia. For a recent Russian study on this issue, see Maslov, Lazareva, and Sukhanova, *Prichiny raspada SSSR.*

1. PRELUDE: YEREVAN 1937

1. This study uses the term "Great Purge" as opposed to "Great Terror." The term "Great Terror" was coined by Robert Conquest, and as historian David Hoffmann reminds us, this name "implies that the purpose of the arrests and executions was to

terrorize the population." In fact, as Hoffmann stresses, "the arrests and executions of the mass operations were conducted in secret, and their [stated] purpose was to eliminate enemies, not to frighten people into submission," although "doubtlessly, Stalinist violence did terrorize victims and their families, and in fact Soviet leaders had no compunction about using terror." "In other words," he concludes, "these actions were not exemplary violence aimed at terrorizing the population." (Hoffmann, *Stalinist Era,* 108.)

2. The 1937 Yerevan intervention is referred to as the "Armenian Affair" (*Armianskoe delo*) by Russian historian Andrei Sorokin. (Sorokin, *"Prakticheskii rabotnik" Georgii Malenkov,* 102–109.)

3. On the Transcaucasian SFSR, see Forestier-Peyrat, "Soviet Federalism at Work," 529–559.

4. For example, Miklós Kun contends that Mikoyan and Malenkov "had instigated a bloodbath in Armenia," even though the Great Purge was already well underway in the republic. The theory that Mikoyan and Malenkov independently "instigated" the Purges in Armenia also removes the agency of Stalin, Beria, and the local Armenian leadership. See Kun, *Stalin,* 290.

5. Suny, *Looking toward Ararat,* 156–157.

6. Aghayan, *Nersik Stepanian,* 39–41. On Beria's history of the Bolsheviks in Transcaucasia, see Suny, *Making of the Georgian Nation,* 265–266.

7. Aghayan, *Nersik Stepanian,* 24–25, 36, 43–47. In addition to his efforts to preserve Armenian national culture, Stepanyan was known for his sensitivity to the cultures of Armenia's Kurdish and Tatar (Azerbaijani) minorities.

8. HAA 1191/4/100/1–7, 17.

9. Aghayan, *Nersik Stepanian,* 39.

10. HAA 1191/4/102/221, 1191/4/103/287, and 1191/4/104/328.

11. Alazan, *Tarapank'i ughinerov,* 64.

12. The thorough Thaw-era investigation included consultation with A. A. Ivanova, an investigator of the all-union Party Control Committee who was present in the building of the Transcaucasian Kraikom at the time of Khanjyan's murder. According to Ivanova, she and her colleagues heard two gunshots emanating from Beria's office. Ivan Korotkov, chairman of the Party Control Committee, rushed to the scene to investigate. He later privately revealed to Ivanova that Beria had personally shot Khanjyan. However, he declined her proposal to inform Moscow about the murder, and he forbade her from doing so, believing that the "story will sort itself out." Later, on the train back to Moscow, Korotkov, who "loved to draw," reportedly drew a sketch from memory of Beria's office, with Khanjyan's dead body on the floor. The sketch was destroyed by Ivanova. The investigative report further revealed that Harutyun Mirza-Avagyan (Mirza-Avakov), the surgeon in Yerevan who initially examined Khanjyan's body, concluded that the wound had been inflicted by a gun fired at a distance and not at close range. Mirza-Avagyan himself later became a victim of Stalin's repressions, reportedly for concluding that Khanjyan had been murdered. See

Artizov et al., *Reabilitatsiia*, 1:314–316, 1:411n18. See also HAA 1191/12/2117/31–39 and RGASPI 17/171/442/72–76.

13. Anahit Charents, "Yeghishe Charents's Final Years: His Life and His Work from 1934–1937," trans. Aris G. Sevag and Sylvia Dakessian, in Nichanian, *Yeghishe Charents*, 86.

14. Lavrentii Beria, "Razveiat' v prakh vragov sotsializma," *Pravda*, August 19, 1936, 2–4. The article was also published on the front page of the Russian-language Soviet Georgian newspaper *Zaria Vostoka* the following day. See Lavrentii Beria, "Razveiat' v prakh vragov sotsializma," *Zaria Vostoka*, August 20, 1936, 1–2.

15. Beria, "Razveiat' v prakh vragov sotsializma," 2. Beria specifically wrote that Chobanian raised the issue of Armenian national-territorial claims to Khanjyan in a letter from 1936 in connection with the development of the 1936 constitution. "I'm talking not only about Ani, Ararat, Kars, and Surmalu, which were transferred to Turkey," wrote Chobanian, "but also about Akhalkalaki and [Mountainous] Karabakh . . . and about Nakhichevan', which has always been part of Armenia."

16. Marshall, *Caucasus under Soviet Rule*, 239–240.

17. Medvedev, *K sudu istorii*, 283.

18. For instance, in the village of Tegh, near Goris in Armenia's Syunik marz, an elderly man in 2015 recounted Mughdusi's active role in the repressions, noting that one of the local victims, Avetis Sargsyan, was the grandfather of future Armenian President Serzh Sargsyan. "Mughdusi was a rare bastard," the man recalled. "Every single person hated and feared him at the same time." See David Stepanyan, "We Had to Cheer when Serzh Sargsyan's Grandfather Was Taken Away," *ArmInfo*, June 1, 2015, https://arminfo.info/full_news.php?objectid=24F7DE10-082E-11E5-A8420EB7C0D21663.

19. For Stalin's March 3 speech at the plenum and the plenary resolution on Ezhov's report "exposing" the activities of "Japanese-German-Trotskiite agents," see Khaustov, Naumov, and Plotnikova, *Lubianka*, 95–114.

20. Petrov and Jansen, *"Stalinskii pitomets" Nikolai Ezhov*, 175–183. For the abstracts from Ezhov's report at the June plenum, see Danilov and Manning, *Tragediia Sovetskoi Derevni*, vol. 5, bk. 1, 306–308.

21. HAA 1/17/66/30–31. For Amatuni's letter to Stalin, see HAA 1/17/66/27–36.

22. HAA 1/17/66/27–30. According to Mary Kilbourne Matossian, "the Specifists might be best described as 'national marxists' rather than 'marxist nationalists'; like members of the Jewish Bund, their principal point of disagreement with the Bolsheviks and the Mensheviks was on the issue of permitting the existence of autonomous ethnic units within the R.S.D.R.P. organization." Formed in 1903, the Specifists "never acquired a large following," but they nevertheless "represented a tendency of long-range significance: the tendency to demand greater consideration for national peculiarities in the implementation of overall social-democratic policies." (Kilbourne Matossian, *Impact of Soviet Policies*, 23–24, 50–51.) For additional information on the Specifists, see Ter Minassian, *Nationalism and Socialism*, 33–37.

23. HAA 1/17/66/27.

24. HAA 1/17/66/28.

25. The death of Ter-Gabrielyan reportedly had a lasting impact on Mikoyan. In his memoirs, Anton Kochinyan recounted that, during a trip to southern Armenia in the late 1960s, he, Mikoyan, and other officials stopped at the village of Tegh, near Goris. From Tegh, locals pointed out the location of the birthplace of Ter-Gabrielyan in nearby Nagorno-Karabakh. Upon hearing the name of Ter-Gabrielyan, Mikoyan reportedly felt "deep sorrow," recalling the Armenian leader's "tragic death" in August 1937. (Kochinyan, *Anavart husher*, 287.)

26. These quotes are derived from the testimony of Liparit Barseghyan, a member of the Soviet Communist Party in Armenia since 1925, who served as a member of the Armenian Central Committee Secretariat in the 1930s. A victim of the Stalinist repressions, Barseghyan sent his testimony to the deputy head of the Investigative Department of the Armenian KGB Col. Ruben Piruzyan and Armenian First Secretary Suren Tovmasyan on November 18, 1955. For the full text, see HAA 1191/9/1078/294–299.

27. HAA 1191/9/1078/388 and 1191/9/1077/18–20.

28. HAA 1191/9/1078/387 and 1191/9/1077/119–122.

29. HAA 1191/9/1078/389. The exact location of the third-floor window from which Ter-Gabrielyan fell is marked with a red "x" in a schematic plan of the Armenian State Security (NKVD/KGB) building marked "secret" in the files of Ter-Gabrielyan in the repressed persons fond (1191) of the HAA. According to the plan, the distance from the windowsill to the ground was ten meters (thirty-three feet). (HAA 1191/9/1078/376.)

30. For Stalin's letter, see GARF R-5446/120/607/18–19. According to the December 1957 testimony of Malenkov's assistant Dmitrii Sukhanov, when Stalin heard the news of Ter-Gabrielyan's death, he wrote a short note to Malenkov stating, "I don't believe that Ter-Gabrielyan would jump out of the window. He was thrown out. This case needs to be investigated." Sukhanov claimed that he personally saw this note and that Malenkov drafted the September 8 letter based on it, on the orders of Stalin. (RGANI 6/19/12/42.) However, in his testimony to Nikolai Shvernik from June 30, 1958, Malenkov asserted that the letter was dictated to him personally by Stalin and that Stalin then gave him the short note afterward, before his departure for Yerevan. (RGANI 6/19/10/1–2.) Stalin's personal records indicate that he received Malenkov at 6:40 p.m. (18:40) on the evening of September 8, 1937. (Chernobaev, *Na priiome u Stalina*, 219.)

31. GARF R-5446/120/607/18.

32. GARF R-5446/120/607/18.

33. GARF R-5446/120/607/18–19.

34. RGASPI 17/171/499/6–7, 11; and RGANI 6/19/12/43.

35. On April 25, 1955, at the Chief Military Prosecutor's Office in Moscow, Arsenovich testified to Colonel of Justice A. N. Vitievskii and Senior Lieutenant of

Justice Rygalin that Stalin personally selected Litvin to participate in the 1937 Yerevan intervention. (HAA 1191/12/2115/125.) The following year, in 1938, Litvin would commit suicide in Leningrad, leaving the note "I can no longer take part in the murder of innocent people and the fabrication of spurious cases." According to Anton Antonov-Ovseenko, when Mikoyan heard about Litvin's suicide note, "he muttered, 'at least one honest man was found among that gang.'" (Antonov-Ovseenko, *Time of Stalin*, 160.)

36. RGANI 6/19/12/43. Donskoi and Smirnov, along with Sukhanov and Litvin, also attended the plenum. (HAA 1/17/24/8.)

37. RGANI 6/19/12/42–43.

38. N. Khrushchev, *Memoirs of Nikita Khrushchev*, 2:202.

39. Fitzpatrick, *On Stalin's Team*, 127; and Sorokin, *"Prakticheskii rabotnik" Georgii Malenkov*, 89–109.

40. RGASPI 17/171/499/3, 7; RGANI 6/19/12/43; and HAA 1191/12/2115/125–216.

41. Georgia under Beria held the dubious distinction of having one of the USSR's highest rates of executions and arrests per head of population during 1937–38. According to historian Alex Marshall, "30,512 citizens [in the republic] underwent arrest, and between March 1937 and September 1938 some 3,486 individuals were sentenced to death, which placed Georgia in third place nationally behind Moscow oblast' and the Ukrainian SSR, and even higher if one takes into account the per capita percentage of the overall population affected." (Marshall, *Caucasus under Soviet Rule*, 238.)

42. RGANI 6/19/12/44–45.

43. For Malenkov's speech at the plenum of the Tatar obkom of August 23–25, 1937, see RGASPI 83/1/10/89–103. See also Sorokin, *"Prakticheskii rabotnik" Georgii Malenkov*, 100–101.

44. HAA 1191/9/1078/295; and RGASPI 17/171/500/83, 92.

45. RGANI 6/19/12/43; and RGASPI 17/171/499/3, 7.

46. Bagirov's presence in Yerevan is recounted in both the December 27, 1957, testimony of Dmitrii Sukhanov (RGANI 6/19/12/43, 45) and the September 15, 1953, testimony of Georgii Tsaturov (HAA 1191/9/1078/332 and 1191/12/2115/159–160).

47. RGASPI 17/171/500/83–84.

48. RGASPI 17/171/499/3 and 17/171/500/84; and HAA 1191/1/48/101–106 and 1191/12/2115/131.

49. RGASPI 17/171/499/4 and 17/171/500/84, 92–93.

50. RGASPI 17/171/500/84.

51. RGASPI 17/171/499/4 and 17/171/500/85. In his April 1955 testimony, Arsenovich recounted that Mughdusi was "badly beaten" under interrogation and that "his face was covered with bruises." (HAA 1191/12/2115/128.)

52. This account was related by former Armenian NKVD lieutenant Bagrat Kostikyan to Liparit Barseghyan while in jail. Like Barseghyan, Kostikyan was also arrested by the NKVD brigade during the Yerevan intervention. (HAA 1191/9/1078/296–297.)

53. RGASPI 17/171/499/4 and 17/171/500/85.

54. RGASPI 17/171/500/84.
55. RGASPI 17/171/500/85.
56. RGASPI 17/171/499/4–8.
57. RGANI 6/19/12/43.
58. RGASPI 17/171/499/5. For Gor'kii's article from which Malenkov quoted, see Maksim Gor'kii, "Esli vrag ne sdaetsia—ego unichtozhaiut," *Pravda*, November 15, 1930, 2. Notably, at the meeting of the Party Control Committee of the CPSU Central Committee of July 1, 1958, Malenkov confessed to personally participating in the beatings, although he initially denied it. (RGASPI 17/171/500/86, 95–96.)
59. HAA 1191/12/2115/127.
60. RGASPI 17/171/500/52, 91. As Arsenovich testified, the "whole brigade moved into the Armenian NKVD building and lived there for 3–4 days." (HAA 1191/12/2115/126.)
61. HAA 1/17/61/32.
62. RGASPI 17/171/500/87. In his testimony before the July 1958 meeting of the Party Control Committee, Petrov noted that he attended the plenum and sat in the first row. (RGASPI 17/171/500/85.) His attendance is confirmed in the existing *protokoly* recorded by Mushegh Danelyan. (HAA 1/17/24/8.)
63. RGASPI 17/171/500/51, 88, 90.
64. RGASPI 17/171/500/90.
65. RGASPI 17/171/500/51.
66. According to Armen Ananyan and Liparit Barseghyan, in the text that Malenkov read before the plenum, Guloyan "confessed" to being a member of a "Transcaucasian counter-revolutionary right-Trotskiite insurgent center." Ananyan added that the alleged aim was to launch an "armed uprising" to split off the entirety of Transcaucasia from the USSR and "to establish a bourgeois order in Transcaucasia." Barseghyan further testified that Malenkov also read aloud the "confession" of Mughdusi, who "revealed" that he had been recruited by Khanjyan into a "counter-revolutionary organization" as early as 1933. According to the text, Mughdusi likewise "confessed" to running his own separate "counter-revolutionary organization" within Armenia's state security apparatus and that his organization was responsible for throwing Ter-Gabrielyan out the window because Ter-Gabrielyan planned to "expose" them. For Ananyan's testimony, from July 1, 1958, see RGASPI 17/171/500/90. For Barseghyan's testimony, from November 18, 1955, see HAA 1191/9/1078/295.
67. RGASPI 17/171/500/90–91. These quotes are from Armen Ananyan's testimony against Malenkov from July 1, 1958. No transcript of the plenum is known to exist in either the HAA or the archive of the National Security Service of Armenia. Only two copies of Mushegh Danelyan's *protokoly* of the plenum, both in Russian, are held at the HAA's Social-Political Archive (formerly the Armenian Party Archive) in Yerevan. (HAA 1/17/24/8–11 and 1/17/25/7–10.) In a top secret letter to Khrushchev from August 5, 1957, Armenian First Secretary Suren Tovmasyan noted the following: "After checking the archival materials of the Armenian Central Committee, it was

not possible to find any traces of the minutes and transcript of the September (1937) plenum of the Central Committee of Armenia. Probably, Comrade Malenkov seized the documents of the plenum at that time, and they are possibly in the archives of the Central Committee of the CPSU." (RGASPI 17/171/498/121.) However, there is also no transcript of the plenum in the CPSU Central Committee files in RGASPI.

68. Artizov et al., *Reabilitatsiia*, 2:586.

69. TsA FSB RF 3/4/149/66. The document, dated September 15, 1937, is reproduced in Petrov and Jansen, *"Stalinskii pitomets" Nikolai Ezhov*, 251. It is also quoted in Nikolai Shvernik's January 1958 report to Khrushchev about Malenkov's role in the Yerevan intervention. (RGASPI 17/171/499/11.) See also Artizov et al., *Reabilitatsiia*, 2:586.

70. RGASPI 17/171/499/11. According to Sukhanov, who misidentified Agrba as the "secretary of the Nagorno-Karabakh Obkom," Malenkov summoned the Abkhaz leader to a meeting in the office of the Armenian first secretary. After a brief conversation, he promptly instructed Litvin to arrest Agrba. (RGANI 6/19/12/45.) On September 21, Ezhov ominously ordered Litvin to send both Agrba and Akopov to Moscow "urgently." (TsA FSB RF 3/4/149/120.)

71. HAA 1/17/24/9–10.

72. RGANI 6/19/12/44.

73. RGASPI 17/171/499/11.

74. HAA 1/17/24/10.

75. TsA FSB RF 3/4/149/85.

76. HAA 1/17/24/10.

77. HAA 1191/16/2297/2. After four years of investigation, the Military Collegium of the Soviet Supreme Court sentenced Hovhannisyan to an eight-year imprisonment on July 9, 1941, with the loss of civil rights and confiscation of all property. He was later released early on April 15, 1943, and permitted to leave the Gulag labor camps of the Komi Republic and return to Armenia. (GARF R-5446/120/1100/59.) However, he was never legally exonerated, and after the death of Stalin, he appealed to Voroshilov and the Soviet military prosecutor on June 12 and December 31, 1953, respectively. (GARF R-5446/120/1100/59–66.) Finally, Hovhannisyan met personally with Mikoyan in Yerevan on March 12, 1954, one day after the statesman's call to rehabilitate Charents. (GARF R-5446/120/1113/3.) As a result of this meeting, he provided Mikoyan with copies of his earlier appeals, as well as a direct appeal to Mikoyan for his full rehabilitation and support for the publication of his scientific historical works. (GARF R-5446/120/1100/55–58.) Hovhannisyan would be fully rehabilitated by the Soviet government on August 11, 1954. (HAA 1191/1/48/113.) Upon his arrival in Moscow from Yerevan on November 4, he telegrammed Mikoyan seeking a meeting, presumably to thank him for his assistance. (GARF R-5446/120/1100/67–68.) Significantly, although Mikoyan mentioned Hovhannisyan's repression in his memoirs, he did not discuss his personal role in his rehabilitation. (A. Mikoyan, *Tak bylo*, 47.)

78. For the full letter, see HAA 1191/16/2297/2–25. After the September 1937 intervention, Hovhannisyan again provided testimonies to the NKVD about various political and cultural figures in Armenia from January 27 to 31, 1938. (HAA 1191/16/2297/30–107.)

79. For the section on Amatuni in the September 19 letter, see HAA 1191/16/2297/19–23.

80. HAA 1191/12/2116/171–173; and GARF R-5446/120/607/20–21.

81. GARF R-5446/120/607/20. The same *delo* includes an excerpt from Amatuni's autobiography about his departure from Armenia in 1930 in connection with his involvement in the Lominadze group. (GARF R-5446/120/607/23.) On the Lominadze affair, see Khlevniuk, *In Stalin's Shadow*, 30–39, 69–77. Lominadze's widow, Nina, was arrested by the NKVD on January 9, 1938. For the crime of being the spouse of an "enemy of the people," she spent eight years in a Gulag labor camp at Akmolinsk in Soviet Kazakhstan. After her release in 1946, she was arrested again in Tbilisi in 1951 and sentenced to a second exile in Kazakhstan. Her son, Sergo, was arrested in 1943 and sentenced to a ten-year imprisonment that he served in camps in the Far East and Far North. Amnestied in March 1953, Nina appealed to Mikoyan for her rehabilitation in May 1954. (GARF R-5446/120/1100/134–134ob, 136–138.) Mikoyan forwarded her request to Roman Rudenko and asked to be updated about the results of her case. (GARF R-5446/120/1100/135.)

82. GARF R-5446/120/607/22.

83. GARF R-5446/120/607/21.

84. GARF R-5446/120/607/22.

85. GARF R-5446/120/607/21. In his letter, Amatuni further instructed Hovhannisyan to send his response through Gumedin. (GARF R-5446/120/607/22.) A close friend of Aghasi Khanjyan, Gumedin (born Gurgen Dadayan or Melik-Dadayan) was known to be skeptical of the official explanation regarding the death of Armenia's former first secretary. According to the August 12, 1953, testimony of Evgeniia Baghdasaryan, the sister of Gumedin's wife Asya, an "agitated" Gumedin once said in a private family conversation that "the death of Khanjyan was the work of Beria." He also claimed that Beria had suggested to Khanjyan that he commit suicide but that Khanjyan refused. (Mozokhin, *Politbiuro i delo Beria*, 251–254.) Gumedin was arrested by the NKVD brigade in Yerevan on September 18, 1937, and executed on September 16, 1938. He was later rehabilitated on February 2, 1956. ("Gumedin, Gurgen Khorenovich," *Stalinskie rasstrel'nye spiski (Mezhdunarodnyi Memorial)*, accessed January 1, 2025, https://stalin.memo.ru/persons/p42568/; RGASPI 17/171/498/124; and HAA 1191/12/2115/142, 194.)

86. GARF R-5446/120/607/21. Hovhannisyan wrote more directly about Amatuni's address in his letter to the Soviet military prosecutor from December 31, 1953, in Yerevan. (GARF R-5446/120/1100/63–66.) For Amatuni's speech, see Amatuni Amatuni, "Ob itogakh plenuma TsK KP(b) Armenii," *Zaria Vostoka*, October 30, 1936, 2–4.

87. HAA 1/17/52/156, 159–160.

88. HAA 1/17/52/147–155, 161–163, 167.

89. For the full record of the meeting, see HAA 1/17/58/1–10.

90. HAA 1/17/58/6. The official was R. Galstyan of the Agricultural Department of the Armenian Central Committee.

91. For examples, see the testimonies given by Armenian officials to Malenkov regarding "sabotage" in the Alaverdi and Stepanavan raions in HAA 1/17/58/1–4.

92. In one case, Kh. Smbatyan of the Armenian Party Control Committee informed Malenkov that Shamshadin Raikom Secretary Gevorgyan once drank a toast to Khanjyan's health. (HAA 1/17/58/5.) In another case, Armenian Central Committee propaganda chief Gino Shaghgamyan informed Malenkov that "there were facts" that the wife of Ijevan's Second Secretary B. Sargsyan "made counter-revolutionary statements after the death of Khanjyan." (HAA 1/17/58/6.)

93. For example, in the case of Stepanavan, Malenkov proposed setting up an investigative team to examine the problem with "Trotskiites" and "sabotage" in the area more closely. (HAA 1/17/58/3–4.)

94. By the time Mikoyan arrived in Yerevan, Stalin already had knowledge of the sabotage allegations. He instructed Malenkov to update Mikoyan on the matter. (TsA FSB RF 3/4/149/105.)

95. TsA FSB RF 3/4/149/85, 105; and Danilov and Manning, *Tragediia Sovetskoi Derevni*, vol. 5, bk. 1, 605n70. Relying on Mushegh Danelyan's *protokoly* of the plenum, scholars previously assumed that Mikoyan had arrived with Malenkov and Litvin at the start of the Yerevan intervention but remained in the background during the first few days. For example, in her account, Sheila Fitzpatrick wrote that Mikoyan, "discomforted by the presence of so many friends and clients," decided to keep "as much as possible in the background at the party plenum and let Malenkov do the talking." (Fitzpatrick, *On Stalin's Team*, 127.)

96. Chernobaev, *Na priiome u Stalina*, 220.

97. TsA FSB RF 3/4/149/85. The document is reproduced in Petrov and Jansen, *"Stalinskii pitomets" Nikolai Ezhov*, 251, although the *list* number is given as 65 rather than 85. On the execution of the Baku 26, see Suny, *Baku Commune*, 337–343. For Mikoyan's personal account, see A. Mikoyan, *Tak bylo*, 94–110.

98. TsA FSB RF 3/4/149/85.

99. TsA FSB RF 3/4/149/105. On September 17, Stalin instructed Malenkov to return on September 25 or 26 and stated that Litvin should remain in Yerevan and wait for orders from Ezhov. (TsA FSB RF 3/4/149/85.)

100. Malenkov attended the final session of the plenum on September 23. (HAA 1/17/24/11.)

101. The typewritten copy of Malenkov's testimony to Nikolai Shvernik from June 30, 1958, notes that although Mikoyan participated in the plenum, he did not participate directly in the actual investigation. (RGANI 6/19/10/2.) The existing evidence and testimonies confirm this statement.

102. "Nash kandidat—tovarishch Mikoian" and "Kak odin otdadim nashi golosa t. Mikoianu," *Kommunist*, November 11, 1937, 1.

103. A. Mikoyan, *Tak bylo*, 629.

104. Well-known examples of Mikoyan's interventions include his colleague Napoleon Andreasyan, the poet Avetik Isahakyan, Marshal Ivan (Hovhannes) Baghramyan, the sculptor Yervand Kochar, and the Bonner family. In fact, Ruth Bonner's husband (Elena's father) was Gevorg Alikhanyan (Alikhanov), a former classmate of Mikoyan's at the Nersisyan School in Tiflis. Mikoyan also attempted to save Aleksei Snegov. On Andreasyan, see RGASPI 84/3/348/106; and A. Mikoyan, *Tak bylo*, 629. On Isahakyan, see Ashkhen Mikoyan, "Avetik Isaakian i Anastas Mikoian," *Aravot*, June 2, 2014, https://ru.aravot.am/2014/06/02/180030/. On Baghramyan, see Sergo Mikoyan, *Hayrs Anastas Mikoyane*, 50; and Medvedev, *Oni okruzhali Stalina*, 152–153. On Kochar, see Haykaz Kochar's account in Hovhannisyan and Martirosyan-Kochar, *Maestro K'ochare*, 173. On the Bonner family, see Bonner, *Mothers and Daughters*, 323–324. On Snegov, see Sergo Mikoyan, "Aleksei Snegov v bor'be za 'destalinizatsiiu,'" 69–70; and Medvedev, *Oni okruzhali Stalina*, 153–155.

105. Stepan Mikoyan, *Vospominaniia voennogo liotchika-ispytatelia*, 40.

106. Pavlov, *Anastas Mikoian*, 92.

107. Sergo Mikoyan, "Stalinism as I Saw It," 185–186.

108. A. Mikoyan, *Tak bylo*, 628–629.

109. Ibid., 629. Similarly, in his June 1958 testimony to Nikolai Shvernik, Malenkov noted that Mikoyan arrived in Armenia with a mandate from the CPSU Central Committee. (RGANI 6/19/10/2.)

110. Sergo Mikoyan, "Stalinism as I Saw It," 157.

111. Fitzpatrick, *On Stalin's Team*, 127.

112. A. Mikoyan, *Tak bylo*, 629.

113. For a list of Party members invited to the evening plenary proceedings of September 22, see HAA 1/17/32/6–9; and GARF R-5446/120/607/33–36.

114. At the September 19 meeting with Malenkov, Armenian ORPO instructor S. Gasparyan highlighted Galustyan's impressive administrative record in Amasia, praising him as a "highly respected" and "very energetic worker" who "enjoys great authority" and did "a great job during his short time" in the district. (HAA 1/17/58/4.) More sinisterly, during the first phase of the Great Purge in Armenia, Galustyan also reported to Amatuni on alleged "Dashnaks" and "Trotskiites" in Amasia, in a letter dated May 14, 1937. (GARF R-5446/120/607/30.)

115. HAA 1/17/24/10.

116. HAA 1/17/58/9. In his December 1957 testimony, Sukhanov also discusses Shaghgamyan's speech. (RGANI 6/19/12/44.)

117. A. Mikoyan, *Tak bylo*, 629–630.

118. The attendee was A. A. Isahakyan, a Party member since 1929. (RGASPI 17/171/499/5–6.) Isahakyan was among the Armenian Party members invited to attend the September 22 evening session of the plenum. (HAA 1/17/32/7; and GARF R-5446/120/607/34.)

119. The notes are held in GARF R-5446/120/607/1–17. They appear to have been hastily assembled at the last minute by Mikoyan in advance of his plenary address. Such a practice was not uncommon for Mikoyan. His ability to improvise speeches was a skill that he first developed during his revolutionary years. As he stressed in his memoirs, "speeches were not read from a piece of paper, but delivered on the fly, often improvised." (A. Mikoyan, *Tak bylo*, 27.) This point was raised by Azerbaijani Old Bolshevik Mamed Veisov during Mikoyan's meeting with Old Bolsheviks in Baku in March 1964. Veisov recalled attending an underground Bolshevik meeting in 1919 in which Mikoyan spoke but did not have a written speech and only used notes. "You also spoke without a summary," he told Mikoyan, "but you frequently took out individual quotes on cigarette paper from your left and then your right pockets." "We didn't have briefcases," Mikoyan jokingly responded. (GARF R-5446/120/1844/26.)

120. GARF R-5446/120/607/2. In his memoirs, Mikoyan further recounted having to read (*zachitat'*) a letter at the plenum, although he did not specify the author of the document. (A. Mikoyan, *Tak bylo*, 629.)

121. HAA 1/17/24/10.

122. Haroot, "Purges in Soviet Armenia," 138. The *Armenian Review* editorial note accompanying the account identifies the author, writing under the pseudonym "Arman Haroot," as a former member of the editorial staff of *Khorhrdayin Hayastan* who fled to Germany and then to the United States. An anti-Stalinist émigré, Haroot maintained a pro-Bukharin position, referring in his text to Nikolai Bukharin as "a second Lenin, the latter's dearest comrade." (Haroot, "Purges in Soviet Armenia," 134.)

123. Haroot, "Purges in Soviet Armenia," 138. Vardges Vardapetyan was also arrested in 1937. (HAA 1191/12/2115/2 and 1191/12/2116/8.)

124. Cohen, *Victims Return*, 91. Two well-known instances of Mikoyan dissenting on the use of force from later in his career include his stances on Hungary in 1956 and on Novocherkassk in 1962. On Novocherkassk, see Baron, *Bloody Saturday*, 47. On Hungary, see Taubman, *Khrushchev*, 294. See also S. Khrushchev, *Nikita Khrushchev: Rozhdenie sverkhderzhavy*, 161–163.

125. Sergo Mikoyan, "Zhizn', otdannaia narodu," in A. Mikoyan, *Tak bylo*, 18. The quote was paraphrased by Sergo from Natalia Mostovenko, who was present when Mikoyan made his remarks at a gathering commemorating the one-year anniversary of the death of Lev Shahumyan. For Mostovenko's full account, see Mostovenko, *Odin god*, 147–148. Although Mostovenko was uncertain if Mikoyan used the word "scoundrels" (*negodiai*) or "bastards" (*merzavtsy*), Sergo noted that his father would most likely have used the latter term. (Sergo Mikoyan, "Aleksei Snegov v bor'be za 'destalinizatsiiu,'" 84; and Casper, "Bolshevik Afterlife," 33.)

126. The existing evidence indicates that the 1915 Genocide weighed heavily on Mikoyan, as reflected in his later writings. See A. Mikoyan, *Tak bylo*, 41, 194–195; and GARF R-5446/120/1110/327.

127. RGASPI 17/171/498/126. For the full report, entitled "On the Work to Uncover and Liquidate the Counter-revolutionary Underground in Armenia," see RGASPI

17/171/498/123–129. The copy held in RGASPI was sent by Armenian State Security (later KGB) Chairman Georgi Badamyants to Armenian First Secretary Tovmasyan on July 10, 1957. Tovmasyan then sent it directly to Khrushchev on August 5, in the aftermath of the defeat of the "Anti-Party Group." (RGASPI 17/171/498/120–122.)

128. For the full text of Order 00447, see Danilov and Manning, *Tragediia Sovetskoi Derevni*, vol. 5, bk. 1, 330–337; and Khaustov, Naumov, and Plotnikova, *Lubianka*, 273–281. The quoted text is derived from the English translation in Getty and Naumov, *Road to Terror*, 473–480.

129. For Amatuni's message to Ezhov and Stalin, see RGASPI 17/166/575/140. Incidentally, together with Voroshilov, Kaganovich, and Chubar', Mikoyan was one of those who signed off on Amatuni's note. In Transcaucasia, the numbers for Category 1 repressions as established with Order 00447 on July 30, 1937, were 2,000 for the Georgian SSR, 1,500 for the Azerbaijan SSR, and 500 for the Armenian SSR. The numbers for Category 2 were 3,750 for the Azerbaijan SSR, 3,000 for the Georgian SSR, and 1,000 for the Armenian SSR. (Danilov and Manning, *Tragediia Sovetskoi Derevni*, vol. 5, bk. 1, 331–332; and Khaustov, Naumov, and Plotnikova, *Lubianka*, 375.)

130. RGASPI 17/171/498/126.

131. During the Ezhovshchina, the common practice was for the highest-ranking official in the republic (usually the first secretary) to determine the quotas for Category 1 and Category 2 repressions, which would then be sent to Stalin and Ezhov for approval. This fact alone makes the Mikoyan-Malenkov-Litvin request of September 22 so exceptional, as it was a request advanced by three men as opposed to one. Overall, the fact that Mikoyan was expected to take on the responsibilities of the local first secretary in this instance is significant, as it again reflects the degree to which the Armenian government was being directly run from Moscow during the intervention period.

132. Danilov and Manning, *Tragediia Sovetskoi Derevni*, vol. 5, bk. 1, 367. A copy of the document is reproduced in Sorokin, *"Prakticheskii rabotnik" Georgii Malenkov*, 107; and Petrov and Jansen, *"Stalinskii pitomets" Nikolai Ezhov*, 252. In *Tragediia Sovetskoi Derevni* (published in 2004), the original document was cited as APRF 3/58/212/113. However, the much more recent Sorokin and Petrov-Jansen publications note that the document is now held in RGANI, although they do not provide a specific archival cipher. The original message arrived in Moscow at 11:00 p.m. (23:00) on September 22, 1937.

133. RGASPI 17/166/580/10 and 17/162/22/12. A copy of the first of these two documents is reproduced in Sorokin, *"Prakticheskii rabotnik" Georgii Malenkov*, 108; and Petrov and Jansen, *"Stalinskii pitomets" Nikolai Ezhov*, 252. See also Khaustov, Naumov, and Plotnikova, *Lubianka*, 376.

134. Sorokin, *"Prakticheskii rabotnik" Georgii Malenkov*, 107.

135. A. Mikoyan, *Tak bylo*, 629–630.

136. Ibid., 630.

137. Ibid., 38, 41–43.

138. HAA 1191/1/47/4 and 1191/1/45/2.

139. HAA 1191/1/47/10 and 1191/1/45/1.

140. HAA 1191/1/48/122–123. A victim of the Purges, Adoyan spent six months with Shahverdyan in an Armenian NKVD jail cell beginning in October 1937. Shahverdyan told Adoyan about his refusals to endorse Beria's historical "interpretations." He recounted that during the one of his interrogations, one of the investigators told him that "for refusing to carry out Beria's order, your death in prison is sufficient." The investigator added, "Understand, you old dog, that your main act against the revolution is your malicious refusal of Beria." Shahverdyan told Adoyan, "Do not forget that my sole 'crime' was my refusal to write memoirs to Beria's taste."

141. HAA 1191/1/47/212–216.

142. HAA 1191/1/47/215–216. The text is an excerpt of the protocol from Mughdusi's interrogation, conducted by Litvin, Al'tman, and Geiman.

143. Mikhail Kotliarov, "Dela vragov Armianskogo naroda," *Pravda*, September 28, 1937, 2.

144. A. Mikoyan, *Tak bylo*, 630.

145. HAA 1191/1/49/111.

146. A. Mikoyan, *Tak bylo*, 630.

147. Shahverdyan's first appeal, from August 4, 1939, was addressed to Mikoyan, Beria, Soviet Prosecutor General Mikhail Pankrat'ev, Soviet Supreme Court Chairman Ivan Goliakov, and Chairman of the Military Collegium of the Soviet Supreme Court Vasilii Ul'rikh. (HAA 1191/1/48/3–12.) His second appeal, from January 29, 1940, was a direct, handwritten appeal addressed only to Mikoyan. (HAA 1191/1/48/13–20.) Shahverdyan addressed a similar direct appeal to Stalin on February 14, 1940. (HAA 1191/1/48/22–26.)

148. HAA 1191/1/49/111.

149. HAA 1/17/24/10. For an earlier draft of the letter, see GARF R-5446/120/607/54–57.

150. HAA 1/17/24/12–15.

151. HAA 1/17/24/13.

152. HAA 1/17/24/14.

153. HAA 1/17/24/15.

154. HAA 1/17/24/11.

155. RGASPI 17/171/500/51.

156. HAA 1191/9/1078/256; and RGASPI 17/171/498/125.

157. HAA 1191/12/2115/126.

158. HAA 1191/9/1078/256–263. According to the report of Armenian KGB captain Kostandyan, no records of Amatuni's interrogation exist before October 7, 1937.

159. RGASPI 17/171/413/105, 17/171/414/378, 17/171/416/68, and 17/171/417/213. Despite documented evidence of Amatuni's active involvement in Stalin's Purges as an ally of Beria, he was posthumously rehabilitated in 1977 by the all-union Military Commission and the KGB. Inexplicably, the KGB's investigative report

from November 4, 1977, concluded that there was "no sufficient evidence of Amatuni's involvement in illegal repressions." (HAA 1191/12/2117/145.) He was posthumously reinstated to full membership in the Party on February 8, 1978. (Filippov, *Territorial'nye rukovoditeli VKP(b)*, 95.) An earlier effort to rehabilitate Amatuni during the Khrushchev era was rejected by the Soviet government due to his role in the Purges. In a letter to the all-union Central Committee on June 15, 1956, Armenian First Secretary Suren Tovmasyan detailed Amatuni's crimes and named several of his victims, including Mahari, Alazan, Norents, Totovents, Bakunts, Shahverdyan, Adoyan, and many others. He also drew special attention to the case of Charents. (HAA 1191/12/2117/12–15.) Tovmasyan's letter was based on the official May 1956 report on the Amatuni case by a special commission of the Armenian Central Committee, which consisted of Shmavon Arushanyan, Hrachya Margaryan, A. R. Ayvazyan, Georgi Badamyants, and V. S. Zakharyan. (HAA 1191/12/2115/188–193.) On September 1, 1977, Badamyants testified that his role in the commission was "very passive" and "almost formal." He likewise cast doubt on its conclusions, noting that, except for himself, most of the members were in Armenia during 1936–37, and therefore their findings were influenced by their "purely subjective experiences and personal perceptions" of Amatuni's leadership. (HAA 1191/12/2116/4–5.) Nevertheless, the report of the commission does reflect the existing archival record regarding Amatuni's active role in the Purges, as evidenced by his June 1937 letter to Stalin on the "struggle against counter-revolution" and his July 1937 message to Stalin and Ezhov on setting quotas for Category 1 and Category 2 repressions. (HAA 1/17/66/27–36; and RGASPI 17/166/575/140.)

160. N. Mikoyan, *Svoimi glazami*, 62.

161. Ibid., 44.

162. Ibid., 65. In 1926, Geurkov began studying in Moscow at the Scientific Automotive Institute (NAMI). When Nami was born, her parents originally considered giving her the traditional Armenian name Gayane after her grandmother in Telavi, Georgia. However, in a burst of revolutionary enthusiasm befitting the NEP era, her parents decided to name her Nami after the Scientific Automotive Institute instead. "My father lived in the future," she recalled in her memoirs. (N. Mikoyan, *Svoimi glazami*, 17–18.)

163. GARF R-5446/120/607/58. In the document, the section on Galustyan is underlined in red.

164. GARF R-5446/120/607/59–60.

165. HAA 1/17/24/11. As plenary chairman, Danelyan also wrote out and signed the *protokoly* of the September plenum. (HAA 1/17/24/8–11.) His surname is alternatively spelled "Danelyan" on some documents and "Danielyan" on others.

166. Chernobaev, *Na priiome u Stalina*, 220–221.

167. HAA 1/17/37/1–6.

168. For the materials dealing with Mikoyan's trip to Yerevan in relation to the Supreme Soviet elections of December 1937, see GARF R-5446/120/605–606, 608–611.

Mikoyan was to hold his Supreme Soviet post long after Arutinov's eventual dismissal in 1953, stepping down only in 1974 under backstage pressure from Brezhnev. (Sergo Mikoyan, "Anastas Mikoian," 451.)

169. N. Mikoyan, *Svoimi glazami*, 132.

170. Khvorostian was also awarded the Order of the Red Star on December 19, 1937. He remained Armenia's internal affairs chief until his arrest in February 1939 and later died in Moscow's Butyrka prison on June 6 of that same year. (Petrov and Skorkin, *Kto rukovodil NKVD*, 428.)

171. Khaustov, Naumov, and Plotnikova, *Lubianka*, 379–380.

172. Danelyan was arrested by the NKVD brigade in Yerevan on October 19, 1937, executed on July 18, 1938, and posthumously rehabilitated on September 24, 1955. ("Danelian, Musheg Nersesovich," *Stalinskie rasstrel'nye spiski (Mezhdunarodnyi Memorial)*, accessed January 1, 2025, https://stalin.memo.ru/persons/p30050/; RGASPI 17/171/498/124; and HAA 1191/12/2115/127–128, 139, 181.) Galustyan was arrested by Beria's Georgian NKVD on October 31, 1937, executed in Yerevan on September 16, 1938, and posthumously rehabilitated on December 28, 1955. (Filippov, *Territorial'nye rukovoditeli VKP(b)*, 187–188.) Margaryan was also arrested by the Georgian NKVD, but just over two weeks later, on November 16. He was executed on December 29, 1937, in Tbilisi and posthumously rehabilitated on August 8, 1956. (Filippov, *Territorial'nye rukovoditeli VKP(b)*, 388.)

173. Minasyan, *How Did I Survive?*, 36–38. At the time, Minasyan was temporarily working in the local Party leadership of the Nakhichevan' ASSR.

174. RGASPI 17/166/575/58.

175. Khaustov and Samuelson, *Stalin, NKVD i repressii*, 300.

176. On Nazi Germany's relations with Kemalist Turkey, see Ihrig, *Atatürk in the Nazi Imagination*.

177. RGASPI 17/166/580/47–50. At the time, the raions of Amasia, Artik, Sardarabad, and Ghamarlu also included the territories of the future raions of Ghukasyan, Ani, Baghramyan, and Masis, respectively. For an administrative map of Soviet Armenia during this period, see Vardanyan, Sargsyan, and Nazaryan, *National Atlas of Armenia*, 2:117.

178. Tsutsiev, *Atlas of Ethno-Political History*, 74–76; and Hewsen, *Armenia*, 266–267. See also Burdett, *Caucasian Boundaries*, 1:745, 1:780; and Burdett, *Armenia*, 1:670, 1:678.

179. Bournoutian, "Iran-Turkey-Armenia Borders," 99–102. See also Burdett, *Caucasian Boundaries*, 1:744, 1:780; and Burdett, *Armenia*, 1:670, 1:677.

180. Tsutsiev, *Atlas of Ethno-Political History*, 96–97. According to scholar Pavel Polian, "a total of 40 border districts of Georgia, Armenia, Azerbaijan, Turkmenistan, Uzbekistan and Tajikistan were assigned [by Soviet authorities] to be cleansed of 'unreliable elements.' In particular, 1,325 Kurds that had resided in the frontier zone were resettled to [the] Kyrgyz Republic and Kazakhstan. At the end of 1937, 1,121 Kurd and Armenian families from Armenia and Azerbaijan arrived in Kazakhstan (Alma-Ata

and South Kazakhstan Obls.)." (Polian, *Against Their Will*, 102.) See also Pobol' and Polian, *Stalinskie deportatsii*, 75–80.

181. RGASPI 17/166/580/47.

182. For further background, see Omarkhali, "Kurds in the Former Soviet States," 133. See also Goff, *Nested Nationalism*, 47–48; and Michiel Leezenberg, "Soviet Kurdology and Kurdish Orientalism," in Kemper and Conermann, *Heritage of Soviet Oriental Studies*, 91. Initially, even after the September 27 resolution, the Armenian government continued to highlight the promotion of Kurdish culture in Armenia as one of the successes of the Soviet nationality policy. For instance, during the Supreme Soviet elections in December 1937, a female Kurdish representative (Javahir Sukiasyan) spoke not only in favor of Mikoyan's election as a Supreme Soviet deputy but also about Kurdish cultural achievements in the republic, including the publication of the Kurdish-language newspaper *Rya T'eze*. ("Predvybornaia vstrecha tovarishcha Mikoiana s izbirateliami," *Kommunist*, December 8, 1937, 1.) However, the gradual repression against Kurdish culture continued. *Rya T'eze* ceased publication in 1938 and did not resume publication until the Thaw, in 1955. ("Rya T'aza," in Hambardzumyan and Aruzmanyan, *Haykakan Sovetakan Hanragitaran*, 9:679.)

183. RGASPI 17/166/580/48–49.

184. For instance, on September 23, an article was published in Yerevan's *Kommunist* newspaper by Khachik Beroyan about the allegations of mass sabotage, under the ominous title "Enemies Operate in the Kolkhoz." (Khachik Beroyan, "Vragi oruduiut v kolkhoze," *Kommunist*, September 23, 1937, 3.) The focus was the Alaverdi raion, specifically the village of Shnogh, a community that was among those singled out by local Armenian officials in their demands for more repressions to deal with "Dashnak-Trotskiite sabotage" in their September 19 meeting with Malenkov. (HAA 1/17/58/1–2.) In his article, Beroyan claimed that the primary Party organization in Shnogh had been "infiltrated by counter-revolutionary sabotage elements" who, "in turn, accepted a number of Dashnaks to the kolkhoz and therefore hindered its growth and consolidation."

185. HAA 1191/12/2116/14–15.

186. HAA 1/17/66/35–36.

187. HAA 1191/12/2116/15. In his interview with KGB investigator Lt. Nikolai Oleshko, Kotliarov claimed that he spoke to Mikoyan on September 19. However, he apparently misremembered the exact date of their conversation, as Mikoyan did not arrive in Yerevan until September 20. Oleshko conducted the interview with Kotliarov on August 29, 1977, in connection with the reinvestigation of the case of Amatuni during the Brezhnev era. (HAA 1191/12/2116/12–17.)

188. "Hay zhoghovrdi aryune tstsogh izhere" and "Informats'ion haghordagrut'yun," *Khorhrdayin Hayastan*, September 26, 1937, 1; and "Besposhschadno gromit' i vykorchiovyvat' vragov naroda" and "Informatsionnoe soobshchenie," *Kommunist*, September 26, 1937, 1.

189. Mikhail Kotliarov, "Dela vragov Armianskogo naroda," *Pravda*, September 28, 1937, 2. Kotliarov also attended the Armenian Party plenum in Yerevan. (HAA 1/17/24/8 and 1/17/32/6; and GARF R-5446/120/607/33.)

190. See Mikhail Kotliarov, "Hay zhoghovrdi ts'hnamineri gortsere," *Khorhrdayin Hayastan*, September 29, 1937, 1; and Mikhail Kotliarov, "Dela vragov Armianskogo naroda," *Kommunist*, September 29, 1937, 2.

191. See, for example, "Kauch'uki kombinati ashkhatoghnere voghjunum en Enker Mikoyanin," *Khorhrdayin Hayastan*, November 11, 1937, 1; and "Haykakan khoh bolor ehntroghnerin" and "Avetik' Abovyani voghjuyni khosk'e," *Khorhrdayin Hayastan*, December 8, 1937, 2. In these pieces, the authors praised Mikoyan for his role in "exposing" and purging Amatuni, Akopov, Guloyan, Mughdusi, and other "Dashnak-Trotskiite" and "Bukharinite" "enemies" on the "instructions of Great Stalin." See also the November 1937 letter of the Armenian Composers' Union to Mikoyan in GARF R-5446/120/605/1–2ob. Notably, the narrative of the September 1937 events presented years later in the *Sketches of the History of the Communist Party of Armenia* did not mention Mikoyan or even Malenkov. (Aghayan et al., *Ocherki istorii kommunisticheskoi partii Armenii*, 387.)

192. As Armenian First Secretary Suren Tovmasyan reported in his top secret letter to Khrushchev on August 5, 1957, the memory of Malenkov's role in the repressions in Armenia fueled widespread popular support for Khrushchev's actions against the "Anti-Party Group." Tovmasyan noted that the resolution of the Central Committee's June Plenum "On the Anti-Party Group of Malenkov, Kaganovich, and Molotov" received "unanimous approval from the entire [Armenian] Party organization and all the working people of the republic." As one Armenian Party veteran remarked during a meeting of activists at Yerevan State University, "Malenkov is guilty and should be punished not only for the 'Leningrad Affair', but also for the fact that in 1937, upon his arrival in Armenia, he subjected many, many honest communists to repression without any reason." (RGASPI 17/171/498/120.) See also Tomilina et al., *Boi s "ten'iu" Stalina*, 123, 287–289.

193. As Mikoyan later wrote in his memoirs, "Stalin's main mistake [in nationality affairs], which was condemned by Lenin, was the attempt to lower the status of the independent Soviet republics to the position of powerless autonomies." (A. Mikoyan, *Tak bylo*, 557.)

2. YEREVAN 1954

1. GARF R-5446/120/1113/1. The Stalin statue was removed by the Soviet Armenian government in 1962 and later replaced by Ara Harutyunyan's Mother Armenia monument in 1967. (Panossian, *Armenians*, 349; Kaplanova, *Ara Arutiunian*, 86–88.) Armenian First Secretary Yakov Zarobyan did not rush in removing the statue and approached the matter carefully, out of sensitivity to neighboring Georgia, in the aftermath of the 1956 Tbilisi riots. (N. Zarobyan, *Iakov Zarobian*, 92–93.)

2. For the published booklet of the speech, see A. Mikoyan, *Rech' na sobranii izbiratelei*. An Armenian translation was also published that same year with a print run of ten thousand. (A. Mikoyan, *Char Yerevani*.) It was also published in the Russian-language Armenian daily *Kommunist* (A. Mikoyan, "Rech' tovarishcha A. I. Mikoiana," *Kommunist*, March 12, 1954, 2–4), and an Armenian translation was correspondingly

published in the daily *Sovetakan Hayastan* (A. Mikoyan, "Enker A. I. Mikoyani chare," *Sovetakan Hayastan*, March 12, 1954, 4–5). Additionally, an abridged version, notably without Mikoyan's invocations of Raffi, Patkanyan, Charents, and Myasnikyan and without his condemnation of national nihilism, also appeared in *Pravda* (A. Mikoyan, "Rech' tovarishcha A. I. Mikoiana," *Pravda*, March 12, 1954, 3).

3. Suny and Kivelson, *Russia's Empires*, 330.

4. For further discussion of the idea of "Apricot socialism," see Lehmann, "Apricot Socialism," 9–31.

5. See Cohen, *Victims Return*, 89–91; Casper, "Bolshevik Afterlife," 33–77; Fitzpatrick, *On Stalin's Team*, 241–246; Lewin, *The Soviet Century*, 246–247; Medvedev, *Oni okruzhali Stalina*, 163–166; Pavlov, *Anastas Mikoian*, 269–295; K. Smith, *Moscow 1956*, 32–46; and Taubman, *Khrushchev*, 278.

6. See Kilbourne Matossian, *Impact of Soviet Policies*, 201; Mouradian, *De Staline à Gorbatchev*, 206; Panossian, *Armenians*, 288–289; Suny, *Looking toward Ararat*, 180–181; Virabyan, *Hayastane Stalinits' minch'ev Khrushch'ov*, 212; and Walker, *Armenia*, 371.

7. On the 1965 Yerevan demonstrations, see Lehmann, "Apricot Socialism," 9–31; and Saparov, "Re-negotiating the Boundaries," 862–883. On the Karabakh movement, see Malkasian, *"Gha-ra-bagh!"* For an overview of these events in the context of Armenian history, see Panossian, *Armenians*, 319–323, 384–388.

8. Panossian, *Armenians*, 323.

9. Shepilov further noted that Beria's "manifesto on the nationalities question" was an "an artfully composed document with a good share of demagoguery" that was "calculated to sow divisions among the various nationalities rather than promote closer relations" and "to exploit precisely these antidemocratic, nationalist sentiments to his own advantage." (Shepilov, *Kremlin's Scholar*, 260–261.)

10. Loader, "Beria and Khrushchev," 1760–1761.

11. Risch, *Ukrainian West*, 20; Amar, *Paradox of Ukrainian Lviv*, 15–16; and Chernyshova, "De-Stalinisation and Insubordination," 387–409.

12. For the best overview, see Loader, "Beria and Khrushchev," 1759–1792.

13. Sergei Khrushchev, interview by Pietro Shakarian, Cranston, RI, May 3, 2019.

14. Sergo Mikoyan, *Hayrs Anastas Mikoyane*, 50.

15. On Arushanyan's criticisms of Arutinov at the Armenian Central Committee plenum of July 14–15, 1953, see Khlevniuk et al., *Regional'naia politika N. S. Khrushcheva*, 38–40. For accounts of Arutinov's downfall from the perspective of Armenian officials, see Astsatryan, *XX dar*, 127–131; and Kochinyan, *Anavart husher*, 173–178. Western scholarship traditionally attributes Arutinov's downfall to his ties with Beria, an argument first advanced by Mary Kilbourne Matossian. (Kilbourne Matossian, *Impact of Soviet Policies*, 200.) However, this explanation, based entirely on the limited information presented in the Soviet press in the 1950s, obscures the reality of the more complicated relationship between Arutinov and Beria.

16. The plenum lasted from November 28 to November 30. For the full transcript, see HAA 1/33/10–12.

17. Astsatryan, *XX dar*, 129–130.

18. Filippov, *Territorial'nye rukovoditeli VKP(b)*, 111.

19. HAA 1/33/12/97–99.

20. Filippov, *Territorial'nye rukovoditeli VKP(b)*, 111.

21. GARF R-5446/120/1268/33.

22. GARF R-5446/120/1721/12–13.

23. Casper, "Bolshevik Afterlife," 44. For the letters sent to Mikoyan, see GARF R-5446/120/1099–1101.

24. A. Mikoyan, *Tak bylo*, 636.

25. Casper, "Bolshevik Afterlife," 42–44.

26. A. Mikoyan, *Tak bylo*, 34. On Rafael Patkanyan and Raffi, see Hacikyan et al., *Heritage of Armenian Literature*, 3:316–318, 3:345–348.

27. On the "return to Leninism" during the Thaw, see Polly Jones, "From the Secret Speech to the Burial of Stalin: Real and Ideal Responses to De-Stalinization," in Jones, *Dilemmas of De-Stalinization*, 42–43.

28. Cohen, *Victims Return*, 91.

29. Mikoyan later recounted the following in his memoirs: "Many of my classmates are no longer alive. Unfortunately, some of them—[Gevorg] Alikhanyan, [Artak] Stamboltsyan, [Haykaz] Kostanyan, [Vahan] Balyan, [Garegin] Gardashyan, [Suren] Hakobyan, [Vahan] Yeremyan, [Sedrak] Margaryan—fell victim to the repressions of 1937–38. All were posthumously rehabilitated, and their honor was fully restored." (A. Mikoyan, *Tak bylo*, 45.)

30. Shatunovskaia not only worked alongside Mikoyan in Baku but also claimed to have shared a romantic relationship with him at one point, which she loved to recount years later. For details, see Shatunovskaia, *Ob ushedshem veke*, 90–101; and see also K. Smith, *Moscow 1956*, 96–97.

31. For Mikoyan's personal account of the Leningrad Affair, see A. Mikoyan, *Tak bylo*, 603–614. For another perspective from the Mikoyan family, see Stepan Mikoyan, *Vospominaniia voennogo liotchika-ispytatelia*, 198–202. Sergo Mikoyan likewise recounted his experience of the Leningrad Affair, as well as his marriage with Alla and her tragic passing from leukemia, in "Anastas Mikoian," 314–321, 703–707.

32. A. Mikoyan, *Tak bylo*, 609–610.

33. Ibid., 614.

34. For Mikoyan's account of the plenum and Stalin's attacks against him, see A. Mikoyan, *Tak bylo*, 618–627.

35. Stepan Mikoyan, *Vospominaniia voennogo liotchika-ispytatelia*, 200.

36. Vladimir Mikoyan, interview by Pietro Shakarian, St. Petersburg, January 14, 2023. According to Vladimir Mikoyan, "Zinaida Dmitrievna had been condemned in October 1950 (one year after execution of her husband) for ten years of imprisonment [in Vladimir] as the spouse of 'the enemy of the people.'" See also Stepan Mikoyan, *Vospominaniia voennogo liotchika-ispytatelia*, 200.

37. Artizov et al., *Reabilitatsiia*, 1:392n8.

38. On Charents, see Hacikyan et al., *Heritage of Armenian Literature*, 3:958–963.

39. HAA 1191/1/962/105–106, 129, 195–196.

40. HAA 1191/1/962/99, 196. A medical report from November 28, 1937, concluded that Charents's death was caused by echinococcus of the liver, enterocolitis, and effects of his morphine addiction, combined with a general exhaustion of the body. (HAA 1191/1/962/154–154a.) However, according to Charents's daughter, Anahit, "in 1955, following Stalin's death, I received my father's 'death certificate' from the State Security Committee of Armenia. A line was drawn opposite the 'cause of death,' while November 27, 1937 was recorded as the date of death. The site of his grave is unknown." (Anahit Charents, "Yeghishe Charents's Final Years: His Life and His Work from 1934–1937," trans. Aris G. Sevag and Sylvia Dakessian, in Nichanian, *Yeghishe Charents*, 101.)

41. RGANI 6/19/12/43–44.

42. RGASPI 17/171/500/87.

43. Minasyan, *How Did I Survive?*, 38.

44. HAA 1/17/73/180.

45. For the *protokoly* of the commission, see HAA 1/17/98. The *delo* notes that the work of the commission began on September 26, 1937, but the cases of *listy* 1–22 are undated, while only the cases beginning from *list* 23 are dated from September 26. The absence of a date for the first twenty-two *listy* suggests that work of the commission began earlier, likely on September 25, with intervening breaks on September 27 and 30. For additional materials related to the commission's work, see HAA 1/17/98–106 and 1/17/73/180–185, 187–188.

46. HAA 1/17/98/29.

47. HAA 1/17/73/180–185, 187–188.

48. RGASPI 17/171/500/80.

49. RGASPI 17/171/499/6. The eyewitness was G. A. Jalladyan, the former chairman of the Armenian Gosplan and later Soviet Armenia's permanent representative in Moscow.

50. For Izabella Charents's original handwritten letter to Mikoyan in Russian, see HAA 1/17/104/138–139. For a printed version of her letter in both Russian and Armenian, see D. Gasparyan, *Yeghishe Ch'arents'*, 620–621.

51. HAA 1191/1/964/1–2 and 1191/1/967/1.

52. HAA 1191/1/962/164.

53. Anahit Charents, "Yeghishe Charents's Final Years," 96.

54. Ibid., 101.

55. HAA 1191/1/962/186.

56. HAA 1/34/1/64. In the Armenian edition of Tovmasyan's speech, the phrase "cult of personality" is rendered as "*anhati pashtamunk'*." (Tovmasyan, *Hashvetu zekuts'um*, 80.) As historian Amatuni Virabyan notes, "It is true that the 'cult of personality' was addressed [by Tovmasyan] in an indirect and abstract way. However, it testifies to the fact that two years before the Twentieth Party Congress, there were already tendencies within the Party leadership in 1954 to overcome the 'cult.'" (Virabyan, *Hayastane Stalinits' minch'ev Khrushch'ov*, 210–211.)

57. For Pospelov's notes of Malenkov's remarks, see RGASPI 629/1/54/68–70. See also Sorokin, *"Prakticheskii rabotnik" Georgii Malenkov*, 517–524.

58. For Kochar's speech in Russian, see HAA 1/34/2/72–79. For the Armenian version, see HAA 1/34/4/12–23. Kochar's speech is also discussed by Virabyan in his study of postwar Soviet Armenia. (Virabyan, *Hayastane Stalinits' minch'ev Khrushch'ov*, 211–212.)

59. HAA 1/34/2/72 and 1/34/4/12. Pospelov referred to the concept of national nihilism in his criticism of Armenia's former first secretary Arutinov in the final morning session of the November 1953 plenum. (HAA 1/33/12/83.)

60. HAA 1/34/2/72–74 and 1/34/4/12–15. Subsequently, during his March 1954 visit to Armenia, Mikoyan met personally with Demirchyan on March 12, one day after his Yerevan speech. (GARF R-5446/120/1113/3.)

61. HAA 1/34/2/75 and 1/34/4/17–18.

62. Panossian describes Raffi and Abovyan as the "two towering giants of eastern Armenian literature" in the nineteenth century. Abovyan accompanied explorer Friedrich Parrot on the first recorded ascent of Mount Ararat in 1829 and later became the first Armenian author to write in vernacular Eastern Armenian rather than Classical Armenian (*grabar*). On Abovyan, see Hacikyan et al., *Heritage of Armenian Literature*, 3:211–214. On the significance of Abovyan and Raffi in the context of Armenian history, see Panossian, *Armenians*, 142–145.

63. For an English translation of *Khent'e*, see Raffi, *The Fool*.

64. Suny and Kivelson, *Russia's Empires*, 322; and Kilbourne Matossian, *Impact of Soviet Policies*, 168.

65. HAA 1/34/2/75 and 1/34/4/17–18.

66. HAA 1/34/2/75 and 1/34/4/17–18. On Shirvanzade, see Hacikyan et al., *Heritage of Armenian Literature*, 3:480–483.

67. HAA 1/34/2/75–76 and 1/34/4/18–19. Charents's "Along the Crossroads of History" expressed the poet's "bitterness and disappointment over Armenia's leadership, particularly during the eighteenth and nineteenth centuries, and ends with the sarcastic observation that in order to be saved, Armenia should perhaps attempt, like the camel in the parable, to pass through the eye of a needle (Matt. 19:24)." (Hacikyan et al., *Heritage of Armenian Literature*, 3:962.)

68. HAA 1/34/2/76 and 1/34/4/19.

69. On the Altai deportations, see Aleksanyan, *Sibirskii dnevnik*.

70. HAA 1/34/2/78 and 1/34/4/22–23. The Altai exiles were also addressed at the Seventeenth Armenian Party Congress by Georgii Martirosov, then the interior minister of Soviet Armenia. In his speech, Martirosov emphasized that the security forces were working to redress this "mistake," which he stated was the result of a trumped-up case against alleged "Dashnaks." This case, he claimed, was approved by former Armenian interior minister Sergei Korkhmazyan and former prosecutor Isahak Isagulov. (HAA 1/34/2/81–82.) However, as Virabyan notes, Isagulov became the republic's prosecutor only in December 1949, when the exile "had already long been an established fact." (Virabyan, *Hayastane Stalinits' minch'ev Khrushch'ov*, 212.)

Ironically, Martirosov himself was expelled from the Party a year later for his role in creating a trumped-up case against alleged "Dashnak counter-revolutionaries" as the head of the NKVD in Gagra, Abkhazia, in 1937, resulting in the execution of eighteen people and the long-term imprisonment of twelve more. (Artizov et al., *Reabilitatsiia*, 1:249.) Notably, in his speech at the Seventeenth Armenian Party Congress, Martirosov remarked that after the Central Committee plenum of July 1953 (in which Beria was expelled from the Party), his ministry already began "receiving a large number of appeals for the revision of investigative cases of individuals previously convicted, especially in 1936–37." (HAA 1/34/2/81.)

71. *Sovetakan Hayastan, № 8, Mart 1954.*

72. Ibid.; and A. Mikoyan, "Rech' na sobranii izbiratelei," March 11, 1954. Mikoyan commenced and concluded the speech in Armenian. In addition, he originally planned to read a quote from Hovhannes Tumanyan's poem "The Dog and the Cat" in Armenian when discussing the need to improve services in the republic. (GARF R-5446/120/1111/38–40.) However, he read this text in Russian when he delivered the final version of the speech.

73. For the first and earliest known draft of Mikoyan's speech, see GARF R-5446/120/1112/2–98. For the second draft, see GARF R-5446/120/1111/60–165 and R-5446/120/1083/1–89. For the third draft, see GARF R-5446/120/1111/2–55. GARF holds two copies of the second draft, one dated March 5, the other March 6. Although earlier versions of this study considered them to be separate drafts, they are in fact identical copies of the same draft with mostly the same handwritten editorial notes by Mikoyan.

74. GARF R-5446/120/1110/321–327. In the *delo*, this text is listed as "Materials handed over by Comrade Arzumanyan" ("*Materialy, peredannye t. Arzumanianom*"), although the authorship is unmistakably that of Mikoyan, given the style, tone, and political perspective of the writer, the accompanying corrections in Mikoyan's handwriting, and the fact that entire sections later appeared in the second and third drafts of the 1954 Yerevan speech. At the same time, it cannot be excluded that "Comrade Arzumanyan" (likely Mikoyan's close friend Anushavan Arzumanyan) assisted Mikoyan in developing the speech.

75. A. Mikoyan, *Tak bylo*, 195.

76. GARF R-5446/120/1112/1.

77. A. Mikoyan, *Rech' na sobranii izbiratelei*, 39–41. On the Baku Commune, see Suny, *Baku Commune*. On Sayat-Nova, see Hacikyan et al., *Heritage of Armenian Literature*, 2:869–880. On Tumanyan, see Hacikyan et al., *Heritage of Armenian Literature*, 3:619–622.

78. A. Mikoyan, *Rech' na sobranii izbiratelei*, 42.

79. Ibid. Until the Sovietization of Armenia in 1920, Mount Ararat had been part of Russian Armenia. The volcanic massif became part of Turkey as a result of the treaties of Moscow and Kars negotiated between the Bolsheviks and the Turkish Kemalists. (Panossian, *Armenians*, 248.) Nevertheless, Ararat was retained as a

national symbol by Soviet Armenia. In his memoirs, Khrushchev recalled the ways in which this situation impacted Soviet-Turkish relations: "On the Armenian flag there was a coat of arms depicting Mount Ararat, and Ararat is now located on Turkish territory. The Turks even complained to us, asking why Armenia had Mount Ararat on its flag. Was it making a claim to Turkish territory? Our reply to the Turks was this: 'Why do you have a half moon depicted on your flag? After all, the moon doesn't belong to Turkey, not even half the moon. What's going on? Do you want to take over the whole universe, and did you choose the moon as a symbol of that?' The border dispute was dropped. Istanbul withdrew its objections." (N. Khrushchev, *Memoirs of Nikita Khrushchev*, 3:467–468.)

80. A. Mikoyan, "Rech' na sobranii izbiratelei," March 11, 1954. The line "in full view of you, from Yerevan" was improvised by Mikoyan when he delivered the speech.

81. On Mikoyan's concern for Yerevan's security, see pages 87–88. For an English translation of Griboedov's play, see Griboedov, *Woe from Wit*.

82. Iosif Stalin, "Riech' t. Stalina," *Pravda*, May 24, 1918, 2. The Constituent Congress of the Tatar-Bashkir Soviet Republic was held on May 10–16, 1918, in Moscow. For Stalin's opening speech from the congress, see Stalin, "Riech' Stalina," *Pravda*, May 18, 1918, 1–2.

83. GARF R-5446/120/1112/92.

84. A. Mikoyan, *Rech' na sobranii izbiratelei*, 43.

85. A. Mikoyan, "Rech' na sobranii izbiratelei," March 11, 1954.

86. Ibid. Mikoyan ad-libbed the latter part of this line. In the published version, his words were toned down to "and strangely enough, by people with Party cards." (A. Mikoyan, *Rech' na sobranii izbiratelei*, 43.)

87. A. Mikoyan, "Rech' na sobranii izbiratelei," March 11, 1954.

88. See the first draft of Mikoyan's speech in GARF R-5446/120/1112/85–97.

89. GARF R-5446/120/1111/148–165.

90. GARF R-5446/120/1112/45–55.

91. A. Mikoyan, *Tak bylo*, 34.

92. GARF R-5446/120/1111/157.

93. For the overview, see GARF R-5446/120/1110/321–327.

94. GARF R-5446/120/1110/321–322. On Nazaryan, see Hacikyan et al., *Heritage of Armenian Literature*, 3:219–220.

95. HAA 1/34/64/54–58.

96. GARF R-5446/120/1110/299–303.

97. A. Mikoyan, "Rech' na sobranii izbiratelei," March 11, 1954.

98. Ibid.

99. For the first draft, see GARF R-5446/120/1112/92, and for the second, see GARF R-5446/120/1111/158 and R-5446/120/1083/7.

100. GARF R-5446/120/1110/299–303.

101. GARF R-5446/120/1111/52.

102. A. Mikoyan, "Rech' na sobranii izbiratelei," March 11, 1954.

103. Saparov, *From Conflict to Autonomy*, 103–106; and Hovannisian, *Republic of Armenia*, 4:406. On Lenin's position toward Georgia, see Suny, *Making of the Georgian Nation*, 210–220.

104. Nansen, *Armenia and the Near East*, 316.

105. Y. Charents, *Across Two Worlds*, 52.

106. Rayfield, *Stalin and His Hangmen*, 465–466.

107. A. Mikoyan, *Rech' na sobranii izbiratelei*, 44.

108. Myasnikyan's leadership in Armenia was later the subject of Frunze Dovlatyan's epic 1976 film *Yerkunk'* (*Delivery*), with renowned Armenian actor Khoren Abrahamyan as Myasnikyan. See Dovlatyan, *Yerkunk'*.

109. GARF R-5446/120/1111/159.

110. GARF R-5446/120/1110/299–301.

111. Mnatsakanyan, *Alek'sandr Myasnikyan*, 6.

112. A. Mikoyan, *Rech' na sobranii izbiratelei*, 44.

113. See J. Smith, "Battle for Language," 983–1002; and Loader, "Rebellious Republic," 113–139.

114. Peter Blitstein, "Nation-Building or Russification? Obligatory Russian Instruction in the Soviet Non-Russian School, 1938–1953," in Suny and Martin, *State of Nations*, 253.

115. A. Mikoyan, "Rech' na sobranii izbiratelei," March 11, 1954. The last two sentences were added by Mikoyan when he delivered the address. He was supposed to read the following text, which was to be added to the final version of the speech: "Azerbaijanis, Georgians, Armenians, Latvians, and Soviet citizens of any other nationality who graduate from secondary schools should be fluent in Russian and graduating students at the universities should know it perfectly." (GARF R-5446/120/1111/59.) In the end, this text was included in the published version of the address. (A. Mikoyan, *Rech' na sobranii izbiratelei*, 45.)

116. A. Mikoyan, "Rech' na sobranii izbiratelei," March 11, 1954. In the first and second drafts of his speech, Mikoyan's quote from Maiakovskii's poem was originally more extensive. (GARF R-5446/120/1112/95–96, R-5446/120/1111/161, and R-5446/120/1083/5.)

117. GARF R-5446/120/1111/160 and R-5446/120/1112/94.

118. A. Mikoyan, *Rech' na sobranii izbiratelei*, 45.

119. A. Mikoyan, "Rech' na sobranii izbiratelei," March 11, 1954.

120. GARF R-5446/120/1111/55.

121. Sergo Mikoyan, *Hayrs Anastas Mikoyane*, 113.

122. Casper, "Bolshevik Afterlife," 54.

123. Regina Ghazaryan, "Husher Ch'arents'i masin," in D. Gasparyan, *Ch'arents'i het*, 357.

124. Vartan Matiossian, "A Tale of Neglected Relation: Yeghishe Charents and Constant Zarian," in Nichanian, *Yeghishe Charents*, 235.

125. Dzarugian, *Hin yerazner, nor chambaner,* 106–107.
126. Kilbourne Matossian, *Impact of Soviet Policies,* 201.
127. HAA 1/34/54/26 and GARF R-5446/120/1099/1.
128. GARF R-5446/120/1099/2.
129. HAA 1/33/218/6–12.
130. HAA 1191/4/2081/106–107.
131. On the housing issue in the postwar USSR, see M. Smith, *Property of Communists.*
132. A. Mikoyan, *Rech' na sobranii izbiratelei,* 36. On mass housing and urban development in the Khrushchev era, see Harris, *Communism on Tomorrow Street;* Varga-Harris, *Stories of House and Home;* and Kalemeneva, "From New Socialist Cities," 426–449.
133. GARF R-5446/120/1098/19.
134. GARF R-5446/120/1099/3. Among the other received letters, eighty-two were "requests for personal reception," thirty-eight were "complaints against judicial and investigative bodies," thirty-three concerned employment assistance, twenty-eight were personal requests, eighteen were "complaints about the poor work of various institutions and enterprises," eleven dealt with wrongful exile to the Altai krai, and eleven more focused on issues related to Party membership—that is, either reinstatement to the Party or complaints of refusal of admission to the Party. The remaining letters concerned the division of kolkhozes (six) and rationalization requests (two).
135. GARF R-5446/120/1099/2.
136. GARF R-5446/120/1104/42.
137. GARF R-5446/120/1104/47.
138. For example, in a note to Kochinyan from June 7, 1954, referring to letters from Soviet Armenian citizens on pensions, Mikoyan originally instructed his colleague in Yerevan to "inform the applicants and me" of the outcomes. However, in this particular instance, Mikoyan decided to cross out the "and me" part. (GARF R-5446/120/1104/54.)
139. HAA 1191/1/48/2.
140. GARF R-5446/120/1101/103.
141. HAA 1191/1/48/112.
142. HAA 1191/1/45/41–42, 1191/1/47/253–257, and 1191/1/49/78–80a.
143. Vladimir Mikoyan, interview by Pietro Shakarian, Moscow, March 11, 2020.
144. HAA 1191/12/2117/31.
145. Artizov et al., *Reabilitatsiia,* 1:411n18. See also RGASPI 17/171/442/72–76.
146. HAA 1191/9/1078/387–390, 1191/4/103/301–304, and 1191/4/104/329–331ob.
147. Shelepin, *Rech' na XXII s"ezde KPSS,* 10. As a booklet, Shelepin's speech had a print run of fifty thousand copies.
148. In his memoirs, Mikoyan claims to have sent requests only to Rudenko, but extensive documentation in GARF R-5446/120/1104 also shows that he forwarded

requests to other Party leaders, especially Anton Kochinyan in cases specifically related to Armenia.

149. These lists, with Mikoyan's personal signature next to virtually every case, form the vast bulk of the documents in GARF R-5446/120/1104.

150. A. Mikoyan, *Tak bylo*, 637.

151. Stepan Mikoyan, *Vospominaniia voennogo liotchika-ispytatelia*, 45–46.

152. Sergo Mikoyan, "Aleksei Snegov v bor'be za 'destalinizatsiiu,'" 70. On Lev's 1918 imprisonment with Mikoyan, Suren Shahumyan, and Samson Kandelaki at Krasnovodsk, see A. Mikoyan, *Tak bylo*, 110–111.

153. Tatiana Shahumyan, interview by Pietro Shakarian, Moscow, February 12, 2020.

154. RGASPI 84/3/53/154.

155. A. Mikoyan, *Tak bylo*, 637.

156. RGASPI 84/3/53/153.

157. A. Mikoyan, *Tak bylo*, 637.

158. Eimermacher et al., *Doklad N. S. Khrushcheva*, 186.

159. A. Mikoyan, *Tak bylo*, 637.

160. GARF R-5446/120/1844/15.

161. Sergo Mikoyan, "Anastas Mikoian," 367–368.

162. Arzumanyan was arrested in Tbilisi by Beria's Georgian NKVD men on November 10, 1937, and then transferred to Yerevan, where he was held until his release in May 1939. (Arzumanyan, "Iskusheniia," 167–170.)

163. Mil'chakov, *Molodost' svetlaia i tragicheskaia*, 94–99.

164. Cohen, *Victims Return*, 87–89.

165. A. Mikoyan, *Tak bylo*, 636.

166. Sergo Mikoyan, "Aleksei Snegov v bor'be za 'destalinizatsiiu,'" 70.

167. Ibid.; and Tatiana Shahumyan, interview by Pietro Shakarian, Moscow, February 12, 2020.

168. A. Mikoyan, *Tak bylo*, 636.

169. Sergo Mikoyan, "Aleksei Snegov v bor'be za 'destalinizatsiiu,'" 70–71.

170. Tatiana Shahumyan, interview by Pietro Shakarian, Moscow, February 12, 2020.

171. Sergo Mikoyan, "Aleksei Snegov v bor'be za 'destalinizatsiiu,'" 69.

172. Ibid., 74–75.

173. S. Khrushchev, *Reformator*, 353.

174. Sergo Mikoyan, "Aleksei Snegov v bor'be za 'destalinizatsiiu,'" 69–70.

175. Medvedev, *Khrushchev*, 69.

176. Lenoe, *Kirov Murder and Soviet History*, 562.

177. A. Mikoyan, *Tak bylo*, 636.

178. Sergo Mikoyan, "Aleksei Snegov v bor'be za 'destalinizatsiiu,'" 72.

179. A. Mikoyan, *Tak bylo*, 636.

180. Sergo Mikoyan, "Aleksei Snegov v bor'be za 'destalinizatsiiu,'" 77. See also Taubman, *Khrushchev*, 277–278; and K. Smith, *Moscow 1956*, 32–34.

181. Shatunovskaia, *Ob ushedshem veke*, 286. See also K. Smith, *Moscow 1956*, 99.

182. HAA 1191/1/962/178.

183. The exact text in the report reads, "The Armenian poet CHARENTS Yeghishe was rehabilitated, as evidenced by the speech of Comrade Mikoyan A. I. on 11 March 1954 at a meeting with voters in Yerevan." (HAA 1191/4/102/232.)

184. HAA 1191/1/962/195–198 and 1191/12/2115/196.

185. HAA 1/34/64/95. This document, dated September 20, 1954, is a handwritten note instructing the Armenian official Astvatsaturyants to "expedite" ("*uskorit'*") the return of the Charents family to his Yerevan home (today the Yeghishe Charents House-Museum in Yerevan). On July 25, 1955, the issue was marked as "resolved" ("*reshion*"). The *delo* containing this note also originally included a letter written by Arpenik Charents to Mikoyan, dated September 11, 1954. However, this document is not present in the *delo*, and its whereabouts are not known.

186. Izabella Charents, "Yeghishe Ch'arents'i kyank'i verjin orere," in D. Gasparyan, *Ch'arents'i het*, 383–384.

187. Arpenik Charents, "Svetlyi, dobryi obraz ottsa navsegda ostalsia v moei pamiati," *Armianskii muzei Moskvy i kul'tury natsii*, November 27, 2018, https://www.armmuseum.ru/news-blog/charents.

188. I. Charents, "Yeghishe Ch'arents'i kyank'i verjin orere," 384. On Izabella's remarriage, see Arpenik Charents, "Svetlyi, dobryi obraz ottsa navsegda ostalsia."

189. Ghazaryan, "Husher Ch'arents'i masin," 358.

190. I. Charents, "Yeghishe Ch'arents'i kyank'i verjin orere," 384.

191. Ibid.

192. GARF R-5446/120/1720/8. For his arrest and rehabilitation, see HAA 1191/12/2115/195 and 1191/1/962/197.

193. Ashkhen Mikoyan, "Avetik Isaakian i Anastas Mikoian," *Aravot*, June 2, 2014, https://ru.aravot.am/2014/06/02/180030/. For a testimony against Isahakyan in the interrogation protocol of Semion Pirumov from the Soviet Georgian Interior Ministry from June 23, 1937, see HAA 1191/9/1077/76–78. For a biographical overview of Isahakyan, see Hacikyan et al., *Heritage of Armenian Literature*, 3:734–736.

194. GARF R-5446/120/1268/73. Mikoyan originally concluded this text with "this grave, irreparable loss, suffered by the Soviet people and Soviet socialist culture," but simply shortened it to "this grave, irreparable loss." For the telegram that Mikoyan received on Isahakyan's passing from Eduard Topchyan (the first secretary of the Armenian Writers' Union), see GARF R-5446/120/1268/74.

195. For the signed book, see RGASPI 84/3/389.

196. For the autographed book, see RGASPI 84/3/382. The Armenian-language inscription by Kochar reads, "With warmest feelings, to my dear elder comrade of my youth, Anastas Mikoyan, with love from Yervand Kochar, 7-VII-71, Yerevan."

197. Hovhannisyan and Martirosyan-Kochar, *Maestro K'ochare*, 173. Mikoyan's role in saving Kochar is recounted by Kochar's son, Haykaz.

198. Ibid., 87.

199. For Mikoyan's speech, see A. Mikoyan, *Rech' na XX s"ezde KPSS*.

200. Salisbury, *To Moscow—and Beyond*, 167.

201. A. Mikoyan, *Tak bylo*, 642.

202. Harrison E. Salisbury, "Fifty Years That Shook the World" in Salisbury, *Soviet Union*, 18. In his speech before the congress, Mikoyan even remarked that "it would be no exaggeration to state that the Twentieth Party Congress is the most important congress in the history of our Party after Lenin." (A. Mikoyan, *Rech' na XX s"ezde KPSS*, 38.)

203. Astsatryan, *XX dar*, 66.

204. The place of Mikoyan's 1954 Yerevan speech as an indicator of major change was likewise reflected in the *Sketches of the History of the Communist Party of Armenia*, although its major political, cultural, and historical impact was not analyzed. (Aghayan et al., *Ocherki istorii kommunisticheskoi partii Armenii*, 470–471.)

205. Angaladian, *Armenian Avant Garde*, 20.

206. Panossian, *Armenians*, 323.

207. Tromly, *Making of the Soviet Intelligentsia*, 225.

208. HAA 1/34/54/34. For the published Armenian translation, see A. Mikoyan, *Char Yerevani.*

209. S. Takaryan, "Proizvedeniia Ov. Tumaniana i. E. Charentsa v hudozhestvennom chtenii," *Kommunist*, April 14, 1954, 3.

210. See Y. Charents, *Lenin–Poemner yev Banasteghtsut'yunner.*

211. See Y. Charents, *Entir Yerker.*

212. Yeghishe Charents, "Ballada o Vladimire Il'iche, muzhike i pare sapog," *Kommunist*, January 30, 1955, 3.

213. GARF R-5446/120/1101/10–18.

214. Anahit Charents, "Yeghishe Charents," 248–249.

215. GARF R-5446/120/1101/15. For the original manuscript, see RGALI 613/1/8159.

216. Anahit Charents, "Yeghishe Charents," 250.

217. GARF R-5446/120/1101/12–13.

218. GARF R-5446/120/1101/13–15.

219. GARF R-5446/120/1101/16.

220. GARF R-5446/120/1101/10. Postupal'skii was not the only individual to invoke the name of Charents in an appeal to Mikoyan. On September 10, 1954, Ekaterina Surkhatyan, the widow of Armenian writer and literary critic Harutyun Surkhatyan, another victim of the Purges, appealed to Mikoyan to "return [her husband] to literature." "Who was the first critic who uncovered the talent of Charents and wrote so much about him? Surkhatyan," she wrote. "In a fit of his painful condition, Charents was about to destroy his works, believing that no one needed them. Only Surkhatyan, whose authority Charents acknowledged, was able to calm him by force of persuasion when he was too far gone." (HAA 1/34/64/83–84.)

221. RGALI 613/7/631/2.

222. See Y. Charents, *Izbrannoe.*

223. S. Sarinyan, "K novomu izdaniu sochinenii Raffi," *Kommunist*, January 13, 1956, 3. For the ten-volume series, see Raffi, *Yerkeri zhoghovatsu.*

224. Hamazasp Harutyunyan, *Zapiski diplomata*, 166–168. Harutyunyan served as the Soviet Union's ambassador to Canada during the Khrushchev era.

225. For the work, see Bakunts, *Yerker*. For a biographical sketch of Bakunts, see Hacikyan et al., *Heritage of Armenian Literature*, 3:988–990. Although best known for his prose, Bakunts also worked as a screenwriter for the Haykino (Armenkino) film studio. According to Ashot Hovhannisyan, it was Mikoyan who suggested the idea for the film *Zangezur*, for which Bakunts wrote the initial screenplay. (HAA 1191/4/102/236.) As director Hamo Bek-Nazaryan recounted, Bakunts, who was himself a native of Zangezur, was "an eyewitness to many of the events that he was going to discuss in the scenario." Unfortunately, the writer ceased participating in the production due to his repression in 1936, and he was ultimately left uncredited on the finished film. (Bek-Nazaryan, *Zapiski aktiora i kinorezhissiora*, 201–203; and Bek-Nazaryan, *Zangezur*.)

226. HAA 1191/4/102/231–245. With Amatuni's approval, Bakunts was arrested on August 9, 1936, as part of the case against Nersik Stepanyan. (HAA 1191/4/100/33, 40.) He was executed by the Armenian NKVD on July 8, 1937. (HAA 1191/4/102/221.) In the HAA, the files of Bakunts in the repressed persons fond (1191) are held with those of Stepanyan, Drastamat Ter-Simonyan, and others arrested in this case. On the case of Totovents, who was arrested on July 20, 1936, see HAA 1191/12/2115/196.

227. Gurgen Boryan, "Master novelly," *Kommunist*, March 30, 1956, 3.

228. HAA 1/36/2/57. See also Tovmasyan, *Otchiotnyi doklad*, 78–79. Additionally, in the published booklet version, Tovmasyan inserted the following between the final two sentences: "The fundamental problem of literary and artistic activity—the problem of creating new, full-fledged plays, operas, and ballets on the Soviet theme—continues to remain unresolved. This is a big question—the question of repertory policy."

229. HAA 1/36/2/58–59. See also Tovmasyan, *Otchiotnyi doklad*, 80–81.

230. CPSU, *XX s"ezd Kommunisticheskoi Partii Sovetskogo Soiuza*, 1:495.

231. N. Khrushchev, *Rech' na torzhestvennom zasedanii*, 25; and RGANI 52/1/366/24, 61, 103.

232. RGANI 5/31/52/44. Tovmasyan's report, dated April 12, 1956, was specifically addressed to the Department of the Union Republic Party Organs of the CPSU Central Committee. For the full report, see RGANI 5/31/52/44–49. For an abridged version, see Eimermacher et al., *Doklad N. S. Khrushcheva*, 471–473.

233. RGANI 5/31/52/41–42. For an abridged version of Tovmasyan's March 23 report, see Eimermacher et al., *Doklad N. S. Khrushcheva*, 419–421.

234. RGANI 5/31/52/42.

235. RGANI 5/31/52/41–42. Barseghyan was rehabilitated by the Soviet government on November 20, 1954. (HAA 1191/12/2115/143, 181.)

236. RGANI 5/31/52/42.

237. Eimermacher et al., *Doklad N. S. Khrushcheva*, 553.

238. RGANI 5/31/52/47.

239. Eimermacher et al., *Doklad N. S. Khrushcheva*, 553.

240. RGANI 5/31/52/46.

241. RGANI 5/31/52/47.

242. Eimermacher et al., *Doklad N. S. Khrushcheva*, 554.

243. RGANI 5/31/52/47.

244. Eimermacher et al., *Doklad N. S. Khrushcheva*, 554. Similar complaints about the Soviet response to the Istanbul pogrom were raised at the Armenian Writers' Union meeting concerning the Twentieth Party Congress. (Eimermacher et al., *Doklad N. S. Khrushcheva*, 552.) On the Istanbul pogrom of September 1955, see Zürcher, *Turkey*, 233. These events are also discussed by Turkish author Orhan Pamuk in his portrait of Istanbul. (Pamuk, *Istanbul*, 173–175.)

245. "Document 97: Memorandum of Conversation (Foreign Relations of the United States, 1958–1960, Volume X, Part 1, Eastern Europe Region; Soviet Union; Cyprus)," *Office of the Historian, US Department of State*, July 25, 1959, https://history.state.gov/historicaldocuments/frus1958-60v10p1/d97.

246. Eimermacher et al., *Doklad N. S. Khrushcheva*, 554. Dzarugian noted similar shortcomings of Soviet "democracy" in his account of Mikoyan's 1958 visit to Yerevan. "It's a country where people have no choice but have the right to cast their votes to the only candidate on the ballot," he wrote. "The whole thing looks like a comedy of sorts, the comic stage of an unimaginative play. But when one experiences the solemnity of the people, their enthusiasm and their religious-like devotion to the process, a person has no choice but to become serious and make an effort to understand the meaning of all that is happening around him." During Mikoyan's Russian-language speech, Dzarugian, who did not understand Russian, went out for a smoke and met a well-known Armenian writer (whom he did not name) in the hall of the Opera Theatre. Noting the length of Mikoyan's speech, Dzarugian remarked, "Listen, in my country [Lebanon] if a candidate speaks this long, we do not vote him." In response, the anonymous Armenian writer jested, "This one has his re-election guaranteed. That is why he cares less." (Dzarugian, *Hin yerazner, nor chambaner*, 100–101, 104.)

247. RGANI 5/31/52/47–48; and Eimermacher et al., *Doklad N. S. Khrushcheva*, 555.

248. RGANI 5/31/148/43.

249. Risch, *Ukrainian West*, 121.

250. See Tromly, *Making of the Soviet Intelligentsia*, 217–243; and Tromly, "Unlikely National Revival," 607–622.

251. On Latvia, see Prigge, *Bearslayers*; and Loader, "Stalinist Purge," 244–282.

252. On the 1956 events in Tbilisi, see Kaiser, *Georgian and Soviet*; Blauvelt and Smith, *Georgia after Stalin*; and V. Kozlov, *Mass Uprisings in the USSR*, 112–135.

3. APRICOT PATRONAGE

1. On Thaw-era patronage networks, see Nikolai Mitrokhin, "The Rise of Political Clans in the Era of Nikita Khrushchev," in J. Smith and Ilic, *Khrushchev in the Kremlin*, 26–40.

2. On Mikoyan's Baku network, see Casper, "Bolshevik Afterlife," especially the first chapter.

3. Willerton, *Patronage and Politics*, 223–224.
4. RGASPI 84/3/37/17.
5. Lehmann, "Apricot Socialism," 13.
6. Historians have traditionally (and logically) concluded that Zarobyan's departure from Armenia's highest office in 1966 was related to the 1965 demonstrations in Yerevan. (For example, see Saparov, "Re-negotiating the Boundaries," 863n2.) However, in his memoirs, Yeghishe Astsatryan maintained that Zarobyan's departure was caused more by backstage Soviet political intrigues than by the Yerevan demonstrations or the Genocide issue. Specifically, Astsatryan recounted that, with the changing political climate in Moscow associated with the downfall of Khrushchev, Zarobyan's political opponents in Armenia sensed an opportune time to remove him from office. However, as Astsatryan also noted, "it is difficult to assert conclusively which factor played the decisive role in the ouster of Zarobyan: the Moscow factor, or the local Armenian factor." (Astsatryan, *XX dar*, 179–184.) See also N. Zarobyan, *Iakov Zarobian*, 103–107.
7. After his work in Mongolia during World War II, Astsatryan was elected by the all-union Central Committee to become the chairman of the Soviet-German Joint Stock Company in Germany. However, he wanted to pursue his career in Armenia instead. Astsatryan had already been in contact with Mikoyan during the war and appealed to him for support. Mikoyan endorsed Astsatryan's move, reasoning that "Armenia is in great need of qualified personnel at this time." He then asked the minister of nonferrous metallurgy, Piotr Lomako, to assign Astsatryan to a suitable position in the Armenian Republic. Lomako arranged for Astsatryan to be appointed to the post of deputy director of the Kanaker Aluminum Plant. From this position, Astsatryan moved through the ranks of the Party, eventually becoming deputy chairman of Armenia's Council of Ministers. Astsatryan recounted that he first met Mikoyan in person in Arutinov's office at the end of his tenure and that his first long meeting with the statesman took place during his March 1954 trip to Armenia. (Astsatryan, *XX dar*, 63–66.)
8. Mikoyan articulated this view in his writings and public speeches. For example, see A. Mikoyan, *Sovetskomu Soiuzu piat'desiat let*, 57–70; and RGASPI 84/3/53/13.
9. N. Khrushchev, *O Programme Kommunisticheskoi partii*, 89. Citing the Virgin Lands campaign in Kazakhstan as an example, Khrushchev emphasized that the "economic development of every Soviet republic is the result of the fraternal cooperation and mutual assistance of all Soviet peoples." On relations among nationalities in the Virgin Lands, see Michaela Pohl, "From White Grave to Tselinograd to Astana: The Virgin Lands Opening, Khrushchev's Forgotten First Reform," in D. Kozlov and Gilburd, *Thaw*, 269–307.
10. Astsatryan, *XX dar*, 77. The Khrushchev government employed a similar approach toward Soviet Central Asia, highlighting that region as a model for development in the Global South. See Cucciolla, "Sharaf Rashidov," 185–201; Kalinovsky, *Laboratory of Socialist Development*; and Kirasirova, *Eastern International*, chap. 5.
11. For example, in November 1959, while in Mexico City for the opening of the Soviet Exhibition, Mikoyan began chatting with a local woman in a language

unknown to his translator, Nikolai Leonov. "I didn't understand a word," Leonov recalled. "Anastas Ivanovich then turned to me and asked: 'Well, why don't you translate?' I answered: 'I do not understand it, Anastas Ivanovich. This is not Spanish. Apparently, it is some sort of language of the Indians from southern Mexico.'" Mikoyan laughed and responded, "You passed the honesty test! I really thought that you would start translating something. She speaks Armenian and she is welcoming me on behalf of the Armenian community of Mexico." He then proceeded to speak with her in Armenian and asked Leonov to "apologize on his behalf to the entire hall." (Sergo Mikoyan, "Anastas Mikoian," 674.)

12. One account by Astsatryan reveals that Mikoyan was cognizant of this contradiction. Once, in the early 1960s, there was a great need for cement in Armenia, and Kosygin, then the chairman of the Council of Ministers, decided to grant Uzbekistan's unused cement allocation to the republic. Astsatryan hoped that Kosygin would promptly finalize his decision and that Yerevan would receive it soon ("*vaghemyus ore*"). However, the official decision was delayed because Kosygin had already left for his vacation in Sochi. "Mikoyan did not want to sign that decision," recalled Astsatryan. "I called Anastas Ivanovich, explained the situation, and asked him to sign off on it. He then told me, 'Think deeply for a minute, if I sign this decision, will not the Uzbeks say that I have taken their cement and given it to Armenia?' Finally, I called Kosygin in Sochi. The government released the cement to us with his signature." (Astsatryan, *XX dar*, 84–85.)

13. In his speech, Zarobyan emphasized that "the unprecedented dramatic flowering of Soviet Armenia's economy, science, and culture represents a new demonstration of the victory of the general line of our Party and its wise Leninist nationality policy." (Y. Zarobyan, *Otchiotnyi doklad*, 8.)

14. Sergo Mikoyan, "Anastas Mikoian," 671.

15. Sergo Mikoyan, *Hayrs Anastas Mikoyane*, 182.

16. Mikoyan's son Sergo recalled that his father "was always visiting his native village" but that he also "regretted that the city of Alaverdi had 'gone up' to, and in fact merged with, his native Sanahin." However, "he was told that the city had nowhere else to grow." (Sergo Mikoyan, "Anastas Mikoian," 403.) Elaborating on the expansion of Alaverdi into Sanahin, Astsatryan wrote, "There was no room for new construction in the narrow valley of Alaverdi. Therefore, to create environmentally friendly living conditions for the population, the Sovnarkhoz and Gosstroi decided to construct Alaverdi's subsequent housing, cultural-domestic, and other civic structures on the Sanahin Plateau, in the vicinity of Mikoyan's native village." (Astsatryan, *XX dar*, 75.)

17. Sergo Mikoyan, "Anastas Mikoian," 671.

18. GARF R-5446/120/1113/7–8.

19. GARF R-5446/120/1113/20.

20. Sergo Mikoyan, "Anastas Mikoian," 671.

21. Astsatryan, *XX dar*, 75. See also "Tovarishch A. I. Mikoian v Armenii," *Kommunist*, March 16, 1962, 1.

22. GARF R-5446/120/1720/12.
23. "Tovarishch A. I. Mikoian v Armenii," March 16, 1962, 1.
24. Astsatryan, *XX dar*, 67.
25. "Tovarishch A. I. Mikoian v Armenii," March 16, 1962, 1.
26. Astsatryan, *XX dar*, 67–68.
27. HAA 113/50/152/5–7.
28. HAA 1/41/130/4.
29. HAA 113/50/152/5.
30. "Prebivaniie tov. A. I. Mikoiana v Armenii," *Kommunist*, March 15, 1962, 4.
31. Ibid. See also GARF R-5446/120/1720/7.
32. Astsatryan, *XX dar*, 68.
33. "Prebivaniie tov. A. I. Mikoiana v Armenii," 4.
34. GARF R-5446/120/1337/2.
35. Kochinyan, *Anavart husher*, 394. On Zotov, see Piruzyan, *Pishchevaia industriia*, 30–35.
36. Kochinyan, *Anavart husher*, 357, 393–394.
37. Ibid., 394–395. According to Aram Piruzyan, Mikoyan personally defended Zotov when Stalin wanted to remove him from his post after the war. (Piruzyan, *Pishchevaia industriia*, 34.)
38. Kochinyan, *Anavart husher*, 357, 395.
39. GARF R-5446/120/1720/3.
40. "Tovarishch A. I. Mikoian v Armenii," *Kommunist*, March 13, 1962, 1. Mikoyan echoed these remarks in his speech at the Yerevan Opera Theatre on March 14. (Anastas Mikoyan, "Enker A. I. Mikoyani chare," *Sovetakan Hayastan*, March 15, 1962, 1.)
41. Kochinyan, *Anavart husher*, 358.
42. Ibid., 396.
43. Ibid., 231–233.
44. Ibid., 397.
45. On Mikoyan's visits to Zangezur and Daralagyaz, see GARF R-5446/120/1720/5–7; RGASPI 84/3/342/1–4; Astsatryan, *XX dar*, 71–74; Kochinyan, *Anavart husher*, 287–288, 396–404; "Hevale A. I. Mikoyan li Ermenistane," *Rya T'eze*, March 18, 1962, 3; and E. Melik-Nubarov and R. Karagyozyan, "Tovarishch A. I. Mikoian v Armenii," *Kommunist*, March 14, 1962, 1. For coverage of Mikoyan's 1962 visit to Zangezur in the local Party newspapers of Kajaran and Meghri, see "K'ajarants'inere ayd vore yerbek' ch'en morrana," *K'ajaran*, March 15, 1962, 1; and "Enker A. I. Mikoyane Agarakum," *Koltntesayin Gyugh*, March 18, 1962, 1. Footage of the 1962 trip to Zangezur can be seen in Zhamharyan, *A. I. Mikoyane Hayastanum*.
46. GARF R-5446/120/1720/4–5. The meeting with Hambardzumyan was also attended by other prominent members of the Armenian Academy of Sciences, including the painter Martiros Saryan. (Zhamharyan, *A. I. Mikoyane Hayastanum*.) Mikoyan earlier met with Hambardzumyan at Byurakan Observatory during his 1958 trip to Armenia. (GARF R-5446/120/1337/3 and R-5446/120/1344; and *Sovetakan*

Hayastan, № 8, Mart 1958.) He would later visit Byurakan once more during his November 1970 trip to the republic. (RGASPI 84/3/342/11.)

47. Astsatryan, *XX dar,* 72. Like the Russian *sovnarkhoz* (*sovety narodnogo khoziaistva*), the Armenian *zhoghtntkhorh* is a contraction of *zhoghovrdakan tntesut'yan khorhurd,* or "people's economic council." As Nataliya Kibita notes, there were 105 sovnarkhozes in the Soviet Union, as established in May–June 1957. These included "70 in the RSFSR, 11 in Ukraine, nine in Kazakhstan, four in Uzbekistan and one in each of the other republics," including Armenia. (Kibita, *Soviet Economic Management under Khrushchev,* 41.)

48. Astsatryan, *XX dar,* 72–73.

49. HAA 113/50/67/24.

50. HAA 113/50/53/34–35.

51. RGASPI 84/3/342/3.

52. Kochinyan, *Anavart husher,* 387–388.

53. Ibid.

54. Astsatryan, *XX dar,* 69.

55. GARF R-5446/120/1113/1–2.

56. GARF R-5446/120/1113/6, 20.

57. GARF R-5446/120/1113/2.

58. GARF R-5446/120/1113/17.

59. GARF R-5446/120/1113/6, 19.

60. Harris, *Communism on Tomorrow Street,* 92.

61. GARF R-5446/120/1113/7.

62. GARF R-5446/120/1113/19–20.

63. "Tovarishch A. I. Mikoian v Armenii," March 16, 1962, 1. The spring remains standing today, and among those honored is Mikoyan's son, Vladimir, who was killed in a dogfight over Stalingrad in 1942. (Vladimir Mikoyan, interview by Pietro Shakarian, St. Petersburg, January 18, 2023.)

64. Kochinyan, *Anavart husher,* 403–404.

65. Khachikyan and Hakhverdyan, *T'umanyan 100: Hobelyanakan taregrut'yun,* 10–12, 63. For more on the organization of the festivities, see Permiakov et al., *Sekretariat TsK KPSS: 1968 g.,* 788n639.

66. The celebrations are chronicled in detail in Khachikyan and Hakhverdyan, *T'umanyan 100: Hobelyanakan taregrut'yun.* An abridged Russian translation was published two years later. (See Khachikyan and Hakhverdyan, *Tumanian 100: Iubileinaia letopis'.*) The festivities received extensive press coverage and were the subject of Suren Arakelyan's 1969 documentary film *Hovhannes T'umanyan.* (Arakelyan, *Hovhannes T'umanyan.*)

67. Khachikyan and Hakhverdyan, *Tumanian 100: Iubileinaia letopis',* 89. Kochinyan's complete speech, with the Mikoyan reference, is available only in the Russian edition of the Khachikyan-Hakhverdyan book.

68. Anastas Mikoyan, "Mets lorets'in," *Grakan T'ert',* September 24, 1969, 2. For a Russian translation, see Khachikyan and Hakhverdyan, *Tumanian 100: Iubileinaia*

letopis', 314–315. In his dedication, Mikoyan wrote that the poetry recitation, which occurred in the spring of 1914, was the only time that he personally encountered Tumanyan and that, even then, he and his fellow students regretted not taking the opportunity to speak to him directly. Mikoyan did not recount this moment in his memoirs, although he noted that he was "lucky to know [Tumanyan] personally." He added, "In his books, I became particularly captivated by his descriptions of the people and places close to me in my native region of Lori. In the language of Tumanyan, I met many words and expressions of our Lori dialect [*Lorva barbar* in Armenian]." He likewise referred to Tumanyan as his "*rodstvennik*," given that the family of his wife, Ashkhen Mikoyan (née Tumanyan), was distantly related to the poet. (A. Mikoyan, *Tak bylo*, 34; and Stepan Mikoyan, *Vospominaniia voennogo liotchika-ispytatelia*, 15.)

69. In conversation with the writer Marietta Shahinyan, Mikoyan later noted, "If only you were in Armenia now, at least at the celebrations marking the centenary of Tumanyan, you would look around and be stunned. So much has been accomplished in Armenia during the years of Soviet power, with the help of the Russian proletariat and the commonwealth our peoples. As an artist, you could describe very well—and with great force—the Leninist legacy that unites our peoples [*nashi narody*] around the Party." (RGASPI 84/3/119/44.)

70. Sergo Mikoyan, "Anastas Mikoian," 671.

71. In addition to addressing him formally in person, Mikoyan addressed Kochinyan in Russian-language letters with the formal, capitalized "You" (*Vy*). For examples, see GARF R-5446/120/1104/42, 47, 54.

72. Kochinyan, *Anavart husher*, 393.

73. Ibid., 399–400.

74. Ibid., 393.

75. Ibid., 387.

76. N. Zarobyan, *Iakov Zarobian*, 95–96.

77. "Kukuruzu—na polia Armenii!," *Kommunist*, March 26, 1955, 3. On Khrushchev's corn campaign, see Hale-Dorrell, *Corn Crusade*.

78. According to Zarobyan's son, Nikita, this amount still represented a significant increase in corn cultivation in Armenia (by over two times) compared to the yield of 1950. Moreover, he noted that the "gross corn harvest increased by more than 2.8 times." (N. Zarobyan, *Iakov Zarobian*, 61.)

79. A. Mikoyan, *Tak bylo*, 565.

80. Arushanyan, *Yakov Zarobyane*, 11.

81. Sergo Mikoyan, *Hayrs Anastas Mikoyane*, 122–123.

82. GARF R-5446/120/1843/7.

83. Astsatryan, *XX dar*, 77.

84. Sergo Mikoyan, "Anastas Mikoian," 399.

85. Astsatryan, *XX dar*, 70; and Kochinyan, *Anavart husher*, 389.

86. GARF R-5446/120/1113/15–16.

87. RGASPI 84/3/342/3.

88. GARF R-5446/120/1113/19, 21.

89. GARF R-5446/120/1113/5, 18, 20. Tragically, Spitak would later become known for its close proximity to the epicenter of the 1988 Armenian earthquake. On the fate and rebuilding of Spitak after 1988, see Katja Doose, "Spitak: The Last Petrified Soviet Utopia," in T. Harutyunyan, *Yerevan Architectural Guide*, 268–289.

90. Piruzyan, *Zhizn' strany—sud'ba moia*, 67.

91. Ibid., 112–113. As Piruzyan recounted, "Once, I was attending a reception at Mikoyan's place, and he suggested that I start creating the book *Armenian Cooking*. I replied that this matter was very complicated and that I would hardly be up to completing such a task. But he insisted that I do it."

92. For the first edition, see Piruzyan, *Armianskaia kulinariia* (Moscow: Gostorgizdat, 1960). The second and third editions were published in 1971 and 1983, respectively. In his memoirs, Piruzyan incorrectly asserted that the first edition was printed in East Germany and that the print run was five hundred thousand copies. However, the publication information of the first edition indicates that it was printed in Leningrad with an initial print run of fifty thousand. A second print run of the first edition followed with fifty thousand more copies, for a total circulation of one hundred thousand.

93. Piruzyan, *Zhizn' strany—sud'ba moia*, 113.

94. See Piruzyan, *Haykakan khohanots'*. The print run of this sole Armenian edition was sixty thousand.

95. Kochinyan, *Anavart husher*, 207–208.

96. GARF R-5446/120/1113/21.

97. Kochinyan, *Anavart husher*, 209.

98. Piruzyan, *Zhizn' strany—sud'ba moia*, 86.

99. Grigoryan, *Ploshchad' Lenina v Erevane*, 28–29.

100. Piruzyan, *Zhizn' strany—sud'ba moia*, 67–68.

101. The Lenin monument was designed by Sergei Merkurov, while the architects of the pedestal were Natalia Paremuzova and Levon Vartanov, supervised by Yerevan's chief architect, Mark Grigoryan. On the history of the monument, see Grigoryan, *Ploshchad' Lenina v Erevane*, 61–70.

102. GARF R-5446/120/1113/1.

103. According to Kochinyan, Mikoyan liked the Hrazdan Gorge so much that he "made it into a place of rest." (Kochinyan, *Anavart husher*, 385.)

104. Poghosyan and Ter-Minasyan, *Ararman ughin*, 34, 49.

105. RGASPI 84/3/342/12.

106. Poghosyan and Ter-Minasyan, *Ararman ughin*, 51.

107. A. Mikoyan, *Tak bylo*, 683.

108. Yuzefovich, *Aram Khachaturyan*, 128–133. Mikoyan also claimed to have provided the inspiration for Khachaturian's *Spartacus* (A. Mikoyan, *Tak bylo*, 683), and attended a performance of this work at the Yerevan Opera Theatre during his March 1962 trip to Armenia (GARF R-5446/120/1720/2). However, in an interview with musicologist Grigorii Shneerson, Khachaturian maintained that the idea for the ballet

belonged to the Creative Workshop of the Bolshoi Theatre, specifically to Konstantin Vladimirov, a friend of Anatolii Lunacharskii. (Shneerson, *Aram Khachaturian*, 129.) Regardless of the origins of the ballet, Mikoyan and Khachaturian remained good friends for the rest of their lives. During his illness in the 1970s, Khachaturian was visited by Mikoyan twice at his suburban Moscow hospital, including on the composer's seventieth birthday. (A. Mikoyan, *Tak bylo*, 682–684.)

109. Grigorian, *Erevan*, 197–199.

110. Astsatryan, *XX dar*, 71.

111. Kochinyan, *Anavart husher*, 391–392.

112. Astsatryan, *XX dar*, 71.

113. For the resolutions on Charentsavan, see HAA 207/60/57/47–48. For Mikoyan's recommendation to rename the town, see Sergo Mikoyan, *Hayrs Anastas Mikoyane*, 113. Mikoyan similarly advised renaming Elar (Abovyan) and Chatghran (Nor Geghi) during his 1954 trip to Armenia. See GARF R-5446/120/1113/15.

114. Yeghenian, *Red Flag at Ararat*, 42–43.

115. Kochinyan, *Anavart husher*, 383–384.

116. Doose, "Green Nationalism," 185; and Coumel, "Failed Environmental Turn," 178–179.

117. "Enker A. I. Mikoyane Agarakum," 1.

118. GARF R-5446/120/1113/7, 15–16, 18, 20.

119. GARF R-5446/120/1113/15.

120. GARF R-5446/120/1113/5, 19.

121. Kochinyan, *Anavart husher*, 386.

122. A. Mikoyan, *Rech' na sobranii izbiratelei*, 34.

123. RGASPI 84/3/53/10.

124. RGASPI 84/3/53/11–12.

125. Sergo Mikoyan, "Anastas Mikoian," 671.

126. For Manaseryan's pamphlet (written under the pseudonym S. E. Serian'), see Manaseryan, *Ispariaiushchiesia milliardy*.

127. On the history and architecture of the Sevan Island (now Sevan Peninsula), see Mnatsakanian, *Documents of Armenian Architecture 18*.

128. Grossman, *Armenian Sketchbook*, 49.

129. Martynov and Grigoryan, *Razvitie energeticheskoi bazy Sovetskoi Armenii*, 269–272, 278–285, 291–292. See also HAA 1/36/79.

130. For the full letter, see GARF R-5446/95/311/1–3.

131. GARF R-5446/95/311/2.

132. GARF R-5446/95/311/4–5.

133. Sergo Mikoyan, "Anastas Mikoian," 399.

134. Ibid., 671–672.

135. Ibid.

136. Bedrosov, *40 let Sovetskoi Armenii*, 14.

137. Astsatryan, *XX dar*, 166; and N. Zarobyan, *Iakov Zarobian*, 76.

138. Sergo Mikoyan, *Hayrs Anastas Mikoyane,* 182.

139. For example, in the big speech that Khrushchev delivered in Yerevan on May 6, he recalled meeting young Soviet Armenian commanders at Port Arthur in China and in the Soviet Far East and afterward jokingly accused Mikoyan of "spreading Armenians everywhere." (N. Khrushchev, *Rech' na torzhestvennom zasedanii,* 15; RGANI 52/1/366/90, 113, 124; and A. Mikoyan, *Tak bylo,* 531.) The next day, at a mass gathering at Yerevan's Dinamo (later Republican) Stadium, Khrushchev noted that Mikoyan had advised him on the popularity of the Armenian national treat *matsun.* (RGANI 52/1/366/140.) On same day, in a meeting with representatives from the Armenian diaspora, Khrushchev referenced both Mikoyan and his brother Artiom while discussing successful Armenians in the USSR. "For example, take my first deputy Anastas Ivanovich Mikoyan. Apparently, you know him, and if you don't, then I will tell you a secret—he is an Armenian," he playfully noted. (HAA 1/127/141/42–43; and RGANI 52/1/366/144, 155.)

140. GARF R-5446/95/311/7–11. Khlebnikov's assessment was dated February 20, 1961, while Tikhomirov's assessment was dated May 4, 1961, on the eve of Khrushchev's Armenia visit.

141. GARF R-5446/95/311/6.

142. Bedrosov, *40 let Sovetskoi Armenii,* 164.

143. Ibid., 167. Baghramyan can also be seen in the footage of the trip in Zhamharyan, *Ts'ntsum e Hayastane.*

144. Astsatryan, *XX dar,* 167–168. See also Grigorian, *Erevan,* 233–235.

145. Astsatryan, *XX dar,* 168–169.

146. N. Zarobyan, *Iakov Zarobian,* 79.

147. Bedrosov, *40 let Sovetskoi Armenii,* 165–166.

148. Kochinyan, *Anavart husher,* 390–391.

149. Bedrosov, *40 let Sovetskoi Armenii,* 166–167. Footage of the boat excursion, including the *ishkhan* feast, can be seen in Zhamharyan, *Ts'ntsum e Hayastane.*

150. Arushanyan, *Yakov Zarobyane,* 11–12. On Khrushchev's sampling of Armenian wine, see Bedrosov, *40 let Sovetskoi Armenii,* 17, 174. Khrushchev delivered toasts in Yerevan and Byurakan. For the texts of these toasts, both dated May 7, 1961, see RGANI 52/1/366/165–170.

151. Arushanyan, *Yakov Zarobyane,* 12.

152. N. Zarobyan, *Iakov Zarobian,* 79. In his memoirs, Astsatryan recalled that Zarobyan raised the issue of Sevan's diminution to Khrushchev earlier, as the party caught the first glimpse of the lake. (Astsatryan, *XX dar,* 169–170.)

153. Sergo Mikoyan, "Anastas Mikoian," 672.

154. Arushanyan, *Yakov Zarobyane,* 12.

155. N. Zarobyan, *Iakov Zarobian,* 79.

156. GARF R-5446/95/311/11. Separately, Tikhomirov noted that the cost for "switching the Hrazdan-Sevan irrigation systems from Lake Sevan to other water sources" would be approximately 610 million rubles.

157. Sergo Mikoyan, "Anastas Mikoian," 672.

158. N. Zarobyan, *Iakov Zarobian*, 81.

159. A. Mikoyan, "Enker A. I. Mikoyani chare," 1.

160. GARF R-5446/95/311/12. Additionally, the Arpa-Sevan resolution was referenced by Zarobyan in his speech before the Twenty-Second Armenian Party Congress on September 21, 1961. (Y. Zarobyan, *Otchiotnyi doklad*, 17.)

161. Martynov and Grigoryan, *Razvitie energeticheskoi bazy Sovetskoi Armenii*, 324–326.

162. RGANI 5/31/164/73.

163. Y. Zarobyan, *Otchiotnyi doklad*, 17–18.

164. For the drafts of Mikoyan's speech, and specifically the opening with his discussion on the Sevan issue, see GARF R-5446/120/1720/91–92; and R-5446/120/1722/1–2, 39–40, 42–43. In earlier drafts, Mikoyan also mentioned the role of the Arpa River in the process of replenishing Sevan.

165. A. Mikoyan, "Rech' na sobranii izbiratelei," March 14, 1962. For the Armenian-language drafts of the opening of Mikoyan's speech, see GARF R-5446/120/1722/111–112, 114–116.

166. A. Mikoyan, "Enker A. I. Mikoyani chare," 1.

167. A. Mikoyan, "Rech' na sobranii izbiratelei," March 14, 1962. In an early draft of his speech, Mikoyan almost decided against including the references to de-Stalinization in his praise for Khrushchev. (GARF R-5446/120/1722/2.) However, he ultimately retained them in the final version of the address. Mikoyan's initial hesitation may have been conditioned by the local Caucasian context and the sensitivity in neighboring Georgia toward de-Stalinization. During the 1956 Tbilisi riots, Mikoyan and ethnic Armenians generally were singled out for especially harsh criticism by Georgian nationalists. (Kaiser, *Georgian and Soviet*, 123–124.)

168. Kochinyan, *Anavart husher*, 391.

169. Astsatryan, *XX dar*, 70–71.

170. RGASPI 84/3/342/3, 12.

171. "Tovarishch A. I. Mikoian v Armenii," March 13, 1962, 1.

172. GARF R-5446/120/1720/1–2. These scenes can be seen in Zhamharyan, *A. I. Mikoyane Hayastanum*.

173. "Ot'ezd tov. A. I. Mikoiana iz Erevana," *Kommunist*, March 17, 1962, 1.

174. Dzarugian, *Hin yerazner, nor chambaner*, 100–101.

175. Kochinyan, *Anavart husher*, 403.

176. Grossman, *Armenian Sketchbook*, 24. In the 1967 Soviet edition of Grossman's work, this reference to Mikoyan was edited out by Brezhnev-era censors. (Grossman, *Dobro vam! Rasskazy*, 207.) For the original, uncensored Russian text, see Grossman, *Dobro vam! (Iz putevykh zametok): Rasskazy*, 31.

177. HAA 1/127/141/42–43; and RGANI 52/1/366/144, 155.

178. Lehmann, "Apricot Socialism," 14–18. On the Karabakh movement, see Malkasian, *"Gha-ra-bagh!"*

179. For an account of Mikoyan's trip to Agarak, see "Enker A. I. Mikoyane Agarakum," 1.

180. "Tovarishch A. I. Mikoian v Armenii," March 16, 1962, 1.

181. Astsatryan recalled that he and other officials were on their way to an important meeting with Zarobyan when Kochinyan reported that "Mikoyan had notified him about his arrival in Yerevan and that he absolutely wanted to visit the city of Alaverdi, his native village of Sanahin, and his ancestral home." (Astsatryan, *XX dar*, 74–75.)

182. GARF R-5446/120/1720/13. See also "Tovarishch A. I. Mikoian v Armenii," March 16, 1962, 1. Footage of the massive crowd scenes can be seen in Zhamharyan, *A. I. Mikoyane Hayastanum*.

183. Astsatryan, *XX dar*, 75.

184. The doves and balloons can be seen in Zhamharyan, *A. I. Mikoyane Hayastanum*.

185. On Mikhail Bakhtin's concept of *carnival*, see Bakhtin, *Problems of Dostoevsky's Poetics*, 122–123.

186. "Tovarishch A. I. Mikoian v Armenii," March 16, 1962, 1.

187. "Enker A. I. Mikoyann Alaverdum," *Dzulogh*, March 17, 1962, 1.

188. "Tovarishch A. I. Mikoian v Armenii," March 16, 1962, 1; and "Enker A. I. Mikoyann Alaverdum," 1.

189. "Enker A. I. Mikoyann Alaverdum," 1. On the Soviet tradition of giving gifts to political leaders, see Ssorin-Chaikov and Sosnina, *Dary vozhdiam*.

190. GARF R-5446/120/1720/13.

191. "Enker A. I. Mikoyann Alaverdum," 1.

192. Astsatryan, *XX dar*, 75.

193. Zhamharyan, *A. I. Mikoyane Hayastanum*.

194. Kochinyan, *Anavart husher*, 402. The phrase is a common set expression in the Armenian language.

195. Astsatryan, *XX dar*, 75–76.

196. GARF R-5446/120/1720/13; and "Tovarishch A. I. Mikoian v Armenii," March 16, 1962, 1. Footage of the first tree-planting ceremony can be seen in Zhamharyan, *A. I. Mikoyane Hayastanum*. According to Ter-Ghazaryants, Mikoyan later visited his father's grave again during a return trip to Sanahin after his retirement. (Sergo Mikoyan, "Anastas Mikoian," 672.)

197. GARF R-5446/120/1720/13.

198. Astsatryan, *XX dar*, 76.

199. Kochinyan, *Anavart husher*, 397–398. The flags and slogans are also described in the account of Mikoyan's 1962 visit to Kajaran in the town's local Party newspaper. ("K'ajarants'inere ayd vore yerbek' ch'en morrana," 1.) According to Kochinyan, it was Mikoyan who, years earlier, suggested giving the mine the name "Kajaran," after the nearby village that eventually grew into the major industrial town. (Kochinyan, *Anavart husher*, 397–398.)

200. Zhamharyan, *A. I. Mikoyane Hayastanum*.

201. "K'ajarants'inere ayd vore yerbek' ch'en morrana," 1; and "Enker A. I. Mikoyane Agarakum," 1.

202. Astsatryan, *XX dar*, 72.

203. Kochinyan, *Anavart husher*, 287–288, 400.

204. Ibid., 399, 401–403. Both the town and the raion of Yeghegnadzor were known as Mikoyan, after Anastas, from 1935 to 1957. The historical name was restored by the Soviet government in accordance with the decree (*ukaz*) on place names adopted by the Presidium of the Supreme Soviet on September 11, 1957. The decree mandated that localities could be named in honor of renowned public figures only posthumously, consistent with the ideological struggle against the "cult of personality." It was introduced by Khrushchev's government in the aftermath of the defeat of the "Anti-Party Group" in June 1957, providing it with a convenient pretext to change the names of places and institutions named after the disgraced officials Malenkov, Molotov, and Kaganovich. For the September 1957 decree, see Mandelshtam, *Sbornik zakonov SSSR*, 621–624. The decision of the Supreme Soviet of Armenia to restore Yeghegnadzor's historical name was formally made on December 6, 1957. (HAA 207/60/31/14–15.) Prior to assuming the name Mikoyan on January 3, 1935, the town was known by the Turkish name of Keshishkend. Before that time, it was also known as Yeghegik and Yeghegyats. (Aslanyan and Grgearyan, *Haykakan SSH*, 67.) As of 2025, many residents in Yeghegnadzor and neighboring communities such as Areni, including many born after 1991, continue to colloquially refer to the town as "Mikoyan."

205. Kochinyan, *Anavart husher*, 399. Since the time of Mikoyan's visit, Shurnukh's Azeri population fled as part of the population exchange between Armenia and Azerbaijan amid the onset of tensions over Nagorno-Karabakh.

206. GARF R-5446/120/1720/6.

207. In August 1993, Zangelan was seized from Azerbaijan by Karabakh Armenian forces. From 1993 to 2020, they administered Zangelan (also known as Kovsakan) as part of the Kashatagh district of the "outer security zone" of the Nagorno-Karabakh (Artsakh) Republic. Meanwhile, Azerbaijan viewed the Zangelan raion as one of seven "occupied districts" surrounding Mountainous Karabakh. During the 2020 Karabakh war, Zangelan was retaken by Azerbaijani forces and now remains under their control. For further information, see Chrysanthopoulos, *Caucasus Chronicles*, 102–106; and Tsutsiev, *Atlas of Ethno-Political History*, 114–116.

208. Medvedev, *Oni okruzhali Stalina*, 130.

209. N. Khrushchev, *O Programme Kommunisticheskoi partii*, 9.

210. Saparov, *From Conflict to Autonomy*, 33.

211. A. Mikoyan, *Tak bylo*, 171. Given the political sensitivity over this issue, Mikoyan's discussion of the Shushi pogrom does not appear in the Russian or Armenian editions of his memoirs published in the Soviet Union during his lifetime.

212. RGASPI 17/6/95/5. As with the discussion of the Shushi pogrom in Mikoyan's memoirs, this section of Mikoyan's report is conspicuously edited out of the version published in Anikeev et al., *Perepiska sekretariata TsK RKP(b)*, 7:442. However, a

similar statement in Sergei Kirov's summary of Mikoyan's report was left unedited in Pavlov, *S. M. Kirov*, 1:143.

213. Hovannisian, *Republic of Armenia*, 1:88–90, 1:156–164.

214. Saparov, *From Conflict to Autonomy*, 93–95.

215. For Mikoyan's full report from Baku dated May 22, 1919, see RGASPI 17/6/95/5–8. According to Mikoyan, the report was delivered to Lenin personally by two young Baku communists, Shura Bertsinskaia and Tigran Askendaryan. (A. Mikoyan, *Mysli i vospominaniia*, 25–27.) Mikoyan likewise recounted that the Baku Party organization sent a third courier, Khoren Boryan, to Moscow with an analogous letter. (A. Mikoyan, *Tak bylo*, 139.) In addition, Kirov, who was then the head of the Political Department of the Eleventh Red Army, prepared a summary of Mikoyan's report for Lenin and Stalin on June 3, 1919. (Pavlov, *S. M. Kirov*, 1:143–145.)

216. RGASPI 17/6/95/5ob.

217. RGASPI 17/6/95/6. Mikoyan similarly noted in his memoirs years later that, in some cases, "Azerbaijani and Armenian peasants acted jointly together and very amicably" against the Musavatist regime in these uezds. (A. Mikoyan, *Tak bylo*, 145.) Within Russian Transcaucasia, Zangezur and Mountainous Karabakh comprised part of the Elizavetpol' guberniia. (Tsutsiev, *Atlas of Ethno-Political History*, 59.)

218. RGASPI 17/6/95/6. This section is also edited out of the version in Anikeev et al., *Perepiska sekretariata TsK RKP(b)*, 7:444. Again, however, a similar statement in Kirov's summary of Mikoyan's report was left unedited in Pavlov, *S. M. Kirov*, 1:144.

219. HAA 199/1/38/27.

220. A. Mikoyan, *Mysli i vospominaniia*, 34. According to Mikoyan, Lenin at the time did not even know where Karabakh was, let alone Dagestan or Chechnia, and relied on the Caucasian Bolsheviks to provide him with details on the dynamics in the region. (A. Mikoyan, *Tak bylo*, 166.) The Kazakh uezd (also known as Kazakh-Shamshadin) encompassed the present-day Tavush marz of Armenia and the Qazax, Aghstafa, and Tovuz raions of Azerbaijan. After the Sovietization of Azerbaijan and Armenia in 1920, the Soviet government divided the uezd between the two republics along geographic and ethnographic lines. The mountainous Armenian-inhabited area became part of Soviet Armenia, while the lowland Tatar (Azerbaijani) area became part of Soviet Azerbaijan. (Tsutsiev, *Atlas of Ethno-Political History*, 81.)

221. For the best historical overview of the decision to incorporate Nagorno-Karabakh into Soviet Azerbaijan, see Saparov, *From Conflict to Autonomy*, 90–124. See also Pisarenko, *Sergei Kirov*, 300–311.

222. Although Mikoyan played no such role, both Azerbaijani and Armenian scholars have scrutinized his early statements on the Karabakh question in the crucial period of 1920 between the Sovietization of Azerbaijan and the Sovietization of Armenia. This was a unique period during which the dispute over Mountainous Karabakh became one between Soviet Azerbaijan and the Dashnak-led First Armenian Republic. Soviet Azerbaijani claims over both the disputed province and neighboring Zangezur were backed by Ordzhonikidze and the Eleventh Red Army, with the aim

of advancing the Sovietization of the region. (Saparov, *From Conflict to Autonomy,* 98.) Lenin favored a much more cautious approach, advising Ordzhonikidze "not to hurry" with further Bolshevik expansion into Transcaucasia. (Kvashonkin et al., *Bol'shevistskoe rukovodstvo,* 123–124n7.) In this instance, Mikoyan supported the position of Ordzhonikidze, as evidenced by his telegram from June 29, 1920. (RGASPI 64/1/17/133–135.) Overall, it must be emphasized that statements from Caucasian Bolsheviks in this period should be considered within this very specific historical context. In the final analysis, they had no impact on the decisions made *after* Armenia's Sovietization, when the status of Mountainous Karabakh became an internal Soviet question involving two republics within the same state.

223. Shatunovskaia, *Ob ushedshem veke,* 119. Although not mentioning Mountainous Karabakh explicitly, Mikoyan himself also noted that one of Stalin's "violations of the nationality policy" was his role in "fixing borders between republics that did not always correspond to the actual settlement of peoples." (A. Mikoyan, *Tak bylo,* 556–557.)

224. HAA 1/2/1/26.

225. Saparov, *From Conflict to Autonomy,* 117. On Stepanakert, see Hewsen, *Armenia,* 265.

226. Mandelshtam, *Sbornik zakonov SSSR,* 6. The NKAO and the Nakhichevan' ASSR were also the only autonomies where the majority nationalities already possessed titular union republics of their own. By contrast, the Gorno-Badakhshan AO served as an autonomy for the Pamiri peoples, while the Dagestan ASSR served as an autonomy for the various peoples of Dagestan.

227. On national identity in Soviet Azerbaijan over the *longue durée* of Soviet history, see Goff, *Nested Nationalism.*

228. Astsatryan, *XX dar,* 81–82. On Adamyan's activities, see Hamlet Harutyunyan, *Nakhagahe.*

229. Astsatryan, *XX dar,* 82–83. Although historically inhabited by a mixed population of Armenians and Tatars (Azerbaijanis), the Nakhichevan' region became overwhelmingly Azerbaijani during the twentieth century. (Mouradian, *De Staline à Gorbatchev,* 414.) On the Armenian history and cultural heritage of the Nakhichevan' ASSR, see Ayvazian, *Historical Monuments of Nakhichevan.*

230. Sergo Mikoyan, "Anastas Mikoian," 404–405. For an Armenian translation, see Sergo Mikoyan, *Hayrs Anastas Mikoyane,* 123–124.

231. Ibid.

232. HAA 1/25/49/73.

233. Goff, *Nested Nationalism,* 81–82.

234. Mandelshtam, *Sbornik zakonov SSSR,* 6.

235. RGANI 5/31/52/47; and Eimermacher et al., *Doklad N. S. Khrushcheva,* 472, 552.

236. HAA 409/1/5787/7. To Bulganin, Vazgen wrote, "While abroad, many [diasporan Armenians] asked us whether the time had arrived for a fair resolution regarding the question of the autonomous oblast' of Nagorno-Karabakh, the Nakhichevan'

ASSR, and the Akhalkalaki raion [Javakhk/Javakheti in Soviet Georgia]. These territories are mainly populated by Armenians but continue to remain outside the borders of Soviet Armenia. Thus, foreign Armenians are hopeful that the benevolent Soviet government will create the necessary land (territorial), economic, and housing conditions for their return to the Homeland in order to reunite their compatriots with their native land."

237. Khrushchev's meeting with the diasporan representatives took place on May 7, 1961. (Bedrosov, *40 let Sovetskoi Armenii*, 155–156.) Among those present, Artin Djerejian, a Hunchak Party leader from Lebanon, asked the premier directly about the status of the NKAO and the Nakhichevan' ASSR. Lebanese Armenian composer Hampartzoum Berberian echoed Djerejian's remarks, expressing hope that "in a peaceful way, Comrade Khrushchev would make [an] exceptional surprise" for his diasporan guests and for "the entire Armenian people," implicitly referring to Mountainous Karabakh. (HAA 1/127/141/33–37.)

238. Astsatryan, *XX dar*, 172–173. Zarobyan's son, Nikita, further noted that his father sought to use the meeting to "demonstrate to Khrushchev the unity of the Armenian people and the mindset of the politically influential diaspora." (N. Zarobyan, *Iakov Zarobian*, 121–122.)

239. HAA 1/127/141/29, 44; RGANI 52/1/366/146, 157; and Astsatryan, *XX dar*, 173.

240. On this matter, Khrushchev stated, "It is clear that the question of the reunification of the Armenian people will occur, but we must have patience. This question cannot be resolved by war, but by reason, by the advantage of the [political] system." (HAA 1/127/141/45; and RGANI 52/1/366/147, 158.)

241. For the official transcript of Khrushchev's remarks, see HAA 1/127/141/42–51; and RGANI 52/1/366/142–164.

242. Astsatryan, *XX dar*, 173. On Mountainous Karabakh, Zarobyan later recounted Khrushchev telling him, no less evasively, that it would be best to "leave the issue for the future." (Arushanyan, *Yakov Zarobyane*, 33.)

243. Astsatryan, *XX dar*, 83.

244. For the appeal, see HAA 207/26s/140/1–6. A samizdat Armenian translation was later leaked to the Armenian diasporan press and published in the Beirut-based Armenian newspaper *Sp'iurk'* in December 1963. According to the newspaper, approximately 2,500 Karabakh Armenians signed the appeal. ("Yushagir Sovetakan Miut'ean Ministrneri Soveti nakhagah, Sovetakan Miut'ean Komunistakan Partiayi Kentkomi k'artughar Enker N. S. Khrushch'ovin," *Sp'iurk'*, December 31, 1963, 2–3.) The original Russian-language letter to Khrushchev was made on behalf of the residents of the NKAO and the Armenians of the Shamkhor, Khanlar, and Shahumyan raions of Soviet Azerbaijan. The Armenian translation also includes Dashkesan among the listed raions. Historically, the Armenian communities of these districts (located north of the NKAO) referred to their native region as Gandzak. For a detailed map of the Gandzak area, see Vardanyan, *Atlas of the Nagorno-Karabagh Republic*, 38.

245. Lehmann, "Apricot Socialism," 24.

246. For the appeal and list of signatories, see HAA 1/46/65b/1–51. The appeal is dated to 1966, without an exact date specified. Saryan's name is listed first among those who signed. Significantly, in their joint response letter to the CPSU Central Committee from September 1966, Anton Kochinyan and Badal Muradyan noted that the signatories (whom they identified as "scientific and cultural figures of the Armenian SSR") also raised the issue of the Nakhichevan' ASSR, in addition to the NKAO. They further noted a reference to the "generally well-known historical fact that forty-six years ago [in 1920], the government of the Azerbaijan SSR proclaimed a declaration acknowledging these territories as indivisible parts of the Armenian SSR, but that their actual unification was delayed." (HAA 1/46/65a/1.) However, the copies of the appeal held in the HAA (in both Armenian and Russian) mention only the NKAO and not Nakhichevan', while the 1920 declaration from Soviet Azerbaijan is not discussed. The absence of these passages suggests that these texts may be abridged versions of the appeal to Moscow.

247. Permiakov et al., *Sekretariat TsK KPSS: 1965–1967 gg.*, 65.

248. HAA 1/46/65a/1–9.

249. Kochinyan, *Anavart husher*, 421.

250. For Kochinyan's full account of his activities in relation to the NKAO, see Kochinyan, *Anavart husher*, 418–428.

251. Astsatryan, *XX dar*, 83–84.

252. Sergo Mikoyan, *Hayrs Anastas Mikoyane*, 173.

253. On socialist legality, see Dobson, *Khrushchev's Cold Summer*.

254. "Sergei Mikoyan Sees New Opportunities for Armenians to Claim Gharabagh," *Armenian Mirror-Spectator*, October 24, 1987, 1, 18; and Ara Kalaydjian, "Mikoyan and Balayan Optimistic on Karabagh Reunification with Armenia," *Armenian Mirror-Spectator*, February 6, 1988, 1, 8–9.

255. "Ot'ezd tov. A. I. Mikoiana iz Erevana," 1.

256. "K'ajarants'inere ayd vore yerbek' ch'en morrana," 1.

257. Arushanyan, *Yakov Zarobyane*, 34. For more on Mikoyan's friendship with Baghramyan, see A. Gasparyan, *I. Kh. Bagramian*, 298–303.

258. Dzarugian, *Hin yerazner, nor chambaner*, 103–105.

259. Sergo Mikoyan, "Anastas Mikoian," 672–673.

4. *DRUZHBA* DEFENDED

1. Riga, *Bolsheviks and the Russian Empire*, 221.
2. For further information, see Lehmann, "Apricot Socialism," 9–31.
3. Hirsch, *Empire of Nations*, 5.
4. A. Mikoyan, *Rech' na XX s"ezde KPSS*, 34–36.
5. On developments in Soviet historical sciences during the Thaw, see Roger D. Markwick, "Thaws and Freezes in Soviet Historiography, 1953–64," in Jones, *Dilemmas of De-Stalinization*, 173–192; and Markwick, *Rewriting History in Soviet Russia*.

6. On the *druzhba narodov* concept and its NEP-era predecessor *bratsvo narodov*, see Martin, *Affirmative Action Empire*, 432–461. For an earlier Western study on this concept, see Tillett, *Great Friendship*. Tillett's study remains an essential work on the *druzhba narodov* concept in Soviet historical literature, although its analysis is clouded by Cold War–era Western biases.

7. Martin, *Affirmative Action Empire*, 432–433.

8. On the concept of "brotherhood and unity" in Yugoslavia, see Haug, *Creating a Socialist Yugoslavia*, 122.

9. A. Mikoyan, *USSR*, 32–33.

10. GARF R-5446/120/1288/9, 13. Mikoyan wrote the inscription on January 23, 1957, in a visitor's book kept at the border post at Firiuza (misspelled as "Fiuriza" in the documents), while meeting with Soviet border guards and inspecting the frontier with Iran.

11. Haug, *Creating a Socialist Yugoslavia*, 85.

12. GARF R-5446/120/1110/327. In this text, Mikoyan crossed out the adjective "final" (*okonchatel'nyi*) in the phrase "final physical annihilation," likely because he concluded that the 1915 Genocide ultimately failed to achieve the objectives of the Young Turk/Ittihadist regime, as evidenced by the existence of Soviet Armenia.

13. GARF R-5446/120/1110/327.

14. For the most comprehensive history of the Genocide, see Kévorkian, *Armenian Genocide*.

15. Panossian, *Armenians*, 228.

16. GARF R-5446/120/1110/326–327. On the relationship between the Armenians and the tsarist state, see Badalyan Riegg, *Russia's Entangled Embrace*. For a detailed history of the Russian expansion into the larger region, see Bournoutian, *From the Kur to the Aras*.

17. This argument was echoed by Bournoutian, who contended that the security umbrella of Imperial Russian rule allowed for significant political, social, and economic development in Eastern Armenia, setting the stage for the much greater changes of the Soviet era. See Bournoutian, *Armenia and Imperial Decline*.

18. The quotes that Mikoyan used include "The valiant spirit of the Russians saved us" and "The power of Russian philanthropy . . . softened these very rocks—the desolate, lifeless fields of Armenia settled by a people, who are now restoring their sacred country again under the care of the Russian nation." (GARF R-5446/120/1110/325.) For Abovyan's novel, see Abovyan, *Verk' Hayastani*.

19. GARF R-5446/120/1110/325.

20. GARF R-5446/120/1110/324.

21. A. Mikoyan, *Tak bylo*, 41, 195.

22. Ibid., 194–195.

23. Ibid., 195.

24. Ibid.

25. On the history of the Armenian revolutionary movement, see Ter Minassian, *Nationalism and Socialism*.

26. GARF R-5446/120/1110/323. On Nalbandyan, see Hacikyan et al., *Heritage of Armenian Literature,* 3:291–294.

27. GARF R-5446/120/1110/324–325.

28. A. Mikoyan, *Rech' na sobranii izbiratelei,* 43. For an English translation of Chernyshevskii's novel, see Chernyshevskii, *What Is to Be Done?* Mikoyan was not alone in highlighting the connection between Chernyshevskii and Nalbandyan. In his book, Tillett reflects on the effort of Soviet historians from other republics to stress the link between Russian revolutionary figures and non-Russian national revolutionaries. (Tillett, *Great Friendship,* 387–392.)

29. On the Dashnaks, see Ter Minassian, *Nationalism and Socialism.*

30. Panossian, *Armenians,* 245–248.

31. Lehmann, "Apricot Socialism," 11.

32. Riga has even speculated that Mikoyan may have been a member of the ARF before he became a Bolshevik. (Riga, *Bolsheviks and the Russian Empire,* 218.) In his memoirs, Simon Vratsyan claimed that Mikoyan had been a member of the party. (Vratsyan, *Keank'i Ughinerov* 3:34.) However, no archival evidence supports this claim, and such assertions are rejected by the Mikoyan family.

33. GARF R-5446/120/1343/16. Of this private meeting, Antranig Dzarugian wrote, "Yesterday evening, two carloads, some forty people, arrived from Tiflis. They were not officials from the other republics. Nor were they representatives of the Party. They were his [Mikoyan's] one-time classmates from the Nersesian School: most of them ordinary citizens. He spent the whole evening with them feasting, dancing and singing. He was transferred to a different world." (Dzarugian, *Hin yerazner, nor chambaner,* 105–106.) In addition to the 1958 reunion, Mikoyan would participate in at least two more reunions with Nersisyan School alumni in 1967 and 1968. (Avagyan and Perikhanyan, *Nersisyants'iner, 1824–1924,* 250–251, 260, 263.)

34. GARF R-5446/120/1343/5. Even Mikoyan's Dashnak opponents begrudgingly admitted being impressed by his speaking abilities. As Andre Amourian, the editor of the Armenian American *Asbarez* newspaper, recounted in January 1959, "The thing I remember particularly about him was that he was such a good speaker. He spent more of his time in classrooms and outside arguing in favor of Marxism. Fortunately we had some good Dashnak speakers who could keep up with him." (John M. Bernier, "Editor of 'Asbarez' Newspaper Recalls Having Met 'Guest' Anastas Mikoyan," *Hairenik Weekly,* January 15, 1959, 2.)

35. GARF R-5446/120/1343/7. Kajaznuni was the first prime minister of the First Republic of Armenia of 1918–20. The statement on the Dashnaks "not being able to do anything" is reminiscent of his 1923 report calling for Dashnak recognition of Soviet Armenia, entitled *Dashnaktsutyun Has Nothing More to Do.* For Kajaznuni's report, see *H. H. dashnakts'ut'yune anelik' ch'uni aylevs.*

36. A. Mikoyan, *Tak bylo,* 75–79.

37. Although the Dashnaks held a hostile attitude toward Mikoyan, there were also groups within the Armenian diaspora who admired him as an Armenian "success story" in the Soviet context. The Armenian Social Democrats (Hunchaks) were

especially favorably disposed toward Mikoyan. In an interview with the Beirut-based Armenian literary periodical *Ahken* in 1968, the leader of the Hunchaks, Harutiun Kuzhuni (Cherechian), said, "If the Georgians had Stalin and Beria for years, then we also had Mikoyan for years, and we still have him today." (Shahinian, "Sots'ial Demokrat Hnch'akean Kusakts'ut'iune," 98.)

38. Vratsyan, "How Armenia Was Sovietized, Part III," 70.

39. "Mi zroyts' pataskhanatu bolsheviki het," *Droshak*, December 1929, 285.

40. James H. Tashjian, "Anastas Mikoyan: The Man We Are Dining and Wining, He's Purged Thousands of Armenians, Helped Wreck Armenian Freedom; He's No More 'Armenian' Than Khrushchev (Anastas Mikoyan: The False Legend)," *Hairenik Weekly*, January 15, 1959, 1, 4–5.

41. A. Mikoyan, *Rech' na sobranii izbiratelei*, 41.

42. GARF R-5446/120/1110/324.

43. RGASPI 84/3/53/8.

44. GARF R-5446/120/1721/9.

45. Bournoutian, *Armenia and Imperial Decline*, 97.

46. RGASPI 84/3/53/12–13.

47. RGASPI 84/3/53/9.

48. GARF R-5446/120/1343/17.

49. For Hovhannisyan's letter to Mikoyan, Tumyan's full manuscript, and the map of the NKAO, see RGASPI 84/3/81. In the *delo*, Tumyan's surname is misspelled as "Tunyan" due to a typo in Hovhannisyan's original Armenian-language letter to Mikoyan. Tumyan's manuscript, entitled *Depk'ere Lernayin Gharabaghum 1917–1920 t't'*. (*Events in Nagorno-Karabakh in 1917–1920*), was originally completed in 1964. Although it was never published during the Soviet era, it was eventually published in post-Soviet Armenia in 2008 with the support of the Matenadaran in Yerevan. See Tumyan, *Depk'ere Lernayin Gharabaghum 1917–1920 t't'*.

50. RGASPI 84/3/81/2. For Tumyan's epilogue, see RGASPI 84/3/81/323–330. In a concluding comment (not included in the 2008 published edition of the book), Tumyan bemoaned the fact that the 1962 appeal to Khrushchev, like earlier appeals, remained unanswered ("*dzayn barbaroy yanapati*"). (RGASPI 84/3/81/330.)

51. RGASPI 84/3/81/3.

52. For Mikoyan's critique of Stalin's *Short Course*, see A. Mikoyan, *Rech' na XX s"ezde KPSS*, 34–36.

53. Markwick, "Thaws and Freezes," 174.

54. Ibid., 173–177.

55. Ibid., 185.

56. GARF R-5446/120/1720/8.

57. The completed book was eventually published in 1967 in Yerevan. See Aghayan et al., *Ocherki istorii kommunisticheskoi partii Armenii*.

58. GARF R-5446/120/1721/1.

59. Sergo Mikoyan, *Hayrs Anastas Mikoyane*, 122.

60. GARF R-5446/120/1721/1–2.

61. A. Mikoyan, *Tak bylo*, 39–41. On Iran in World War I, see Atabaki, *Iran and the First World War*. Regarding General Andranik, during the 1960s, Soviet Armenian authorities initiated a limited "rehabilitation" of him, given his conflicts with the Dashnaks and the fact that he once pledged allegiance to the Baku Commune. However, the effort was highly contested, in particular by observers from Azerbaijan who accused Andranik of being responsible for the ethnic cleansing of Azeri civilians during the civil war in Transcaucasia. (Saparov, "Re-negotiating the Boundaries," 873–874.) Significantly, Mikoyan himself participated in this effort to "rehabilitate" Andranik. In the Soviet-era edition of his memoirs, he recounted Andranik's expression of loyalty to the Baku Commune, his conflicts with the Dashnaks, and his donation of his saber as a gift to the State Historical Museum in Yerevan "as a sign of admiration for Soviet Armenia." (A. Mikoyan, *Dorogoi bor'by*, 42–43.)

62. Years later, Sergo Mikoyan noted that his father had become "blinded [to internationalism] by the role of 'proletarian Baku' in the revolution." (Sergo Mikoyan, "Anastas Mikoian," 32.)

63. For Mikoyan's full report to Lenin on the Armenian question from early December 1919, see RGASPI 5/1/1202/8–9ob.

64. RGASPI 5/1/1202/8.

65. RGASPI 5/1/1202/8–9.

66. In his letter, Mikoyan wrote that the national liberation struggle of the Western Armenians could be interpreted as an objective revolutionary struggle, "albeit not entirely fairly." (RGASPI 5/1/1202/8.)

67. GARF R-5446/120/1721/7.

68. RGASPI 5/1/1202/9ob.

69. In his proposal, Shahumyan outlined that the Georgian region (Western Transcaucasia) would encompass the Kutais guberniia, the Batum oblast', and part (presumably most) of the Tiflis guberniia, while the Armenian region (Eastern Transcaucasia) would include the Erivan guberniia, the Kars oblast', and parts of the Tiflis and Elizavetpol' guberniias. He envisioned that the Tatar/Azerbaijani region (Baku) would include the Baku guberniia, the Dagestan oblast', and part of the Elizavetpol' guberniia. On the question of Ottoman Armenia, Shahumyan stressed that the local population "must decide its own fate" and that "if they decide to join Russia, they should be joined with the Armenians." (Belova, Ohanjanyan, and Barseghyan, *S. G. Shaumian*, 2:103–105.)

70. GARF R-5446/120/1721/7. See also A. Mikoyan, *Tak bylo*, 64–65; and Suny, *Baku Commune*, 207n94.

71. GARF R-5446/120/1721/5–6.

72. On the 1918 Armenian Communist Party, see Hovannisian, *Republic of Armenia*, 1:408–415. See also A. Mikoyan, *Tak bylo*, 160.

73. RGASPI 84/3/282/91–94ob.

74. RGASPI 84/3/282/95.

75. GARF R-5446/120/1721/5. In addition, Mikoyan discussed his position on Haykuni's Armenian Communist Party in *Tak bylo*, 164; and *Mysli i vospominaniia*, 38.

76. GARF R-5446/120/1721/6–7. In his December 1919 report to Lenin, Mikoyan also attacked Haykuni's Armenian Communist Party over its territorial claims on Ottoman Armenia, which he claimed encouraged the "massacre of Muslims" under the guise of the "struggle for Soviet power" and the "sauce of communism covered with Armenian chauvinism." (RGASPI 5/1/1202/90b.) This strong critique served to bolster Mikoyan's more central argument against Haykuni's party and its position toward the Transcaucasian Kraikom.

77. GARF R-5446/120/1721/5.

78. RGASPI 84/3/282/97–141.

79. Obichkin, Shanshiev, and Shahumyan, "Nekotorye voprosy," 78–86. Among his cited quotes, Mikoyan noted that Haykuni's insistence on complete independence from the Transcaucasian Kraikom, if realized, would be "disastrous in the conditions of Caucasian reality."

80. For Haykuni's letters to Mikoyan, see GARF R-5446/120/1629, 1791. Haykuni was repressed in 1937 and exiled for over ten years. Upon release, he worked in Russia before returning to Yerevan in 1954. (Volobuev, *Politicheskie deiateli Rossii 1917*, 13.) Although Haykuni was repressed under Stalin's regime, Mikoyan asserted that Stalin had earlier supported Haykuni's Armenian Communist Party during the revolutionary period. (A. Mikoyan, *Tak bylo*, 376–377.)

81. For a detailed overview of the May Uprising, see Hovannisian, *Republic of Armenia*, 3:209–253. After the uprising was violently crushed by the Dashnak-led Armenian government, rumors spread that Mikoyan had been among those executed, even though Mikoyan did not participate in the May Uprising and was not in Armenia at the time. (Hovannisian, *Republic of Armenia*, 3:252.)

82. Although the Dashnak government succeeded in suppressing the uprising in its main center, it faced greater difficulty in crushing the rebellion in northeastern Armenia, especially in Shamshadin, a stronghold for the Armenian Bolsheviks. (Hovannisian, *Republic of Armenia*, 3:243–247.) After receiving an appeal for assistance, Mikoyan sent a telegram to Ordzhonikidze, requesting aid to the Armenian Bolshevik partisans. However, although Ordzhonikidze and the Eleventh Red Army provided support to the rebels, it was already too late. The telegram is reproduced by Mikoyan in his memoirs. (A. Mikoyan, *Tak bylo*, 175–176.)

83. A. Mikoyan, *Tak bylo*, 176.

84. GARF R-5446/120/1721/8.

85. While in Cuba, Mikoyan regularly met not only with Castro but also with his revolutionary associate, Ernesto "Che" Guevara, who was known for his intransigence in negotiations. In an interview with Iosif Grigulevich, Mikoyan later recounted that once, he even joked that Guevara "lived up to the name 'Che', because 'che' means 'no' in Armenian." The statesman recalled that "upon hearing this, he [Guevara] affably and heartily roared with laughter." (Sergo Mikoyan, *Anatomiia Karibskogo Krizisa*, 619.)

86. GARF R-5446/120/1721/8–9.

87. RGASPI 84/3/53/8.

88. RGASPI 84/3/53/8–9.

89. On the Bolshevik-Kemalist collaboration and its impact on Armenia, see Hovannisian, *Republic of Armenia*, vol. 4. On Soviet perceptions of Kemalism, see Ter-Matevosyan, *Turkey, Kemalism and the Soviet Union*.

90. For the texts of the treaties, see Burdett, *Caucasian Boundaries*, 1:743–753, 1:779–784; and Burdett, *Armenia*, 1:669–689. See also Tsutsiev, *Atlas of Ethno-Political History*, 74–76. On the historical and cultural significance of Ani to the Armenians, see Cuneo et al., *Documents of Armenian Architecture 12*.

91. HAA 113/3/21/27, 100–101, 103–105, 140–142ob, and 113/3/23/49, 56, 59–60ob, 101–102.

92. On the atrocities committed by Kemalist forces against Armenians, see Kerr, *The Lions of Marash*.

93. As Lenin wrote in his *Materialism and Empirio-criticism*, "in following *along the path* of Marxist theory, we will approach closer and closer to objective truth, without exhausting it." (Lenin [as Vl. Il'in"], *Materializm" i empiriokrititsizm"*, 160.)

94. GARF R-5446/120/1721/9–10.

95. GARF R-5446/120/1721/11.

96. GARF R-5446/120/1721/11. The Shakhty Trial of 1928 was one of the most important show trials in the history of the Soviet Union. For a documentary history, see Krasil'nikov, *Shakhtinskii protsess 1928 g.*

97. GARF R-5446/120/1721/11–12.

98. GARF R-5446/120/1721/12.

99. GARF R-5446/120/1721/12–13.

100. RGANI 5/31/148/43. For the full report of Viktor Churaev and Vasilii Snastin to the CPSU Central Committee on Tovmasyan (dated November 16, 1960), see RGANI 5/31/148/41–46. See also Grybkauskas, *Governing the Soviet Union's National Republics*, 97–99.

101. GARF R-5446/120/1721/13.

102. GARF R-5446/120/1721/16; and RGASPI 84/3/282/142.

103. Mikoyan even stressed this point in his account of the Baku Commune in the Soviet-era edition of his memoirs. "Naturally, I cannot claim to have made an exhaustive analysis of the events that occurred in this period," he wrote. "That is the business of scientific historians." (A. Mikoyan, *Dorogoi bor'by*, 249.)

104. For the article, see Mamikonyan, "Mi ej St. Shahumyani," 113–130.

105. For the classic English-language account of the Baku Commune, see Suny, *Baku Commune*. For Mikoyan's personal account, see A. Mikoyan, *Tak bylo*, 65–110.

106. The Baku 26 included Stepan Shahumyan, Prokofii "Aliosha" Japaridze, Mashadi Azizbekov, Ivan Fioletov, Mir Hasan Vezirov, Grigorii Korganov, Iakov Zevin, Grigorii Petrov, Vladimir Polukhin, Arsen Amiryan, Suren Hovsepyan, Ivan Malygin, Baghdasar Avagyan, Meer Basin, Mark Koganov, Fiodor Solntsev, Aram

Kostandyan, Solomon Bogdanov, Anatolii Bogdanov, Armenak Boryan, Eizhen Berg, Ivan Gabyshev, Tadevos Amirov (Amiryan), Iraklii Metaksa, Ivan Nikolaishvili, and Isai Mishne. For Mikoyan's account of the fall of the commune, see A. Mikoyan, *Tak bylo*, 85–110. On the British role in the execution of the Baku 26, Suny notes that "while the more exaggerated claims by Soviet historians of British responsibility in the death of the Twenty-six cannot be substantiated, there is enough evidence to conclude that the British agents in Transcaspia could have prevented the execution if they had been interested in doing so. This they simply were not, and British protests were filed only after the fact." (Suny, *Baku Commune*, 340–341.)

107. A. Mikoyan, *Rech' na sobranii izbiratelei*, 44.

108. GARF R-5446/120/1111/49; and A. Mikoyan, "Rech' na sobranii izbiratelei," March 11, 1954. Significantly, in the original speech that Mikoyan delivered in Yerevan, he mentioned Fioletov's name first after Shahumyan's. In the published version, the order was changed by either Mikoyan or the publisher, with Japaridze's name appearing first after Shahumyan's followed by Fioletov's. (A. Mikoyan, *Rech' na sobranii izbiratelei*, 41.)

109. Harrison E. Salisbury, "Preface," in A. Mikoyan, *Memoirs of Anastas Mikoyan*, xiii.

110. According to Suren Shahumyan, the other six included Samson Kandelaki, Varvara Japaridze, Olga Fioletova, Maria Amirova, Satenik Martikyan, and Maro Tumanyan. (A. Mikoyan, *Tak bylo*, 102.) On his specific case, Mikoyan noted the following in his memoirs: "As a member of the Baku Party Committee, I stayed behind there [in Baku] for illegal Party work against the counter-revolutionary [Musavatist] authorities and after the victory of the Turks. While at liberty, I took measures to save my arrested comrades. It is precisely because I was not arrested in Baku at that time that my surname was not on the above-mentioned list of the prison bailiff. Nor did my name appear on a similar list published in the newspapers, according to which the Baku commissars were arrested in Krasnovodsk later. Moreover, this list excluded the names of the wives of the commissars—the Bolsheviks Varvara Japaridze and Olga Fioletova—who were also not arrested in Baku." (A. Mikoyan, *Tak bylo*, 102–103.)

111. Salisbury, "Preface," xiii.

112. A. Mikoyan, *Tak bylo*, 100; and Suny, *Baku Commune*, 342.

113. A. Mikoyan, *Tak bylo*, 100–101.

114. Salisbury, "Preface," xiii.

115. GARF R-5446/120/1844/3.

116. A. Mikoyan, *Rech' na XX s"ezde KPSS*, 35.

117. RGANI 5/31/52/42; and Eimermacher et al., *Doklad N. S. Khrushcheva*, 420.

118. RGASPI 84/3/251/107. For the full dedication in Russian, see RGASPI 84/3/251/100–108. For the Armenian version, see Anastas Mikoyan, "Step'an Shahumean," *Khorhrdayin Hayastan*, September 20, 1922, 2.

119. A. Mikoyan, "Obrazets revoliutsionera leninskoi gvardii—K 90-letiiu so dnia rozhdeniia S. G. Shaumiana," *Pravda*, October 13, 1968, 3. The draft material for the article can be found in RGASPI 84/3/251/1–39.

120. A. Mikoyan, "Obrazets revoliutsionera leninskoi gvardii," 3. Additionally, Mikoyan reflected on Shahumyan's correspondences with Lenin on nationality concerns in A. Mikoyan, *Sovetskomu Soiuzu piat'desiat let*, 19–23. For more on the exchanges between Lenin and Shahumyan on the national question, see Suny, *Stalin*, 513–515.

121. See A. Mikoyan, "Arajaban," in Barseghyan, *Step'an Shahumyan*, 7–10; and A. Mikoyan, "Kniga o plamennom internatsionaliste," in Hakobyan, *Stepan Shaumian*, iii–xii.

122. The material for the 1977 article can be found in RGASPI 84/3/251/41–99.

123. "Vruchenie ordena Lenina Turkmenskoi SSR," *Pravda*, January 22, 1957, 1.

124. Mikoyan's trip to Soviet Turkmenia took place on January 19–24, 1957. His itinerary included attending, among other events, Turkmen equestrian and national wrestling competitions and a performance of the Turkmen national opera *Shahsenem and Gharib* by Dangatar Ovezov and Adrian Shaposhnikov at the Ashkhabad Makhtumkuli Opera and Ballet Theatre. For Mikoyan's full itinerary, see GARF R-5446/120/1288/6–10.

125. "Prebyvanie A. I. Mikoiana v Maryiskoi oblasti," *Turkmenskaia Iskra*, January 22, 1957, 1.

126. GARF R-5446/120/1288/18–19; and "Pribyte v Ashkhabad tovarishcha A. I. Mikoiana," *Turkmenskaia Iskra*, January 22, 1957, 1.

127. GARF R-5446/120/1288/19.

128. GARF R-5446/120/1844/2.

129. Mikoyan was praised for this feat by Azerbaijani Old Bolshevik Mamed Veisov in his meeting with Old Bolsheviks on the final day of the same Baku visit of March 1964. (GARF R-5446/120/1844/26.)

130. Sergo Mikoyan, *Soviet Cuban Missile Crisis*, 72–74, 82.

131. GARF R-5446/120/1844/2.

132. GARF R-5446/120/1844/3.

133. GARF R-5446/120/1844/5.

134. GARF R-5446/120/1844/5.

135. Tonoyan, *Black Garden Aflame*, xix. In the same vein, Russian ethnologist Victor Schnirelmann wrote of the "rich palette of ethno-political relations and tensions that literally permeated Soviet reality and, in the final analysis, served as a catalyst for the bloody ethnic conflicts that destroyed the beautiful, but far from reality, myth of the '*druzhba narodov*', forged over decades of Soviet propaganda." (Schnirelmann, *Voiny pamiati*, 10.)

136. GARF R-5446/120/1844/7.

137. GARF R-5446/120/1844/6.

138. GARF R-5446/120/1844/7, 37.

139. GARF R-5446/120/1844/7.

140. GARF R-5446/120/1844/60.

141. GARF R-5446/120/1844/55–58.

142. GARF R-5446/120/1844/7.

143. GARF R-5446/120/1844/65.

144. GARF R-5446/120/1844/63.

145. GARF R-5446/120/1844/38. Mikoyan remarked, "Imagine if such a woman were to give such a speech in the 1920s, with an open face. She wouldn't be able to open her face to look at the people. The women [of Azerbaijan] walked with their faces covered. And how many talented women were killed under this blanket-chador? There are as many talented Azerbaijani women in the Azerbaijani Republic today." For the best overview of the unveiling campaign from the perspective of local women in another traditionally Islamic part of the Soviet Union, see Kamp, *New Woman in Uzbekistan*.

146. GARF R-5446/120/1844/38–39. Mikoyan later expressed similar sentiments in his meeting with Baku Old Bolsheviks on March 30, the final day of his 1964 Baku trip. Marveling at Ibrahimova as a symbol of revolutionary success, he remarked, "Imagine how much knowledge that girl has in her head! This is a symbol that we have won. You must be proud of the results of all your labors, which have borne such fruits today." (GARF R-5446/120/1844/19.)

147. GARF R-5446/120/1844/40–41. On Sumgait during the civil war era, Mikoyan recalled, "In 1918, when there were battles not far from here, this place was empty. There was only one water tower [*vodokachka*], a pumping station. In 1920, on April 27, we went to Baku in an armored train to protect supplies from destruction. The first military skirmishes took place here. That was Sumgait. The name was unknown. Just the station and the water tower. There was nothing else and there was no water. Just the water tower and that was it."

148. GARF R-5446/120/1844/44–45.

149. GARF R-5446/120/1844/8, 53. In his Sumgait speech, Mikoyan also discussed the Cold War arms race and foreign affairs, including his meeting with Cyrus Eaton in Cleveland in 1959. (GARF R-5446/120/1844/48–52.)

150. GARF R-5446/120/1845/21–22 and R-5446/120/1844/67.

151. A. Mikoyan, *Mysli i vospominaniia*, 28.

152. GARF R-5446/120/1844/31.

153. After the fall of his predecessor Imam Mustafaev, Akhundov was known for taking a more cautious approach toward Azeri nationalism. As historian Krista Goff notes, "Akhundov clarified a strategy to emphasize economic problems rather than national issues in an attempt to avoid many of the bigger conflicts that had developed in republic governance." (Goff, *Nested Nationalism*, 140.)

154. GARF R-5446/120/1844/9.

155. GARF R-5446/120/1844/9–11.

156. GARF R-5446/120/1844/11.

157. GARF R-5446/120/1844/12–13.

158. GARF R-5446/120/1844/14.

159. GARF R-5446/120/1844/22.

160. GARF R-5446/120/1844/35.
161. GARF R-5446/120/1844/24.
162. GARF R-5446/120/1844/26–28. Veisov also discussed Mikoyan's role in defusing the Cuban Missile Crisis. "We will never forget," he told Mikoyan, "that when you were in Cuba, [your wife] Ashkhen *Badji* [honorific title for an Armenian woman] died at that moment, but you, with Fidel Castro and Comrade Khrushchev directly led this major historical operation. And [during the crisis] the rhythm of your heart, as well as the rhythm of the hearts of Fidel Castro and Nikita Sergeevich Khrushchev, beat simultaneously with the heart of the entire Soviet people, especially the people of Baku." (GARF R-5446/120/1844/27.) On Mikoyan and the Cuban Missile Crisis, see Sergo Mikoyan, *Anatomiia Karibskogo Krizisa* and *Soviet Cuban Missile Crisis.*
163. GARF R-5446/120/1844/19.
164. GARF R-5446/120/1844/24, 22.
165. GARF R-5446/120/1844/21–22. For Olga Shatunovskaia's account of the arrests of Ruhulla Akhundov and Frida Shlemova, see Shatunovskaia, *Ob ushedshem veke*, 163–165.
166. GARF R-5446/120/1844/31.
167. On the pro-Stalinist disturbances in Sumgait, see V. Kozlov, *Mass Uprisings in the USSR*, 295–298.
168. GARF R-5446/120/1844/45, 48.
169. GARF R-5446/120/1844/15.
170. GARF R-5446/120/1844/15–16.
171. GARF R-5446/120/1844/16.
172. GARF R-5446/120/1844/16–17.
173. GARF R-5446/120/1844/17.
174. GARF R-5446/120/1844/17–18.
175. GARF R-5446/120/1844/30–31.
176. Taubman, *Khrushchev*, 615.
177. Cohen, *Victims Return*, 87–112.
178. GARF R-5446/120/1844/20.
179. GARF R-5446/120/1844/21.
180. GARF R-5446/120/1844/30.
181. GARF R-5446/120/1844/31–32.
182. GARF R-5446/120/1844/33. On Old Bolshevik survivors of the Gulag and their continued commitment to the Party, see Adler, *Keeping Faith with the Party.*

5. THE PEOPLES' RETURN

1. As Sergo Mikoyan once recalled, his father was highly regarded in Estonia for respecting the republic's distinctive national identity and not treating it condescendingly "like a 'younger brother'" or "a mute part of the Soviet Union." He recalled similar attitudes toward his father in Turkmenia and Tajikistan. (Sergo Mikoyan, *Soviet Cuban Missile Crisis*, 24.)

2. On Serov, see Petrov, *Ivan Serov.*

3. The idea of *korenizatsiia* refers to the "twin policies of promoting national languages and national elites" in the context of the USSR in the 1920s. For more background, see Martin, *Affirmative Action Empire,* 10–12.

4. Sergo Mikoyan, *Soviet Cuban Missile Crisis,* 13.

5. On the civil war in the North Caucasus, see Korenev, *Revoliutsiia na Tereke;* and Dzidzoev, *Ot Soiuza ob"edinennykh gortsev.* For an overview in English, see Marshall, *Caucasus under Soviet Rule,* 51–146.

6. Gatagova et al., *TsK RKP(b)-VKP(b) i natsional'nyi vopros,* 1:84. On the Gorskaia Republic, see Daudov, *Gorskaia ASSR.*

7. A. Mikoyan, *Tak bylo,* 244–245. For a concise overview of the region before Soviet rule, see Marshall, *Caucasus under Soviet Rule,* 10–34.

8. For the two best studies on local elite involvement in Soviet nation-building (both in the context of Central Asia), see Edgar, *Tribal Nation;* and Khalid, *Making Uzbekistan.*

9. Anastas Mikoyan, "Vmesto predisloviia (Rech' tov. Mikoiana)," in Aliev, *Natsional'nyi vopros i natsional'naia kul'tura,* 9.

10. Ibid., 3–4. On Aliev, see Laipanov and Batchaev, *Umar Aliev.*

11. Tsutsiev, *Atlas of Ethno-Political History,* 83–84.

12. A. Mikoyan, *Tak bylo,* 246.

13. Gatagova et al., *TsK RKP(b)-VKP(b) i natsional'nyi vopros,* 1:84–85.

14. A. Mikoyan, *Tak bylo,* 246.

15. Ibid., 247.

16. Marshall, *Caucasus under Soviet Rule,* 163.

17. Gatagova et al., *TsK RKP(b)-VKP(b) i natsional'nyi vopros,* 1:84.

18. A. Mikoyan, *Tak bylo,* 246.

19. Ibid.

20. Gatagova et al., *TsK RKP(b)-VKP(b) i natsional'nyi vopros,* 1:87.

21. A. Mikoyan, *Tak bylo,* 247.

22. Gatagova et al., *TsK RKP(b)-VKP(b) i natsional'nyi vopros,* 1:88–89.

23. Ibid., 89n2.

24. Marshall, *Caucasus under Soviet Rule,* 164.

25. Gatagova et al., *TsK RKP(b)-VKP(b) i natsional'nyi vopros,* 1:88–89. According to the 1926 Soviet census, ethnic Russians comprised 70 percent of the Groznyi okrug, followed by Ukrainians (8%), Armenians (6%), Tatars (3%), Jews and Mountain Jews (3%), and only then Chechens (2%). Together, East Slavs (Russians, Ukrainians, and Belorussians) comprised 80 percent of the population of the Groznyi okrug. (Severo-Kavkazskoe kraevoe statisticheskoe upravlenie (Otdel perepisi), *Poselionnye itogi perepisi 1926 goda,* 440.)

26. A. Mikoyan, *Tak bylo,* 249.

27. Tsutsiev, *Atlas of Ethno-Political History,* 91–92.

28. A. Mikoyan, *Tak bylo,* 249.

29. Ibid., 249–253; and Marshall, *Caucasus under Soviet Rule*, 171–173.

30. Vladimir Mikoyan, interview by Pietro Shakarian, St. Petersburg, December 3, 2022.

31. Sergo Mikoyan, *Soviet Cuban Missile Crisis*, 13.

32. Marshall, *Caucasus under Soviet Rule*, 164.

33. In his memoirs, Mikoyan recounted that on his return trip from the US on a Scandinavian Airlines flight in 1959, two of the plane's four engines failed over the Atlantic Ocean. When Mikoyan arrived safely in Moscow, his mother told him that she had prayed "constantly" for him. Surprised, Mikoyan asked, "Mayrik, can it be that you still believe in God?" She responded simply, "And how can one live without God?" (A. Mikoyan, *Tak bylo*, 62–63.) In later years, Mikoyan also maintained good relations with Catholicos Vazgen I of the Armenian Apostolic Church. During Mikoyan's 1958 trip to Armenia, at a reception in Yerevan, the republic's leadership arranged for him to meet the Armenian spiritual leader. Mikoyan poured a glass of wine and walked over to Vazgen, accompanied by the Armenian leadership. As he recalled, "Approaching the Catholicos, I greeted and, smiling, said in a joking manner, that I felt some guilt before the Armenian Church because I did not live up to her hopes and efforts invested in my education. 'Speaking in the language of economics,' I said, 'as a student of the Armenian Theological Academy, I turned out to be a 'faulty product.' Everyone laughed. The Catholicos smiled and responded, 'You are mistaken! We are not only not upset with you, but we are even proud that a man like you left the walls of our academy. If only we had a few more 'faulty products!'" (A. Mikoyan, *Tak bylo*, 48. See also Dzarugian, *Hin yerazner, nor chambaner*, 108–109.)

34. A. Mikoyan, "Vmesto predisloviia (Rech' tov. Mikoiana)," 12.

35. A. Mikoyan, *Tak bylo*, 248.

36. Marshall, *Caucasus under Soviet Rule*, 164.

37. Tsutsiev, *Atlas of Ethno-Political History*, 91–93.

38. Polian, *Against Their Will*, 145.

39. Ibid., 146.

40. Tsutsiev, *Atlas of Ethno-Political History*, 98–99.

41. A. Mikoyan, *Tak bylo*, 555.

42. Marshall, *Caucasus under Soviet Rule*, 265.

43. A. Mikoyan, *Tak bylo*, 555.

44. Sergo Mikoyan, "Anastas Mikoian," 174. According to Vladimir Mikoyan, the information on the potential deportation of Dagestanis originated from Koroliov. (Vladimir Mikoyan, interview by Pietro Shakarian, St. Petersburg, January 11, 2023.)

45. Tsutsiev, *Atlas of Ethno-Political History*, 98.

46. Tishkov, *Chechnya*, 26.

47. Polian, *Against Their Will*, 147.

48. Tsutsiev, *Atlas of Ethno-Political History*, 98.

49. Tishkov, *Chechnya*, 27.

50. Polian, *Against Their Will*, 161.

51. Ibid., 181–182.

52. Artizov et al., *Reabilitatsiia,* 1:61–62.

53. Bugaev et al., *Vosstanovlenie Checheno-Ingushskoi ASSR,* 1:38–43.

54. Artizov et al., *Reabilitatsiia,* 1:158–159.

55. Ibid., 1:396n52. "Andersovtsy" refers to the "former servicemen of the Polish Army under the command of [Władysław] Anders, who had arrived on repatriation in the USSR from England in the second half of the 1940s and were relocated in 1951 with their families from Western Ukraine, Byelorussia and Lithuania to special settlements." (Bougai, *Deportation of Peoples,* 167.)

56. Bugaev et al., *Vosstanovlenie Checheno-Ingushskoi ASSR,* 1:46.

57. Artizov et al., *Reabilitatsiia,* 1:161–162.

58. Bugaev et al., *Vosstanovlenie Checheno-Ingushskoi ASSR,* 1:49–50, 1:55–57.

59. Artizov et al., *Reabilitatsiia,* 1:224–225.

60. Ibid., 1:226–227.

61. Ibid., 1:289.

62. N. Khrushchev, *Doklad na zakrytom zasedanii XX s"ezda KPSS,* 40.

63. Ibid.

64. Mikoyan expressed these sentiments at a meeting of the CPSU Central Committee Presidium on February 9, 1956. See Artizov et al., *Reabilitatsiia,* 1:350.

65. For the resolutions on the Kalmyks (March 12, 1956) and the remaining nationalities (April 19, 1956), see Eimermacher et al., *Doklad N. S. Khrushcheva,* 266, 296–297. For the recommendation on lifting the restrictions on the remaining nationalities by Roman Rudenko, Nikolai Dudorov, Ivan Serov, and P. Kudriavtsev, see Eimermacher et al., *Doklad N. S. Khrushcheva,* 278–279.

66. For the full letter, see RGANI 5/31/56/12–21. An abridged version can be found in Eimermacher et al., *Doklad N. S. Khrushcheva,* 267–270. This version omits a section of text regarding the history of the Ingush people and the role of the Ingush in the October Revolution. The letter is dated "no later than March 17, 1956."

67. Eimermacher et al., *Doklad N. S. Khrushcheva,* 269.

68. Bugaev et al., *Vosstanovlenie Checheno-Ingushskoi ASSR,* 1:77.

69. Ibid., 1:79.

70. Ibid.

71. Ibid., 1:79–80.

72. Eimermacher et al., *Doklad N. S. Khrushcheva,* 292–294.

73. Ibid., 293.

74. Ibid., 307–308.

75. Desheriev, *Zhizn vo mgle i borbe,* 236.

76. Bugaev et al., *Vosstanovlenie Checheno-Ingushskoi ASSR,* 1:4.

77. Desheriev, *Zhizn vo mgle i borbe,* 236.

78. The delegation of fourteen consisted of Iunus Desheriev, Idris Bazorkin, Abbas Gaisumov, Zhanetta Ziazikova, Aki Mataev, Khadzhibikar Mutaliev, Akhmet (Akhmad) Saidov, Alaudin Taisumov, Osman Tashtiev, Eset (Aset) Tashukhadzhieva,

Khadzhibikar Khamatkhanov, Sultan Khamiev, Magomed (Magomet) Shataev, and Dzhabrail El'murziev. (Patiev, *Ingushi,* 405.) Curiously, in his account, Desheriev listed only thirteen delegates and did not include El'murziev. (Desheriev, *Zhizn vo mgle i borbe,* 238.) However, according to the account of Idris Bazorkin from June 1956, El'murziev not only was present but even spoke at the meeting. (Patiev, *Ingushi,* 400.)

79. Desheriev, *Zhizn vo mgle i borbe,* 236–238. In his account, Bazorkin likewise indicates June 9 as the date of the reception. (Patiev, *Ingushi,* 397.) However, elsewhere in his memoirs, Desheriev gives the alternative date of June 12. (Desheriev, *Zhizn vo mgle i borbe,* 10–11.)

80. Patiev, *Ingushi,* 397. For the delegation's request for a meeting with Khrushchev, see Desheriev, *Zhizn vo mgle i borbe,* 10.

81. Patiev, *Ingushi,* 399.

82. Ibid., 399–400.

83. Ibid., 400.

84. Desheriev, *Zhizn vo mgle i borbe,* 239.

85. Patiev, *Ingushi,* 400.

86. Desheriev, *Zhizn vo mgle i borbe,* 239.

87. Ibid. For a biography of Ziazikov, see Iandiev, *Iarkii primer sluzheniia narodu.* According to Iandiev, Ziazikov and his wife Zhanetta were first arrested on October 9, 1930, on charges of organizing the murder of Iosif Chernoglaz, Ziazikov's successor as the first secretary of the Ingush Obkom. In that case, Ziazikov was sentenced to death on June 11, 1932. However, after the intervention of Mikoyan, Ordzhonikidze, and "a number of other eminent Party figures," the sentence was commuted to ten years imprisonment. After an early release, Ziazikov was arrested again in October 1937 on charges of being involved in a "bourgeois-nationalist Trotskiite counter-revolutionary organization" and for being "an agent of foreign intelligence." He died in NKVD custody in Groznyi on July 5, 1938, and was later rehabilitated on May 6, 1957. (Iandiev, *Iarkii primer sluzheniia narodu,* 317, 337–342.) For documentary materials on the Ziazikov case, see Iandiev, *Zhizn', otdannaia narodu.*

88. Patiev, *Ingushi,* 400.

89. Desheriev, *Zhizn vo mgle i borbe,* 239.

90. Ibid., 238.

91. Patiev, *Ingushi,* 400–401.

92. Ibid., 400. By contrast, in his account, Desheriev wrote that the meeting lasted for "over two hours," but this statement is almost certainly an exaggeration, especially because he also notes that the meeting, which Bazorkin recounted starting at 5:00 p.m., concluded at 6:00 p.m. (18:00). (Desheriev, *Zhizn vo mgle i borbe,* 239.)

93. Desheriev, *Zhizn vo mgle i borbe,* 239. Russian ethnologist Valery Tishkov notes that this stigma was "common among many deported or otherwise victimized peoples." (Tishkov, *Chechnya,* 25–26.)

94. Patiev, *Ingushi,* 401.

95. Desheriev, *Zhizn vo mgle i borbe,* 239–240.

96. Patiev, *Ingushi*, 401.
97. Desheriev, *Zhizn vo mgle i borbe*, 240.
98. Patiev, *Ingushi*, 401–402.
99. Desheriev, *Zhizn vo mgle i borbe*, 240–241.
100. Ibid., 240.
101. Ibid., 241.
102. Sergo Mikoyan, "Anastas Mikoian," 55. When the Karachai returned to their homeland in 1957, Mikoyan advised that "Karachaevsk" be used for the restored name of the Karachai capital, rather than "Mikoyan-Shakhar." (A. Mikoyan, *Tak bylo*, 282n.)
103. Eimermacher et al., *Doklad N. S. Khrushcheva*, 323–324.
104. Ibid., 324.
105. Ibid., 323n1.
106. Artizov et al., *Reabilitatsiia*, 2:805n5.
107. A. Mikoyan, *Tak bylo*, 556.
108. Bugaev et al., *Vosstanovlenie Checheno-Ingushskoi ASSR*, 1:4; and Artizov et al., *Reabilitatsiia*, 2:10.
109. Artizov et al., *Reabilitatsiia*, 2:805–806n5.
110. Eimermacher et al., *Doklad N. S. Khrushcheva*, 348.
111. Artizov et al., *Reabilitatsiia*, 2:162–163.
112. Bugaev et al., *Vosstanovlenie Checheno-Ingushskoi ASSR*, 1:81.
113. A. Mikoyan, *Tak bylo*, 556.
114. Bugaev et al., *Vosstanovlenie Checheno-Ingushskoi ASSR*, 1:90–92.
115. The greatest number of letters were received by the government from Chechen and Ingush deportees. For the report to Pervukhin by the employees of the Council of Ministers tasked with handling the letters, see Artizov et al., *Reabilitatsiia*, 2:176–180.
116. Michaela Pohl, "From White Grave to Tselinograd to Astana: The Virgin Lands Opening, Khrushchev's Forgotten First Reform," in D. Kozlov and Gilburd, *Thaw*, 280.
117. Artizov et al., *Reabilitatsiia*, 2:179–180.
118. Ibid., 176n.
119. For Gromov's full report, see Eimermacher et al., *Doklad N. S. Khrushcheva*, 387–389. The exact names of the employees are not known.
120. Eimermacher et al., *Doklad N. S. Khrushcheva*, 388–389.
121. Ibid., 388; and Patiev, *Ingushi*, 416.
122. Patiev, *Ingushi*, 408–409.
123. Bugaev et al., *Vosstanovlenie Checheno-Ingushskoi ASSR*, 1:101–105.
124. Desheriev, *Zhizn vo mgle i borbe*, 248–249.
125. Patiev, *Ingushi*, 405.
126. See the letter of Soviet interior minister Nikolai Dudorov to Brezhnev from December 28, 1956, in Bugaev et al., *Vosstanovlenie Checheno-Ingushskoi ASSR*, 1:106.
127. A. Mikoyan, *Tak bylo*, 556.

128. Polian, *Against Their Will*, 201.

129. Patiev, *Ingushi*, 414.

130. As Polian wrote, "It is noteworthy that [the] Crimean Tatars were persistent in fighting for their rights during the entire period of their exile and under any circumstances. Their preparedness to move to their homeland immediately and under any conditions was almost unanimous." (Polian, *Against Their Will*, 214.)

131. A. Mikoyan, *Tak bylo*, 556.

132. Pohl, "From White Grave to Tselinograd," 281.

133. Polian, *Against Their Will*, 201.

134. Cohen, *End to Silence*, 240.

135. Ibid., 243.

136. According to Krista Goff, the Crimean Tatars organized a similar delegation to visit Mikoyan in the late 1950s and received a similar response from him. (Goff, *Nested Nationalism*, 278n2.)

137. As Vladimir Mikoyan noted in an interview with this author, "They [the Volga Germans] wanted to return exactly to their original settlements. But my grandfather remarked that their houses were already inhabited by the new settlers and the state faced a problem—what to do with them? He obviously was sympathetic to the plea of the Volga Germans but quite upset, I was sure. He displayed at least two arguments to me. First, there was a lack of money to relocate the numerous Russian settlers and, second, there was disagreement within the top leadership as far as the German request was concerned. This argument was split into two: firstly, giving land to the Germans might not produce a desirable impact within the country—the memories of the war were still quite vivid. Secondly, if the Germans would have abandoned their settlements and left Kazakhstan, there would be no volunteers to take their place. And who will cultivate the Virgin Lands and grow wheat instead in those unfavorable living conditions?" Vladimir Sergeevich further noted that he did not discuss the status of the Crimean Tatars with his grandfather. (Vladimir Mikoyan, interview by Pietro Shakarian, St. Petersburg, December 3, 2022.)

138. Polian, *Against Their Will*, 201.

139. Bugaev et al., *Vosstanovlenie Checheno-Ingushskoi ASSR*, 1:107–109; and Patiev, *Ingushi*, 418–420.

140. Tsutsiev, *Atlas of Ethno-Political History*, 101–103.

141. GARF R-5446/120/1268/168.

142. GARF R-5446/120/1268/169.

143. In the period of 1956–58, the name "Prigorodnyi raion," or simply "Prigorodnyi," referred specifically to the area that is now known as "East Prigorodnyi" in the Republic of North Ossetia-Alania in today's Russian Federation. The territory of "West Prigorodnyi" (i.e., the former Ordzhonikidze raion) was never part of the Ingush-Ossetian dispute. For a 1958 administrative map of the North Ossetian ASSR with the Ordzhonikidze raion, see Kocheshkova, *Severo-Osetinskaia ASSR*.

144. Patiev, *Ingushi*, 405–406.

145. GARF R-5446/120/1268/170.

146. GARF R-5446/120/1268/169.

147. GARF R-5446/120/1268/169.

148. Tsutsiev, *Atlas of Ethno-Political History*, 101–103.

149. Patiev, *Ingushi*, 406.

150. Polian, *Against Their Will*, 197.

151. During NEP, Ordzhonikidze (then still known as Vladikavkaz) was administered by the Soviet government as a separate political entity, like Groznyi. As Marshall writes, the city served as "a 'shared' capital between North Ossetia and Ingushetia until 1933–34, when Ingushetia merged with the Chechen AO, and Vladikavkaz became North Ossetia's official capital; the earlier compromise position nonetheless fomented for the rest of the 1920s what local historians in retrospect labelled an era of ethnic 'parity' between the two sides regarding control of the city." (Marshall, *Caucasus under Soviet Rule*, 188.)

152. Patiev, *Ingushi*, 417.

153. Ibid., 406.

154. Tsutsiev, *Atlas of Ethno-Political History*, 103.

155. Patiev, *Ingushi*, 417.

156. Desheriev, *Zhizn vo mgle i borbe*, 250.

157. Patiev, *Ingushi*, 406.

158. Desheriev, *Zhizn vo mgle i borbe*, 249.

159. Ibid.

160. Patiev, *Ingushi*, 406–407.

161. Ibid., 428–429.

162. Ibid., 429–430.

163. Ibid., 406–407.

164. Desheriev, *Zhizn vo mgle i borbe*, 250.

165. On an example of the peaceful reintegration of one group of deported peoples (the Balkars), see Lanzillotti, *Land, Community, and the State*, 205–210; and Marshall, *Caucasus under Soviet Rule*, 288–289.

166. V. Kozlov, *Mass Uprisings in the USSR*, 88.

167. Ibid., 108–109.

168. Without specifying a date, Medvedev wrote that Mikoyan flew to the Checheno-Ingush ASSR at Khrushchev's request "when riots flared up in Groznyi due to hostile relations between the Russian population and the Chechens and the Ingush returning to the republic." According to Medvedev, Mikoyan managed to calm tensions "without bloodshed or mass arrests." (Medvedev, *Oni okruzhali Stalina*, 168.) The English translation of Medvedev's book by Harold Shukman is even more curious because it specifies the exact year of Mikoyan's alleged visit to be 1961. (Medvedev, *All Stalin's Men*, 50.) However, there is no evidence to suggest that Mikoyan traveled to Groznyi at any time in 1961 with a mandate from Khrushchev to calm ethnic unrest.

169. Bugaev et al., *Vosstanovlenie Checheno-Ingushskoi ASSR*, 1:3.

6. TOWARD A MORE PERFECT UNION?

1. For examples, see Conquest, *Russia after Khrushchev*, 207; Connor, *National Question*, 398–399; Goff, *Nested Nationalism*, 150; Michael Loader, "The Centre-Periphery Relationship during Khrushchev's Thaw: The View from Latvia," *Peripheral Histories*, January 7, 2017, https://www.peripheralhistories.co.uk/post/the-centre-periphery-relationship-during-khrushchev-s-thaw-the-view-from-latvia; Risch, *Ukrainian West*, 22; and Simon, *Nationalism and Policy*, 245–258.

2. A. Mikoyan, *Tak bylo*, 557.

3. John McGarry and Brendan O'Leary, "Territorial Pluralism," in Basta, McGarry, and Simeon, *Territorial Pluralism*, 34.

4. RGASPI 84/3/37/64–78.

5. Alexander Titov, "The 1961 Party Programme and the Fate of Khrushchev's Reforms," in J. Smith and Ilic, *Soviet State and Society*, 8–9.

6. Titov, "1961 Party Programme," 9.

7. See Khrushchev's remarks at the meeting of the Presidium of the Central Committee on the draft Party Program held on December 14, 1959, in Fursenko et al., *Prezidium TsK KPSS*, 1:415–417. In his discussions on democracy and democratization, Khrushchev placed especially strong emphasis on the need to place term limits on Soviet officials. However, as Titov notes, "this proposal met fierce opposition from the Party ranks." (Titov, "1961 Party Programme," 17.)

8. At the Central Committee Presidium meeting of December 14, 1959, Khrushchev stated the following on Stalin: "Comrades, I am reading many letters now, and I have spoken with workers. They say that if Stalin had died ten years earlier, how our country now would breathe. But this is a fact, comrades. We saw everything, but there was nothing that we could do. None of us could raise our voices, or else we would have been swept away. When he [Stalin] said at the Nineteenth Party Congress 'I want to leave,' he himself was watching us at that time. If somebody would have said 'you are right,' then he would have had him arrested. It was arbitrary. We should prevent it. This arbitrariness can be repeated. We must stipulate, by program, statute, and practice, that it be excluded." (Fursenko et al., *Prezidium TsK KPSS*, 1:416.)

9. As Titov notes, "Kuusinen was soon sidelined in the work of the commission and Ponomarev assumed direct control over the commission's work. This represented a victory for the middle line in terms of ideology, as Kuusinen was considered an ideologist keen on revising Stalin's legacy." (Titov, "1961 Party Programme," 10.) On Kuusinen's role in the development of the Party Program, see Renkama, *Ideology and Challenges*, 284–332.

10. For the full section, see CPSU, *Programma Kommunisticheskoi partii*, 112–116.

11. RGASPI 84/3/37/59.

12. RGASPI 84/3/37/60. As if to emphasize this point, the word "*sblizhenie*" was underlined in the nationality section of the typed Party Program drafts from 1961. (GARF R-5446/120/1616/121 and R-5446/120/1618/136.) In his work on the peoples

of the Russian Far North, Yuri Slezkine translates *sblizhenie* as "merger" and interprets the term as being a form of *sliianie*. (Slezkine, *Arctic Mirrors*, 343–344.) However, the archival materials of Mikoyan's contributions to the Third Party Program indicate that *sblizhenie* was adopted by the Party as a rejection of *sliianie*. Outside of nationality policy, Soviet leaders also used *sblizhenie* in reference to international relations. For instance, Mikoyan invoked the term in this way during his visit to L'viv in Western Ukraine in June 1959. (A. Bogma, "Nagrada Vdokhnovlyayet—Vrucheniie ordena Lenina L'vovskoi oblasti," *Pravda*, June 3, 1959, 2.)

13. Stalin, *Marksizm i voprosy iazykoznaniia*, 53–54; and "Tovarishchu A. Kholopovu," *Pravda*, August 2, 1950, 2.

14. GARF R-5446/120/1619/38.

15. GARF R-5446/120/1616/122.

16. GARF R-5446/120/1619/14 and R-5446/120/1618/137.

17. Titov, "1961 Party Programme," 15. Kuusinen's letter is reproduced in Pyzhikov, *Khruchshevskaia "ottepel',"* 341–345. The archival cipher is RGASPI 586/1/214/2–7.

18. GARF R-5446/120/1616/122.

19. GARF R-5446/120/1619/14–15 and R-5446/120/1618/138.

20. CPSU, *Programma Kommunisticheskoi partii*, 112–113.

21. GARF R-5446/120/1616/125.

22. The language issue was a major point of contention between the republics and Moscow during the Thaw, especially in relation to Khrushchev's 1958 educational reform. For further information, see J. Smith, "Battle for Language," 983–1002; and Loader, "Rebellious Republic," 113–139.

23. GARF R-5446/120/1616/125.

24. GARF R-5446/120/1619/15 and R-5446/120/1618/141.

25. CPSU, *Programma Kommunisticheskoi partii*, 115–116.

26. GARF R-5446/120/1616/124.

27. GARF R-5446/120/1619/15 and R-5446/120/1618/140.

28. CPSU, *Programma Kommunisticheskoi partii*, 115.

29. GARF R-5446/120/1616/124.

30. GARF R-5446/120/1619/15 and R-5446/120/1618/140; and CPSU, *Programma Kommunisticheskoi partii*, 115.

31. GARF R-5446/120/1616/121, R-5446/120/1618/136, and R-5446/120/1619/14.

32. GARF R-5446/120/1616/121.

33. CPSU, *Programma Kommunisticheskoi partii*, 113.

34. Zgorzhel'skaia, "Kontseptsiia," 182–183; and Pyzhikov, *Khruchshevskaia "ottepel',"* 413. On the legal status of the individual in the 1964 constitution, see Zgorzhel'skaia, "Kontseptsiia," 175–191. Zgorzhel'skaia has authored perhaps the most comprehensive overview of the Khrushchev-era constitutional reform in any language.

35. GARF R-5446/120/1616/126 and R-5446/120/1618/141.

36. As Titov notes, "According to [Fiodor] Burlatskii [a member of the draft commission for the Third Party Program], Khrushchev wanted to provide guarantees against 'excessive concentration of power in single hands, stagnation and ageing among party cadres on all levels', thus creating mobility and greater accountability within the governing institutions in the Soviet Union." (Titov, "1961 Party Programme," 17.)

37. CPSU, *Programma Kommunisticheskoi partii*, 116.

38. N. Khrushchev, *O Programme Kommunisticheskoi partii*, 88–90.

39. Ibid., 88.

40. Ibid., 91. Francine Hirsch likewise observed that although Khrushchev believed that the merger of nations was "inevitable," he still maintained that such a process "should not be forced." (Hirsch, *Empire of Nations*, 319.)

41. A. Mikoyan, *Rech' na XXII s"ezde KPSS*, 18.

42. Zgorzhel'skaia, "Kontseptsiia," 71.

43. N. Khrushchev, *Otchiot Tsentral'nogo Komiteta*, 128.

44. A. Mikoyan, *Rech' na XXII s"ezde KPSS*, 20–21.

45. Zgorzhel'skaia, "Kontseptsiia," 71–72, 120–121. According to Zgorzhel'skaia, the early draft constitution was "developed under the editorship of Brezhnev, with an accompanying note by Leonid Il'ichev." However, she further notes that this "draft constitution" was in fact only "a list of proposals for changing the basic law then in force" and that even this document "has not been preserved in its entirety."

46. Ibid., 75–77, 133–134.

47. Renkama, *Ideology and Challenges*, 308–309; and Zgorzhel'skaia, "Kontseptsiia," 44–45.

48. Zgorzhel'skaia, "Kontseptsiia," 103, 178.

49. Ibid., 75–77.

50. Ibid., 85–88.

51. Nikita Khrushchev, "O vyrabotke proekta novoi konstitutsii SSSR—Vystuplenie Tovarishcha N. S. Khrushcheva na sessii Verkhovnogo Soveta SSSR 25 aprelia 1962 goda," *Pravda*, April 26, 1962, 1. Khrushchev's speech was also published in CPSU, *Zasedaniia Verkhovnogo Soveta SSSR shestogo sozyva*, 130–132; and Lepioshkin, *Sbornik ofitsial'nykh dokumentov*, 95–97.

52. N. Khrushchev, "O vyrabotke proekta," 1.

53. Ibid.

54. Ibid. For details on the democratization of the Soviet system as envisioned in the 1964 constitution, see Zgorzhel'skaia, "Kontseptsiia," 160–175, 185–188, 193–194.

55. Khrushchev specifically stated, "In the process of drafting the new constitution, it is necessary to use and to base all of our work on the great ideological heritage of Vladimir Il'ich Lenin—the creator of the first constitutions of the world's first socialist state." He further stressed that the constitution must "fully embody the Leninist principles of social and political life as well as the organization and activities of

the socialist state, as reflected and developed in the Communist Party Program of the Soviet Union." (N. Khrushchev, "O vyrabotke proekta," 1.)

56. N. Khrushchev, "O vyrabotke proekta," 1.

57. "Postanovlenie Verkhovnogo Soveta SSSR o vyrabotke proekta novoi konstitutsii SSSR," *Pravda*, April 26, 1962, 1. See also CPSU, *Zasedaniia Verkhovnogo Soveta SSSR shestogo sozyva*, 166–167; Lepioshkin, *Sbornik ofitsial'nykh dokumentov*, 93–94; and RGANI 52/1/440/11–15. The number of members was later de facto reduced to ninety-six, after the untimely death of Fiodor Generalov on May 3, 1962.

58. The nine subcommittees included the Editorial Subcommittee (chairman: Leonid Il'ichev), and the Subcommittees on General Political and Theoretical Questions (chairman: Nikita Khrushchev); on Public and State Organization (chairman: Frol Kozlov, then Nikolai Podgornyi); on Public and State Management and the Activities of Soviets and Public Organizations (chairman: Leonid Brezhnev); on Economic Questions and National Economic Management (chairman: Aleksei Kosygin); on Nationality Policy and National-State Construction (chairman: Anastas Mikoyan); on Science, Culture, Public Education, and Healthcare (chairman: Mikhail Suslov); on People's Control and Socialist Law and Order (chairman: Nikolai Shvernik); and on Foreign Policy and International Relations (chairman: Otto Kuusinen, then Boris Ponomarev). See RGANI 5/30/466/22–24; and Zgorzhel'skaia, "Kontseptsiia," 195.

59. RGANI 5/30/466/18–19.

60. RGANI 5/30/466/23. The full name of the subcommittee literally translates as "Subcommittee on Questions of Nationality Policy and National-State Construction" (*Podkomissii po voprosam natsional'noi politiki i natsional'no-gosudarstvennogo stroitel'stva*). The Russian acronym for the subcommittee could be rendered as "NPNGS."

61. RGASPI 84/3/37/17.

62. RGASPI 84/3/37/22; and Zgorzhel'skaia, "Kontseptsiia," 195.

63. RGANI 5/30/466/19–20.

64. Sergo Mikoyan, "Anastas Mikoian," 662.

65. For Chistov's comparative report, see RGASPI 84/3/37/24–30.

66. For the transcript of the meeting, see RGASPI 84/3/37/46–63. The individuals present included Piotr Romashkin and Viktor Kotok of the Institute of State and Law of the Soviet Academy of Sciences; Anushavan Arzumanyan of the Institute of World Economy and International Relations of the Soviet Academy of Sciences; Mikhail Kammari and Ivan Tsameryan of the Institute of Philosophy of the Soviet Academy of Sciences; Aleksei Lepioshkin and David Zlatopol'skii of Moscow State University; Hatik Azizyan, head of the Department of Science at *Pravda*; and Aleksei Orlov of the Legal Department of Administrative Affairs of the USSR Council of Ministers.

67. RGASPI 84/3/37/46–47.

68. A. Mikoyan, *Tak bylo*, 557.

69. Fursenko et al., *Prezidium TsK KPSS*, 1:905n5.

70. Fursenko et al., *Prezidium TsK KPSS,* 2:223–224.

71. Fursenko et al., *Prezidium TsK KPSS,* 1:905n5.

72. Ibid., 83.

73. Ibid., 135.

74. A. Mikoyan, *Tak bylo,* 557–558. See also Fursenko et al., *Prezidium TsK KPSS,* 2:943n6. Mikoyan later discussed this issue in his July 1964 speech before the Constitutional Commission, summarizing the recommendations of the NPNSC Subcommittee. (RGASPI 84/3/37/216.)

75. RGASPI 84/3/37/52–53.

76. RGASPI 84/3/37/50–51.

77. RGASPI 84/3/37/56. The quote is from the legal scholar Viktor Kotok.

78. RGASPI 84/3/37/53.

79. National okrugs were officially redesignated as "autonomous okrugs" beginning with the adoption of the 1977 Soviet constitution. (CPSU, *Konstitutsiia,* 25.)

80. RGASPI 84/3/37/48.

81. RGASPI 84/3/37/54–55, 57–58.

82. RGASPI 84/3/37/48.

83. RGASPI 84/3/37/49–50. The Soviet government eventually elevated the Adyghe AO to the status of an ASSR within the Russian SFSR during perestroika, on July 3, 1991, five months before the dissolution of the USSR. See "Osnovnye svedeniia," *Respublika Adygeia,* accessed January 1, 2025, http://www.adygheya.ru/about/information/.

84. RGASPI 84/3/37/58–59.

85. RGASPI 84/3/37/55.

86. RGASPI 84/3/37/80–81, 106.

87. RGASPI 84/3/37/51–52.

88. A. Mikoyan, *Rech' na XXII s"ezde KPSS,* 17.

89. A. Mikoyan, *Tak bylo,* 276.

90. As discussed in chapter 4, Shahumyan advocated the creation of three autonomous regions in Transcaucasia at the RSDRP(b) all-Caucasus Congress of October 1917 in Tiflis. These proposed regions would correspond to the future republics of Georgia, Armenia, and Azerbaijan, as part of a larger Soviet federation. In his address before the congress, Shahumyan defined a "federation" (*federatsiia*) as a "union of equal units" (*soiuz ravnykh edinits*) with each having its own constituent assembly. "We are close to a social revolution," he maintained, "so we shouldn't be so afraid of de-centralization." (Belova, Ohanjanyan, and Barseghyan, *S. G. Shaumian,* 2:103–105.)

91. See A. Mikoyan, *Tak bylo,* 195; and GARF R-5446/120/1110/324.

92. Zgorzhel'skaia, "Kontseptsiia," 182–183; and Pyzhikov, *Khruchshevskaia "ottepel',"* 413.

93. RGASPI 84/3/37/62.

94. RGASPI 84/3/37/61–62. In addition to the Russian SFSR, Mikoyan cited Soviet Georgia and Soviet Azerbaijan as examples of federative union republics, even though both were technically only union republics with autonomous units and not officially federations.

95. RGASPI 84/3/37/62.
96. RGASPI 84/3/37/62.
97. RGASPI 84/3/37/209.
98. RGASPI 84/3/37/84–85.
99. RGASPI 84/3/37/47.
100. Mandelshtam, *Sbornik zakonov SSSR*, 7.
101. On nontitular nationalities in the context of Soviet Azerbaijan, see Goff, *Nested Nationalism*.
102. A. Mikoyan, *Sovetskomu Soiuzu piat'desiat let*, 67–68.
103. GARF R-5446/120/1845/21–22.
104. RGASPI 84/3/37/50–51.
105. RGASPI 84/3/37/64.
106. RGASPI 84/3/37/65.
107. Tumanov's report was entitled "Note on the Coverage of Soviet Nationality Policy and National-State Construction in Bourgeois Literature" ("*Spravka ob osveshchenii v burzhuaznoi literature sovetskoi natsional'noi politiki i natsional'no-gosudarstvennogo stroitel'stva*"). For the full text, see RGASPI 84/3/37/65–78.
108. RGASPI 84/3/37/65, 66, 68, 74, 77.
109. RGASPI 84/3/37/66.
110. RGASPI 84/3/37/65, 67–68.
111. RGASPI 84/3/37/70–71.
112. RGASPI 84/3/37/74–75.
113. RGASPI 84/3/43/52–60, 69–74.
114. Renkama reflected on the "Yugoslav model" and its parallels with the 1961 Party Program in Renkama, *Ideology and Challenges*, 231–260. For Khrushchev's assessments of the Yugoslav system, see N. Khrushchev, *Memoirs of Nikita Khrushchev*, 3:544–546. On the 1963 Yugoslav constitutional reform, see Haug, *Creating a Socialist Yugoslavia*, 180–183.
115. Haug, *Creating a Socialist Yugoslavia*, 185–186.
116. RGASPI 84/3/43/1–29.
117. RGASPI 84/3/37/65–67.
118. For all reports on the contents of these letters, see RGASPI 84/3/39–42.
119. Zgorzhel'skaia, "Kontseptsiia," 124–125. Unfortunately, according to Zgorzhel'skaia, the original citizens' letters are thought to be lost.
120. RGASPI 84/3/40/2–3.
121. RGASPI 84/3/39/98.
122. RGASPI 84/3/42/79. On Russians in the Soviet Union, see Hosking, *Rulers and Victims*.
123. RGASPI 84/3/39/23, 56–57, 116; 84/3/40/95; and 84/3/42/23–28, 76–78. On the Soviet internal passport, see Baiburin, *Soviet Passport*.
124. RGASPI 84/3/39/21–22, 84/3/40/38, and 84/3/42/82.
125. RGASPI 84/3/39/56; 84/3/40/43, 45, 94; and 84/3/42/81.

126. RGASPI 84/3/40/42.
127. RGASPI 84/3/40/123–124.
128. RGASPI 84/3/42/81.
129. RGASPI 84/3/39/23.
130. RGASPI 84/3/42/81–82. In addition, the Karabakh Armenians who appealed to Khrushchev in 1962 framed their demand to join the Armenian SSR or the Russian SFSR within the context of the constitutional reform initiative. (See the handwritten Armenian-language note addressed to the chairman of the forthcoming [October 1962] session of the Armenian Supreme Soviet in HAA 207/26s/140/1–1ob.) Meanwhile, outside the USSR, observers in the Armenian diaspora hoped that the Armenian cases for Nagorno-Karabakh and Nakhichevan' would be raised amid the constitutional proceedings. These hopes were heightened by the fact that an Armenian (Mikoyan) headed the NPNSC Subcommittee and that it included Armenia's first secretary (Zarobyan), as well as input from prominent Soviet Armenian intellectuals, like Arzumanyan. (See "Khmbagrakan: Nergaght' yev haykakan hogheru harts'e," *Sp'iurk'*, July 26, 1962, 1; and "Khmbagrakan: Nor sahmanadrut'ean anhrazheshtut'iune," *Ararat*, August 5, 1962, 2.) In the end, however, only Hatik Azizyan of *Pravda* raised the Armenian case for Nakhichevan' during Mikoyan's July 1962 meeting with the Soviet legal scholars. (RGASPI 84/3/37/59.)
131. RGASPI 84/3/40/39–41.
132. RGASPI 84/3/39/87.
133. RGASPI 84/3/40/42 and 84/3/39/87.
134. RGASPI 84/3/37/41, 42, and 84/3/39/88, 86.
135. RGASPI 84/3/37/146.
136. Zgorzhel'skaia, "Kontseptsiia," 196–197. The Kosygin subcommittee submitted its proposals in April 1963.
137. For the letters of Kozlov and Kulatov, see RGASPI 84/3/37/79–91.
138. RGASPI 84/3/37/83, 91.
139. RGASPI 84/3/37/182–189.
140. RGASPI 84/3/37/146.
141. For Kunaev's letter, see RGASPI 84/3/37/106–112. Kunaev later reassumed his position as Kazakhstan's first secretary after his close friend and ally, Leonid Brezhnev, assumed power in 1964. (Schattenberg, *Brezhnev*, 138.) Despite his demotion by Khrushchev, Kunaev enjoyed good relations with Mikoyan and later recounted that Mikoyan sought his assistance on the rehabilitation of Mikhail Iakubovich, a victim of Stalin's repressions, who resided in Karaganda. (Kunaev, *Ot Stalina do Gorbacheva*, 102.)
142. RGASPI 84/3/37/113–119. On the "cult of personality" in reference to point 8, see Zgorzhel'skaia, "Kontseptsiia," 157. On point 9, in the summer draft of the 1964 constitution, the commissions of the Supreme Soviet (renamed the "Supreme People's Soviet," or *Verkhovnyi Narodnyi Sovet*) were to include not only Supreme Soviet deputies but also "representatives of public organizations as well as ordinary citizens."

These commissions would be granted "an expanded right of legislative initiative, as well as the right to conduct legislative advisory activity, on behalf of the Supreme People's Soviet and its chambers, as well as on their own initiative." (Zgorzhel'skaia, "Kontseptsiia," 146–148, 152. See also Pyzhikov, *Khruchshevskaia "ottepel',"* 436–437.)

143. RGASPI 84/3/37/120.

144. RGASPI 84/3/37/122–123.

145. N. Khrushchev, *O Programme Kommunisticheskoi partii*, 89.

146. RGASPI 84/3/37/121, 124.

147. RGASPI 84/3/37/125–145.

148. RGASPI 84/3/37/147–157.

149. RGASPI 84/3/37/158–165.

150. RGASPI 84/3/37/146, 173, 191.

151. RGASPI 84/3/37/174, 181.

152. RGASPI 84/3/37/141, 185.

153. RGASPI 84/3/37/136, 141, 164, 188.

154. RGASPI 84/3/37/110, 125, 189.

155. RGASPI 84/3/37/125, 139, 187.

156. RGASPI 84/3/37/191.

157. For Kulatov's proposal, see RGASPI 84/3/37/88.

158. RGASPI 84/3/37/23.

159. RGASPI 84/3/37/192–202.

160. RGASPI 84/3/37/203–210.

161. RGASPI 84/3/37/209–210. In these final draft articles, the number of deputies elected from each autonomous republic was set at eleven, while the number of deputies for each autonomous oblast' and each national okrug remained undetermined. In the summer draft of the 1964 constitution, eleven deputies would be elected from each autonomous republic, five from each autonomous oblast', and one from each national okrug. (Zgorzhel'skaia, "Kontseptsiia," 137; and Pyzhikov, *Khruchshevskaia "ottepel',"* 430.)

162. RGASPI 84/3/37/207.

163. RGASPI 84/3/37/209.

164. RGASPI 84/3/37/192–193.

165. Malkasian, *"Gha-ra-bagh!,"* 30–32.

166. RGASPI 84/3/37/211–212.

167. RGASPI 84/3/37/212–213.

168. RGASPI 84/3/37/213–215.

169. RGASPI 84/3/37/215–218.

170. RGASPI 84/3/37/218. On Khrushchev's 1964 decision to replace Brezhnev with Mikoyan as chairman of the Presidium of the Supreme Soviet, see Schattenberg, *Brezhnev*, 165–166; and Sergo Mikoyan, "Zhizn', otdannaia narodu," in A. Mikoyan, *Tak bylo*, 10.

171. RGASPI 84/3/37/218–219.

172. RGASPI 84/3/37/220–224.

173. Zgorzhel'skaia, "Kontseptsiia," 135–136, 179–180. For the full text of the summer 1964 draft constitution, see Pyzhikov, *Khruchshevskaia "ottepel',"* 395–458.

174. Zgorzhel'skaia, "Kontseptsiia," 157–160.

175. Ibid., 136.

176. On Khrushchev's fall, see Taubman, *Khrushchev,* 3–17.

177. A. Mikoyan, *Tak bylo,* 678; and Permiakov et al., *Sekretariat TsK KPSS: 1965–1967 gg.,* 328.

178. On the trial, see Hayward, *On Trial.*

179. Instead of a criminal case against Siniavskii and Daniel', Mikoyan proposed a compromise solution that would have left the matter within the remit of the Soviet Writers' Union. Brezhnev initially agreed with this compromise. However, according to Sergo Mikoyan, Suslov intervened and convinced Brezhnev to proceed with a criminal trial. (Sergo Mikoyan, "Zhizn', otdannaia narodu," in A. Mikoyan, *Tak bylo,* 11.)

180. As Sergo Mikoyan noted, his father continued to enjoy popular respect as a member of the Presidium of the Supreme Soviet for several years after retirement. "His appearance in the stands [at Supreme Soviet sessions] was invariably met with much lengthier applause than that received by Brezhnev himself," he recalled. "As a matter of fact, the very duration of that applause, much like Anastas Ivanovich's remaining authority, unnerved the vain Leonid Il'ich." (Sergo Mikoyan, "Zhizn', otdannaia narodu," in A. Mikoyan, *Tak bylo,* 11.)

181. RGASPI 84/3/50/50–55. See also Anastas Mikoyan, "Rech' tov. A. I. Mikoiana," *Kommunist,* June 5, 1966, 2.

182. For the booklet, see A. Mikoyan, *Sovetskomu Soiuzu piat'desiat let.* For the Armenian translation, see Mikoyan, *Sovetakan Miut'yune hisun tarekan e.* For the English translation, see Mikoyan, *USSR.*

183. A. Mikoyan, *Tak bylo,* 648.

184. The message of Malyan's film, based on Matevossian's story, is that local residents can manage their affairs more effectively with greater local control. For the film, see Malyan, *Menk' enk', mer sarere.* For Matevossian's original 1962 story, see Matevossian, *Ogostos,* 3–127, and for the Russian translation, see Matevossian, *Avgust,* 5–106.

185. For a comparison of the 1964 and 1977 constitutions, see Pyzhikov, *Khruchshevskaia "ottepel',"* 313–314.

186. CPSU, *Konstitutsiia,* 21–23.

BIBLIOGRAPHY

ARCHIVES

APRF	Arkhiv prezidenta rossiiskoi federatsii Archive of the President of the Russian Federation, Moscow
GARF	Gosudarstvennyi arkhiv rossiiskoi federatsii State Archive of the Russian Federation, Moscow
HAA	Hayastani azgayin arkhiv National Archives of Armenia, Yerevan
RGALI	Rossiiskii gosudarstvennyi arkhiv literatury i iskusstva Russian State Archive of Literature and Arts, Moscow
RGANI	Rossiiskii gosudarstvennyi arkhiv noveishei istorii Russian State Archive of Contemporary History, Moscow
RGASPI	Rossiiskii gosudarstvennyi arkhiv sotsial'no-politicheskoi istorii Russian State Archive of Socio-Political History, Moscow
TsA FSB RF	Tsentral'nyi arkhiv federalnoi sluzhby bezopasnosti rossiiskoi federatsii Central Archive of the Federal Security Service, Russian Federation, Moscow

NEWSPAPERS

Soviet Union

Dzulogh (Alaverdi), Armenian (Eastern)

Grakan T'ert' (Yerevan), Armenian (Eastern)

K'ajaran (Kajaran), Armenian (Eastern)

Khorhrdayin Hayastan (from 1940 *Sovetakan Hayastan*, Yerevan), Armenian (Eastern)

Kommunist (Yerevan), Russian

Koltntesayin Gyugh (Meghri), Armenian (Eastern)
Pravda (Moscow), Russian
Rya T'eze (Yerevan), Kurdish (Kurmanji)
Turkmenskaia Iskra (Ashkhabad), Russian
Zaria Vostoka (Tbilisi), Russian

Armenian Diaspora

Ararat (Beirut), Armenian (Western)
The Armenian Mirror-Spectator (Watertown, MA), English
Droshak (Paris), Armenian (Western)
Hairenik Weekly (Boston), English
Sp'iurk' (Beirut), Armenian (Western)

ONLINE RESOURCES

Aravot (https://www.aravot.am/)
Armianskii muzei Moskvy i kul'tury natsii (https://www.armmuseum.ru/)
ArmInfo (https://arminfo.info/)
Office of the Historian, US Department of State (https://history.state.gov/)
Peripheral Histories (https://www.peripheralhistories.co.uk/)
Respublika Adygeia (http://www.adygheya.ru/)
Stalinskie rasstrel'nye spiski (Mezhdunarodnyi Memorial) (https://stalin.memo.ru/)

DOCUMENTARY COMPILATIONS

Anikeev, Vasilii Vasil'evich, et al., eds. *Perepiska sekretariata TsK RKP(b) s mestnymi partiinymi organizatsiiami (Aprel'–mai 1919 g.): Sbornik dokumentov.* Vol. 7. Moscow: Politizdat, 1972.

Artizov, Andrei Nikolaevich, et al., eds. *Reabilitatsiia: Kak eto bylo, Dokumenty Prezidiuma TsK KPSS i drugie materialy.* 3 vols. Moscow: Demokratiia and Materik, 2000–04.

Bedrosov, Ruben Sergeyi, ed. *40 let Sovetskoi Armenii: Sbornik*. Yerevan: Haypethrat, 1961.

Belova, T. N., B. S. Ohanjanyan, and Khikar Barseghyan, eds. *S. G. Shaumian: Izbrannye Proizvedeniia.* 2 vols. Moscow: Gospolitizdat, 1957–58.

Bugaev, Abdullah Makhmudovich, et al., eds. *Vosstanovlenie Checheno-Ingushskoi ASSR (1953–1962): Sbornik dokumentov i materialov.* 2 vols. Nal'chik: Pechatnyi dvor, 2013–16.

Burdett, Anita L.P., ed. *Armenia: Political and Ethnic Boundaries, 1878–1948.* 2 vols. London: Archive Editions, 1998.

———, ed. *Caucasian Boundaries, 1802–1946.* 2 vols. London: Archive Editions, 1996.

Charents, Anahit Yeghishei, ed. "Yeghishe Charents: Stat'i. Pis'ma. Dnevniki." *Voprosy literatury,* no. 11 (November 1987): 225–257.

Cohen, Stephen F., ed. *An End to Silence: Uncensored Opinion in the Soviet Union.* Translated by George Saunders. New York: W. W. Norton, 1982.

CPSU (Communist Party of the Soviet Union). *Materialy XXII S"ezda KPSS*. Moscow: Gospolitizdat, 1961.

Danilov, Viktor Petrovich, and Roberta Manning, eds. *Tragediia Sovetskoi Derevni: Kollektivizatsiia i Raskulachivanie, Dokumenty i Materialy, 1927–1939*. Vol. 5, *1937–1939*, bk. 1, *1937*. Moscow: ROSSPEN, 2004.

Eimermacher, Karl, et al., eds. *Doklad N. S. Khrushcheva o kul'te lichnosti Stalina na XX s"ezde KPSS: Dokumenty*. Moscow: ROSSPEN, 2002.

Fursenko, Aleksandr Aleksandrovich, et al., eds. *Prezidium TsK KPSS: 1954–1964*. 2nd ed. 3 vols. Moscow: ROSSPEN, 2015.

Gasparyan, Davit Vazgeni, ed. *Yeghishe Ch'arents': Norahayt ejer*. Yerevan: Yerevani hamalsarani hratarakch'ut'yun, 1996.

Gatagova, Liudmila Sultanovna, et al., eds. *TsK RKP(b)-VKP(b) i natsional'nyi vopros*. 2 vols. Moscow: ROSSPEN, 2005–09.

Hayward, Max, ed. *On Trial: The Soviet State versus "Abram Tertz" and "Nikolai Arzhak."* New York: Harper and Row, 1966.

Iandiev, Abdulazis Dzhabrailovich, ed. *Zhizn', otdannaia narodu*. Saratov: Regional'noe Privolzhskoe izdatel'stvo "Detskaia kniga," 1996.

Khachikyan, Artavazd V., and Levon H. Hakhverdyan, eds. *Tumanian 100: Iubileinaia letopis'*. Yerevan: Hayastan, 1974.

———. *T'umanyan 100: Hobelyanakan taregrut'yun*. Yerevan: Hayastan, 1972.

Khaustov, Vladimir Nikolaevich, V. P. Naumov, and N. S. Plotnikova, eds. *Lubianka: Stalin i glavnoe upravlenie gosbezopasnosti NKVD. Dokumenty 1937–1938*. Moscow: Demokratiia and Materik, 2004.

Khlevniuk, Oleg Vital'evich, et al., eds. *Regional'naia politika N. S. Khrushcheva: TsK KPSS i mestnye partiinye komitety. 1953–1964 gg*. Moscow: ROSSPEN, 2009.

Krasil'nikov, Sergei Alexandrovich, ed. *Shakhtinskii protsess 1928 g.: Podgotovka, provedenie, itogi*. 2 vols. Moscow: ROSSPEN, 2010–11.

Kvashonkin, Aleksandr Vasil'evich, et al., eds. *Bol'shevistskoe rukovodstvo: Perepiska. 1912–1927. Sbornik dokumentov*. Moscow: ROSSPEN, 1996.

Lepioshkin, Aleksei Il'ich, ed. *Sbornik ofitsial'nykh dokumentov (primenitel'no k kursu sovetskogo gosudarstvennogo prava)*. Moscow: Iuridicheskaia literatura, 1964.

Mandelshtam, L. I., ed. *Sbornik zakonov SSSR i ukazov prezidiuma verkhovnogo soveta SSSR (1938 g.–noiabr' 1958 g.)*. Moscow: Gosudarstvennoe izdatel'stvo iuridicheskoi literatury, 1959.

Martynov, Vladimir Pavlovich, and R. L. Grigoryan, eds. *Razvitie energeticheskoi bazy Sovetskoi Armenii za 50 let: Dokumemty i materialy*. 2nd ed. Yerevan: Hayastan, 1978.

Mozokhin, Oleg Borisovich, ed. *Politbiuro i delo Beria: Sbornik dokumentov*. Moscow: Kuchkovo Pole, 2012.

Patiev, Iakub Sultanovich, ed. *Ingushi: Deportatsiia, vozvrashchenie, reabilitatsiia, 1944–2004, Dokumenty, materialy, kommentarii*. Magas: Serdalo, 2004.

Pavlov, M., ed. *S. M. Kirov: Stat'i, rechi, dokumenty*. Vol. 1, *1912–1921*. Moscow: Partizdat, 1936.

Permiakov, Igor Al'bertovich, et al., eds. *Sekretariat TsK KPSS: Rabochie zapisi i protokoly zasedanii 1968 g.* Moscow: IstLit, 2021.

———. *Sekretariat TsK KPSS: Zapisi i stenogrammy zasedanii 1965–1967 gg.* Moscow: IstLit, 2020.

Pobol', N. L., and Pavel Polian, eds. *Stalinskie deportatsii, 1928–1953.* Moscow: Demokratiia and Materik, 2005.

Tomilina, Natalia Georgievna, et al., eds. *Boi s "ten'iu" Stalina: Prodolzhenie: Dokumenty i materialy ob istorii XXII s"ezda KPSS i vtorogo etapa destalinizatsii.* Moscow: Nestor-Istoriia, 2015.

SPEECHES, TREATISES, AND OFFICIAL REPORTS

Aliev, Umar Dzhashuevich. *Natsional'nyi vopros i natsional'naia kul'tura v Severo-Kavkazskom krae (itogi i perspektivy) k predstoiashchemu s"ezdu gorskikh narodov.* Foreword by Anastas Mikoyan. Rostov-on-Don: Sevkavkniga, Krainatsizdat, 1926.

CPSU (Communist Party of the Soviet Union). *Konstitutsiia (Osnovnoi Zakon) Soiuza Sovetskikh Sotsialisticheskikh Respublik: Priniata na vneocherednoi sed'moi sessii Verkhovnogo Soveta SSSR deviatogo sozyva 7 oktiabria 1977 goda.* Moscow: Izdanie verhovnogo soveta SSSR, 1977.

———. *Programma Kommunisticheskoi partii Sovetskogo Soiuza.* Moscow: Gospolitizdat, 1961.

———. *XX s"ezd Kommunisticheskoi Partii Sovetskogo Soiuza, 14–25 fevralia 1956 goda. Stenograficheskii otchiot.* 2 vols. Moscow: Gospolitizdat, 1956.

———. *XXII s"ezd Kommunisticheskoi Partii Sovetskogo Soiuza, 17–31 oktiabria 1961 goda. Stenograficheskii otchiot.* 3 vols. Moscow: Gospolitizdat, 1961.

———. *Zasedaniia Verkhovnogo Soveta SSSR shestogo sozyva: Pervaia sessiia (23–25 aprelia 1962 g.): Stenograficheskii otchiot.* Moscow: Izdanie verhovnogo soveta SSSR, 1962.

Kajaznuni, Hovhannes Matevosi. *H. H. dashnakts'ut'yune anelik' ch'uni aylevs.* Tiflis: Zh.T.G.Kh. Poligr. Bazh, 1923.

Khrushchev, Nikita Sergeevich. *Doklad na zakrytom zasedanii XX s"ezda KPSS: "O kul'te lichnosti i ego posledstviiakh."* Moscow: Gospolitizdat, 1959.

———. *O Programme Kommunisticheskoi partii Sovetskogo Soiuza: Doklad na XXII s"ezde Kommunisticheskoi partii Sovetskogo Soiuza 18 oktiabria 1961 goda.* Moscow: Gospolitizdat, 1961.

———. *Otchiot Tsentral'nogo Komiteta Kommunisticheskoi partii Sovetskogo Soiuza XXII s"ezdu partii: 17 oktiabria 1961 goda.* Moscow: Gospolitizdat, 1961.

———. *Rech' na torzhestvennom zasedanii v gorode Erevane, posviashchennom 40-letiyu ustanovleniia Sovetskoi vlasti i sozdaniia Kommunisticheskoi partii Armenii, 6 maia 1961 goda.* Yerevan: Haypethrat, 1961.

Lenin (as Il'in"), Vladimir Il'ich. *Materializm" i empiriokrititsizm": Kriticheskiia zamietki ob" odnoi reaktsionnoi filosofii.* Moscow: Zveno, 1909.

Manaseryan (as Serian'), Sukias Yepremi. *Ispariaiushchiesia milliardy i inertnost' russkago kapital.* Moscow: Kul'tura, 1910.

Mikoyan, Anastas Ivani (Hovhannesi/Ivanovich). *Char Yerevani Stalinyan entrakan okrugi entroghneri zhoghovum 1954 t'vakani marti 11-in*. Yerevan: Haypethrat, 1954.

———. *Rech' na sobranii izbiratelei Erevanskogo-Stalinskogo izbiratel'nogo okruga goroda Erevana, 11 marta 1954 goda*. Moscow: Gospolitizdat, 1954.

———. *Rech' na XX s"ezde KPSS, 16 fevralia 1956 goda*. Moscow: Gospolitizdat, 1956.

———. *Rech' na XXII s"ezde KPSS, 20 oktiabria 1961 goda*. Moscow: Gospolitizdat, 1961.

———. *Sovetakan Miut'yune hisun tarekan e*. Translated by K. S. Vardanyan. Yerevan: Hayastan, 1972.

———. *Sovetskomu Soiuzu piat'desiat let*. Moscow: Politizdat, 1972.

———. *USSR: A United Family of Nations*. Translated by David Skvirsky. Moscow: Progress, 1972.

Severo-Kavkazskoe kraevoe statisticheskoe upravlenie (Otdel perepisi). *Poselionnye itogi perepisi 1926 goda po Severo-Kavkazskomu kraiu*. Rostov-on-Don: Gostipografiia imeni Kominterna Sekkavpolygraftresta, 1929.

Shelepin, Aleksandr Nikolaevich. *Rech' na XXII s"ezde KPSS, 26 oktiabria 1961 goda*. Moscow: Gospolitizdat, 1961.

Stalin, Iosif Vissarionovich. *Marksizm i voprosy iazykoznaniia*. Moscow: Gospolitizdat, 1953.

Tovmasyan, Suren Hakobi. *Hashvetu zekuts'um Hayastani kompartiayi XVII hamagumarin HKP kentkomi ashkhatank'i masin, 14 p'etrvari 1954 t'*. Yerevan: Haypethrat, 1954.

———. *Otchiotnyi doklad Tsentral'nogo Komiteta Kommunisticheskoi partii Armenii XVIII s"ezdu KPA, 19 ianvaria 1956 goda*. Yerevan: Haypethrat, 1956.

Zarobyan, Yakov Nikitayi. *Otchiotnyi doklad Tsentral'nogo Komiteta Kommunisticheskoi partii Armenii XXII s"ezdu Kompartii Armenii, 21 sentiabria 1961 g*. Yerevan: Armgosizdat, 1961.

MEMOIRS AND ACCOUNTS

Alazan, Vahram Martirosi. *Tarapank'i ughinerov*. Yerevan: Khorhrdayin grogh, 1990.

Aleksanyan, Arpenik Arayi. *Sibirskii dnevnik, 1949–1954 gg*. Edited by El'za-Bair Guchinova and Harutyun Marutyan. Foreword by Sergei Arutiunov. Yerevan: Izdatel'stvo "Gitutiun" NAN RA, 2007.

Arushanyan, Ruben Grigori. *Yakov Zarobyane im husherum: Mard, k'aghak'ats'i, petakan gortsich'*. Yerevan: Evroprint, 2007.

Astsatryan, Yeghishe Tevosi. *XX dar: Hayastani karuts'man chanaparhin (Husher)*. Yerevan: Edit Print, 2004.

Bek-Nazaryan (as Bek-Nazarov), Hamo Ivani (Ivanovich). *Zapiski aktiora i kinorezhissiora*. Moscow: Iskusstvo, 1965.

Bonner, Elena Georgievna. *Mothers and Daughters*. Translated by Antonina W. Bouis. New York: Vintage Books, 1993.

Charents, Yeghishe Abgari. *Across Two Worlds: Selected Prose of Eghishé Charents.* Translated by Jack Antreassian and Marzbed Margossian. New York: Ashod, 1985.

Chrysanthopoulos, Leonidas T. *Caucasus Chronicles: Nation-Building and Diplomacy in Armenia, 1993–1994.* London: Gomidas Institute, 2006.

Desheriev, Iunus Desherievich. *Zhizn' vo mgle i borbe: O tragedii repressirovannykh narodov, Tom I.* Moscow: Paleia, 1995.

Dzarugian, Antranig Torosi. *Hin yerazner, nor chambaner.* Beirut: Mekhak, 1960. [Unpublished translations from Western Armenian by Vahe Apelian.]

Gasparyan, Davit Vazgeni, ed. *Ch'arents'i het: Husher.* Yerevan: Nairi, 1997.

Grigoryan, Mark Vladimiri. *Ploshchad' Lenina v Erevane: Vospominaniia o proektirovanii i stroitel'stve.* Yerevan: Hayastan, 1969.

Grossman, Vasilii Semionovich. *An Armenian Sketchbook.* Translated by Robert and Elizabeth Chandler. New York: NYRB Classics, 2013.

———. *Dobro vam! (Iz putevykh zametok): Rasskazy.* Moscow: Tekst, 2018.

———. *Dobro vam! Rasskazy.* Moscow: Sovetskii Pisatel', 1967.

Haroot, Arman. "The Purges in Soviet Armenia." *Armenian Review* 4, no. 3 (Autumn 1951): 133–139.

Harutyunyan, Hamazasp Hovakimi. *Zapiski diplomata.* Edited by Albert Nalbandyan. Yerevan: Edit Print, 2017.

Harutyunyan, Hamlet, ed. *Nakhagahe: Suren Adamyane zhamanakakits'neri husherum.* Yerevan: Zangak, 2010.

Hovhannisyan, Anatoli Hranti, and Lala Martirosyan-Kochar, eds. *Maestro K'ochare: Husheri andradardzum.* Yerevan: Antares, 2016.

Kerr, Stanley E. *The Lions of Marash: Personal Experiences with American Near East Relief, 1919–1922.* Foreword by Bayard Dodge. Introduction by Richard G. Hovannisian. Albany: SUNY Press, 1973.

Khrushchev, Nikita Sergeevich. *Memoirs of Nikita Khrushchev.* Edited by Sergei Khrushchev. Translated by George Shriver. 3 vols. University Park: Penn State University Press, 2005–07.

Khrushchev, Sergei Nikitich. *Khrushchev on Khrushchev: An Inside Account of the Man and His Era.* Boston: Little, Brown, 1990.

———. *Nikita Khrushchev and the Creation of a Superpower.* Translated by Shirley Benson. University Park: Penn State University Press, 2001.

———. *Nikita Khrushchev: Rozhdenie sverkhderzhavy.* Moscow: Veche, 2019.

———. *Nikita Khrushchev: Tvorets ottepeli.* Moscow: Veche, 2017.

———. *Pensioner soiuznogo znacheniia.* Moscow: Veche, 2018.

———. *Reformator.* Moscow: Veche, 2016.

———. *Reformator na zakate vlasti.* Moscow: Veche, 2017.

Kochinyan, Anton Yervandi. *Anavart husher.* Edited by Vladimir Petrosyan. Yerevan: Heghinakayin hratarakut'yun, 2008.

Kunaev, Dinmukhamed Akhmedovich. *Ot Stalina do Gorbacheva (V aspekte istorii Kazakhstana).* Alma-Ata: Sanat, 1994.

Mikoyan, Anastas Ivani (Hovhannesi/Ivanovich). *Dorogoi bor'by*. Moscow: Politizdat, 1971.

———. *K'sanakan t'vakanneri skzbin*. Translated by L. T. Meliksetyan. Yerevan: Hayastan, 1978.

———. *The Memoirs of Anastas Mikoyan*. Vol. 1, *The Path of Struggle*. Edited by Sergo Mikoyan. Translated by Katherine T. O'Connor and Diana L. Burgin. Foreword by W. Averell Harriman. Preface and annotations by Harrison E. Salisbury. Madison, CT: Sphinx, 1988.

———. *Mysli i vospominaniia o Lenine*. Moscow: Politizdat, 1970.

———. *Payk'ari ughiov*. Translated by L. T. Meliksetyan. Yerevan: Hayastan, 1972.

———. *Tak bylo: Razmyshleniia o minuvshem*. Edited by Sergo Mikoyan. Moscow: Tsentrpoligraf, 2014.

———. *V nachale dvadtsatykh . . . .* Moscow: Politizdat, 1975.

Mikoyan (Geurkova), Nami Artiomievna. *Svoimi glazami s liubov'iu i pechal'iu . . .* 4th ed. Moscow: SNC, 2018.

Mikoyan, Sergo Anastasi (Anastasovich). "Aleksei Snegov v bor'be za 'destalinizatsiiu.'" *Voprosy istorii* 4 (April 2006): 69–84.

———. "Anastas Mikoian: Zhizn', otdannaia narodu." Unpublished manuscript, Autumn 2009, typescript.

———. *Anatomiia Karibskogo Krizisa*. Moscow: Academia, 2006.

———. *Hayrs Anastas Mikoyane*. Translated by Eduard Avagyan and Svetlana Avagyan. Yerevan: Nairi, 2007.

———. *The Soviet Cuban Missile Crisis: Castro, Mikoyan, Kennedy, Khrushchev, and the Missiles of November*. Edited by Svetlana Savranskaya. Washington, DC: Woodrow Wilson Center Press, 2012.

———. "Stalinism as I Saw It." In *The Stalin Phenomenon*, edited by Alec Nove, 152–196. New York: St. Martin's, 1992.

Mikoyan, Stepan Anastasi (Anastasovich). *Memoirs of Military Test-Flying and Life with the Kremlin's Elite*. Translated by Aschen Mikoyan. Shrewsbury: Airlife, 1999.

———. *Vospominaniia voennogo liotchika-ispytatelia*. Moscow: Tsentrpoligraf, 2014.

Mil'chakov, Aleksandr Ivanovich. *Molodost' svetlaia i tragicheskaia*. Moscow: Moskovskii rabochii, 1988.

Minasyan, Artavazd Mikaeli. *How Did I Survive?* Edited and translated by Aleksandr V. Gevorkyan. 2nd ed. Newcastle upon Tyne: Cambridge Scholars, 2015.

Mostovenko, Natalia Pavlovna. *Odin god: Dnevnik optimistki v inter'ere utrat*. 2nd ed. Moscow: Voskresen'e, 1999.

Nansen, Fridtjof. *Armenia and the Near East*. London: George Allen and Unwin, 1928.

Pamuk, Orhan. *Istanbul: Memories and the City*. Translated by Maureen Freely. New York: Alfred A. Knopf, 2005.

Piruzyan, Aram Sergeyi. *Pishchevaia industriia: Gody, liudi*. Moscow: Nauka, 1999.

———. *Razmyshleniia o proidennom puti*. Yerevan: Hayastan, 1989.

———. *Zhizn' strany—sud'ba moia: K 50-letiiu Pobedy v Velikoi Otechestvennoi voine*. Moscow: Nauka, 1995.

Shahinian, Grigor. "Sots'ial Demokrat Hnch'akean Kusakts'ut'iune yev Hay Date." *Ahekan* 68, no. 3–4 (1968): 84–109.

Shatunovskaia, Olga Grigorevna. *Ob ushedshem veke*. Edited by Zhana Kut'ina, Andrei Broido, and Anton Kut'in. La Jolla, CA: DAA Books, 2001.

Shepilov, Dmitrii Trofimovich. *The Kremlin's Scholar: A Memoir of Soviet Politics under Stalin and Khrushchev*. Edited by Stephen V. Bittner. Translated by Anthony Austin. New Haven, CT: Yale University Press, 2007.

Shneerson, Grigorii Mikhailovich. *Aram Khachaturian, Stranitsy zhizni i tvorchestva*. Moscow: Sovetskii Kompozitor, 1982.

Vratsyan, Simon Ghazarosi. "How Armenia Was Sovietized, Part III." *Armenian Review* 1, no. 3 (Summer 1948): 59–75.

———. *Keank'i Ughinerov: Depk'er, Demk'er, Aprumner*. 6 vols. Beirut: Yusaber, Mshak, and Hamazgayin, 1955–67.

Yeghenian, Aghavnie Yeghia. *The Red Flag at Ararat*. Introduction by Pietro A. Shakarian. London: Sterndale Classics (Gomidas Institute), 2013.

Zarobyan, Nikita Yakovi. *Iakov Zarobian i ego epokha*. Yerevan: Rossiisko-Armianskii (Slavianskii) universitet (RAU), 2008.

LITERARY WORKS AND ANTHOLOGIES

Abovyan, Khachatur Avetiki. *Verk' Hayastani, Voghb Hayrenasiri: Patmakan vep bazhaneal yeris masuns*. Edited by Gurgen Gasparyan and Pion Hakobyan. Preface translated by Vahe Baladouni and John Gery. Yerevan: Grakanut'ean yew aruesti t'angarani hratarakch'ut'iwn, 2004.

Bakunts, Aksel Stepani. *Yerker: Ardzak*. Edited by Sergo Payazat and Ruben Bedrosov. Introduction by Ruben Zaryan. Yerevan: Haypethrat, 1955.

Charents, Yeghishe Abgari. *Entir Yerker*. Edited by Eduard Topchyan, Soghomon Tarontsi, and Garegin Hovsepyan. Yerevan: Haypethrat, 1954.

———. *Izbrannoe*. Edited by Igor Postupal'skii and Hakob Salakhyan. Moscow: Gosudarstvennoe izdatel'stvo khudozhestvennoi literatury, 1956.

———. *Lenin–Poemner yev Banasteghtsut'yunner*. Yerevan: Haypethrat, 1954.

Chernyshevskii, Nikolai Gavrilovich. *What Is to Be Done?* Translated by Michael R. Katz. Annotated by William G. Wagner. Ithaca, NY: Cornell University Press, 1989.

Griboedov, Aleksandr Sergeevich. *Woe from Wit: A Verse Comedy in Four Acts*. Translated by Betsy Hulick. Introduction by Angela Brintlinger. New York: Columbia University Press, 2020.

Matevossian, Hrant Ignati. *Avgust*. Translated by Anahit Bayandur. Moscow: Izvestiia, 1972.

———. *Ogostos*. Yerevan: Hayastan, 1967.

Raffi. *The Fool: Events from the Last Russo-Turkish War, 1877–78*. Translated by Donald Abcarian. London: Gomidas Institute, 2021.

———. *Yerkeri zhoghovatsu*. Edited by Suren Harutyunyan and Khachik Samvelyan. 10 vols. Yerevan: Haypethrat, 1955–59.

DOCUMENTARY AND FEATURE FILMS

Arakelyan, Suren Hakobi, dir. *Hovhannes T'umanyan*. Yerevan: Yerevan Chronicle-Documentary Film Studio, 1969.

Bek-Nazaryan (Bek-Nazarov), Hamo Ivani, dir. *Zangezur*. Yerevan: Haykino (Armenkino), 1938.

Dovlatyan, Frunze Vaghinaki, dir. *Yerkunk'*. Yerevan: Hayfilm (Armenfilm), 1976.

Malyan, Henrik Sureni, dir. *Menk' enk', mer sarere*. Yerevan: Hayfilm (Armenfilm), 1969.

Sovetakan Hayastan, № 8, Mart 1954. Yerevan: Yerevan Chronicle-Documentary Film Studio, 1954.

Sovetakan Hayastan, № 8, Mart 1958. Yerevan: Yerevan Chronicle-Documentary Film Studio, 1958.

Zhamharyan, Jergiz Khachiki, dir. *A. I. Mikoyane Hayastanum*. Yerevan: Yerevan Chronicle-Documentary Film Studio, 1962.

———, dir. *Ts'ntsum e Hayastane*. Yerevan: Yerevan Chronicle-Documentary Film Studio, 1961.

AUDIO RECORDINGS

Mikoyan, Anastas Ivani (Hovhannesi/Ivanovich). "Rech' na sobranii izbiratelei Erevanskogo-Leninskogo izbiratel'nogo okruga goroda Erevana." March 14, 1962. Yerevan. Audio recording, 73:79. HAA.

———. "Rech' na sobranii izbiratelei Erevanskogo-Stalinskogo izbiratel'nogo okruga goroda Erevana." March 11, 1954. Yerevan. Audio recording, 121:48. HAA.

SECONDARY SOURCES

Adler, Nanci. *The Gulag Survivor: Beyond the Soviet System*. New Brunswick, NJ: Transaction Publishers, 2002.

———. *Keeping Faith with the Party: Communist Believers Return from the Gulag*. Bloomington: Indiana University Press, 2012.

Aghayan, Tsatur Paveli. *Nersik Stepanian*. Yerevan: Hayastan, 1967.

Aghayan, Tsatur Paveli, et al. *Ocherki istorii kommunisticheskoi partii Armenii*. Yerevan: Hayastan, 1967.

Amar, Tarik Cyril. *The Paradox of Ukrainian Lviv: A Borderland City between Stalinists, Nazis, and Nationalists*. Ithaca, NY: Cornell University Press, 2015.

Anderson, Benedict. *Imagined Communities: Reflections on the Origin and Spread of Nationalism*. New York: Verso, 2006.

Angaladian, Ruben Sargsi. *The Armenian Avant Garde of the 1960s: Seven Fates*. Translated by Kenneth MacInnes. Yerevan: R. Angaladian, 2006.

Antonov-Ovseenko, Anton Vladimirovich. *The Time of Stalin: Portrait of a Tyranny*. Translated by George Saunders. Introduction by Stephen F. Cohen. New York: Harper and Row, 1981.

Arzumanyan, Gagik Grigori. "Iskusheniia." *Druzhba narodov*, no. 12 (2004): 167–170.

Atabaki, Touraj, ed. *Iran and the First World War: Battleground of the Great Powers*. London: I. B. Tauris, 2006.

Avagyan, Smbat, and Georg Perikhanyan. *Nersisyants'iner, 1824–1924*. Yerevan: Haykakan SSH Gitut'yunneri Akademiayi Hratarakch'ut'yun, 1975.

Ayvazian, Argam Ararati. *The Historical Monuments of Nakhichevan*. Translated by Fr. Krikor H. Maksoudian. Detroit: Wayne State University Press, 1990.

Badalyan Riegg, Stephen. *Russia's Entangled Embrace: The Tsarist Empire and the Armenians, 1801–1914*. Ithaca, NY: Cornell University Press, 2020.

Baiburin, Albert Kashfullovich. *The Soviet Passport: The History, Nature and Uses of the Internal Passport in the USSR*. Translated by Stephen Dalziel. Foreword by Catriona Kelly. Cambridge: Polity, 2021.

Bakhtin, Mikhail Mikhailovich. *Problems of Dostoevsky's Poetics*. Translated by Caryl Emerson. Minneapolis: University of Minnesota Press, 1984.

Baron, Samuel H. *Bloody Saturday in the Soviet Union: Novocherkassk, 1962*. Stanford, CA: Stanford University Press, 2001.

Barseghyan, Khikar Hakobi. *Step'an Shahumyan: Kyank'i yev gortsuneut'yan vaveragrakan taregrut'yun: 1878–1918 t't'*. Introduction by Anastas Mikoyan. Edited by Lev Shahumyan. Yerevan: Hayastan, 1968.

Basta, Karlo, John McGarry, and Richard Simeon, eds. *Territorial Pluralism: Managing Difference in Multinational States*. Vancouver: UBC Press, 2015.

Bittner, Stephen V. *The Many Lives of Khrushchev's Thaw: Experience and Memory in Moscow's Arbat*. Ithaca, NY: Cornell University Press, 2008.

Blauvelt, Timothy K., and Jeremy Smith, eds. *Georgia after Stalin: Nationalism and Soviet Power*. London: Routledge, 2015.

Blitstein, Peter A. "Researching Stalin's Nationality Policy in the Archives." *Cahiers du monde russe: Russie—Empire russe—Union soviétique et États indépendants* 40, no. 1–2 (1999): 125–138.

———. "Stalin's Nations: Soviet Nationality Policy between Planning and Primordialism, 1936–1953." PhD diss., University of California, Berkeley, 1999.

Bohn, Thomas M., Rayk Einax, and Michel Abeßer, eds. *De-Stalinisation Reconsidered: Persistence and Change in the Soviet Union*. Frankfurt: Campus, 2014.

Bougai, Nikolai Fiodorovich. *The Deportation of Peoples in the Soviet Union*. New York: Nova Science, 1996.

Bournoutian, George A. *Armenia and Imperial Decline: The Yerevan Province, 1900–1914*. London: Routledge, 2018.

———. *From the Kur to the Aras: A Military History of Russia's Move into the South Caucasus and the First Russo-Iranian War, 1801–1813*. Leiden: Brill, 2021.

———. "The Iran-Turkey-Armenia Borders as Depicted in Various Maps." *Iran and the Caucasus* 19, no. 1 (2015): 97–107.

Burbank, Jane, and Frederick Cooper. *Empires in World History: Power and the Politics of Difference*. Princeton, NJ: Princeton University Press, 2011.

Casper, Samuel A. "The Bolshevik Afterlife: Posthumous Rehabilitation in the Post-Stalin Soviet Union, 1953–1970." PhD diss., University of Pennsylvania, 2018.

Chakars, Melissa. *The Socialist Way of Life in Siberia: Transformation in Buryatia*. Budapest: Central European University Press, 2014.

Chernyshova, Natalya. "De-Stalinisation and Insubordination in the Soviet Borderlands: Beria's Attempted National Reform in Soviet Belarus." *Europe-Asia Studies* 73, no. 2 (2021): 387–409.

Cohen, Stephen F. *Bukharin and the Bolshevik Revolution: A Political Biography, 1888–1938*. New York: Alfred A. Knopf, 1973.

———. *Rethinking the Soviet Experience: Politics and History Since 1917*. Oxford: Oxford University Press, 1985.

———. *The Victims Return: Survivors of the Gulag after Stalin*. Exeter, NH: PublishingWorks, 2010.

Cohen, Stephen F., Alexander Rabinowitch, and Robert Sharlet, eds. *The Soviet Union since Stalin*. Bloomington: Indiana University Press, 1980.

Connor, Walker. *The National Question in Marxist-Leninist Theory and Strategy*. Princeton, NJ: Princeton University Press, 1984.

Conquest, Robert. *Russia after Khrushchev*. New York: Praeger, 1965.

Coumel, Laurent. "A Failed Environmental Turn? Khrushchev's Thaw and Nature Protection in Soviet Russia." *Soviet and Post-Soviet Review* 40 (2013): 167–189.

Cucciolla, Riccardo Mario. "Sharaf Rashidov and the International Dimensions of Soviet Uzbekistan." *Central Asian Survey* 39, no. 2 (April 2020): 185–201.

Cuneo, Paolo, et al. *Documents of Armenian Architecture 12: Ani*. Translated by Bryan Fleming. Milan: Edizioni Ares, 1984.

Daudov, Abdulla Khamidovich. *Gorskaia ASSR (1921–1924 gg.): Ocherki sotsial'no-ekonomicheskoi istorii*. St. Petersburg: Izdatel'stvo S.-Peterburgskogo universiteta, 1997.

Dobson, Miriam. *Khrushchev's Cold Summer: Gulag Returnees, Crime, and the Fate of Reform after Stalin*. Ithaca, NY: Cornell University Press, 2009.

Doose, Katja. "Green Nationalism? The Transformation of Environmentalism in Soviet Armenia, 1969–1991." *Ab Imperio* 1 (2019): 181–205.

Dzidzoev, Valerii Dudarovich. *Ot Soiuza ob"edinennykh gortsev Severnogo Kavkaza i Dagestana do Gorskoi ASSR (1917–1924 gg.): Nachal'nyi etap natsional'no-gosudarstvennogo stroitel'stva narodov Severnogo Kavkaza v XX veke*. Vladikavkaz: Izdatel'stvo Severo-Osetinskogo gosudarstvennogo universiteta im. K. L. Khetagurova, 2003.

Edgar, Adrienne Lynn. *Tribal Nation: The Making of Soviet Turkmenistan*. Princeton, NJ: Princeton University Press, 2004.

Fitzpatrick, Sheila Mary. *On Stalin's Team: The Years of Living Dangerously in Soviet Politics*. Princeton, NJ: Princeton University Press, 2015.

Forestier-Peyrat, Etienne. "The Cold War Politics of Soviet Federal Structures, 1945–1965: International Dimensions and Domestic Consequences." *Journal of Cold War Studies* 23, no. 3 (2021): 175–207.

———. "Soviet Federalism at Work: Lessons from the History of the Transcaucasian Federation, 1922–1936." *Jahrbücher für Geschichte Osteuropas, Neue Folge* 65, no. 4 (2017): 529–559.

Gasparyan, Albert. *I. Kh. Bagramian*. Moscow: MaRafon, Panas, Innovation and World, 1992.

Gerasimov, Ilya. "The Great Imperial Revolution." *Ab Imperio* 2 (2017): 21–44.

Getty, J. Arch, and Oleg V. Naumov, eds. *The Road to Terror: Stalin and the Self-Destruction of the Bolsheviks, 1932–1939*. Translations by Benjamin Sher. New Haven, CT: Yale University Press, 2002.

Glushchenko, Irina Viktorovna. *Obshchepit: Mikoian i sovetskaia kukhnia*. Moscow: Izdatel'skii dom Gosudarstvennogo universiteta—Vysshei shkoly ekonomiki, 2010.

Goff, Krista A. *Nested Nationalism: Making and Unmaking Nations in the Soviet Caucasus*. Ithaca, NY: Cornell University Press, 2020.

Grigorian, Mark Vladimiri. *Erevan: Biografiia goroda*. Moscow: Slovo, 2022.

Grybkauskas, Saulius. *Governing the Soviet Union's National Republics: The Second Secretaries of the Communist Party*. Translated by Diana Bartkute Barnard. Edited by Michael Loader. London: Routledge, 2020.

Hacikyan, Agop J., et al., eds. *The Heritage of Armenian Literature*. 3 vols. Detroit: Wayne State University Press, 2000–05.

Hakobyan (Akopyan), Grigori Sargsi. *Stepan Shaumian: Zhizn' i deiatel'nost'*. Introduction by Anastas Mikoyan. Edited by Lev Shahumyan. Moscow: Politizdat, 1973.

Hale-Dorrell, Aaron Todd. *Corn Crusade: Khrushchev's Farming Revolution in the Post-Stalin Soviet Union*. Oxford: Oxford University Press, 2018.

Harris, Steven E. *Communism on Tomorrow Street: Mass Housing and Everyday Life after Stalin*. Washington, DC: Woodrow Wilson Center Press, 2013.

Harutyunyan, Tigran Mihrani, ed. *Yerevan Architectural Guide*. Berlin: DOM, 2018.

Haug, Hilde Katrine. *Creating a Socialist Yugoslavia: Tito, Communist Leadership and the National Question*. London: I. B. Tauris, 2012.

Hirsch, Francine. *Empire of Nations: Ethnographic Knowledge and the Making of the Soviet Union*. Ithaca, NY: Cornell University Press, 2005.

Hoffmann, David L. *The Stalinist Era*. Cambridge: Cambridge University Press, 2018.

Hornsby, Robert. *The Soviet Sixties*. New Haven, CT: Yale University Press, 2023.

Hosking, Geoffrey A. *Rulers and Victims: The Russians in the Soviet Union*. Cambridge, MA: Belknap Press of Harvard University Press, 2006.

Hovannisian, Richard G. *The Republic of Armenia*. 4 vols. Berkeley: University of California Press, 1971–96.

Iandiev, Abdulazis Dzhabrailovich. *Iarkii primer sluzheniia narodu*. 2nd ed. Nazran': OOO "KEP," 2018.

Ihrig, Stefan. *Atatürk in the Nazi Imagination*. Cambridge, MA: Belknap Press of Harvard University Press, 2014.

Jones, Polly, ed. *The Dilemmas of De-Stalinization: Negotiating Cultural and Social Change in the Khrushchev Era*. London: Routledge, 2006.

———. *Myth, Memory, Trauma: Rethinking the Stalinist Past in the Soviet Union, 1953–70*. New Haven, CT: Yale University Press, 2013.

Kaiser, Claire P. *Georgian and Soviet: Entitled Nationhood and the Specter of Stalin in the Caucasus*. Ithaca, NY: Cornell University Press, 2022.

Kalemeneva, Ekaterina Alekseevna. "From New Socialist Cities to Thaw Experimentation in Arctic Townscapes: Leningrad Architects Attempt to Modernise the Soviet North." *Europe-Asia Studies* 71, no. 3 (March 2019): 426–449.

Kalinovsky, Artemy M. *Laboratory of Socialist Development: Cold War Politics and Decolonization in Soviet Tajikistan*. Ithaca, NY: Cornell University Press, 2018.

Kamp, Marianne. *The New Woman in Uzbekistan: Islam, Modernity, and Unveiling under Communism*. Seattle: University of Washington Press, 2008.

Kaplanova, Sofia Georgievna. *Ara Arutiunian*. Moscow: Sovetskii khudozhnik, 1968.

Kemper, Michael, and Stephan Conermann, eds. *The Heritage of Soviet Oriental Studies*. London: Routledge, 2013.

Kévorkian, Raymond. *The Armenian Genocide: A Complete History*. London: I. B. Tauris, 2011.

Khalid, Adeeb. *Making Uzbekistan: Nation, Empire, and Revolution in the Early USSR*. Ithaca, NY: Cornell University Press, 2015.

Khalpakhchian, Hovhannes Khachaturi, and Adriano Alpago-Novello. *Documents of Armenian Architecture 3: Sanahin*. Translated by Susan Bassnett and Gisella Waldman. 3rd ed. Milan: Edizioni Ares, 1980.

Khaustov, Vladimir Nikolaevich, and Lennart Samuelson. *Stalin, NKVD i repressii 1936–1938 gg*. Moscow: ROSSPEN, 2010.

Khlevniuk, Oleg Vital'evich. *In Stalin's Shadow: The Career of "Sergo" Ordzhonikidze*. Edited by Donald J. Raleigh and Kathy S. Transchel. Translated by David J. Nordlander. Armonk: M. E. Sharpe, 1995.

Kibita, Nataliya. *Soviet Economic Management under Khrushchev: The Sovnarkhoz Reform*. London: Routledge, 2015.

Kilbourne Matossian, Mary Allerton. *The Impact of Soviet Policies in Armenia*. Leiden: Brill, 1962.

Kirasirova, Masha. *The Eastern International: Arabs, Central Asians, and Jews in the Soviet Union's Anticolonial Empire*. Oxford: Oxford University Press, 2024.

Korenev, Dmitrii Zakharovich. *Revoliutsiia na Tereke, 1917–1918 gody*. Ordzhonikidze: Severo-Osetinskoe knizhnoe izdatel'stvo, 1967.

Kozlov, Denis, and Eleonory Gilburd, eds. *The Thaw: Soviet Society and Culture during the 1950s and 1960s*. Toronto: University of Toronto Press, 2014.

Kozlov, Vladimir Aleksandrovich. *Mass Uprisings in the USSR: Protest and Rebellion in the Post-Stalin Years*. Translated by Elaine McClarnand Mackinnon. Armonk: M. E. Sharpe, 2002.

Kun, Miklós. *Stalin: An Unknown Portrait*. Translated by Miklós Bodóczky and Rachel Hideg. Budapest: Central European University Press, 2003.

Laipanov, Kazi Tanaevich, and Mussa Batchaev. *Umar Aliev*. Cherkessk: Karachaevo-Cherkesskoe otdelenie Stavropol'skogo knizhnogo izdatel'stva, 1986.

Lanzillotti, Ian T. *Land, Community, and the State in the Caucasus: Kabardino-Balkaria from Tsarist Conquest to Post-Soviet Politics*. London: Bloomsbury Academic, 2022.

Lehmann, Maike. "Apricot Socialism: The National Past, the Soviet Project, and the Imagining of Community in Late Soviet Armenia." *Slavic Review* 74, no. 1 (Spring 2015): 9–31.

Lenoe, Matthew E. *The Kirov Murder and Soviet History*. New Haven, CT: Yale University Press, 2010.

Lewin, Moshe. *The Soviet Century*. London: Verso, 2016.

Lincoln, W. Bruce. *Red Victory: A History of the Russian Civil War, 1918–1921*. New York: Da Capo, 1999.

Loader, Michael. "Beria and Khrushchev: The Power Struggle over Nationality Policy and the Case of Latvia." *Europe-Asia Studies* 68, no. 10 (December 2016): 1759–1792.

———. "The Death of 'Socialism with a Latvian Face': The Purge of the Latvian National Communists." *Journal of Baltic Studies* 48, no. 2 (July 2017): 161–181.

———. "The Rebellious Republic: The 1958 Education Reform and Soviet Latvia." *Journal of the Institute of Latvian History* 100, no. 3 (November 2016): 113–139.

———. "Restricting Russians: Language and Immigration Laws in Soviet Latvia, 1956–1959." *Nationalities Papers* 45, no. 6 (September 2017): 1082–1099.

———. "A Stalinist Purge in the Khrushchev Era? The Latvian Communist Party Purge, 1959–1963." *Slavonic and East European Review* 96, no. 2 (April 2018): 244–282.

Malkasian, Mark. *"Gha-ra-bagh!": The Emergence of the National Democratic Movement in Armenia*. Detroit: Wayne State University Press, 1996.

Mamikonyan, Karapet Aveti. "Mi ej St. Shahumyani kyank'i taregrut'yunits'." *Banber Hayastani arkhivneri* 21, no. 3 (1968): 113–130.

Markwick, Roger D. *Rewriting History in Soviet Russia: The Politics of Revisionist Historiography, 1956–1974*. New York: Palgrave Macmillan, 2001.

Marshall, Alex. *The Caucasus under Soviet Rule*. London: Routledge, 2012.

Martin, Terry. *The Affirmative Action Empire: Nations and Nationalism in the Soviet Union, 1923–1939*. Ithaca, NY: Cornell University Press, 2001.

Maslov, Dmitrii Vladimirovich, Liubov' Lazareva, and Natalia Sukhanova. *Prichiny raspada SSSR: Voprosy metodologii issledovaniia*. Moscow: ROSSPEN, 2022.

Medvedev, Roy Aleksandrovich. *All Stalin's Men*. Translated by Harold Shukman. Garden City, NY: Anchor/Doubleday, 1984.

———. *Khrushchev: Politicheskaia biografiia*. Edited by Semyon Reznik. Benson, VT: Chalidze, 1986.

———. *K sudu istorii: O Staline i stalinizme*. Moscow: Vremia, 2011.

———. *Oni okruzhali Stalina*. Benson, VT: Chalidze, 1984.

Mnatsakanian, Stepan Khachaturi. *Documents of Armenian Architecture 18: Sevan*. Translated by Bryan Fleming. Milan: Edizioni Ares, 1987.

Mnatsakanyan, Aramayis Navasardi. *Alek'sandr Myasnikyan (Al. Martuni)*. Yerevan: Haypethrat, 1955.

Mouradian, Claire. *De Staline à Gorbatchev: Histoire d'une république soviétique, l'Arménie*. Paris: Ramsay, 1990.

Mukhanov, Vadim Mikhailovich. *Kavkaz v perelomnuiu epokhu (1917–1921)*. Moscow: Modest Kolerov, 2019.

Nichanian, Marc, ed. *Yeghishe Charents: Poet of the Revolution*. Costa Mesa: Mazda, 2003.

Obichkin, Gennadii Dmitrievich, Gazanfer Shanshiev, and Lev Shahumyan. "Nekotorye voprosy istorii Kommunisticheskoi partii Armenii." *Kommunist*, April 1962, 78–86.

Omarkhali, Khanna. "The Kurds in the Former Soviet States from Historical and Cultural Perspectives." *Copernicus Journal of Political Studies* 2, no. 4 (2013): 128–142.

Panossian, Razmik. *The Armenians: From Kings and Priests to Merchants and Commissars*. New York: Columbia University Press, 2006.

Pavlov, Mikhail Iur'evich. *Anastas Mikoian: Politicheskii portret na fone sovetskoi epokhi*. Moscow: Mezhdunarodnye otnosheniia, 2010.

Petrov, Nikita Vasil'evich. *Ivan Serov—predsedatel' KGB*. Moscow: ROSSPEN, 2021.

Petrov, Nikita Vasil'evich, and Mark Jansen. *"Stalinskii pitomets" Nikolai Ezhov*. Moscow: ROSSPEN, 2020.

Piruzyan, Aram Sergeyi, ed. *Armianskaia kulinariia*. Moscow: Gostorgizdat, 1960.

———. *Armianskaia kulinariia*. 2nd ed. Moscow: Ekonomika, 1971.

———. *Armianskaia kulinariia*. 3rd ed. Yerevan: Hayastan, 1983.

———. *Haykakan khohanots'*. Yerevan: Hayastani Petakan Hratarakch'ut'yun, 1963.

Pisarenko, Konstantin Anatol'evich. *Sergei Kirov: Nesbyvshaiasia nadezhda vozhdia*. Moscow: ROSSPEN and Veche, 2023.

Poghosyan, Anahit, and Anush Ter-Minasyan, eds. *Ararman ughin: Chartarapet Gurgen Musheghyan*. Yerevan: Tapan, 2019.

Polian, Pavel Markovich. *Against Their Will: The History and Geography of Forced Migrations in the USSR*. Translated by Anna Yastrzhembska. Budapest: Central European University Press, 2004.

Pomerants, Grigorii Solomonovich. *Sledstvie vediot katorzhanka*. Moscow and St. Petersburg: Tsentr gumanitarnykh initsiativ, Universitetskaia kniga, 2017.

Prigge, William D. "The 1959 Latvian Purges: A Revision Study." *Journal of Baltic Studies* 35, no. 3 (Fall 2004): 211–230.

———. *The Bearslayers: The Rise and Fall of the Latvian National Communists*. New York: Peter Lang, 2015.

———. "Power, Popular Opinion, and the Latvian National Communists." *Journal of Baltic Studies* 45, no. 5 (September 2014): 305–319.

Pyzhikov, Aleksandr Vladimirovich. *Khruchshevskaia "ottepel'", 1953–1964*. Moscow: OLMA, 2002.

Rayfield, Donald. *Stalin and His Hangmen: The Tyrant and Those Who Killed for Him*. New York: Random House, 2004.

Renkama, Jukka. *Ideology and Challenges of Political Liberalisation in the USSR, 1957–1961: Otto Kuusinen's "Reform Platform", the State Concept, and the Path to the 3rd CPSU Programme*. Helsinki: Suomalaisen Kirjallisuuden Seura, 2006.

Riga, Liliana. *The Bolsheviks and the Russian Empire*. Cambridge: Cambridge University Press, 2012.

Risch, William. *The Ukrainian West: Culture and the Fate of Empire in Soviet Lviv*. Cambridge, MA: Harvard University Press, 2011.

Salisbury, Harrison E., ed. *The Soviet Union: The Fifty Years*. New York: Harcourt, Brace and World, 1967.

———. *To Moscow—and Beyond: A Reporter's Narrative*. New York: Harper and Brothers, 1960.

Saparov, Arsène Kareni. *From Conflict to Autonomy in the Caucasus: The Soviet Union and the Making of Abkhazia, South Ossetia and Nagorno Karabakh*. London: Routledge, 2015.

———. "Re-negotiating the Boundaries of the Permissible: The National(ist) Revival in Soviet Armenia and Moscow's Response." *Europe-Asia Studies* 70, no. 6 (July 2018): 862–883.

Schattenberg, Susanne. *Brezhnev: The Making of a Statesman*. London: I. B. Tauris, 2021.

Schnirelmann, Viktor Aleksandrovich. *Voiny pamiati: Mify, identichnost' i politika v Zakavkaz'e*. Moscow: IKTs "Akademkniga," 2003.

Scott, Erik R. *Familiar Strangers: The Georgian Diaspora and the Evolution of Soviet Empire*. Oxford: Oxford University Press, 2017.

Simon, Gerhard. *Nationalism and Policy towards the Nationalities in the Soviet Union: From Totalitarianism to Post-Stalinist Society*. Translated by Karen Forster and Ostwald Forster. Boulder, CO: Westview, 1991.

Slezkine, Yuri L'vovich. *Arctic Mirrors: Russia and the Small Peoples of the North*. Ithaca, NY: Cornell University Press, 1994.

———. "The USSR as a Communal Apartment, or How a Socialist State Promoted Ethnic Particularism." *Slavic Review* 53, no. 2 (Summer 1994): 414–452.

Smith, Jeremy. "The Battle for Language: Opposition to Khrushchev's Education Reform in the Soviet Republics, 1958–59." *Slavic Review* 76, no. 4 (Winter 2017): 983–1002.

———. "Was There a Soviet Nationality Policy?" *Europe-Asia Studies* 71, no. 6 (July 2019): 1–23.

Smith, Jeremy, and Melanie Ilic, eds. *Khrushchev in the Kremlin: Policy and Government in the Soviet Union, 1953–1964*. London: Routledge, 2011.

———, eds. *Soviet State and Society under Nikita Khrushchev*. London: Routledge, 2009.

Smith, Kathleen E. *Moscow 1956: The Silenced Spring*. Cambridge, MA: Harvard University Press, 2017.

Smith, Mark B. *Property of Communists: The Urban Housing Program from Stalin to Khrushchev*. DeKalb: Northern Illinois University Press, 2010.

Sorokin, Andrei Konstantinovich. *"Prakticheskii rabotnik" Georgii Malenkov*. Moscow: ROSSPEN, 2021.

Ssorin-Chaikov, Nikolai Vladimirovich, and Olga A. Sosnina, eds. *Dary vozhdiam, Gifts to Soviet Leaders*. Introduction by Elena Gagarina. Moscow: Pinakoteka, 2006.

Suny, Ronald Grigor. *The Baku Commune, 1917–1918: Class and Nationality in the Russian Revolution*. Princeton, NJ: Princeton University Press, 1972.

———. *Looking toward Ararat: Armenia in Modern History*. Bloomington: Indiana University Press, 1993.

———. *The Making of the Georgian Nation*. 2nd ed. Bloomington: Indiana University Press, 1994.

———. *Stalin: Passage to Revolution*. Princeton, NJ: Princeton University Press, 2020.

Suny, Ronald Grigor, and Valerie A. Kivelson. *Russia's Empires*. Oxford: Oxford University Press, 2017.

Suny, Ronald Grigor, and Terry Martin, eds. *A State of Nations: Empire and Nation-Making in the Age of Lenin and Stalin*. Oxford: Oxford University Press, 2001.

Taubman, William. *Khrushchev: The Man and His Era*. New York: W. W. Norton, 2003.

Terian, Abraham, ed. *The Life of Mashtots' by His Disciple Koriwn, Translated from the Classical Armenian with Introduction and Commentary*. Oxford: Oxford University Press, 2022.

Ter-Matevosyan, Vahram Hamazaspi. *Turkey, Kemalism and the Soviet Union: Problems of Modernization, Ideology and Interpretation*. New York: Palgrave Macmillan, 2019.

Ter Minassian, Anaide. *Nationalism and Socialism in the Armenian Revolutionary Movement (1887–1912)*. Translated by A. M. Berrett. Cambridge, MA: Zoryan Institute, 1984.

Tillett, Lowell. *The Great Friendship: Soviet Historians on the Non-Russian Nationalities*. Chapel Hill: University of North Carolina Press, 1969.

Tishkov, Valery Aleksandrovich. *Chechnya: Life in a War-Torn Society*. Foreword by Mikhail Gorbachev. Berkeley: University of California Press, 2004.

Tompson, William James. *Khrushchev: A Political Life*. New York: Palgrave Macmillan, 1995.

Tonoyan, Artyom Henri, ed. *Black Garden Aflame: The Nagorno-Karabakh Conflict in the Soviet and Russian Press*. Minneapolis: East View, 2021.

Tromly, Benjamin. *Making of the Soviet Intelligentsia: Universities and Intellectual Life under Stalin and Khrushchev*. Cambridge: Cambridge University Press, 2014.

———. "An Unlikely National Revival: Soviet Higher Learning and the Ukrainian 'Sixtiers,' 1953–65." *Russian Review* 68, no. 4 (October 2009): 607–622.

Tumyan, Harutyun Grigori. *Depk'ere Lernayin Gharabaghum 1917–1920 t't'.: Patmakan aknark*. Edited by Ashot Sargsyan. Yerevan: Antares, 2008.

Varga-Harris, Christine. *Stories of House and Home: Soviet Apartment Life during the Khrushchev Years*. Ithaca, NY: Cornell University Press, 2015.

Virabyan, Amatuni Sasuniki. *Hayastane Stalinits' minch'ev Khrushch'ov, Hasarakakan-k'aghak'akan kyank'e (1945–1957 tt.)*. Yerevan: HH GAA "Gitut'yun" Hratarakch'ut'yun, 2001.

Walker, Christopher J. *Armenia: The Survival of a Nation*. 2nd ed. London: Routledge, 1990.

Willerton, John P. *Patronage and Politics in the USSR*. Cambridge: Cambridge University Press, 1992.

Yuzefovich, Victor Aronovich. *Aram Khachaturyan*. Translated by Nicholas Kournokoff and Vladimir Bobrov. New York: Sphinx, 1985.

Zgorzhel'skaia, Svetlana Sergeevna. "Kontseptsiia obshchenarodnogo gosudarstva v proekte Konstitutsii SSSR 1964 g." Kand. iurid. nauk diss., Russian State University of Justice, Moscow, 2006.

Zubkova, Elena Iurievna. *Russia after the War: Hopes, Illusions and Disappointments, 1945–1957*. Translated by Hugh Ragsdale. Armonk: M. E. Sharpe, 1998.

Zürcher, Erik Jan. *Turkey: A Modern History*. 4th ed. London: I. B. Tauris, 2017.

MAPS AND ATLASES

Galichian, Rouben Arami. *Historic Maps of Armenia: The Cartographic Heritage*. London: I. B. Tauris, 2004.

Hewsen, Robert H. *Armenia: A Historical Atlas*. Chicago: University of Chicago Press, 2001.

Kocheshkova, M. N., ed. *Severo-Osetinskaia ASSR* [map]. 1:600,000. Moscow: Glavnoe upravlenie geodezii i kartografii MVD SSSR. 1958.

Tsutsiev, Arthur Arkadevich. *Atlas of the Ethno-Political History of the Caucasus*. Translated by Nora Seligman Favorov. New Haven, CT: Yale University Press, 2014.

Vardanyan, Manuk Razmiki, ed. *Atlas of the Nagorno-Karabagh Republic*. Translated by Arevik Meliksetyan and Ani Adamyan. Stepanakert: State Committee of the Real Estate Cadastre of the Nagorno-Karabagh Republic, 2010.

Vardanyan, Manuk Razmiki, Martin Sargsyan, and Aida Nazaryan, eds. *National Atlas of Armenia*. Translated by Sayat Kuyumcuyan, Arevik Meliksetyan, and Ani Adamyan. 2 vols. Yerevan: Center of Geodesy and Cartography ("Geocart"), 2015–17.

REFERENCE WORKS

Aslanyan, Arsham Arshami, and Hakob Grgearyan. *Haykakan SSH ach-kharhagrakan anunneri hamarot bararan*. Yerevan: Haykakan SSH GA Hratarakch'ut'yun, 1981.

Chernobaev, Anatolii Aleksandrovich, ed. *Na priiome u Stalina: Tetradi (zhurnaly) zapisei lits, prinyatykh I. V. Stalinym (1924–1953 gg.). Spravochnik*. Moscow: Novyi khronograf, 2008.

Filippov, Sergei Georgievich. *Territorial'nye rukovoditeli VKP(b) v 1934–1939 gg. Spravochnik*. Moscow: ROSSPEN, 2016.

Hambardzumyan, Viktor Hamazaspi, and Makich' Aruzmanyan, eds. *Haykakan Sovetakan Hanragitaran*. 13 vols. Yerevan: Haykakan SSH Gitut'yunneri Akademia, 1974–87.

Petrov, Nikita Vasil'evich, and Konstantin Skorkin. *Kto rukovodil NKVD, 1934–1941: Spravochnik*. Moscow: Zven'ia, 1999.

Volobuev, Pavel Vasil'evich, ed. *Politicheskie deiateli Rossii 1917: Biograficheskii slovar'*. Moscow: Bol'shaia Rossiiskaia Entsiklopediia, 1993.

INDEX

Pietro A. Shakarian is a historian of Russia and the Soviet Union and a postdoctoral fellow at the Centre for Historical Research at the National Research University–Higher School of Economics in St. Petersburg, Russia. He earned his PhD in history at the Ohio State University and his MA at the University of Michigan in Ann Arbor. He was previously a lecturer in history at the American University of Armenia in Yerevan.

For Indiana University Press

Sabrina Black, Editorial Assistant
Anna Garnai, Production Coordinator
Sophia Hebert, Assistant Acquisitions Editor
Samantha Heffner, Marketing and Publicity Manager
Katie Huggins, Production Manager
David Miller, Lead Project Manager/Editor
Bethany Mowry, Acquisitions Editor
Dan Pyle, Online Publishing Manager
Pamela Rude, Senior Artist and Book Designer